Andrew Jackson & His Indian Wars

ANDREW JACKSON

&

HIS INDIAN WARS

ROBERT V. REMINI

VIKING

VIKING

Published by the Penguin Group
Penguin Putnam Inc., 375 Hudson Street,
New York, New York 10014, U.S.A.
Penguin Books Ltd, 27 Wrights Lane,
London W8 5TZ, England
Penguin Books Australia Ltd, Ringwood,
Victoria, Australia
Penguin Books Canada Ltd, 10 Alcorn Avenue,
Toronto, Ontario, Canada M4V 3B2
Penguin Books (N.Z.) Ltd, 182–190 Wairau Road,
Auckland 10, New Zealand

Penguin Books Ltd, Registered Offices:
Harmondsworth, Middlesex, England

First published in 2001 by Viking Penguin,
a member of Penguin Putnam Inc.

10 9 8 7 6 5 4 3 2 1

Insert illustration credits:

National Portrait Gallery: page 7, top and bottom; page 8, bottom; page 10, top and bottom; page 11, top and bottom; page 13, top and bottom; page 14, top; page 15, bottom; The Hermitage: Home of President Andrew Jackson, Nashville, Tenn.: page 12, top and bottom; William L. Clements Library, University of Michigan: page 16. All others courtesy of the Library of Congress.

CIP available

ISBN 0-670-91025-2

The book is printed on acid-free paper. ∞

Printed in the United States of America
Set in Adobe Garamond
Designed by Carla Bolte
Maps by Jeffrey L. Ward

For my first child

ELIZABETH M. REMINI-NIELSON

Preface

This is the last book I shall write about Andrew Jackson; at least I hope so. But it is a book I have wanted to write for a long time, not only because it involved an important and highly controversial subject, but because that subject is so charged with prejudice and misunderstanding. However, before proceeding, I want to assure the reader that it is not my intention to excuse or exonerate Andrew Jackson for the role he played in the removal of Native Americans west of the Mississippi River. My purpose is simply to explain what happened and why.

Today Americans are quite prone to fault Jackson for the removal without understanding the circumstances surrounding the event. They have little appreciation of the mood of Americans at the tail end of the eighteenth and beginning of the ninteenth century. They prefer to single out one culprit for blame, just as King George III is singled out for initiating the American Revolution. They do not understand the fear and mistrust that existed between the white and red people during the early years of the Republic. To begin to understand that situation, modern Americans must first appreciate the fact that the mood and temper of Americans during Jackson's lifetime tolerated and actually condoned removal.

And that toleration produced an indifference to the plight of Native Americans after their removal, an indifference that extended from the nineteenth well into the twentieth century. When I went to school, little was taught about Indians, much less their removal, and that was true in high school, college, and graduate school. John Spencer Bassett, the first modern biographer of Jackson, discussed Indian removal in a chapter entitled "Minor Problems of the Two Administrations." Minor problems! This chapter also dealt with payment of the national debt, the distribution of the surplus, and the Specie Circular. The next modern biographer, Marquis James, whose study won him a Pulitzer Prize, devoted only a few paragraphs to Indian removal, and they were scattered in different parts of the book. Not until the civil rights movement began after World War II did Americans suddenly come awake to their violent past and their disregard of the rights of other people. And those acts of violence occurred not only in the seventeenth, eighteenth, and nineteenth centuries, but the twentieth century as well. They occurred as recently as sixty years ago.

I lived through and fought in World War II, and I remember distinctly the fear and revulsion that spread across the country when Japan declared war against the United States by attacking and bombing Pearl Harbor. American hatred toward "Japs" was palpable. I remember sitting in a subway train in New York City and staring at a group of Asians sitting across the aisle—they were probably Chinese-Americans—and wondering if they were Japanese. And I remember overhearing one Caucasian male say to his neighbor, "Do you think they are Japs who are going to blow up the subway system?"

That sounds like a joke, but it was no joking matter at the time. As a result of this climate of fear and mistrust, the administration of President Franklin D. Roosevelt ruthlessly rounded up and removed Japanese-Americans from their homes in California and interned them in concentration camps away from the coast in order to bolster the defense of the country in case of a Japanese invasion. But these people were not foreign enemies. They were American citizens who were denied their basic civil rights as well as their property because of the nation's perceived need and fear.

We today must remember that in the past a great many normally decent and upright Americans have repeatedly mistreated other people: Native Americans, African-Americans, and Japanese-Americans. And invariably those actions were justified under the rubric of national security or economic need or both. Moreover, this did not happen in some bygone era among unenlightened people. The present generation—the so-called greatest generation—let it happen to their fellow citizens. So before anyone today assumes a high moral tone about what happened a century ago, let that person take a long view of American history and remember that fear and mistrust at any time can and probably will lead to despicable crimes that disgrace the nation and blacken its history.

Readers will notice that the word "Indians" is used more often than the acceptable modern term, "Native Americans," and that's because "Indians" was the word that Americans used in the nineteenth century and that is found in all the documents cited in this book. In addition, "mixed bloods" were normally referred to as "half-breeds." Jackson regularly used the words "Indians" (or "savages" or "barbarians") and "half-breeds."

I have been writing this book on and off for many years. In the research and preparation I have to thank many archivists, librarians, historians, and others for their help, but most especially Jeffrey M. Flannery, manuscript reference librarian at the Library of Congress, and my graduate assistant at the University of Illinois at Chicago, Eric Smith. To them I am most grateful, and I hope they know that.

I also wish to acknowledge the assistance of my superb editor at Viking, Wendy Wolf. Traces of her editorial skill can be detected throughout this book, but that skill was always administered with humor, understanding, patience, and the lightest and most deft touch imaginable. I salute her.

Robert V. Remini
Wilmette, Illinois

Contents

Chronology

1765		Jackson family arrives in Waxhaw settlement, South Carolina
1767	March 15	Andrew Jackson born shortly after the death of his father
1780–1781		Serves in American Revolution: captured, mutilated by British officer, imprisoned with his brother in Camden, and later released in a prisoner exchange
1781		Death of Jackson's mother, Elizabeth Hutchinson Jackson
1784–1786		Studies law in Salisbury, North Carolina
1787	September 26	Licensed as an attorney in North Carolina
1788		Appointed public prosecutor for western district of North Carolina and migrates west
	October 26	Settles in Nashville
1789–1796		Serves on various armed groups to fight Indians
1795	December 19	Elected delegate to Tennessee constitutional convention
1796		Elected to U.S. House of Representatives
	November	Defeated in election for major general of Tennessee militia
1797		Elected to U.S. Senate
1798		Resigns Senate seat; elected judge of superior court of Tennessee
1802		Elected major general of Tennessee militia
1804	July 24	Resigns as judge
1812	June	U.S. declares war against Great Britain
1812–1815		Leads troops against Indians and British
1813	January 7–March	Leads troops to Natchez, returns with troops to Nashville; nicknamed Old Hickory
	July 27	Burnt Corn attack

1813	August 30	Fort Mims massacre
	September 4	Gunfight with Jesse and Thomas Hart Benton
	September 14	Ordered to march against Creeks
	October 7	Leads troops against Creeks
	November 3	Victory at Tallushatchee; adopts Lyncoya
	November 9	Victory at Talladega
1813–1814	November–January	Faces mass desertion of troops
	January 22	Emuchfaw engagement
	January 24	Enotachopco engagement
	March 27	Defeats Creek Indians at Horseshoe Bend
	May 28	Commissioned major general in U.S. Army and placed in command of the southern district
	August 9	Imposes Treaty of Fort Jackson on Creek Nation
	August	Nicknamed Sharp Knife by Indians
	August 22	Occupies Mobile and garrisons Fort Bowyer
	October 25	Invades Florida
	November 7	Captures Pensacola
	November 22	Departs for New Orleans to meet British invasion
1814–1815	December 1–January 8	Defeats British army and forces its withdrawal from Louisiana
1815–1821		Evicts white squatters from Indian territory
1816	July 27	Negro Fort destroyed
	September 14–October 4	Signs provisional treaty with Cherokees
	September 20	Signs treaty with Chickasaws
1817	June–1819, January	Supervises building of the Military Road to the Gulf
	July 8	Signs treaty with Cherokees
	October–December	Quarrels with War Department
	December	Assumes command of Florida invasion
1818	January 6	Offers to seize Florida from Spain
	March 15	Invades Florida
	April 6	Captures St. Marks
	April 6	Arrests Alexander Arbuthnot

1818	April 8	Hangs two Red Sticks, Josiah Francis and Himollemico
	April 16	Attacks Bowlegs Towns
	April 29	Executes Alexander Arbuthnot and Robert Ambrister
	May 24	Captures Pensacola
	May 27	Captures Fort Carlos de Barrancas
	June 2	Declares Seminole War ended and returns to Tennessee
	October 19	Signs treaty with Chickasaws
1819	February 8	Congressional censure for seizure of Florida voted down
1820	October 20	Signs treaty with Choctaws
1821	February 11, 19	Appointed and confirmed territorial governor of Florida
	June 1	Resigns army commission
	July 17	Receives Florida from Spanish
	September 18	Meets with Creek and Seminole chiefs
	November 13	Resigns as governor and returns to Florida
1822	July 20	Nominated for President by Tennessee legislature
1823	October 1	Elected U.S. senator
	December	Reconciles with Thomas Hart Benton
1824	March 4	Nominated for President by Pennsylvania convention
	November	Receives plurality of popular and electoral votes in presidential election
1825	February 9	Defeated for President in House election
	October 12	Resigns Senate seat
	October 14	Nominated for President by Tennessee legislature
1828	June 1	His Indian son, Lyncoya, dies
	November	Elected President
	December 22	His wife, Rachel, dies
1829	March 4	Inaugurated seventh President
	December 8	Recommends Indian removal in his first annual message

1829–1830		Begins reorganization of Bureau of Indian Affairs
	May 28	Signs Indian removal bill
	August	Dismisses head of Indian affairs bureau, Thomas L. McKenney
	August 23	Meets with Chickasaw delegation at Franklin
	August 27	Chickasaws agree to remove
	September 27	Treaty of Dancing Rabbit signed arranging removal of Choctaws
1831	March 18	*Cherokee Nation* v. *Georgia* decided by Supreme Court
1832	March 3	*Worcester* vs. *Georgia* decided by Supreme Court
	March 24	Creeks cede land and agree to remove
	April 6–August 2	Black Hawk War
	May 9	Seminoles agree to remove in Treaty of Payne's Landing
	October 22	Chickasaws cede land
1833	April 6	Meets Chief Black Hawk
1834	June 30	Office of Indian Affairs established; Trade and Intercourse Act passed involving Indian emigrants to west
1835	February 5	Confers with Principal Chief John Ross
	December 18–1842	Second Seminole War
	December 28	Treaty of New Echota signed by seventy-nine Cherokees
1836	May 23	Proclaims Cherokee treaty in force
	May–July	Orders military action against Creeks; Creeks forcibly removed
1837	March 4	Retires from presidency and returns to Tennessee
1838	January 31	Osceola dies after being captured under flag of truce and imprisoned
	spring, summer	Trail of Tears
1845	June 8	Jackson dies at Hermitage

Andrew Jackson & His Indian Wars

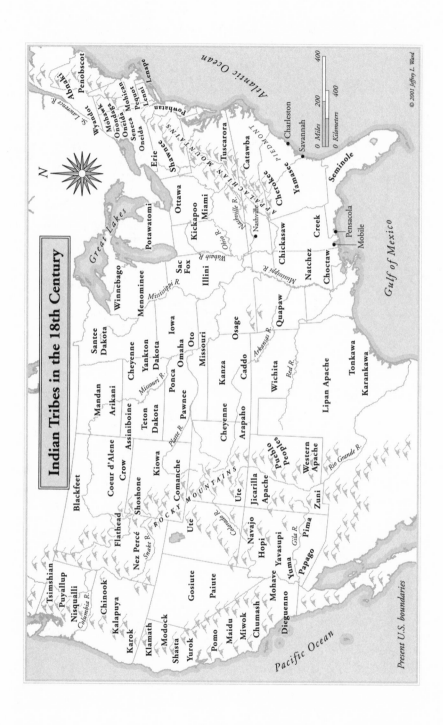

Chapter 1

The Making of an Indian Fighter

The great Shawnee chief Tecumseh let out a terrifying whoop. Six Shawnees, six Kickapoos, and six Winnebagos responded with similar cries. Together, with two Creek warriors as guides, they boarded canoes and headed down the Wabash to the Ohio River on their way south to the country of the Five Civilized Nations: Creeks, Cherokees, Chickasaws, Choctaws, and Seminoles. They were beginning a momentous journey that would change the course of American history in ways they never intended. Tecumseh expected to persuade the southern tribes into joining a stupendous confederation of Native Americans reaching from the Canadian frontier to the Gulf of Mexico with which he would launch a massive Indian attack against white settlements. With such an alliance he expected to sweep the white devils back into the ocean whence they had come and restore the continent to its rightful owners.[1]

After several weeks of overland travel through Kentucky and Tennessee, the chief and his escort arrived in the Alabama Creek territory in October 1811, just in time for the annual grand council of the Creek Nation taking place in the ancient town of Tookabatcha. Tecumseh's fame as an orator and his anticipated address to the council attracted some five thousand Creeks, who had heard about his purpose and had come painted for war. Each night they danced the war dance. Benjamin Hawkins, the veteran American Indian agent in Alabama who espoused the cause of white civilization for Indians and was revered by the Creeks, also attended the grand council, as was his custom.

Finally, after much anticipation, Tecumseh and his warrior party arrived. They strode haughtily to the center of the square of the ancient town and stood "still and erect as so many statues." They were dressed in buckskin hunting shirts and leggings and wore a "profusion of silver ornaments." Their faces were painted red and black, and each warrior carried a rifle, tomahawk, war club, and scalping knife. The muscular six-foot-tall Tecumseh, whose mother was a Creek, looked "austere" and "imperial." He faced the council house and did not turn his head to look to the right or left.

Silence. There was no salutation, no greeting. The Indians waited. Finally Big Warrior (Tustunnuggee Thlucco), a "man of gigantic figure" and the Principal Chief of the Upper Creeks,* slowly approached the visitor and handed his pipe to Tecumseh, who puffed on it and then passed it to his followers. Without saying a word, Big Warrior pointed to a large cabin and Tecumseh and his men entered it. They were seen no more until dark, when they emerged from the cabin and danced the northern war dance, as Creeks crowded around, watching intently but saying nothing.

The following morning one of Tecumseh's escorts presented himself to the Creek Council and announced that his chief would speak at noon; but at that hour the same warrior reappeared and declared that the sun had "traveled too far" and that the talk would be delivered the following day.

This ritual was repeated over the next several days without producing an appearance by the great chief. Finally, in disgust, Hawkins pronounced Tecumseh a fraud and left the council, boasting of his ability to prevent the tribe from entering any agreement that would trigger an uprising. The very next day at noon, Tecumseh and his men emerged from their lodge. It obviously indicated the Shawnee chief's unwillingness to speak in the presence of the white man.

They were naked, except for a "flap about their loins" and a small tobacco pouch suspended under their left arm. They were painted black and each carried a war club. All their other weapons had been laid aside. As an immense throng of Creeks swarmed on either side of them, the visitors moved swiftly into the square, scowling angrily as they walked. At each corner of the square they

---

*Creeks, who actually called themselves Ochese, were given their name by white traders because of the wet and swampy country they inhabited. The Upper Creeks tended to occupy towns in central and southern Alabama along the Coosa and Tallapoosa rivers, while to the east the Lower Creeks occupied towns in west Georgia and east Alabama around the Chattahoochee River. It is unclear how the people in these two regions came to be called Upper and Lower Creeks. Most probably it resulted from the deerskin trade from Charleston, in which the upper path went to the Tallapoosa River and the lower to the Chattahoochee. For the most part they spoke Muskhogean and were often called Muskogees. The Creeks were not so much a tribe as they were a confederacy in which the dominant group was the Muscogees. Michael D. Green, *The Politics of Indian Removal: Creek Government and Society in Crisis* (Lincoln, Neb., and London, 1982), pp. 4, 11–12; Joel W. Martin, *Sacred Revolt: The Muskogees' Struggle for a New World* (Boston, 1991), p. 6; R. S. Cotterill, *The Southern Indians: The Story of the Civilized Tribes Before Removal* (Norman, Okla., 1954), p. 8.

dropped some tobacco and sumac on the ground. By their agitated movements they seemed to be working themselves into a passion, and they strode forward "like a procession of devils."[2] Then they approached the pole in the center of the square, circled it three times, and threw the rest of their tobacco and sumac into a fire at the base of the pole. After that they marched to the huge council chamber or King's House, as it was called in ancient times, and drew up where Big Warrior and other Creek chiefs were seated.

Suddenly, Tecumseh let out a horrendous war whoop, and each of his followers responded with similar shouts, setting up a frightening din. Then the visitor handed Big Warrior a wampum belt of five different strands.

Again silence. A Shawnee pipe was produced. It was large, long, and decorated with shells, beads, eagle feathers, and porcupine quills. Tecumseh and his men each puffed on it and then passed it to the Creek chiefs. All this while not a word was uttered.

At length Tecumseh broke the silence, speaking slowly at first and in guttural tones. But as his words grew more impassioned they came like an avalanche, and "his eyes burned with supernatural luster, and every limb and muscle quivered with emotion."

He began with a brief introduction about his trip from the "great lakes of the North" and how he had passed through many Creek towns "like the wind at night." No whoop was sounded by his followers, he cried, no track was made nor fire kindled, "but see! there is blood on our war clubs!"

"Listen! . . . Oh Muskogees! Brethren of my mother! Brush from your eyelids the sleep of slavery, and strike for vengeance and your country!"

By this time his voice had swelled to a roar and resounded over the square as he called on the Creeks to join their Shawnee brothers to the north and wage war against their common enemy, the white settlers who constantly pressed deeper and deeper into their country. The expression on his face varied with the words he spoke, frequently showing hatred and defiance, occasionally profound sadness. And sometimes his face brightened with a "murderous smile."

"Let the white race perish!" he raged. They seized your lands, corrupted your women, and trampled on the bones of your dead.

"Back whence they came, upon a trail of blood, they must be driven!

"Back—aye, back into the great water whose accursed waves brought them to our shores!

"Burn their dwellings—destroy their stock—slay their wives and children, that the very breed may perish.

"War now! War always! War on the living! War on the dead!"

At the height of this impassioned plea the Shawnee chief assured his listeners that it was the will of the "Great Spirit" who had spoken in the ear of his brother, "the mighty Prophet of the Lakes." And when the white men approach your towns, Tecumseh went on, the earth will open up and swallow them. Then will the Creeks see Tecumseh's strong arm of fire, which will stretch across the sky. "You will know I am on the war-path. I will stamp my foot and the very earth shall shake."

He spoke for an hour. When he finished he had a look of "concentrated vengeance." Not a word was uttered by the immense crowd who heard him. No one let out a war whoop, applauded, shouted, or replied, but a thousand warriors shook with emotion and brandished their tomahawks in the air. Even Big Warrior, who had discouraged the war party among his people, was seen more than once spasmodically clutching the handle of his knife.

A Shawnee pipe was lighted and passed around in solemn silence. Finally Tecumseh's escort let out an "appalling yell" and began their tribal war dance, a descriptive dance that included several individual segments: the scout, the ambush, the surprise, the deadly struggle, and the final evolutions of battle. As they danced they brandished their war clubs and screamed in concert.[3]

After several minutes, Big Warrior regained his composure. His antiwar convictions stirred again and a look of deep sorrow flickered across his face. Slowly he turned toward Tecumseh and said that he would not join the confederation in a war against the United States. He could not. His people would suffer if he did.

Tecumseh reacted in anger and reportedly thrust a finger in Big Warrior's face. "Your blood is white," he shouted. ". . . You do not believe the Great Spirit sent me. You shall believe it. I will leave directly and go straight to Detroit. When I get there I will stamp my foot upon the ground and shake down every house in Tookabatcha."[4]

Several weeks later, after Tecumseh had left and returned to Detroit, an earthquake rocked the Creek territory and severely damaged Tookabatcha. To the superstitious it was a sure sign that Tecumseh had indeed conveyed to them the will of the Great Spirit. As houses collapsed around them the people ran about crying, "Tecumseh has got to Detroit! Tecumseh has got to Detroit! We feel the shake of his foot!" To add further proof of his divine mission the sudden appearance of a comet recalled the Shawnee's claim that his arm of fire would be stretched across the sky.

Although Big Warrior and a number of other chiefs did not cotton to Tecumseh's call to war and publicly scorned the idea, some Upper Creeks, led by a coterie of prophets, formed a war party known as Red Sticks, a name they acquired from their practice of painting their war clubs bright red. The Red Sticks resented the influence of Big Warrior and his faction, as well as the encroachment by whites on their land, the intrusion of white culture, and the building of a federal road from the Georgia frontier to new American settlements along the Alabama River.

A group of them, led by Little Warrior, visited the Shawnees up north. On their way home they killed seven white families on the Duck River just south of Nashville. On learning of these murders, Benjamin Hawkins demanded the arrest and punishment of those involved. The tribal council agreed, and Big Warrior sent out a war party to seize them. The fugitives vainly resisted their capture, and eight of them were executed. The Red Sticks subsequently retaliated by killing nine of the executioners.

Other "rebel" Creeks, led mainly by Peter McQueen (a mixed-blood son of a Scots trader and Creek mother), Josiah Francis (Hilis Hadjo), Paddy Welsh (another mixed-blood), and others, most of them "prophets," formed a mystic order probably created by Seekabo and patterned after the rites developed by Tecumseh's brother, Tenskwatawa, called The Prophet. They claimed they had power to change the direction of bullets in flight, cause earthquakes, or summon lightning to strike a victim.[5]

Over time they attracted a large following, mostly through prophecy, preaching, and magic. As the numbers of Red Sticks swelled, especially among young warriors, they began a systemic assault against their own people, attacking and burning several villages allied with Hawkins, killing livestock, burning homes and fields, and even besieging Big Warrior and his comrades at their fort in Tookabatcha. This civil war broadened into something more ominous when Big Warrior appealed to Hawkins for help. The agent rescued the Principal Chief, but now the United States was involved, and involved at a time when it was already locked in a war against Great Britain that had been declared in June 1812.

A group of so-called War Hawks in the House of Representatives, led by its Speaker, Henry Clay, convinced President James Madison that he should ask Congress for a declaration of war because of Britain's continued violations of American rights. Not only had England impressed our seamen to help fight its war with Napoleon, but it had seized our ships, incited Indians to attack the frontier, and refused to evacuate forts held on American territory along the

Canadian border, which it had promised to do under the peace terms that ended the American Revolution. But even more important was a feeling throughout the country that the United States needed to prove to itself and to foreign countries around the world that it had legitimately won its independence and could maintain American rights against any power that dared infringe them, including the most powerful. Madison complied with the demand of the War Hawks, and on June 4, 1812, the House of Representatives voted a declaration of war against Great Britain, followed by the Senate on June 17. The next day President James Madison signed the bill and the nation went to war.

But now the country was also involved in the Creek War, something Britain would surely exploit to its advantage. Then, in July 1813, at a crossing of Burnt Corn Creek on the Pensacola Road, a group of whites and mixed-blood Creeks attacked a number of Red Sticks, led by Peter McQueen and High Head Jim, who were transporting a packtrain of powder and shot obtained from the Spanish in Florida to their Upper Creek villages. The Red Sticks drove off their attackers but lost their gunpowder. The whites and their friends took refuge in Fort Mims, a makeshift structure built around the house of Samuel Mims, a Georgia trader. It was a mile from the Alabama River in the Mississippi Territory and about forty miles north of the town of Mobile.

At noon on August 30, 1813, the Red Sticks counterattacked. They were led by a new recruit, William Weatherford (Chief Red Eagle). They entered through an open gate and slaughtered the defenders and burned the fort. It was one of the most appalling massacres in frontier history. "The fearful shrieks of women and children put to death in ways as horrible as Indian barbarity could invent" echoed through the fort. They were "butchered in the quickest manner, and blood and brains bespattered the whole earth. The children were seized by the legs, and killed by batting their heads against the stockading. The women were scalped, and those who were pregnant were opened, while they were alive and the embryo infants let out of the womb." Red Eagle wanted no part of this savagery but he could do nothing to stop it. Between 250 and 275 white settlers, friendly Indians, and mixed-bloods were killed; between twenty and forty escaped.[6]

By this action the Red Sticks had dared to war against the United States, had dared to attack an American settlement and slaughter hundreds of its occupants. The Creek civil war had now merged into the War of 1812.

The horror of the massacre at Fort Mims prompted the governor of Tennessee, Willie Blount, to call out the militia. The legislature authorized him to raise five thousand men for a three-month tour of duty, so he ordered Major General Andrew Jackson of the Tennessee militia to "call out organize rendezvous and march without delay" 2,500 volunteers and militia "to repel an approaching invasion . . . and to afford aid and relief to the suffering citizens of the Mississippi Territory."[7]

The James Madison administration responded as well. It recognized that the Creek War had to be extinguished before it expanded into a general uprising among other tribes. Its strategy involved dispatching four armies from Tennessee, Georgia, and the Mississippi Territory into the Creek Nation from different angles with orders to converge at the point where the Coosa and Tallapoosa rivers meet to form the Alabama River.[8] Andrew Jackson, commanding the army from west Tennessee, planned to head directly south, slicing through the heart of the Upper Creek Nation and shredding the power of the Red Sticks as he went. He also planned to lay out a military road through the wilderness that would reach Mobile, thereby providing easy access across the southwestern heartland for future American settlers. As it turned out, the only army to fight the Creek War was Jackson's. The expeditions from Georgia and the Mississippi Territory hardly amounted to more than forays followed by quick retreats.

On taking command, Jackson issued a proclamation to what he called his "*Brave Tennesseans,*" and the Nashville *Whig* published it on September 29, 1813. "Your frontier," he declared, "is threatened with invasion by a savage foe! Already do they advance towards your frontier, with their scalping knives unsheathed, to butcher your wives, your children, and your helpless babes. Time is not to be lost! We must hasten to the frontier, or we will find it drenched in the blood of our fellow-citizens."

The "great Indian fighter of Tennessee" with his troops then headed toward the Creek country and started on a long journey that eventually brought him to the White House. Thus began his celebrated wars against the southern Indian tribes of the United States, which did not end for some twenty-five years, until he had removed them from their ancestral homeland and sent them into a wilderness across the Mississippi River.[9]

———

The making of this Tennessee Indian fighter began some fifty-odd years earlier when a young Scotch-Irish family in Castlereagh on the eastern coast of Northern Ireland—approximately 125 miles from Carrickfergus—decided to flee the miseries of their homeland and follow the path to America taken by thousands

of their countrymen and several of their immediate neighbors and close relatives. His father, also named Andrew Jackson, and his family left Ireland in 1765,
crossed the ocean over a period of many weeks, and suffered the usual agonies
of an eighteenth-century transatlantic passage on a small, frail, and overcrowded
wooden ship.

These Scotch-Irish, who were predominantly Presbyterian in their religious
commitment, had initially moved in the early 1600s from lowland Scotland to
northern Ireland, where they remained for many years, but by the beginning of
the eighteenth century a great number of them had decided for economic reasons, among others, to emigrate to America.

After crossing the ocean they relocated in and around the Philadelphia area,
attracted to the "holy experiment" that the proprietor of the Pennsylvania
colony, William Penn, had established to provide a model of religious liberty
and "Christian living." As their numbers increased, many of them moved westward, until they collided with the mountains and the hostility of the French,
who had infiltrated the area from their strongholds in Canada and forced them
to shift their course toward the southeast. They ultimately settled in the Carolina Piedmont, taking the Great Philadelphia Wagon Road, which passed
through Charlotte in North Carolina. Many of them then moved straight down
to Camden in the northeastern section of South Carolina.

For the most part these very practical and hardheaded Scotch-Irish preferred
to establish themselves on hillside locations near creeks that could be easily
forded and did not flood as readily and as disastrously as large rivers. Hillside locations usually provided natural springs, hence few wells needed to be dug for
water. They planted sweet potatoes, turnips, pumpkins, peas, and beans, and
from the Indians they learned to raise maize (corn) and tobacco.

Naturally the Scotch-Irish in America retained many traits of their Scottish
forebears as well as a few traits acquired in their century-long sojourn among the
Irish. As seen by one contemporary, these American Scotch-Irish were clannish,
impetuous, persistent, "honest and truthful," and able to eke out a livelihood
from "a hard soil and an ungenial clime." They were also hospitable, generous,
and "singularly tender in their feelings." Most particularly, they were contentious for what they thought was right and just. They were also stubborn and
quick to anger and could be most unforgiving. They rarely forgot an offense,
and they carried grudges to inordinate lengths.[10]

Some of these traits were amply demonstrated in the Jackson family. For one
thing, their long, hazardous journey across a turbulent ocean and into a wilder-

ness fraught with both known and unknown perils demonstrated their determination, their fortitude, and their courage. There is little documentary evidence about their journey to their new home in America, but of the surviving reports one of them states that the Jacksons arrived in Charles Town (Charleston), South Carolina, and then moved to the Waxhaw settlement, an area 160 miles northwest from Charleston. Other sources suggest they arrived in Pennsylvania and then traveled south, following a trail taken earlier by other members of the family. It does seem probable that in coming to a foreign land and wishing to be as close to their kin as possible, they took the route south from Philadelphia through Maryland, Virginia, and North Carolina until they reached the hollows and river bottoms of the Blue Ridge. However they arrived, the Jacksons finally settled in the Piedmont or upland area of the Carolinas, known as the Waxhaws, that stretches from North to South Carolina and was the homeland of the Catawba Indians.[11]

Andrew and Elizabeth demonstrated great determination and strength of character as they labored to build a new home in this strange and forbidding country. They settled on new land in the Waxhaws about seven miles from the center of the Scotch-Irish community in the district. Relatives and friends who had accompanied them to America (or who had arrived a short time earlier) helped guide them in their efforts to build a farm and eke out a living. They located on the Twelve Mile Creek, a branch of the Catawba River, and had as neighbors the remaining members of the once powerful Catawba Nation.

Fortunately the tribe posed little threat to the settlers. With one exception these Indians had long been allies of the English against the Spanish and French. They lived along the Catawba River, and their tribe included Waterees, Congarees, Santees, Waxhaws, and Seewees, all of whom belonged to the Siouan group. However, the most dominant Indian tribe in South Carolina was the powerful and fierce Cherokee Nation. Related to the Iroquois of New York, the Cherokees were mountain people and occupied much of the colony's western and northwestern area.

During the early history of the Carolinas there had been several bloody encounters between whites and Native Americans. The recently founded Carolina colonies, along with Georgia, developed a lively trade with coastal Indian hunters, most of whom were Yamasees who lived ninety miles southwest of Charleston. Guns and textiles were traded for deer skins and Indian slaves. Yamasee hunters usually raided Cherokee, Creek, and Tuscarora villages in their search for slaves. When several Cherokees were captured and taken to Charleston to be sold to settlers, the leaders of the Cherokee Nation demanded their release, threatening to exterminate the white settlements if their demands were not met. This filthy traffic in the slave trade among Indians declined shortly thereafter because of white preference for Africans, but the trade in furs and pelts continued, marked by increased cheating and conniving by settlers.

In 1711 the Tuscarora War broke out over the fraudulent activities of white traders and the rumors that the Tuscaroras were to be removed from their land to make room for another colony of European settlers. The savage fighting between whites and Native Americans lasted for nearly two years before the colonial militia succeeded in destroying many Tuscarora villages and taking several hundred prisoners, thereby putting an end to the fighting. But not much later the Yamasees exploded against white atrocities over wrongs committed against their persons, their property, and especially their land. Catawbas joined the fighting against the colonists to stop the unrelenting encroachment of whites on their land and the seizure of their property for unpaid debts. Together the Yamasees and Catawbas nearly wiped out the South Carolina colony in 1715, but they could not rival the fighting resources of their enemy nor the continued infusion of white settlers coming from Europe. After long periods of Indian slaughter as well as the effects of diseases like smallpox and influenza, the tribes virtually disappeared. This was particularly true of the Yamasees. By 1761 it was recorded that only twenty Yamasees survived in South Carolina out of population that had once boasted five thousand or more.[12]

Still the danger of Indian attack did not disappear with the conclusion of the Yamasee War. At any moment war parties from Cherokee, Iroquois, or Shawnee villages might suddenly descend on an isolated settler and burn his house and fields on the excuse that the intruder was infringing on hunting grounds or violating a sacred site—which was often true. Horse-stealing by Indians was a particularly heinous crime and never failed to provoke retaliatory actions by settlers. The white men and women living on the frontier had to maintain a constant vigil against marauding, frequently drunken, and outraged Native Americans. They also got caught up in conflicts among the Indians, especially as different tribes took an active role in the struggle for empire between France and Great Britain that continued over the better part of the eighteenth century. Some tribes fought with the British, others with the French, and many of them with one another.

Of particular concern in South Carolina during these wars was the increasing attempts by Virginia, North Carolina, and Georgia traders to establish monopoly rights to trade with the western tribes. The rivalry encouraged the Cherokees, who lived to the west and in the mountains, to attempt to break the stranglehold exercised by the Charleston mercantile community over the trade by inviting Virginian and Georgian—and even French—traders to visit the Cherokee Nation and negotiate agreements. South Carolina retaliated by instituting a trade embargo by which guns, powder, textiles, and other essentials were cut off from the tribe. The Cherokees had traditionally sided with the British in the imperial wars, but now an active faction sought help from French officials in New Orleans. In the so-called Cherokee War (1760–1761) that resulted from the dispute, the Catawbas aided the Carolinians against both the Cherokees and the French and brought down on themselves the wrath of the Shawnees, who killed their king. The ferocity of the war paralyzed whites with fear because they were caught in the middle. But the Catawbas had their revenge when a few years later they captured a number of Shawnees, tortured them, and put them to death.[13]

Many frontiersmen were also massacred in the fighting, since war parties did not always distinguished between Catawbas and settlers. Finally, smallpox and the unrelenting burning of Cherokee fields and villages by colonial forces brought the killing to an end. Attakullakulla, the "Little Carpenter," and several other Cherokee chiefs petitioned the South Carolina governor for peace in December 1761, and it was granted.

Between the Cherokee War and the French and Indian War (1754–1763), the last war the English and French fought for control of North America, the Catawba Nation was severely reduced in numbers and strength. It was said that the Catawbas were fast sinking into "degeneracy and a state of servility and dependence." By 1765 when the Jacksons arrived, the Catawbas had entered a long period of decline, finding great difficulty in shifting from an economy of hunting and trapping to planting and cattle raising.

Prior to the Cherokee War the Piedmont filled up slowly because of the Indian menace. But now a new wave of Scotch-Irish crowded into the area. Meanwhile a treaty was reached with the Catawbas restricting them to a fifteen-mile square and taking from them their hunting rights outside the area. For the Indians it was virtually impossible to sustain themselves economically on such a reduced "reservation," and they appealed for "gifts" and other "necessities" to keep from starving.[14]

This practice of drawing a line between English territory and Indian territory merely imitated what had become standard practice in the colonies for over a generation. And each succeeding generation would find it needed more Indian land and would redraw the lines and remove the tribes farther west. Removal was a policy nearly as old as the arrival of English settlers almost two centuries earlier. Moreover, the practice of offering Indians "gifts" to stave off starvation soon turned into bribery to entice them into surrendering their land. It was also demoralizing and reduced tribes to dependence and poverty—which is what happened to the Catawbas.

In 1765 the white population of the Piedmont had increased in the previous four years by over 50 percent. The Piedmont attracted not only the predominantly Presbyterian Scotch-Irish but Germans, who were Lutheran, Moravian, or German Reformers, along with some Baptists and Quakers. As the community grew, meetinghouses were built and congregations formed. Among these new arrivals were the Jacksons: Andrew, a poor tenant farmer, his wife, Elizabeth, said to have been a weaver both before and after their marriage, and their two sons, Hugh, aged two, and Robert, six months. Accompanying them was Elizabeth's sister, Jane, the wife of James Crawford. They were welcomed by another sister, the wife of George McCamie, who had preceded them to the Waxhaws, as had two other sisters, the wives of the Leslie brothers. It was a kind of grand reunion for Elizabeth Jackson, who now had an extended family to sustain them as they began their new life in the wilderness.

Because Andrew had little money when he arrived, he was forced to settle on less fertile land.[15] The warm, moist climate and the lack of humus generated iron oxides in the soil, turning it into red clay. Although the soil was ill suited for farming, Jackson and these other Scotch-Irish heroes persisted in tilling it for over 150 years.

Andrew worked himself to death trying to eke out a livelihood from this unpromising location. He built a log cabin, cleared fields, and raised a crop. As far as can be determined he never had clear title to an acre of this land, and after a long battle to make the land yield, he succumbed. Sometime in late winter or early spring 1767, Andrew Jackson died suddenly, leaving a pregnant wife and two small sons.

After the burial, Elizabeth and her children never returned to their homestead at Twelve Mile Creek. Rather they went to the home of Elizabeth's sister, Jane Crawford, where on March 15, 1767, she gave birth to a third son. She named him Andrew after her late husband.

The Jackson family lived with the Crawfords for the next dozen years or so, Elizabeth serving as housekeeper and nurse to her ailing sister. Here young Andrew attended an academy run by Dr. William Humphries and was later sent to a school directed by the Presbyterian minister James White Stephenson, in the hope that he might fulfill his mother's wish that he become a Presbyterian minister. Although he learned to read and write and "cast accounts," young Andrew never received the education commensurate with his intellectual abilities and talents. And his adult life frequently demonstrated the unfortunate effects of this deficiency. James Parton, an early biographer, said that Jackson's "ignorance was as a wall round about him—high, impenetrable. He was imprisoned in his ignorance, and sometimes raged round his little, dim enclosure like a tiger in his den."[16] This characterization is a bit overwrought, but it is true that he never had the essential education that might have properly prepared him for the great office he later achieved.

Just as crucially, he also lacked a father or someone else to provide adult male guidance. Apparently none of his uncles, for whatever reason, took up the role. And the boy never forgot it. Once Andrew left the Waxhaws he never looked back. He never regarded his South Carolina relatives as members of his family. When he became famous a few of these relatives contacted him to ask about their relationship, but he either turned a deaf ear to their inquiries or put them off with a curt response.

On the other hand, Elizabeth, known to her family and friends as Aunt Betty, did what she could to provide the boy with direction and purpose, and as a strong figure herself, she contributed a great deal to his character development. It was reported that Elizabeth taught her son not to steal, lie, or sue for slander or assault. The field of honor was the place to settle personal quarrels, she said. "Sustain your manhood always. . . . Never wound the feelings of others. Never brook wanton outrage upon your own feelings." After his great victory over the British in 1815, General Jackson supposedly said to several friends gathered around him, "Gentlemen, I wish she could have lived to see this day. There never was a woman like her. She was gentle as a dove and as brave as a lioness."[17]

Although the menace of the Catawbas had virtually disappeared during young Andrew's early years, there were always conflicts between Indians and settlers, usually over horse-stealing or unpaid bills, to settle which white frontiersmen seized land in lieu of money. These disputes frequently resulted in violence. And the threat of Indian attacks from some marauding war party from the west or north was a constant fear that pervaded white settlements on the frontier. Children soon learned about the danger and the need to protect themselves and their families. Just who educated Andrew in the art of Indian fighting cannot be documented with any degree of certainty, but the recollections of neighbors suggest that his mother had an enormous influence. According to a neighbor, Susan Alexander, "Aunt Betty" was a "fresh-looking, fair-haired, very conservative, old Irish lady, at dreadful enmity with the Indians."[18]

"At dreadful enmity with the Indians." Alexander seems to think that Elizabeth's oldest son, not Hugh or Robert, was killed by Indians, which, if true, would certainly explain her "dreadful enmity." Moreover, said Alexander, the family "did lament about their eldest son and brother. They took great spells of mourning about him."

Hugh was the eldest son, and he died during the American Revolution, most probably from a heat stroke. There is no documentation supporting the claim that Elizabeth had a fourth child, and Alexander is undoubtedly confused about his identity. After all, she was quite old when she provided these reminiscences, and, as she said, she wished she "had committed better to my memory about matters." But she is certain about one thing: Elizabeth's deadly hatred for Indians that had resulted from the killing of a kinsman.[19]

"Mrs. Jackson and her son, Andrew, came to our house," Alexander remembered, but not the other brothers. "Nor do I recollect hearing them mention any other brother than the one that was killed. I only recollect about the death of that one brother, and I had it as a perfect belief, that he was killed by the Indians—for they often mourned him, and they were inveterate haters of the Indians, on account of their barbarities—both he and his mother."

"Inveterate haters of the Indians." Thus, according to Alexander, Andrew Jackson learned to fear and hate Indians from an early age—as did most frontier settlers. And they never forgot. "Oh!" said Alexander, "we all suffered by those horrid Indians; and the remembrance of it has not gone out of me yet."[20]

Besides Andrew's mother, his older brothers may have had a hand in stirring the boy's great enmity against Native Americans, and possibly his uncles, too. Surely the other boys in the neighborhood with whom he played and attended school reinforced his mistrust and fear.

As he grew, Andrew learned to make bows and arrows, just like the Indians, and in time became something of a marksman in "shooting snipes, partridges and wild turkeys." Alexander remembered him as "a lank, leaning-forward fellow, tall of his age," with a "a large forehead and big eyes." Moreover, she said he "was an independent boy in his manner . . . [and] could not well be idle."[21]

It is also known that early in life he learned to detect the sounds of Indians communicating with one another in the brush when they imitated the call or sounds of animals or birds. He was especially adept at knowing if those sounds meant danger. It was reported that he once saved a party from possible massacre by Cherokees when he recognized that the forest sounds came from humans, not wildlife.[22]

In addition to his hatred, mistrust, and fear, Andrew developed some fixed prejudices about Native Americans by the time he became a teenager: their undeviating enmity toward white society for squatting on their land; the need for constant vigilance against Indian attack; the belief that "savages," as he invariably called them, were barbaric and could not be trusted and regularly violated promises and treaty agreements. Those like Andrew who lived on the frontier accepted as indisputable fact that Indians had to be shunted to one side or removed to make the land safe for white people to settle and cultivate. The removal, if not the elimination of the Indian from civilized society, became ingrained in the culture. And it lodged securely in Andrew's mind as well.[23]

As a teenager he was one of the wildest in the neighborhood. Hot-tempered, easily offended, and ready to fight if insulted, he quickly gained a reputation as an undisciplined youth who seemed hell-bent on mischief and troublemaking. Some writers attributed it to the fact that there was a good deal of Scotch-Irish in him. Like his forebears, young Andrew could be stubborn, impetuous, quick to anger, and extremely contentious when he believed he was right. And he rarely forgot an affront ot insult. At the same time he could be unwavering in his loyalty toward friends and "singularly tender" toward them. One early biographer described him as "a wild, frolicsome, willful, mischievous, daring, reckless boy." A fighting cock all his life, he was very kind to the hens who clucked around him but a savage killer toward any other cock who dared cross him.

On one occasion he was challenged by a group of boys to fire a gun that had been loaded to the muzzle. It was a prank. Apparently they wanted to watch him get thrown to the ground by the discharge. Andrew grabbed the gun, fired it, and was sent sprawling. In a near frenzy, he sprang to his feet and screamed, "By G-d, if one of you laughs, I'll kill him!" And the terrible look in his blazing blue eyes indicated beyond doubt that he meant what he said. No one laughed or made a sound. No one dared.[24]

As a youth Andrew developed a vicious temper that sometimes exploded into violence. But violence was a way of life on the frontier, and he absorbed it as a matter of course.

Violence soon shook the entire country when the American colonies in Philadelphia declared their independence from Great Britain in 1776 and took up arms to defend it. Once the fighting began, the British promptly employed

Indians to assist them in subduing the rebellion. John Stuart was assigned the task of supplying the Cherokees, Creeks, Choctaws, and Chickasaws with guns and ammunition so that they might wipe out frontier settlements in the south. As allies of the British, the Cherokees attacked the new white Watauga communities in the trans-Appalachian area in Tennessee (at that time still part of North Carolina) and then extended their raids eastward into Virginia and North and South Carolina. The frontiersmen, led by James Robertson and John Sevier, drove off the Indians in Tennessee, while other American forces in the east burned the Cherokees' villages and destroyed their crops. The terror ultimately succeeded in forcing the Cherokees to agree to give up their tribal rights in western South Carolina and reaffirm their cession of the Watauga and Nolichucky settlements in eastern Tennessee. But a faction of the Cherokee Nation known as the Chickamauga Cherokees, led by Dragging Canoe and Bloody Fellow, kept up their attacks and were regularly supplied with guns and ammunition by the British. Throughout the Revolution both the frontier and more settled communities like the Waxhaws were on perpetual alert because of the intermittent Indian raids.

General Charles Lee, commander of the Continental forces in the south, blamed the British for inciting these raids. Their plan, as laid out by "his most excellent and clement majesty, George the third," he wrote, was "to lay waste the provinces, burn the habitations, and mix men, women, and children in one common carnage, by the hand of the Indians."[25]

William Henry Drayton, the leader of the revolutionary movement in South Carolina and elected chief justice in 1776, echoed these sentiments and made certain that patriot officers understood clearly the expectations of the people living on the southern frontier with respect to the Indians. *"And now a word to the wise,"* he wrote to the commanders. "It is expected you make smooth work as you go—that is you cut up every Indian corn field, and burn every Indian town—and that every Indian taken shall be the slave and property of the taker; that the nation be extirpated, and the lands become the property of the public." Understand me, he said: "For my part I shall never give my voice for a peace with the Cherokee Nation upon any other terms than their removal beyond the mountains."[26]

Removal was the will of South Carolinians even at the start of the American Revolution. And the greatest South Carolinian of them all, Andrew Jackson, would ultimately make it happen.

The British themselves finally brought the war to the south when they slammed into Georgia and South Carolina and captured Savannah and Charleston. Then, in the spring of 1780, when Andrew was thirteen years of age, some 300 enemy horsemen, commanded by Lieutenant Colonel Banastre Tarleton, rode into the Waxhaws, surprised a group of patriot soldiers, and inflicted heavy losses on them, killing 113 and wounding 150. Most of "the people hided [*sic*] their boys, for fear the British would take them off." Homes were pillaged and the dead and wounded left where they had fallen. The savagery of the British assault resembled Cherokee fighting, and the engagement was rightly called a massacre. The meetinghouse was converted into a hospital, and Elizabeth Jackson with her two younger sons attended the wounded. The oldest son, Hugh, joined the regiment of William Richardson Davie and later died of "the fatigues of the day" at the Battle of Stono Ferry.[27]

After wreaking havoc on the settlers, Tarleton made a serious effort to enlist the aid of the Catawba Nation against the Americans. But the Catawbas were too weak to provide any useful help. Then Lord Rawdon, with an even larger contingent of British soldiers, descended on the hapless Carolinians and sent them fleeing toward the mountains for protection, Elizabeth Jackson and her two sons with them. It soon became a vicious cycle: the British would depart and the settlers would return to their homes; then the enemy would reappear and the Waxhaw inhabitants would scurry back to the interior. As a result, the summer of 1780 became one long horror of "murderous tories" seeking to annihilate the American rebels. The people of the Waxhaws lived in a state of perpetual fright, never knowing when or if the British soldiers or their Indian allies would pounce on them and burn their homes and fields.

In this seesaw kind of existence Andrew Jackson experienced something he never forgot. It gave him firsthand knowledge of how an enemy of his country always engaged Indians in their warfare against the Americans. In his mind, and the minds of most frontiersmen, the Indians were pawns to be used by any foreign power seeking to gain dominance in North America.

At their mother's encouragement, Robert and Andrew attended the drills and general musters of the local militia, where they learned the commands and exercises of military service. Thus, at an early age, Andrew came to appreciate the value and necessity of the militia; he also came to appreciate many of the social and political assets that attended membership in this vital organization.

Because of British and American loyalist or Tory devastation of their community, the people of the Waxhaws kept appealing for help. And it finally came in the person of Colonel William Richardson Davie and a small force intent on avenging the Tarleton massacre. Andrew and his brother joined this force, probably as messengers or errand boys, and at the Battle of Hanging Rock the Americans almost won a victory. But they celebrated too soon and got drunk, and when the British counterattacked they panicked and rode off in wild confusion.

It has been said that if General Jackson had any model for soldiering, that model was Davie. The colonel was bold in planning his operations but very cautious in executing them. He was also untiringly active and ever vigilant. He cared for his troops and tried to provide for their comfort whenever possible.[28]

After the Battle of Hanging Rock the British departed and the settlers returned to their homes—or what was left of them. But the following year the enemy returned and the fighting broke out once more. The month of February 1781 witnessed some of the worst moments of the Revolution for the people of the Waxhaws. It became a vicious civil war in which neighbor fought neighbor. "Men hunted each other like beasts of prey, and the savages were outdone in cruelties to the living and indignities to the dead."[29] For the remainder of his life Andrew Jackson remembered the horror of those days and the madness that prevailed over the entire community. He and his brother took part in many skirmishes in the area and were finally captured when a Tory neighbor notified British dragoons of their presence in the home of Lieutenant Crawford. The house was surrounded; troops burst in and the boys were taken prisoner.

A British officer guarding them ordered Andrew to clean his boots, and when he refused the officer aimed his sword straight at his head. Andrew threw up his left hand to protect himself and received a deep gash on his forehead and fingers, a lifetime reminder of British savagery.

The two boys, along with about twenty other captives, were incarcerated in what can only be described as a concentration camp in Camden, South Carolina. Never would he forget how "harshly & inhumanly" he and the other prisoners were treated. Herded into an area with 250 other prisoners, and lacking adequate food, medicine, or beds, both Jackson boys were robbed and abused. At length they contracted smallpox. Fortunately their mother arrived just as an exchange of prisoners was being arranged between Lord Rawdon and Captain Walker of the American militia. She persuaded the officers to include her boys in the exchange, and they were surrendered, along with five Waxhaw neighbors, in return for a number of British soldiers.[30]

Elizabeth was stunned by the appearance of her children. Wasted by disease and malnutrition, they appeared to be dying. She procured two horses, placed Robert on one—clearly he was the worse off—and rode the other herself. Andrew walked behind them, barefoot and without a jacket, a distance of forty-five miles. When she got them home she put them both to bed and nursed them as best she could; but Robert died two days later and Andrew became delirious and nearly succumbed. Fortunately the skill and attention of his mother, his own strong constitution, and the help of a local doctor eventually brought him around. But it was a slow process and he remained feeble and weak for months. For Elizabeth, "it was a time of great trials," remembered Susan Alexander. "She did think a dreadful deal of that son, Ande, who was her all."[31]

But once "Ande" passed the critical stage his mother decided to travel to Charleston to help nurse prisoners of war held in prison ships, among them two nephews, James and William Crawford. Lord Cornwallis had moved out of South Carolina, leaving a small occupying force in Charleston, and had reached Virginia, where he was presently fortifying Yorktown. It seemed safe enough for Elizabeth to travel, and so with several other nursing companions she journeyed the 160 miles to Charleston, where she later contracted cholera, or ship fever, as it was called, and died.

So, at the age of fifteen, Andrew Jackson was an orphan and a veteran of war with both the British and the Indians. And with it all he had experienced intense personal suffering.

For the next several years a depressed, physically ill, angry, and resentful young man tried to discover what he wanted to do with his life. For a time he continued to live in the house of Thomas Crawford, where he met another boarder, Captain Galbraith. On one occasion Galbraith took offense at something Andrew had said and raised his hand to strike him. Andrew lost complete control of himself. He cursed the captain in a shouted stream of invective and swore that if the hand touched him Galbraith was a dead man. And he vividly remembered what he said when he related the incident decades later. "I had arrived at an age to know my rights," he said, "and although weak and feeble from disease, I had courage to defend them, and if he attempted anything of that kind I would most assuredly Send him to the other world."[32]

Once the Revolution ended and the British evacuated South Carolina, Andrew and a group of other young men rode off to Charleston, where he spent the better part of 1782 drinking, gambling, cockfighting, and mischief-making in a wild, carefree existence that bordered on the manic. It was as though he was attempting to assuage the demons within him. When he dissipated what money he had and found his friends no longer willing to put up with his antics, he returned to the Waxhaws, finished what little formal schooling he could find, and then, in 1784, at the age of seventeen, departed for Salisbury, in Rowan County, North Carolina, to learn enough law to become a lawyer. Apparently he figured that that profession would help him advance in a new nation that had achieved its independence and was in the process of establishing a republican society. It would appear that he had had enough of waywardness and the unbridled indulgence of his anger and grief. From the moment he departed South Carolina, Andrew Jackson set out to make something of himself.

Chapter 2

Fighting Cherokees, Chickasaws, and Creeks

For the next two years, Andrew trained in the law in the office of Spruce McCay, an eminent local barrister. He copied papers, cleaned the office, ran errands, and read law books. Presumably, in a few years, this "course of study" would qualify him for admission to the North Carolina bar. He and a number of other law students found living quarters in the town and regularly indulged their youthful exuberance in evenings of fun and games. Andrew became the group leader, demonstrating at this early age his ability to attract followers and plot their activities. One resident of the town remembered that "Andrew Jackson was the most roaring, rollicking, game-cocking, horse-racing, card-playing mischievous fellow that ever lived in Salisbury." But these activities were unlike his antics in Charleston. He no longer needed to act out an inner rage. What he did was simply let off steam after a long day of monotonous work in McCay's law office.[1]

It was reported that he was not a scholar and preferred the stable and horses to books and office work. Horses and girls were his principal interests, and to amuse his friends he frequently engaged in practical jokes, such as removing gates and signposts and relocating outhouses to remote areas.

For all his juvenile exuberance and horseplay, Andrew was apparently well liked in Salisbury. Something about him was very appealing. Even at the age of eighteen he possessed a charismatic presence that drew people to him. Over the following years he developed a style and dignity that won respect and attention. It was said that if Andrew Jackson joined a party of travelers and they were attacked by Indians, he would instinctively take command and the party would just as instinctively look to him for leadership.[2]

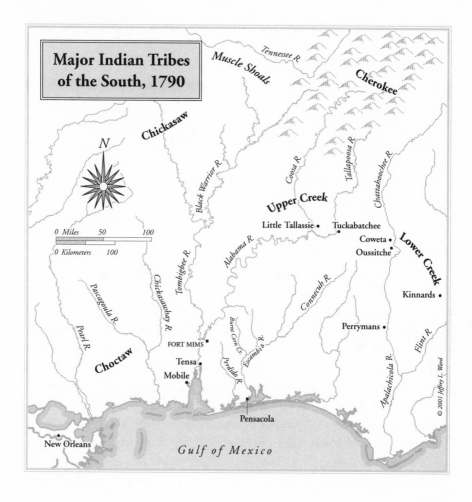

Major Indian Tribes
of the South, 1790

One reason for Andrew's commanding presence was his appearance. Standing tall at six feet one inch, erect in bearing with a shock of sandy-colored, bushy hair that stood straight up and added to his height, he exuded a sense of strength. He had a slender face with a jutting jaw and a long, straight nose that flared slightly at the end. But his most outstanding feature was deep blue eyes that could shower sparks when ignited by passion.

His study of law at McCay's ended in 1786, and he completed his apprenticeship in the office of Colonel John Stokes, regarded as one of the best lawyers in North Carolina. From schools he derived little, and from law books and practicing attorneys less. Still, he learned enough to appear before two judges of the

Superior Court of Law and Equity of North Carolina on September 26, 1787, and win the right to practice as an attorney in the several courts of pleas and quarter sessions within the state.

For the next six months Andrew drifted around North Carolina, trying to establish himself, but his practice did not take hold. Then he heard that John Mc-Nairy, a former fellow student at McCay's, had been elected by the legislature to be the superior court judge for the western district of North Carolina, the area that later became the state of Tennessee, and had the authority to appoint the public prosecutor for the district. McNairy offered the post to Jackson, and since his career in eastern North Carolina seemed to be going nowhere, Andrew accepted. He and Bennett Searcy, another McCay student, who had been appointed clerk of the court, and three or four others, agreed to rendezvous at Morgantown and then head west into eastern Tennessee. Unquestionably life in the wilderness would present numerous problems and dangers, and certainly the post of public prosecutor would not make him popular on the frontier, but Jackson seemed genuinely excited by the prospect and the challenge of a new career, especially in a region that had already tried and failed to cut free of North Carolina and create a new state within the United States. Two western communities, called settlements at the time, had already been formed: one around Knoxville, the other around the Cumberland River Valley centered in Nashville. Both gave promise of further development that could enhance the fortunes of a young, eager, and ambitious young man like Andrew Jackson.

There was, however, a triple-headed menace the settlers constantly faced along the far western frontier: England, Spain, and their Indian allies. In 1783, North Carolina had passed the so-called "Land Grab Act," which permitted citizens of the state to claim Indian land in Tennessee. Less than a year later some two to three million acres of Cherokee and Chickasaw lands were staked out and claimed. Needless to say, that action set off a vicious contest between whites and Indians. The attacks by Cherokees became so numerous that many of Tennessee's earliest settlers fled their homes and traveled as far north as Kentucky. Then militias from several communities counterattacked and forced the Indians to withdraw—all of which only intensified the enmity between the two peoples.

Spain, in possession of East and West Florida and Louisiana by virtue of the treaties that ended the French and Indian War and the American Revolution, contributed to the havoc by supplying the Indians with weapons and urging them to resist American encroachment on their land. Don Esteban Miró, governor at New Orleans, encouraged the dissident Chickamauga Cherokees, led by Dragging Canoe, to accelerate their war against the settlers and promised them a Spanish trading post in Tennessee where they could obtain guns and ammunition. Stamping his foot on the ground, Dragging Canoe swore that he and his Chickamaugans would turn Tennessee into a "bloody ground."[3]

England, too, kept the frontier in turmoil by assisting its Spanish allies in the south with war materials for the Indians and continuing to occupy the forts along the northern frontier on U.S. soil in violation of the Treaty of Paris that ended the Revolution. Thus, from the 31st parallel in the south and up the Mississippi Valley to the northern border with Canada, the American frontier settlements became a battleground between white squatters in search of land and Native Americans intent on driving them away.

Jackson knew the dangers in heading into Tennessee, but they in no way discouraged him. He rather looked forward to it. So he packed a few belongings, a gun, and perhaps a letter or two of introduction and rode off to Morgantown, where he met the other members of his group. In early 1788, they started west across the mountains, heading for Jonesborough. They did not stay long in Jonesborough, just long enough for Jackson to quarrel with another lawyer by the name of Waightstill Avery over what Jackson considered an insult to his legal reputation. They settled the matter with a duel. Fortunately, neither man was injured.[4]

In heading toward the frontier in Nashville, Jackson, McNairy, and the others knew they would travel through dangerous Indian country. They therefore decided to join a large party of settlers that had a sizable escort. There would be greater safety in numbers, and unquestionably they would need it. A notice in the *North Carolina State Gazette* of November 28, 1788, announced the departure of the McNairy party and warned of the perils they faced. "Notice is hereby given, that the new road from Campbell's station to Nashville, was opened on the 25th of September, and the guard attended at that time to escort such persons as were ready to proceed to Nashville; that about sixty families went on, amongst whom were the widow and family of the late General Davidson and John McNairy, judge of the Superior Court; and that on the 1st day of October next, the guard will attend at the same place for the same purpose."[5]

After making all the necessary preparations, the settlers, their escort, and the law enforcement group of McNairy, Jackson, and Searcy headed toward Nashville, some 183 miles to the west. The group numbered about a hundred, including women and children, and the road they traveled sliced through a gap in the Cumberland Mountains and into a wilderness that was considered "more dangerously infested" with hostile Indians than any other area in the western country, and that included the "dark and bloody ground of Kentucky."

Every day and every night, members of the group watched and listened for any sign of hostiles. When they came to what was considered the most hazardous segment of their journey they kept marching, never stopping to rest or make camp. They traveled a night and two days for some thirty-six hours, never halting longer than an hour. They knew that when they reached a certain point along the road they would be relatively safe, allowing them to make camp and rest.

When they reached that point it was night. The exhausted travelers lit fires and set up tents for the women and children to sleep. The men, except for those assigned to sentinel duty, wrapped themselves in blankets and lay down under a tree or alongside fallen logs with their feet toward the fire. Soon everyone but the guards fell asleep and complete silence enveloped the camp.

All slept. Everyone, that is, except Andrew Jackson. He sat on the ground, back against a tree, smoking a corncob pipe. Whether he remained awake to finish his smoke or because he suspected trouble is not known. But about ten o'clock as he started to doze off he heard the hoots of owls in the forest around him. Strange, he thought. Owls in this country? He started dozing again, and once more an owl hooted, only this time it was louder and closer to the camp. Something unusual in the note of the hoot captured his attention and brought him fully awake. From his experience in the Waxhaws he remembered similar sounds, and in a flash he bolted to his feet, grabbed his gun, and raced over to his sleeping friend Bennett Searcy.

"Searcy," Jackson hissed, "raise your head and make no noise."

The dazed and semiconscious Searcy raised his head. "What's the matter?" he asked.

"The owls—listen," commanded Jackson. "There—there again. Isn't that a little *too* natural?"

"Do you think so?" came the reply.

"I know it," said Jackson. "There are Indians all around us. I have heard them in every direction. They mean to attack before daybreak."[6]

They woke up other members of the escort, who confirmed both Jackson's opinion and his advice that the other people in the party be roused and that the march be resumed right away. Very quietly the camp was broken up and the company moved out. In their evacuation they neither saw nor heard a single Indian. But an hour later a party of hunters stumbled on the abandoned camp and decided to take advantage of the still-smoldering fires and get some rest. Just before dawn they were attacked by the Indians and all but one were killed.

The following spring, Judge McNairy had occasion to travel back to Jonesborough, and he passed near the same spot where the hunters had been slain. Without a Jackson in his party to warn him of danger, McNairy and his escort were set upon by the enemy and narrowly escaped with their lives. They fled to a river and swam across to the other side, leaving their horses, bags, and clothing behind. They reckoned themselves lucky to be alive.[7]

By the end of October 1788, Jackson and his train of emigrants reached Nashville. He found lodgings at the blockhouse of the widow Donelson, whose husband, John, had been killed by Indians just a short time before. There the young lawyer met the widow's youngest daughter, Rachel, who was then married to Lewis Robards. Rachel was as carefree and wild as Andrew, and the two fell in love, igniting a terrible family quarrel. Robards returned to Kentucky, where he later began proceedings to obtain a divorce, accusing his wife of desertion and adultery with another man. The divorce was ultimately granted, after which Andrew and Rachel were married in 1793 by the justice of the peace.[8]

Jackson prospered in his new surroundings, successfully prosecuting delinquent debtors, establishing his own private law practice, which mainly involved land titles, sales, debts, and assaults, and winning appointment as attorney general for the district. His law practice expanded very quickly and he later formed partnerships with John Overton and Samuel Donelson, one of Rachel's many brothers, to buy and sell land (much of which was still under Indian title and control) and operate a store on the Cumberland River.

When he first arrived in Nashville in 1788 the several stations set up along the Cumberland River for protection from the Indians guarded approximately five thousand men, women, and children who had been settling the area since 1779. It was indeed the outpost of white civilization, and no one dared live more than five miles from the central stockade for fear of enemy attack. So exposed were they that within a five-mile radius of Nashville the Indians killed a settler every ten days. By the time Jackson arrived, they had killed thirty-three altogether.

The situation grew worse each month. The continued influx of white settlers into Tennessee meant an inevitable invasion of Indian land, and with it ceaseless bloodletting. Both groups despised and feared each other, and this prejudice and mistrust saturated both their cultures.

Jackson was no different from any other settler. To him Indians were "savages," and mixed-bloods were "half-breeds." And he always treated them like children—bloodthirsty children, to be sure—whose barbarism knew no deterrent save the gun.

In establishing himself in Nashville, Jackson became part of the community's efforts to protect and defend itself against the outraged Cherokees who understandably attacked squatters on their land. He "aided alike in garrisoning the forts, and in pursuing and chastising the enemy," reported one early chronicler. And in conducting his legal business during the first seven years of his residence in Tennessee he regularly traveled between Nashville and Jonesborough. He journeyed back and forth between these two communities a total of twenty-two times—this when the Indian menace in the area was at its height.

He usually traveled in the company of other men or guides. As a result he became well versed with the peculiar habits and practices of the Cherokees and soon gained a reputation as an excellent Indian fighter. Shortly after his arrival in Nashville he was conscripted into an expedition to punish the "savages," following their daring attack on the Robertson Station during broad daylight when the men were in the fields. Captain Sampson Williams headed this force of about sixty or seventy men, and they raced to the edge of the Duck River in an attempt to catch the fleeing Indians. But Williams realized that the hostiles were outdistancing them and that so large a force as he had could not overtake the enemy. So with twenty men, among them Jackson, he rushed ahead of the main group. By making forced marches they finally caught sight of their prey encamped on the south side of the river. There were about thirty Cherokees. Stealthily Williams and his men crept forward in the thick cane that concealed their presence. At daybreak they attacked, killing one man, wounding five or six others, and sending the party rushing headlong across the river to the north side, where they disappeared and made good their escape. The Indians left behind sixteen guns, nineteen shot pouches, and all their baggage, consisting of blankets, leggings, moccasins, skins, and other articles.[9]

Williams did not pursue, but met up with the other men of his force and returned to Nashville. So ended Andrew Jackson's "first Indian campaign and Indian fight" in Tennessee. He was a private in this small expedition but, according to Captain Williams, "bold, dashing, fearless, and *mad upon his enemies*." The two men became fast friends and "had great ambition for encounters with the savages." Indeed, they developed a passion about fighting Indians and over the next several years they indulged their passion at every opportunity.[10]

To Jackson, killing Indians and driving them farther south and west was the only way to safeguard the Tennessee frontier. It was a necessary function of life in the wilderness.

During one of his many trips to Jonesborough, Jackson came to a creek that had been swollen by rain and had become a raging torrent. It was night, and the rain kept falling in torrents. He dared not forge the creek and so waited all night, wrapped in a blanket, holding his rifle, and listening to the roaring flood. He was also alert to any sound that might indicate the presence of the enemy. Certain that Cherokees lurked nearby, he kept an all-night vigil. The following morning the rain stopped, the creek subsided, and he mounted his horse and crossed to the other side. He reached Jonesborough without further incident, but on his return he and his three other companions spotted the smoldering fires of a party of hostiles on the opposite side of the Amory River. And it was a large party. Without a moment's hesitation, Jackson assumed command of the group and summoned his friends to follow him as they abandoned the road at different points, erasing all trace of their presence. He then headed into the mountains along the banks of the river. All night they traveled, guided only by the sound of the river. As the hours passed he realized that at some point they must cross the river if they expected to get to Nashville. In the morning Jackson decided to cross it. But in order to keep their powder dry, he directed that they build a raft rather than swim to the other side. On the raft they placed their belongings, including their guns and shot pouches. Two makeshift oars were tightly rigged to either side. Jackson and another man jumped aboard while the other two men tended the horses.

The raft no sooner left the shore than it was seized by the current and carried swiftly downstream. The two men onshore raced alongside and called to Jackson to return, but he kept pulling on his oar, trying to gain the opposite bank. Then suddenly he spotted the edge of a fall in the river and realized he must return immediately or be hurtled with his companion and their belongings over the fall. Straining every nerve and muscle in his body, he tore off one of the oars and extended it to the two men onshore, who had kept abreast of the raft. Fortunately, they grabbed hold of it and pulled the raft to the bank. In their anger and fright the two men screamed at Jackson for failing to respond to their alarm when they first called to him to return. Jackson just laughed. "A miss is as good as a mile," he responded. "*You see how near I can graze danger.* Come on, and I will save you yet."

And he did. They continued their march along the riverbank, spent another night without lighting a fire or eating supper, and finally found a ford the next morning, where they crossed. They then returned to Nashville without hearing or seeing any hostile Indians. But it was a close call.[11]

Jackson had many other close calls. Once, on his way across the wilderness to meet a party of friends, he arrived late at the rendezvous, and his friends had already left. It was dusk and he had ridden as fast as possible, but he would never catch up to them unless he continued traveling through the night. He finally reached the campfires his friends had recently left as they continued their journey. But Jackson also discovered the tracks of Indians who were obviously trailing the Tennesseans. Realizing the danger, he raced on and found the spot where the Indians had left the path and taken to the woods in an effort to circle ahead and set an ambush. He finally reached his friends after they had crossed a deep, half-frozen river and were drying their clothes by the campfires. He burst into the camp, sounding the alarm. The party instantly resumed their march.

All that night and the next day they traveled, not daring to rest or eat until they reached the cabins of a company of hunters. They begged for shelter and protection but were refused, presumably because the hunters suspected the travelers would steal their provisions. Jackson and his party were forced to continue their march in the teeth of a raging snowstorm. Finally they could continue no longer. Utterly exhausted, they dropped in their tracks. They had not slept for sixty hours. Jackson wrapped himself in a blanket, slid to the ground, and fell immediately asleep. The next morning he awoke to find himself buried in six inches of snow.

But the Indians continued their pursuit. At length they came upon the cabins of the hunters and vented their rage by slaughtering every one of them. It was a brutal scene, so much so that the Indians felt satisfied that they had exacted a suitable revenge on the whites. They therefore broke off their pursuit of Jackson and his party and left them to complete their journey unmolested.[12]

The accumulation of such events as these shaped Jackson into a bold and resourceful Indian fighter, thirsting for "encounters with the savages." Within a very short time of his arrival in Tennessee he had become a daring and reckless frontiersman who seemingly placed little value on life—his own or that of the Indians. No matter what he was doing he would instantly drop it to answer the call "to pursue a savage foe." The summons of a trumpeter or one relayed by man, woman, child, or servant could not be disregarded under pain of ostracism. Anyone who dallied when summoned "could not 'hold up his head' among honest and brave men." "Savages" had to be disposed of, one way or another.[13]

As can be seen, Jackson spent a good deal of his early life in Tennessee hunting Indians and being hunted by them. It was a contest that added greatly to the already existing fear and distrust lodged deep in the consciousness of both races.

The continuing problem of the Spanish in Florida and Louisiana, who regularly supplied the Creeks, Chickasaws, and Cherokees with munitions, convinced Jackson and most frontiersmen that Spain, like England, had to be expelled. By its action Spain hoped to form the tribes into a defensive military chain and thereby keep the Americans from advancing farther south and west and threatening its empire. What resulted was a Southern Indian Confederation of sorts, nominally led by a mixed-blood Creek named Alexander McGillivray. The chiefs of these tribes regularly met in Mobile, Pensacola, and New Orleans to confer with Spanish officials.

Another problem with Spain involved control of the Mississippi River. If westerners wished to sell their produce in either Natchez or New Orleans or ship it east by way of the Gulf of Mexico, they had to have Spanish approval. Thus Spain formed a collar around the southwest by which it could squeeze the economic life out of American settlers. Worse, Spanish military posts were built on what was actually American soil (but still claimed by Spain) so as to keep the southern tribes well supplied with guns and ammunition. The main Spanish post was located on the Mississippi River at Chickasaw Bluffs, now the site of Memphis.[14]

The Tennesseans turned to their government for help but received virtually no support. The new Congress formed under the Articles of Confederation sought to establish peace with the tribes by negotiating treaties and restraining belligerent states. Accordingly, Benjamin Hawkins, Andrew Pickens, Joseph Martin, and Lachlan McIntosh were appointed United States commissioners and met with the Cherokees. They drew up the Treaty of Hopewell on November 28, 1785, defining the Cherokees' boundaries and recognizing their right to expel squatters. But white settlers paid little attention to the treaty. Consequently, open warfare with the Indians continued unabated, and grew more intense when a Tennessee land company seized over three million acres of land near Muscle Shoals between 1788 and 1791. Dragging Canoe, who had not attended the Treaty of Hopewell meeting, attacked the Muscle Shoals settlements and drove off the invaders. The Tennesseans responded by executing several suspected murderers. Naturally that action triggered Indian retaliation.

Disgusted with Congress's unwillingness to provide armed support, some frontiersmen intrigued with the Spanish, dangling the prospect of secession from the United States as an inducement to the Spanish to intercede and end the Indian raids. James Robertson, who commanded the original group of explorers to the Cumberland in 1779, indicated what might happen. "In all probability," he wrote in 1788, "we cannot long remain in our present state, and if the British or any commercial nation who may be in possession of the mouth of the

Mississippi would furnish us with trade, and receive our produce there cannot be a doubt that the people on the west side of the Appalachian mountains will open their eyes to their real interest."[15] Anytime farmers on the frontier shipped goods to New Orleans they had to pay a levy of 15 percent. No doubt relief from this burdensome tax and from the devastating assaults by the various tribes— not a particular desire to live under Spanish rule—accounts for the settlers' increasing sympathy for separation from the United States.

This Spanish Conspiracy, as it was sometimes called, infected Andrew Jackson as well as many other settlers. He spoke to one André Fagot, a merchant and officer in Louisiana who Jackson mistakenly believed was related to Esteban Miró, the Spanish governor, in the hope of establishing a regular trade between Nashville and New Orleans as well as persuading Miró to intervene with the Indians. "I think it the only immediate way," Jackson wrote to Brigadier General Daniel Smith, "to obtain a peace with the savage."[16]

Shortly after Jackson wrote this letter a new government under the Constitution was formed in New York City with George Washington as President. Washington immediately appointed a cabinet with Henry Knox as secretary of war; and the War Department was authorized to supervise Indian affairs. Despite the fact that Native Americans lived within the territorial limits of the United States as described in the Treaty of Paris, Knox convinced Washington that the tribes should be treated as sovereign nations with autonomous rights of self-government within their borders. He also believed that the United States had a moral obligation to protect Indians, and that the only way to end the warfare on the frontier was to restrain aggressive whites by legislative action. To implement this policy, the Treaty of Holston was signed with the Cherokees on July 2, 1791; in it the government agreed to pay $5,000 in suitable goods for the Indian land illegally occupied by settlers. The treaty also drew up a new boundary and forbade white encroachment. A process of "civilizing" the Cherokees was also initiated by furnishing farming tools from time to time so that they could become "herdsmen and cultivators" instead of hunters.[17] But like previous treaties, the Treaty of Holston of 1791 was regularly violated by white squatters and was not enforced by the central government. It therefore failed to satisfy either the settlers or the Indians. And it certainly failed to resolve the ongoing problem of two races colliding and quarreling over land on the frontier.

Meanwhile, on May 26, 1790, Congress responded in part to the relentless complaints and demands from frontiersmen by organizing the country between Kentucky and the present territories of Alabama and Mississippi into the "Territory of the United States South of the river Ohio." President Washington named William Blount of North Carolina as governor and Daniel Smith as secretary. Blount was a very clever, sharp-nosed manipulator, politician, land speculator, and financier—and later the first United States senator to be expelled from that body—who was well connected and quickly established himself as a power broker in the new territory. As governor, Blount also served as Indian Affairs superintendent with jurisdiction over the four great southern tribes: the Cherokees, Creeks, Choctaws, and Chickasaws.* But it was made clear to him by the secretary of war that the administration was preoccupied at the time with the northwest Indians who had inflicted a crushing defeat on General Arthur St. Clair in November 1791, and therefore he, Blount, was to pursue a strictly defensive policy toward the southern tribes, using the local militia only to ward off attacks. The governor was specifically instructed not to initiate an aggressive policy toward the Indians. Knox then confirmed the recommendations made by Blount and appointed James Robertson and John Sevier as brigadier generals.

Despite Knox's directive, Blount regularly pestered the government with demands that it rid the southwest of the Indian menace. In a letter to the secretary, he declared that "the Creeks, if not the Cherokees must be chastised by the hand of the Government before they will desist from killing and robbing the Frontier Inhabitants of the United States."[18]

But the Indians, too, had complaints, chiefly the fact that the United States had failed to stop the constant flow of white immigrants into their lands in violation of the boundary provisions of the Treaty of Holston. As a consequence the Chickamauga War broke out in 1792 when followers of Dragging Canoe waged sporadic assaults against American settlers and continued their raids for the next two years. In September 1792 the Chickamauga Cherokees attacked Nashville.

Like Blount, Jackson believed the central government had to step in to stop the killing. He knew firsthand what the horrors of Indian warfare entailed and over time began to formulate an Indian policy, which he expressed openly and frankly. And he expressed it at the highest level, including Governor Blount, whom he sought to cultivate.[19] In an effort to influence the governor and John McKee, Blount's commissioner sent to work out a "general Peace" with the Chickamaugas, he wrote to the commissioner and recited what he and other frontiersmen had come to believe was the proper policy the government should adopt when dealing with Indians.

*The Seminoles in Florida fell under Spanish jurisdiction.

Peace talks are nothing but "Delusions" to put us off our guard, he declared. Why treat with them in the first place when experience "teaches us that Treaties answer No other Purpose than opening an Easy door for the Indians to pass through to Butcher our Citizens." What possible motive prompts Congress to attempt peace talks with them completely escapes me, he added. Some say "humanity dictates it." Well, if that be true, how about a little humanity shown toward our own citizens? By extending "an Equal share of humanity" to us, he went on, Congress would act "Justly and Punish the Barbarians for Murdering her innocent Citizens." Moreover, both the Creek and Cherokee Nations have failed repeatedly to abide by the provisions of existing treaties. For instance, they will not surrender the "butchers" who kill our people as they are required to do under the terms of virtually every treaty that has ever been signed. "If they [the murderers] are not given up it is an infringement of the Treaty and a cause of war and the whole Nation ought to be Scurged for the infringement of the Treaty for as the Nation will not give murderers up when demanded it is a[n] acknowledgement of their Consent to the Commission of the Crime therefore all consenting are Equally guilty." In sum: forget treaties; scourge hostile tribes; protect U.S. citizens at all costs. Jackson concluded his letter with a clear reference to the Spanish Conspiracy. Unless we get adequate protection from the government, he warned, "this Country will have at length to break or seek a protection from some other Source than the present."[20]

It did not take Blount long to become acquainted with Jackson, size up his talents, and decide to cultivate his legal and political support in dealing with the communities in and around Nashville. In fact he developed a lively correspondence with the young man and at one point even asked him to arrange some of his land purchases. Also, he took particular notice of Jackson in several instructions he sent to his generals. In accordance with directives from the government, he informed General Robertson that he wanted the provisions of the treaty with the Cherokees "preserved inviolate and if that can not be done I beg you to make examples of the first violators of it. It will be the Duty of the Attorney of the District Mr. Jackson to prosecute on Information in all such cases and I have no doubt that he will readily do it." When, as always happened, white settlers violated the treaty by disregarding the boundary provisions, Blount did try on occasion to enforce Knox's orders. "Let the District Attorney Mr. Jackson, be informed; he will be certain to do his duty, and the offenders prosecuted."[21]

A pragmatist and a man of increasing political ambition, Jackson provided enough evidence of his loyalty and commitment to the governor's interests and directions to convince Blount that this district attorney could be extremely useful to him as his ally. Several months later, on September 10, 1792, Blount appointed Jackson as judge advocate for the Davidson County cavalry regiment commanded by Lieutenant Colonel Robert Hays, who had married Andrew and Rachel. The appointment was a clear recognition of Jackson's legal ability and usefulness but also an acknowledgment of the young man's long and valued association as a volunteer in the armed militia fighting Indians on the frontier.

Thus, by the age of twenty-five, Jackson had solidly established his reputation in Nashville as a lawyer and businessman with marital connections to one of the first families of the community, and he had valuable ties to the most important political operative in the territory. He was obviously getting ahead rather quickly. Now that he had an official position in the militia, the ambitious district attorney no doubt began to think of future promotions, including that to commanding officer.

A month later, Blount attempted another reward for his western friend. He proposed a promotion for him within the militia. "Can't you contrive for Hay to resign," he asked Robertson, "and I will promote Donelson and appoint Jackson second Major."[22] But Robertson warned against such a move as politically unwise, so the governor backed off.

Over the following months, Jackson got in a lot of military time as the Chickamauga Cherokees continued "to prowl around and infest the settlements" and kill settlers. From their stronghold in the five "Lower Towns" near Chattanooga they orchestrated raids along the Cumberland River, sometimes with the help of neighboring Creeks and Chickasaws. Jackson continued to rail against the "savages" and against Congress for its indifference to what he called the murdering of innocent settlers and the repeated violations of treaties by the Indians. For two years this situation persisted until General Robertson arranged to have a detachment of troops attack the Chickamauga towns. This action was undertaken in a secret arrangement—secret because of the government's order against all but defensive actions against the southern tribes.

On September 6, 1794, Robertson ordered Major James Ore "to defend the District . . . against the Creeks and Cherokees of the Lower Towns," who, he said, were "about to invade it, as also to punish such Indians as have committed recent depredations." The expedition of 550 mounted infantry descended on Nickajack, a small town of three hundred Indians, surrounded it, attacked, and killed "a considerable number of warriors." The neighboring town of Running Water, the presumed capital of the Chickamauga Cherokees, heard the attack and tried to help their brethren but were quickly defeated. "Running Water was counted the largest, and among the most hostile towns of the Cherokees," reported Ore to Blount, and we have destroyed it.

Ore and his men rescued a number of white settlers, who told them that not two days before "a scalp dance had been held" in the town "over the scalps lately taken from Cumberland." Among the war trophies the militia found not only a large number of scalps but a supply of guns and ammunition recently delivered by the "Spanish Government."[23]

According to one report, Jackson participated in this assault, and demonstrated his fitness for command "in planning the attack on Nickajack" as well as "his good conduct generally in the campaign."[24] But other witnesses denied his presence.[25] Whatever the truth, the victory at Nickajack and Running Water forced the Chickamauga dissidents to seek peace with the Americans and return to their allegiance with the Cherokee Nation.

Because Robertson had violated the instructions from the government, he was forced to resign his commission. But no one was chosen to replace him, and so Robertson retained his command as though nothing had happened. This high-handed dismissal of government orders with respect to the Indians only encouraged frontiersmen to disregard federal orders whenever it seemed appropriate to do so. Here again was another lesson Jackson learned from his frontier experience. On more than one occasion in the future he would simply ignore government orders regarding the Indians and act according to his own perception of what was the proper course of action.

Caught between the continued restrictions imposed by the government and the demands of settlers to undertake punitive action against the "savages," Blount decided that the only possible escape from the dilemma was to propose the admission of the territory into the Union as a state. That way it could presumably manage the Indian problem itself without federal interference. Besides, Blount figured that statehood would advance his own interests in land speculation. So, on August 25, 1794, his party newspaper, the Knoxville *Gazette,* initiated the call to begin the process of statehood for Tennessee. He alerted his lieutenants about his intentions and told Robertson that although he believed the Cherokees now wanted peace, the Creeks "must be humbled before you can enjoy peace and I fear that wished for period will never arrive until this Territory becomes a State and is represented in Congress."[26]

Moving with lightning speed, Blount guided the territorial legislature into taking several actions: it called for a plebiscite on the question of statehood and a census to make certain the territory had a sufficient population to qualify, and it arranged for the convocation of a constitutional convention. As expected, the census showed that more than 77,000 white males and females, free blacks, and slaves inhabited the territory. Of that number, 6,504 voted for statehood and 2,562 against, a ratio of 13 to 5 in favor.[27]

An election of delegates to the constitutional convention followed, held on December 18 and 19, 1795, and among the five men elected from Davidson County was Andrew Jackson. His election was another sign of his growing reputation as a community leader in the western district and the esteem in which he was held by his neighbors—and particularly by Governor William Blount. The convention met in Knoxville from January 11 to February 6, 1796, and both Jackson and McNairy represented their county on the twenty-two-member committee that drafted the constitution and declaration of rights. To what extent Jackson materially contributed to these documents cannot be determined. Part of the declaration of rights stated that the people who had pioneered this area had created a barrier between the "savage hostiles" and the older settlements to the east and therefore were entitled to the right of preemption and occupancy. Because these people had exposed themselves to "pillage, starvation and massacre" without a clear title to the land, they deserved the preemption.

Congress approved the admission of Tennessee as a state, and President Washington signed the bill on June 1, 1796. The state legislature then elected William Blount and William Cocke to the U.S. Senate; both came from the eastern districts of Tennessee. It was politically necessary to have a westerner elected to the House of Representatives, and Blount decided the time had come to advance Jackson's career into national politics. Because the young man had "strong western views" on the questions of the Indians, the Spanish, and the English—that is, he regularly thundered imprecations against these "enemies of the people"—it was believed that he would attract a considerable following in the election. And he did. He had no opposition in the western districts and only token opposition in Washington County. He received 1,113 votes to 12 for James Rody.[28]

Before taking his seat in Congress as Tennessee's first and only U. S. representative in the lower house, he made a bold attempt to win election as major general of the state's militia. The selection of commanding officers in the militia in those early years was essentially a democratic process. The state was divided into three districts, each with a brigade, and each county had a regiment; in addition, one cavalry regiment was attached to each brigade. Members of the militia elected regimental and company officers regardless of rank; field officers of each district elected the brigadier generals. Finally the major general who commanded the militia of the entire state was elected by the field officers of all three districts plus the brigadier generals.

It was a bold move for a twenty-nine-year-old to reach so high, but Jackson was intensely ambitious and believed that his experience fighting Indians for the past several years and his obvious leadership ability in numerous engagements against the hostiles qualified him for the post. However, the new governor of the state, John Sevier, had other ideas. He preferred George Conway and by political manipulation defeated Jackson's bid.

But the new congressman learned an important lesson from the experience. If he wanted to be the major general—and he most certainly did, to cap his career in Tennessee—he needed to prepare the ground; he needed to attract a personal following within the militia and show an even greater interest in its affairs than he had in the past, and he needed to participate actively in all future militia elections.

The militia election took place in November 1796. A month later, on December 5, Jackson took his seat in the House of Representatives when the second session of the 4th Congress got underway in Philadelphia, the capital of the new government prior to its removal to Washington, D.C., in 1800. For the most part, Jackson was a silent participant in House proceedings, his votes reflecting his western states' rights, conservative commitment. He preferred to follow the lead of some of the more distinguished members of the chamber, such as James Madison of Virginia, Nathaniel Macon of North Carolina, Albert Gallatin and Edward Livingston of New York, and Fisher Ames of Massachusetts, among others.

But when a petition was received from Hugh Lawson White, a fellow Tennessean, requesting compensation for his services in a campaign against several Cherokee towns led by General Sevier in late 1793, Jackson finally became vocal and active. President Washington had repeatedly refused to honor the petition, and the Committee of Claims reported to the House on December 29, 1796, that although the settlers had been harassed by "thefts and murders," it questioned whether the expedition was "a just and necessary measure." Henry Knox also reported that the attack was offensive, not defensive, and undertaken without presidential authority and in violation of specific orders from the War Department.[29]

Jackson erupted. Without letting a day pass, he gained the floor and insisted that the raids were indeed "just and necessary. When it was seen that war was waged upon the State, that the knife and the tomahawk were held over the heads of women and children, that peaceable citizens were murdered," it was time to take action. He went on to dispute the facts as presented by Secretary Knox, declaring that from June to the end of October 1793, some twelve hundred Indians assaulted the militia, "carried their station, and threatened to carry the Seat of Government." The response of the militia was purely defensive, he stormed, and therefore the claim should be granted. He closed his argument by offering a resolution:

"*Resolved,* That General Sevier's expedition into the Cherokee Nation, in the year 1793 was a just and necessary measure, and that provision ought to be made by law for paying the expenses involved."[30]

Several representatives wanted the resolution tabled or sent back to committee, but Jackson insisted that all the facts had been brought forward by the Claims Committee and therefore there was no need to repeat the process. He also insisted that the expenses for all the participants—not just White's—should be honored by the government. Nevertheless, the House refused to be stampeded and adjourned for the day before taking final action.

The following morning, Jackson followed up his line of argument by insisting that inasmuch as the troops had been called out by a superior officer they were obliged to obey. A "contrary doctrine," he declared, "would strike at the very root of subordination. It would be saying to soldiers, 'Before you obey the command of your superior officer, you have the right to inquire into the legality of the service upon which you are about to be employed, and, until you are satisfied, you may refuse to take the field.' "

Admit to this, he cried, and you destroy the very basis on which military authority rests. Sevier and his officers had been obliged to obey the order to mount the expedition against the Cherokees. They and their men had acted in "full confidence that the United States would pay them, believing that they had appointed such officers as would not call them into the field without proper authority."[31]

Jackson's several speeches on the issue contained a number of principles that remained constant throughout his military career. They involved authority and responsibility, subordination and obedience, disciple and loyalty. He was very rigid in these matters and would brook no opposition to them. Soldiers obeyed orders properly authorized and governments supported and defended their soldiers, no matter the risk or the expense.

The original resolution called for the payment of only one individual, but now Jackson argued for payment for the entire expeditionary force. If the cause was just for one man, he contended, it was just for all the others. A long debate followed, ending with the referral of the matter to a select committee, of which Jackson was named chairman and which included as members Jeremiah Smith of New Hampshire, Thomas Blount of North Carolina, George Dent of Maryland, and Robert Goodloe Harper of South Carolina. To strengthen his case, Jackson prepared a number of supporting documents with a summary he wrote himself in which were listed all the "depredations" contained in the reports of Daniel Smith, secretary of the territory.

A month later the committee issued its report to the full House, and it flatly declared that the expedition was essential for the defense of the frontier and that the authority of the governor of the territory required that the militia obey his orders. The report, written by Jackson, described how a thousand or more Cherokees, Chickamaugans, and Creeks crossed the Tennessee River and marched to within seven miles of Knoxville. The hostiles attacked Caveat's Station and "put Every man woman and Child to Death in the most Cruel and inhuman manner." Sevier was ordered to pursue the "murderers" so as to "inflict if possible a Just punishment upon them for the Cruel murders they had Committed." He did indeed pursue, attack, and rout them, making it possible for Blount, the then territorial governor, to report that "for a Considerable time after Seviers return no Depredations were Committed by the Indians on the frontier and that that Campaign was the Ground work of the Subsequent *present* Tranquility of & Enjoyed by the Holston frontier." Consequently the report recommended full compensation for the entire militia. Without further debate the recommendation went straight to the House Ways and Means Committee for inclusion in the federal appropriations for 1797. The amount granted the militia came to $22,816.[32]

This single success in winning compensation for the militia elevated Jackson's reputation in the west to such a pinnacle that it guaranteed him a second term if he chose to run. "The payment of Seviers expedition," wrote William C. C. Claiborne, a member of Tennessee's constitutional convention and a man Jackson would meet again in New Orleans, where Claiborne was governor during the British invasion in the War of 1812, "has heightened the esteem of the people for the General Government and secured to yourself a permanent interest."[33]

Jackson next addressed the subject of the Nickajack expedition, and he called on the secretary of war and his accountant to provide the muster and pay rolls of that campaign so that he could present a memorial for payment before the full House. He was soon informed that no such papers had ever been submitted. He wrote Ore and informed him of the precedent he had established with the Sevier campaign and of his inability to advance a claim for the Nickajack expedition. You would have been paid, he assured Ore, had the papers been properly submitted. "I wish you to publish this letter," he declared, "for the information of those citizens, who served under your command on the expedition."

Eventually the appropriate papers were assembled and sent to the secretary of war's office, and a payment of $8,773.17 was authorized for the Ore expedition and another $3,302.29 for Thomas Johnson and his men who accompanied Ore.[34]

Jackson also put forward a claim for the mixed-blood Chickasaw chief George Colbert, who was an ally of the Americans against the Creeks. In 1795, Lieutenant Colonel Kasper Mansker and Captain David Smith had led forty-five men into the Chickasaw country to assist Colbert in repelling Creek attacks. Smith had provided supplies for the expedition, and Jackson sought now "to obtain pay for the provisions." But he frankly held out little hope of winning compensation at this time. "I think the claim will be negatived," he wrote. Not until the Chickasaw Treaty of 1818 that Jackson himself negotiated as Indian commissioner was Smith reimbursed in the amount of $2,000. The United States government also agreed to compensate the Indian allies.[35] As was pointed out many times by early biographers, Jackson could be generous toward Indian allies and support their rights if he judged their claims legitimate and not detrimental to the interests of the United States. But let them defend their own rights and claims by raising the tomahawk and he could be savage and unforgiving.

His position on the Indians and their relations with the state and federal governments was further revealed as several incidents were brought to his attention by Governor Sevier in early 1797. First, it seems that two Indians had been killed by John Seviston and Edward Mitchell, a deputy sheriff and captain of the militia respectively, and that the Chickasaws were "much exasperated and threaten to take satisfaction, in case the murderers are not punished." Sevier said he would have attempted to apprehend Seviston and Mitchell if either the Chickasaws or the U.S. Indian agent, David Henley, had lodged a complaint. But they did not, and he suspected that Henley had assured the Indians that the governor had "nothing to do in indian affairs." This may give the tribes "very unfavorable ideas and consider themselves wholly independent of any measures" proposed "or held out" by the state government.

Jackson responded immediately. He regretted that Indians had been wantonly murdered by whites and applauded Sevier's intention to apprehend Seviston and Mitchell and bring them to trial. By their actions these criminals jeopardized "the lives of many of our Innocent Citizens—and perhaps women and Children," he wrote. As for the more important question of the governor's authority in such matters, Jackson had a very clear and precise position. "In you alone is Constitutionally invested the authority and power of protecting the State in case of Invasion," he declared, "and to bring to Condign punishment, (through the medium of the Courts of Justice) any person that may Commit acts, that may tend to Endanger the safety and peace of your Government." You are the proper authority to make these villains pay for their crime, not Henley, and certainly not the "General Government." He then launched into a diatribe against those who would undermine "states' rights," who would "Endanger the safety and peace" of each individual state by attempting to divert legitimate power from the hands of the governor. Sovereignty was retained by the states when the Constitution was written and ratified, he argued, "which never ought on any account to be Surrendered to the General Government, or its officers [like Henley] and when [attempted] . . . it ought to be opposed." Since the inauguration of the current administration, President Washington[36] has been "Grasping after power," and the moment "the Sovereignity of the Individual States is overwhelmed by the General Government, we may bid adieu to our freedom."

A second point raised by Sevier in his letter to Jackson expressed the fear that westerners almost universally entertained. If a war broke out between the United States and any European power, he told Jackson, "we should find in all the southern tribes inveterate enemies." Not only did the young congressman believe this point as absolute truth, it shaped his whole thinking about how the government should handle Indian affairs. As a result, Sevier continued, "traders of every description would conceive it their interest to divert the attention and intercourse of the indians from the United States to a quarter where they could recommence their trading as usual." And the national government was responsible for this looming danger. Its trading and land policies were causing general jealousy among the tribes and among traders. It was seeking to control everything. "Congress was scratching after every bit of a rackoon skin in the nation that was big enough to cover a Squaws' ———." And it had caused "much clamour among the good citizens of this state." He had heard that the Cherokee chief Redheaded Will had seceded from the Cherokee Nation and had led the people of his entire town across the Mississippi River and had settled in Spanish territory. Others would surely follow, Sevier said. The government must change its policy toward the southern tribes, he concluded. Instead of Congress handing out thousands of dollars to them "who despise it," the government should give it to "the lame, the halt, and the blind soldier . . . to whom we are indebted for our existence as a nation."

Jackson agreed totally with the governor's contention. We cannot tolerate investing Henley with the task of superintending the Indians and carrying on a trade with them that excludes citizens of "our State" from that trade. Jackson said he fully intended to propose in the House the repeal of the act that gave the central government authority to regulate trade and intercourse with the Indians on the frontier. It was a mistake, he insisted, and needed to be repealed.

The third and last point raised by Sevier in his letter involved Chief Piomingo, who had led a delegation of Chickasaws to the capital to present their claims and grievances and came away displeased with the treatment they had received. Piomingo told Sevier that "a certain great man there was like unto a cowardly old woman, through fear would treat her enemies better than her friends." Just who Piomingo was referring to is unclear, but Jackson admitted speaking to Piomingo and knew that he and his Chickasaws were dissatisfied with the government's attitude toward them. But what did they expect, Jackson responded. The government's policy only encouraged "hostile acts" by the "savages." The right approach for the Indians was to take their complaints to the states and find justice in American courts.[37]

Clearly, Jackson felt that the states were better suited than the federal government to handle Indian affairs and should have a free hand. But he also insisted that they act legally through American courts. Unfortunately the Indians frequently found American courts unsympathetic to their claims and rights.

Jackson's term as a representative ended before he could propose any changes in the government's Indian policy, and he did not run for a second term. Instead he was elected to the Senate after Blount attempted a coup that brought about his own expulsion from the upper house.

Blount's actions came about in part from rumors that Spain, after agreeing to the Pinckney Treaty of 1795 by which the Mississippi River was opened to Americans, including the right of deposit for storing goods in New Orleans, was on the verge of returning Louisiana to France along with East and West Florida in exchange for part of Santo Domingo. The idea of Napoleon Bonaparte, the master of France, controlling the lower Mississippi Valley alarmed westerners, because they feared he would again close the river to them. Since France and Spain were now locked in a war with Great Britain, William Blount and his brother decided to invite the British to help subsidize American filibusters to seize both Louisiana and Florida. In exchange for this financial support, England would guarantee free navigation of the Mississippi, establish New Orleans as a free port, and make generous land grants to the American "conspirators." But the conspiracy collapsed when a letter written by Blount on April 21, 1797, to James Carey came into the possession of the new administration headed by President John Adams, who had succeeded George Washington in 1797. The letter was turned over to a select House committee, which passed articles of impeachment against Blount, accusing him of conspiring to create within the United States "a military hostile expedition" against Florida and Louisiana "for the purpose of conquering the same for the King of Great Britain." He had, in effect, violated American neutrality and undermined Indian relations with the United States.

Rather than face a trial in the Senate, Blount resigned his office, and Joseph Anderson replaced him. Then, instead of renominating Senator William Cocke, whose loyalty to the Blount faction was questionable, the Blount forces selected Andrew Jackson to run in his place. There was no question of Jackson's commitment to the Blounts, and his record as a representative made him one of the most popular men in western Tennessee. On September 26, 1797, the Tennessee legislature duly elected him to the U.S. Senate by a vote of 20 to 13.

It was a grave mistake. And it soon became evident. The thirty-year-old Jackson was out of his depth in the Senate, and he knew it. He hated his position, and his senatorial record is virtually a blank. One of the few things he did attempt was to do something about the government's Indian policy. Along with two other members of the Tennessee congressional delegation, he complained directly to Adams himself. Settlers were being driven "to the Spanish Dominions," they wrote, because essential treaties to redraw boundaries with the tribes had not been concluded. Furthermore, the people living "on what is called the indian lands" were in "great distress" because of boundary disputes and were regularly assaulted by "savages." To make matters worse, the government had violated the personal liberty of its citizens in its efforts to protect Native Americans. Judge David Campbell of the state's superior court, for example, had been routed out of bed at ten in the evening by U.S. troops on charges of trespassing on Indian lands without a passport. He was taken to the camp as a prisoner and detained until the following day. His arrest, insisted the three congressmen, was a violation of an individual's "Civil liberty"; worse, the sovereignty of the state had been "Outrag'd." Such action by the government was indefensible. At the very least the three demanded the removal of the commander of the U.S. troops, "the author of Such Military Tyranny."[38]

The greatest encroachment on "indian lands" occurred in the Powell Valley of east Tennessee, and the settlers constantly complained to Governor Sevier about the "regid and exorbitant measures" carried out by federal forces "under a pretext that the indian lands are encroached upon." The settlers argued that they had a right to this land, that the Indian claims had been extinguished twenty years ago. "It is painful to hear the cries of the people of this state, against a partial conduct in favour of a Savage tribe," Sevier told Jackson, "that can only be noticed, or favoured for their atrocious murders, robberies, and a desolate wantonness to commit every diabolical crime, that could possibly suggest itself to savage invention." What is more, "I fear one half our citizens will flock over into another government, indeed they are now doing it daily." He urged these people to have "patience and fortitude," but they were becoming "very restless and clamorous."[39]

President Adams very graciously invited the three men to come to his home and discuss these matters directly with him. Their conversation went well and ended with Adams promising to negotiate a new treaty with the Cherokees that would be satisfactory to the settlers. What resulted from all this was the First Treaty of Tellico, signed on October 2, 1798, which gave the settlers title to the land in dispute.[40]

But no sooner was this crisis resolved than Sevier came back at the congressional delegation with a demand to bring about another "extinguishment" of Indian land.[41]

It never seemed to end, this insatiable hunger for Indian land. And Jackson as settler and congressman agreed that the tribes had to yield. He was not the least interested in defending Indian rights. He represented the interests of the people had who elected him. He did what he had to do and wanted to do, and the Indian paid the price.

Despite satisfaction in convincing the Adams administration to make concessions to the Tennessean settlers, Jackson was generally "disgusted with the administration of the government" and convinced that he did not belong in the Senate. Frustrated, weary, and bored, he finally resigned his office on April 16, 1798, without apology or explanation. He served only one session of his term, then simply walked away from the job he loathed.[42]

Perhaps another reason for his sudden and abrupt departure from the nation's capital was the possibility of a judgeship that did not require his absence from home for months on end, yet would advance his political and military ambitions by taking him to all the districts of Tennessee. Shortly after he arrived back in Nashville he was elected without opposition by the legislature to the bench of the state superior court with a salary of $600 per annum. Governor Sevier signed his commission on December 22, 1798. Jackson at this time was thirty-one, and he served on the bench for the next six years.

Although his knowledge of the law was admittedly scanty, the young judge performed his duties tolerably well. "Tradition reports," declared an early biographer, "that he maintained the dignity and authority of the bench, while he was on the bench; and that his decisions were short, untechnical, unlearned, sometimes ungrammatical, and generally right." Respect for the law was something Jackson insisted upon in his courtroom. And woe to him who violated it. On one occasion, Russell Bean, a "great, hulking fellow" who had been indicted for cutting off the ears of his child in a "drunken frolic," swaggered into court, cursed the judge, jury, and all assembled, and then brazenly marched out the door.

"Sheriff," roared Judge Jackson, "arrest that man for contempt of court and confine him."

The sheriff obeyed but soon reported back that he could not apprehend the fellow.

"Summon a posse, then, and bring him before me."

Again the sheriff failed in his duty. No member of the posse dared lay a hand on Bean because he threatened to shoot the "first skunk that came within ten feet of him."

Jackson raged. "Mr. Sheriff," he stormed, "since you can not obey my orders, summon me; yes, sir, summon me."

"Well, judge, if you say so, though I don't like to do it; but if you will try, why I suppose I must summon you."

The judge adjourned court ten minutes as he strode out the door.

He found Bean a short distance away, in the center of a crowd, cursing and flourishing his pistols and threatening death to anyone who might attempt to take him into custody.

Jackson came straight toward the man, a pistol in each hand. "Now," he screamed as he stared into the eyes of the criminal, "surrender, you infernal villain, this very instant, or I'll blow you through."

Bean looked into Jackson's blazing eyes. Suddenly a complete change came over him. "There, judge," he meekly replied, "it's no use, I give in." He dropped his weapons and was carted off to jail.

Several days later the prisoner was asked why he timidly surrendered to Jackson after defying an entire posse. "Why," said Bean, "when he came up, I looked him in the eye, and I saw shoot, and there wasn't shoot in nary other eye in the crowd; and so I says to myself, says I, hoss, it's about time to sing small, and so I did."

It was those eyes. They instantly registered whatever emotion or passion surged within the man. And seeing them ignite signaled anyone in close range to run for cover. Indians came to appreciate what that signal meant. They said he merely had to look at them that way and they dropped lifeless to the ground.[43]

For the next several years, Jackson performed his duties around the state with ever-mounting success, never failing to use the time to improve his relationships with the leading men in the several counties. He paid particular heed to the officers of the militia, cultivating their friendship and demonstrating his concern with and interest in the affairs of their organization. More than anything else he still hungered for the rank of major general. Indeed, it had become an obsession. Unfortunately, John Sevier had run out his constitutional string of three successive terms as governor and could not run again. He was replaced by Archibald Roane, another member of the Blount faction and one of Jackson's friends. So, at the next election for major general, Sevier decided to take command of the militia once again just as the officers put forward Jackson's name for the same position.

Sevier was flabbergasted that Jackson would challenge his right to the office. After all, he was the hero of the Battle of King's Mountain during the Revolution and an acknowledged leader of Tennesseans against the Cherokees, Creeks, and Chickamaugas. To think that a lawyer—a *"poor pitifull petty fogging Lawyer,"* as he called Jackson[44]—with limited experience fighting Indians (compared to his) could presume to run for the rank of major general. Sevier could hardly believe it. His shock turned to cold fury when the results of the election, held on February 5, 1802, were announced.

It was a tie. Both men had seventeen votes, while Brigadier General James Winchester received three.[45] This was an extraordinary accomplishment for Jackson and demonstrates how high his popularity had grown and how skillfully he had used it to win support from the militia officers. No doubt he would have won the election outright had he not run against someone as formidable and experienced as John Sevier.[46]

To break the tie the choice then fell to the new governor, and without a moment's hesitation Roane selected his friend Andrew Jackson. Thus, at the tender age of thirty-five, Mr. Justice Jackson became Major General Andrew Jackson of the Tennessee militia, a position he held until May 1814 when he became a major general in the United States Army.[47]

But the rivalry between the two men continued to escalate over the next several months and finally resulted in a duel. They chose the Indian territory in the neighborhood of South West Point to satisfy their "honor," because Sevier claimed he did not want to pollute the sacred soil of Tennessee with Jackson's blood.

The major general arrived early for the encounter. He waited for days. No Sevier. Not a sign. Beside himself, Jackson headed back for Knoxville to force a showdown. He had not gotten far when he suddenly spotted Sevier riding toward him surrounded by a company of mounted men. The duelists quickly dismounted. Jackson lunged at Sevier and threatened to cane him. Sevier drew his sword, which so frightened his horse that "he ran away with the Governor's Pistols." Jackson drew on him, whereupon Sevier ducked behind a tree. At which point Sevier's son drew on Jackson and Jackson's second drew on the son.

It had become a farce. Jackson's second was aiming at Sevier's son, who was aiming at the general, who was aiming at Sevier, who was hiding behind a tree. The comedy ended when members of Sevier's party rushed forward and persuaded the contestants to end their ridiculous feud. The entire party rode back to Knoxville together. Both sides then resorted to the newspapers to carry on their war, and after a brief period the contest exhausted itself.[48]

Jackson turned to his new duties as major general and performed them with an exactitude and a demonstration of leadership that immediately won the respect and admiration of his officers and men. No *"poor pitifull petty fogging Lawyer"* he. What emerged over the next several years was a genuine military figure of commanding presence, a man who would demonstrate keen military intelligence, and a man who showed concern for his troops and went out of his way to see to their comfort and care.

One of his most obvious responsibilities was the enforcement of the laws and treaties that dealt with whites and Indians and the protection of the tribes within their lands. Shortly after taking up his new duties, Jackson received a letter from Governor Roane informing him that an Indian had been murdered in an area close to the Cherokee boundary and that Major William Russell, a commissioned captain in the South County militia, had raised a party intent on taking the law into its own hands by searching out some Indian camps in the mountains "over our boundary" and "breaking them up." Russell lived near the road that connected east and west Tennessee and ran into the "Wilderness" region that had not yet been acquired from the Cherokees.

On receiving the letter, Jackson immediately contacted Colonel Henry McKinney in Jackson County[49] and ordered him to arrest Russell if he had already carried out his plan; if not, said Jackson, McKinney was to order him to cease and desist. If Russell refused to obey this order, "I command you immediately to arrest him, and to furnish Brigadier genrl. [James] Winchester [of the Mero District militia] with the charges against him so that a court martial may be called and a Speedy enquiry had into his conduct."

In this earliest known action by Jackson as major general he displayed a degree of fairness and sense of justice that regularly characterized most of his behavior when dealing with both Indians and militiamen. As he told McKinney, "the militia are considered to be the bulwark of our national peace prosperity and happiness, and for an officer thus to violate the law and hazard the peace of our country, is Such an example to those of a lower grade, that it ought and must meet, with speedy corrective."[50]

Along with fairness, this letter also reveals Jackson's racism, something shared by most if not all frontiersmen. He referred to the Indians as "those of a lower grade," and he included slaves in that category as well. Much as he might admire those of a "lower grade" for their courage and treat them with respect when they obeyed him, he regarded them as inferior and prone to mischief and troublemaking and barbarism.

To follow through, Jackson then contacted General Winchester and informed him of his action. He feared "still more rash & unwarrentable" actions if justice was not served. He therefore wanted Winchester to investigate the matter and "if the facts are true" to "persue the Legal steps to have a Speedy . . . court martial."

This was the sort of incident that occurred often during his tenure as major general. But Jackson took the necessary moves to put an end to it. Within a relatively short time the militia understood that their commander would not tolerate violations of the laws and treaties of the United States and that they were "guardians of our national peace liberty and happiness."[51]

Throughout the administrations of John Adams and his successor, Thomas

Jefferson, the settlers continued to gain access to Indian land. As in the past, land was frequently transferred to settle debts owed by the tribes to trading companies or to government-operated stores or factories. The Indians usually purchased more than they could afford and were then obliged to cede their land to pay what they owed. From 1791 to 1819 the Cherokees signed twenty-five treaties with the federal government to cancel debts, and the Creeks and Chickasaws signed almost as many. President Jefferson in particular urged the factors or storekeepers to keep the Indians in debt so that they would be obliged to agree to land cessions. And chiefs of each tribe were regularly bribed with goods and annuities to gain their consent or help in winning approval of the treaties.[52]

Indian loss of land because of pressure by federal and state governments became a source of continued irritation and discord and violence. But once the land had been ceded by treaty, Major General Andrew Jackson was there to ensure white and Indian compliance. And he brooked no violations.

Chapter 3

Old Hickory

Over the next several years, Jackson continued in his several occupations as judge, land speculator, businessman, and major general. In the latter role he conducted meetings and regular drills and when necessary "chastised" both whites and Indians for violating the law. In addition to everything else, the presence of the Spanish in Louisiana and the Floridas required constant surveillance. And it became infinitely more worrisome when Napoleon, in the hope of rebuilding a North American empire, demanded that Spain return Louisiana to France, and Spain complied in 1800 in the secret Treaty of San Ildefonso. When rumors of the retrocession reached the United States, President Thomas Jefferson immediately recognized the danger, because it meant that the colossus of Europe would now sit astride New Orleans and the entire Mississippi Valley. Fortunately the problem was happily resolved by the disastrous defeat of Napoleon's army in Santo Domingo. Rebuilding a North American empire was quite impossible, so he agreed to sell Louisiana to the United States for $15 million in 1803.

Once the treaty was ratified, Jackson rather fancied himself territorial governor of this new acquisition and pulled strings to get it, but President Jefferson had other ideas and appointed William C. C. Claiborne instead. He also appointed James Wilkinson as general of U.S. forces in New Orleans, a traitor who soon became a paid informant and spy for the Spanish still present in the Floridas.

Despite the loss of the Louisiana post, Jackson continued to make a reputation for himself as an energetic and skillful commander of the Tennessee militia. He was known and appreciated for his prompt reaction to any hostile activity by the southern tribes. On one occasion he was informed that Creeks had committed "a horrid Carnage on Bradshaws Creek of Elk River" in which twenty-five families were wiped out. He immediately dispatched a division of volunteers to provide relief, but the following day he learned that the "villians" [*sic*] were not Creeks at all but whites who "painted themselves, raised the indian yell" and tried to "get possession of some houses possessed by others." Jackson immediately countermanded his order and directed that the volunteers be discharged. It is uncertain whether the "villians" went unpunished.[1]

A particularly unfortunate incident occurred when he decided to declare war against Silas Dinsmore, the U.S. agent to the Choctaw Indians. Such agents were appointed by the national government, received a salary of $1,800, paid out annual annuities to the tribal chiefs, and were charged with protecting the Indians from exploitation by whites. They were expected to deliver up offending Indians in their care but only *complain* of atrocities by whites. Many of these agents were decent enough men with genuine feeling for their charges. They helped teach the Indian the white man's skills. Apparently Dinsmore was one of these, a true friend of the Choctaws. Because of that friendship there were complaints that he failed to enforce the law, particularly with respect to the interests of slave owners: runaway slaves frequently sought refuge in Indian villages. So in April 1811, Dinsmore put up a sign on the road leading from Nashville through the Choctaw country to the Mississippi River announcing that he would arrest and detain "every negro found traveling in the Choctaw country whose master had no passport and evidence of ownership." And he made good his promise. He detained every black person whose master or companion did not have the requisite papers.

Complaints to the War Department followed, especially when he arrested the servants of well-to-do "gentlemen." Dinsmore was subsequently rebuked by his superiors for getting "carried away" by his responsibilities. He defended himself by declaring that the law required all persons passing through the Indian country to have a passport. Was the law to be enforced or not? But the government responded by telling him to use discretion in making arrests and try to discriminate "between the exterior appearance and the reality of a gentleman."

At this point General Jackson entered the dispute. Never a great friend of agents, and always offended by government officiousness, he happened to pass Dinsmore's agency house with twenty-six slaves belonging to a company in which he was an inactive partner, and he did not have the necessary passports. He was taking them from Natchez to Nashville. On spotting Dinsmore's agency, he armed two of his servants—which on the face of it was quite extraordinary for the time—and ordered them to "FIGHT THEIR WAY, if necessary." He himself carried a rifle. He then directed the slaves to go to the banks of a nearby creek and have their breakfast. He was obviously looking for trouble and anxious to teach Dinsmore a lesson.

He rode up to the agency, where he saw several Choctaws and asked for Dinsmore. When they told him he was away, the general left a message with them. Tell Dinsmore, he said, that General Andrew Jackson had come by with his slaves and without passports. He would have been glad to see him but could not wait. Tell him that the general "was going on homeward, *with his negroes;* intimating that the Choctaw agent might make what he could of it."[2]

Later Dinsmore stopped a "lady who was traveling through the Choctaw country with a train of ten negroes." He not only detained the slaves but published a card dated September 11, 1812, in the Nashville *Clarion* boasting of his action. To Jackson this was "lawless tyranny" by a government official against "peaceful and honest citizens." It was an action against "a defenseless woman, and her property—*and for what?* The want of a passport! And, *my God!* is it come to this? Are we *freemen, or are we slaves?*" He asked his friend George W. Campbell, the current Tennessee senator, to inform the secretary of war that westerners demanded justice; make it clear to him, he wrote, that "both from Indians and Indian agents we will enjoy the rights secured to us by solemn treaty, or we will die nobly in their support."

Jackson was so infuriated that he decided to use his influence to procure Dinsmore's removal as an agent. But he got nowhere. Still he harbored his grudge, and he waited several years to achieve his goal. As it happened the agent was away during the War of 1812 and there was fear that the Choctaws might join Tecumseh's confederation. So the Tennessee authorities took it upon themselves to appoint a replacement, who succeeded in keeping the Choctaws loyal to the United States. When the war ended, Dinsmore tried to get his job back, but Jackson, now a national hero, insisted that the substitute agent be retained, and the War Department bowed to his will. Dinsmore was reduced to poverty and became a "wanderer in the regions" over which he had once held full sway. Eight years later he met Jackson and tried to reconcile with him, but the unyielding general just glared his contempt and walked away.[3]

Jackson had one particular grievance that applied to all government agents, not just Dinsmore: the violation of the right guaranteed "by treaty" that Indians who murdered American citizens should be surrendered when demanded and tried by the laws of the United States and punished. Yet, he said, "the *Creek law says the Creeks will punish them themselves*." And the actions of the Creek agent, Benjamin Hawkins, and the Chickasaw agent, James Robertson, have supported the Indian position. "These innovations," he told Senator Campbell, "without the consent of the constituted power being first had, our citizens do not understand." We are entitled to "*justice,*" and by the eternal we will have it. "We want and do expect the murderers delivered up agreeably to treaty." This may be strong language, he allowed, but "it is the language [freemen] ought to be taught to lisp from their cradles."[4]

The Indians' conviction that they were to punish their own when charged with offenses against whites was something Jackson could not understand and would not accept, insisting that existing treaties required the surrendering of such criminals to white authority. Agents, on the other hand, frequently stood their ground and refused to hand over accused offenders. All of which only added to the constant turmoil on the frontier.

And Jackson was right. The first U.S. treaties with the southern tribes began with the Treaty of Hopewell, in which the Cherokees in 1785 and then the Choctaws and Chickasaws in 1786 agreed in Article 5 that if American citizens violated the boundary of the tribes, they forfeited the protection of the government and could be punished by the tribes as they wished. But Article 6 stated that if an Indian committed a capital crime against an American the tribe must turn the culprit over to U.S. authorities to be punished according to U.S. law. And Article 7 declared that any American who committed a capital crime against an Indian should be tried and punished as if he had committed the crime against another American. The Treaty of New York with the Creeks in 1790 contained similar language. "So Jackson was right," states a historian of the Creek Nation; "the Creeks were bound by treaty to turn over to the U.S. any Creek charged with committing a capital crime against an American."[5]

The more General Jackson dealt with the troublesome Indian/white relations on the frontier, the more he was forced to consider what could be done to settle this and other problems once and for all. As early as 1809, if not earlier, he began discussing the possibility of Indian removal with Willie Blount, the half brother of William and the present leader of the Blount faction. Blount had just become the new governor of Tennessee, and he wrote to the major general his belief that "the time seems to be fast approaching" when the federal government would have to propose to the Cherokees and Creeks "an exchange of territory" by which the tribes would leave their present location and move to "the vacant lands west of the Mississippi" that had been obtained from Napoleon Bonaparte in the Louisiana Purchase of 1803. The United States needed friends on its southern borders, Blount said, and "the conduct of the european nations is such, that neutral rights are now and have been long disregarded, and if the United States should in support of their rights have to contend with those nations, it would be sound policy in us to gain strength in that quarter of our territory, for it is not unreasonable to suppose that a part of foreign policy would be to get possession of that part of the territory of the United States." In brief, the Indians along the Gulf Coast were a threat to national security. Any European power with designs on American territory would surely ally itself to the southern tribes and incite them into declaring war against the United States.

"For our benefit," Blount admitted, ". . . I wish them led away from us—[and] I am willing to act justly towards them." At present "they are surrounded by States thickly populated by people who have different interests," and they would be better off if they moved. Game "is very abundant" on the other side of the Mississippi. The "climate [is] friendly to their constitutions, and much of the country is inhabited by people (Indians) whose manners and customs are more assimilated to their's than those of the people where they now live." Every citizen of Tennessee should promote "this exchange of territory," and "I am convinced," he told Jackson, "yours will not be withheld."

Indeed not. Blount ended his letter by suggesting that it be a subject for conversation the next time they met.[6]

Exchange! That was the answer. The two men obviously talked at length on the question, although no immediate response from Jackson has survived. And Blount returned to the subject in subsequent letters. He spent the winter of 1810–1811 urging "the necessity, expediency &c. of the United States inviting the Southern Indians to settle west of the Mississippi," something as clear as "two and two make four." He took the matter up with the state's legislature in his inaugural address and, over the next several months, continually explored the matter with the General Assembly.[7]

Jackson was probably one of the earlier converts to the notion of Indian removal through an exchange of land, an idea first put forward by Thomas Jefferson and adopted by Blount. To the general the argument about national security resonated in his mind like no other, and he, too, thought it made remarkable good sense. He also came to believe that it was in the Indians' own self-interest to remove. With all the killing that had been going on for decades, with pressure constantly mounting by the invasion of white intruders into Indian lands from every direction, it hardly took much thought or calculation to determine that the annihilation of Native Americans would be the inevitable consequence if they refused to remove—just as had happened among several eastern tribes, such as the Yamasees and Delawares.

The sporadic violence that regularly flared on the frontier with Cherokees, Creeks, Chickasaws, and Choctaws particularly reinforced Jackson's advocacy of Blount's proposal, especially when Little Warrior, leading a party of Creeks who were returning from a visit to the Shawnees on the northern lakes, "massacred" several families living near Duck River on May 12, 1812. They took Martha Crawley captive and "murdered" two of her children, who were playing in the yard. Martha's husband was away at the time, and she managed to hide her two youngest children in a potato cellar under the floor of her home. The Indians broke open the door and dragged Martha outside with the intention of killing her but decided instead to hold her captive. They forced her to cook for them as they headed for Tuckabatchee but committed "no other violence" on her.[8]

The massacre and the treatment of Mrs. Crawley and children "aroused strong feelings against the Creeks among the people of Tennessee," none more so than Major General Andrew Jackson, who had a claim to land along the Duck River. He happened to be on a trip to Georgia to settle land claims that could have landed him in debtor's prison when the incident occurred, but upon returning home he wrote to Blount and gave full vent to his fury against these "murdering Creeks." "My heart bleeds within me," he thundered, "on the recept of the news of the horrid cruelty and murders committed by a party of Creeks, on our innocent, wifes and little babes. . . . *They must be punished*—and our frontier protected—and as I have no doubt but the[y] are urged on by british agents and tools, the sooner the[y] can be attacked, the less will be their resistence, and the fewer will be the nations or tribes that we will have to war with." We must march into the Creek Nation, he insisted, and "demand the perpetrators, at the Point of the Bayonet—if refused—that we make reprisals— and lay their Towns in ashes." The Creeks are preparing for war, he went on, and the Cherokees can be persuaded to "Join us, if we shew an immediate spirit of revenge, and it may deter the bad men of the Choctaws and Chekesaws, from aiding the Creeks." He begged Blount to give him the "provisions and munitions of war," and, he added, "by your orders" he would lead 2,500 volunteers to "quell the Creeks, and bring them to terms without presents or anuities."[9] He was itching to lay hands on the Creeks and show them in clear and unmistakable ways what "retributive justice" meant.

Jackson also wrote to George Colbert, the mixed-blood Chickasaw chief, and said he had learned that the Creek murderers had passed through "your nation carrying along with them stolen horses, scalps, and a white woman prisoner." He also had heard that the Chickasaws had taken two of these horses from these Creeks. "Brother," he scolded, "could you not also have taken the woman?" The "creeks have killed our women and children, we have sent to demand the murderers, if they are not given up, the whole creek nation shall be covered with blood, fire shall consume their Towns and villages: and their lands shall be divided among the whites." You know that "I am your friend, and the friend of your nation," but if you persist in allowing Creeks to have access through your Nation, my friendship and the friendship of the United States "will stop." Remember how the entire Creek Nation came to destroy your towns and how "a few hundred chickasaws aided by a few whites chased them back to their nation, Killing the best of their warriors, and covering the rest with Shame?" Remember? Brother, we will do the same if "the Creeks dare to touch you for your friendship to us." So be warned: "Mark what I say." If you suffer any more scalps or stolen horses to be carried through your Nation by the Creeks, "your Father the President" will know that you have violated your treaty with us and have taken our enemy "by the hand."

Jackson ended his letter by demanding that Colbert give him the names of the Creek murderers, the identity of their towns, and "the place where they have carried the woman prisoner." You say you are the friend of whites—"now prove it to me."[10]

What is instructive here is the manner and tone with which Jackson addressed the chief. And it never varied. He always addressed Indians as though they were children, irrespective of their age, education, or intellectual maturity. The President of the United States was their "Father" and he their "Friend & Brother"—provided they obeyed him and performed exactly as he directed. These he called "true Indians, the natives of the forest."[11] Disobedience to his commands made them not naughty children but enemies who broke treaties, associated with "designing half-breeds and renegade white men," and therefore forfeited the friendship of the United States and deserved to be severely punished. The Indians themselves too often fostered this curious relationship. They always called the President "Father" and referred to themselves as his "red children." For Jackson, then, the relationship of whites to Indians was distinctly that of the superior instructing the inferior. And in this respect he was not different from most Americans living close to Indian tribes.[12]

Like many other Tennesseans he felt that "little confidence . . . ought to be placed in the aid or friendship of Indians." They were not to be trusted. He also believed that sound policy dictated "the propriety of inlisting one nation against another." In this present matter he was especially anxious in "inlisting" the Cherokees against the Creeks. If the Cherokees were engaged, he said, they "will be obliged to be friendly with us to preserve themselfs—I believe self interest and self preservation the most predominant passion—fear is better than love with an indian." Therefore, he told Governor Blount, we must enlist such Cherokee chiefs as Lowry, Walker, and Major Ridge and get them to cooperate in punishing the Creeks.[13]

Fear is better than love with an Indian. That to a large extent describes how Jackson behaved toward Native Americans. Put the fear of everlasting damnation in them, he said. And in this instance he kept badgering Blount for arms and ammunition so that he could dispense that fear across the entire Creek Nation. He finally told the governor that he would march by July 25 at the latest with whatever arms and supplies he could obtain and "penetrate the creek Towns, untill the Captive [Martha Crawley], with her captors are delivered up, and think myself Justified, in laying waste their villiages, burning their homes, killing their warriors and leading into Captivity their wives and Children." No doubt about it, General Andrew Jackson could be savagely cold-blooded and ruthless when punishing Indians. And he always felt "justified." The outrage committed against Martha Crawley and her family was all he needed to justify a campaign of terror.[14]

But it must be remembered that he could also be ruthless toward white men who squatted on Indian land without authority and in violation of government treaties. These were "troublemakers" who by their actions placed the lives of settlers in great jeopardy. Granted the tribes had to be removed, but not by unauthorized squatters who deliberately or not instigated frontier warfare for their own land-hungry purposes. As general of the army he frequently employed his troops in expelling these "robbers" from Indian lands. "I ordered Capt. [Sam] Houston," he reported to the secretary of war on one occasion, "to seize and deliver all intruders over to the Civil Authority, and their stock into the hands of the Marshall" to be sold at public auction. He felt he was under orders "to take all persons and stock, found trespassing on the Indian Territory, and deliver them over to the civil authority for prosecution." Moreover, the civil authority had to cooperate with the military, he insisted, because intruders invariably returned to their settlements after the military had left. It was useless to remove them "without prosecution for the infraction of the law," he added.[15]

Jackson carried his message of vengeance to the people of Tennessee when he published an article in the *Democratic Clarion* on July 8, 1812, to express his concerns. Two months had passed, he ranted, since this "cruel outrage, this act of war . . . [and] no vengeance has yet been taken: no atonement has yet been made." And vengeance and atonement were essential to prevent further depredations. Mrs. Crawley was still held at Tuckabatchee. We cannot, he said, permit the assassinations "of women and children to escape with impunity and with triumph." The "zeal" of your major general "has not been stopped." The Nickajack expedition put an end to the Cherokee War, he declared, and we need another expedition to put down what is obviously a new war by Creeks. "Citizens," he cried, "hold yourselves in readiness: it may be but a short time before the question is put to you: *Are you ready to follow your general to the heart of the Creek nation.*"

Revenge of sorts was achieved when Little Warrior and his band were condemned by Big Warrior, who ordered out a war party that killed eight of them, triggering the outbreak of a Creek civil war. Meanwhile Tandy Walker, who had lived among the Creeks for many years and had been sent by the government as a "public blacksmith" for the benefit of the Indians, visited his old friend Chief Oceocheemotla of the Creek Nation and arranged Martha Crawley's release. He found her "very feeble," her mind "impaired by suffering," and "her limbs and feet" still "wounded" because of the hardships she had endured. She was taken to the home of George Gaines, whose wife ministered to the stricken woman. After a week's nursing, Martha's "mind appeared to be restored."[16]

But no vengeance and no atonement by American authority had yet been visited on the hostile Creeks. And Jackson swore he would have both. Nearly a year passed before he finally laid heavy hands on these "savages," because he was abruptly notified by Governor Blount that the United States had declared war against Great Britain in June 1812.

The War of 1812 was expected to settle many outstanding grievances between the United States and Great Britain, such as seizure of ships, the impressment of seamen, and the need to prove the nation's right to independence. But there was another factor in the declaration of war: the ever-constant desire for American expansion. "I shall never die contented," said Representative Richard M. Johnson of Kentucky, "until I see her [Great Britain's] expulsion from North America, and her territories incorporated with the United States." The acquisition of Spanish East and West Florida also tempted American expansionists. Presently allied to England, although not involved in the conflict, Spain had a long history of encouraging Indian depredations in the south and west, and that activity had to be stopped once and for all.[17]

In prosecuting the war the Madison administration sent Governor Willie Blount seventy blank commissions for volunteers to take part in an expedition to New Orleans, and Blount gave one of them to Jackson, ordering him to proceed directly to New Orleans. Henceforth the militia general was now Major General of United States Volunteers.

Jackson gathered his army at Nashville, and although the weather was brutally cold and the ground covered with snow, the expedition took off on January 7, 1813, and descended the ice-clogged Ohio and Mississippi rivers to Natchez, where it halted. Then, to his shock and amazement, Jackson received an order from the secretary of war, John Armstrong, dismissing his army and instructing him to turn over "all articles of public property" to General James Wilkinson, stationed in New Orleans.[18]

The order scarcely made any sense. Dismissing over two thousand men five hundred miles from home and casting them loose in Indian country was sheer insanity. Jackson had 150 men on sick report, fifty-six of whom could not raise their heads above the ground. Worse, practically all his men were destitute—they had not any means of defraying the expenses involved in getting home.[19] The secretary of war "must have been drunk when he wrote" the order, Jackson told his congressman, Felix Grundy, "or so proud of his appointment as to have lost all feelings of humanity & duty."[20] But he figured that the order was a personal vendetta to punish him for past grievances. And he also figured that the administration guessed that his army would not attempt to return home but would join Wilkinson in New Orleans.

Actually there was no conspiracy. What Jackson did not know was that his army was meant to assist a strike force operating from New Orleans to seize East Florida from Spain. But Spain was allied to Russia, and the Czar was now attempting to mediate an end of the war between Great Britain and the United States. To avoid further international complications the administration decided to abandon the expedition and so sent Jackson the dismissal order. Nonetheless Congress did authorize the seizure of what was left of West Florida, and in the spring of 1813 the United States captured Mobile, claiming it as part of the Louisiana Purchase and forcing the Spanish to withdraw to Pensacola.

Jackson knew none of this. All he knew was that he and his army had been dismissed, and he decided then and there that he would disregard the order. It was another instance of his contempt for any authority that conflicted with what he knew to be the right thing to do. He would not disband his army; rather he would lead it back to Tennessee himself at his own expense if necessary. He dispatched a letter to Armstrong and informed him that "these brave men . . . deserve a better fate and return from their government. . . . They followed me to the field; I shall carefully march them back to their homes."

And he did, in a long, agonizing journey. Something in his character emerged during this trip that helps explain his subsequent military successes. It was willpower. Not the ordinary kind. This was superhuman. Almost demonic. It was sheer, total, concentrated determination to achieve his goals. He became capable of extraordinary feats of courage and perseverance in the face of incredible odds. Victory alone was acceptable, defeat unthinkable. He made up his mind that he would bring his army safely back to Nashville, no matter the cost, "even if it meant carrying every last one of them on his back."[21]

He ordered his officers to turn over their horses to the sick, which he himself had done. Walking alongside his men day after day he never showed signs of fatigue. He cheered his men with words of praise for their heroism. He daily showed his concern for their safety and comfort, and they never forgot it. "It is . . . my duty," he told his wife, "to act as a father to the sick and to the well and stay with them untill I march them into Nashville."[22]

It was during this journey home that the men decided that Andrew Jackson was about as tough as anything they knew. And so they christened him "Old Hickory," and that became his nickname among Americans for the remainder of his life. When the troops finally arrived home, the Nashville *Whig* reported what had happened and what his soldiers thought of him. "Long will their General live in the memory of his volunteers of West Tennessee for his benevolent, humane, and fatherly treatment to his soldiers; if gratitude and love can reward him, General Jackson has them. It affords us pleasure to say, that we believe there is not a man belonging to the detachment but what loves him."

Indeed, and they were not ashamed to admit it. The entire frontier community suddenly had a new regard for their hero. He was now "the most beloved and esteemed of private citizens in western Tennessee."[23]

But this newfound glorification was soon tarnished when he involved himself in a dispute between his brigade inspector, William Carroll, and Jesse Benton, the brother of Thomas Hart Benton, Jackson's aide-de-camp. Old Hickory foolishly agreed to stand as Carroll's second in the resulting duel. Unfortunately, when the order came to fire during the duel, Jesse wheeled around to a very low squatting position. As a consequence, Carroll's bullet inflicted a long, raking wound across both cheeks of Jesse's buttock. This humiliation infuriated both Benton brothers, and they turned their anger against Jackson, because they felt that as an older man and senior officer of the militia he should never have involved himself in a dispute between two young bucks. It was none of his business. Their grievance festered over the next several months until finally they took their revenge by ambushing Old Hickory in a hotel bar. In the struggle Jesse shot Jackson in the arm with a bullet and a slug from a second weapon. The slug shattered Old Hickory's shoulder and the bullet pierced his arm and remained embedded against the upper bone of his left arm. A physician worked over him and managed to stanch the flow of blood with poultices of elm and other wood cuttings as prescribed by Indians. For weeks Jackson lay prostrate from the loss of blood, and it was nearly a month before he could leave his bed.[24]

Years later, Thomas Hart Benton and Jackson reconciled, and Senator Benton became one of President Jackson's leading spokesman in Congress. But Jesse never forgave the general nor his brother for deserting to the enemy. The bullet remained in Jackson's arm until 1832, when a Philadelphia surgeon, operating in the White House without anesthesia (which was not yet in use), removed it.

While Jackson was recovering from his wound, the massacre at Fort Mims occurred on August 30, 1813, when William Weatherford and his Red Stick warriors "murdered" hundreds of American settlers. Governor Blount immediately ordered "the great Tennessee Indian fighter" to call out the militia and march against the Creeks.

At last! At long last! After over a year of waiting, Old Hickory now was given the opportunity of bringing "vengeance and atonment" to the Creek Nation. He would make the Creeks pay dearly for the "massacre of the Tennessee families on Duck River and the treatment of Mrs. Crawley and children." He would teach them a lesson that would not only punish them for their crimes but instruct other tribes on what to expect if they violated treaties and waged war against citizens of the United States.

On September 24 he issued an order to his "Brave Tennesseans" to rendezvous at Fayetteville for immediate duty against the Creeks. We cannot waste time, he told them. We must hasten to the frontier "or we will find it drenched in the blood of our fellow-citizens." His men knew about his physical condition, so he felt obliged to mention it in his order. "The health of your general is restored," he assured them. "He will command in person."[25]

Chapter 4

The Creek War

Three days later, General Jackson broke camp and headed south to link up with his cavalry commanded by Brigadier General John Coffee, which he had sent ahead to Huntsville to prepare a camp for the main army. He also dispatched letters to friendly Creeks and encouraged them to "hold out obstinately" if attacked by Red Sticks. "I will come to your relief," he assured them. To Chief Chennabee, who captured hostiles, recruited warriors for the Americans, and provided valuable information, Jackson wrote: "If one hair of your head is hurt or of your family or of any who are friendly to the whites, I will sacrifice a hundred lives to pay for it. Be of good heart, & tell your men they have nothing to fear." Jackson repeated his promise of protection to Chief Pathkiller, the Principal Chief of the Cherokee Nation, when he heard that Weatherford had threatened to punish all Indians who refused to aid the Red Stick cause. "It is time that all our enemies should feel the force of that power [the United States] which has indulged them so long, & which they have, so long, treated with insult." Many individual Indians responded to the general's promise with pledges of loyalty. In the ensuing military engagements over the long and arduous months ahead, Old Hickory enjoyed the considerable help of many friendly Creeks, including Big Warrior. And Chief Pathkiller helped recruit and organize Cherokee warriors to serve under the American commander.[1]

Speeding along at the incredible rate of thirty-six miles a day, the west Tennessee army joined Coffee at Huntsville, then moved deep into Creek country and halted at the southernmost tip of the Tennessee River, where Jackson built Fort Deposit as a depot for supplies. After completing this fort he pushed on to the Coosa River, slicing a wide path for a road over the mountains as he went,

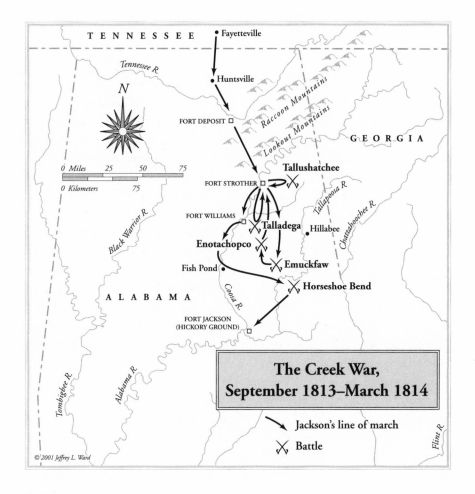

The Creek War,
September 1813–March 1814

Jackson's line of march

Battle

©2001 Jeffrey L. Ward

and establishing a base at Fort Strother on the river in the northern Mississippi Territory in what is presently Alabama.

He and his army were now about thirteen miles to the east of the hostile village of Tallushatchee. On November 3, 1813, General Coffee's brigade surrounded Tallushatchee and systematically slaughtered most of the warriors. It was a quick and bloody operation. "We shot them like dogs," boasted Davy Crockett. The killing was so gruesome that Lieutenant Richard Keith Call became nauseated. "We found as many as eight or ten dead bodies in a single cabin," he declared. "Some of the cabins had taken fire, and half consumed human bodies were seen amidst the smoking ruins. In other instances dogs had torn and feasted on the mangled bodies of their masters. Heart sick I turned from the revolting scene." The town was then burned to the ground.

The Americans lost five men and forty-one wounded in the attack; some 186 Red Sticks were found dead. In this war of unspeakable barbarity only the lives of women and children were spared, but eighty-four women and children were taken as captives in this encounter. "We have retaliated for the destruction of Fort Mims," reported the jubilant General Jackson to Governor Blount.[2]

While inspecting the bloody battleground, soldiers came upon a dead Indian woman still clutching her living ten-month-old male infant. The child was the sole survivor of his family. Some Indian women "wanted to k[ill him] because the whole race & family of his [blood] was destroyed," reported Jackson. But, in an unprecedented act of mercy that not all militiamen approved, one of the interpreters, possibly James Quarles, intervened and lifted the child from the hands of his dead mother. He carried the infant to the commanding general. When Jackson was told that the other Indians wished to kill the infant, he immediately overruled them. Suddenly, he said, he experienced a deep feeling for the boy. "In fact when I reflect that he as to his relations is so much like myself I feel an unusual sympathy for him."

Jackson took the child to his tent. There he dissolved a little brown sugar with water and coaxed the boy, named Lyncoya, to drink. As he watched the infant he kept remembering his own childhood and the many hardships he had suffered and how at the age of fourteen he, too, had become an orphan. In a rather remarkable way he identified with the child, and he decided to keep him. He placed him in the care of Major William White, who was directed to take him to the Hermitage, Jackson's home outside Nashville, and present the boy as a gift to his adopted son, Andrew Jackson, Jr. "Tell my dear little andrew to treat him well," Jackson wrote his wife. "Charity and christianity says he ought to be taken care of." But you must "keep Lyncoya in the house," he warned, because "he is a Savage." Still I "want him well taken care of, he may have been given to me for some Valuable purpose."

Lyncoya was sent first to Huntsville to be nursed and clothed, after which White escorted him to the Hermitage, which they reached in May 1814.[3] The child was raised in the Jackson household and as a youth sometimes terrified visitors to the Hermitage when, smeared with war paint, he would jump out from behind a bush and let out a war whoop—just to see their reaction. Jackson always treated him as a son and considered sending him to West Point, which he regarded as the best school in the country; but the boy wanted to be a saddler, the one occupation Jackson had also favored in his youth. Indeed the two were very much alike, which the general realized and commented on. As he said, "fortune has thrown [Lyncoya] in my h[ands]" for "some Valuable purpose."[4]

After sending the child north, Jackson kept his troops busy strengthening Fort Strother. Running short of supplies to feed his army, he sent off express messages to General James White and General John Cocke, who were commanding the east Tennessee troops, to hurry to his aid. This serious shortage of food and other supplies caused a severe deterioration of morale. By this time General White had arrived at Turkey Town, a Cherokee village about twenty-five miles to the north. Several more pleas followed in which Jackson begged White to bring with him as much food as he had on hand. He said he was desperate. But the appeals went unheeded. White just sat at Turkey Town and did nothing.[5]

Late in the evening of November 7 a friendly Creek chief burst into Jackson's camp with the news that the Red Sticks had massed before the town of Talladega in great numbers with the intention of destroying it because it was allied with the Americans. This chief had managed to make his way through the besiegers cloaked in a hog skin. Talladega was approximately thirty miles south of Fort Strother, and the chief pleaded with Jackson to come immediately to its rescue. Realizing that he now had a splendid opportunity to destroy a large Red Stick force, Old Hickory hurriedly set out for the town with twelve hundred infantry and eight hundred cavalry and mounted riflemen, "leaving behind me the sick and wounded, and all the baggage with what I considered a sufficient force to protect them, until the arrival of Genl White who was hourly expected" with supplies.[6]

At midnight the army departed Fort Strother, advancing in three columns so that if attacked it could quickly form a square to protect itself, and by the evening of November 8 it had arrived within six miles of the Red Sticks. Friendly Creek spies informed Jackson that the hostiles were posted within a quarter of a mile of the Talladega fort but that they could not get close enough to judge their number. Moments later a runner brought news that General White had been ordered by General Cocke to withdraw and proceed to the mouth of Chatuga Creek. Since that was the last order White received, he naturally obeyed it.

Filled "with astonishment and apprehensions" about the safety of Fort Strother, Jackson had no other recourse than to launch an immediate attack on the enemy. At 4:00 A.M. on November 9 the army again advanced. The infantry formed two columns, militia on the left and volunteers on the right, while cavalrymen and mounted riflemen formed two columns on the flanks and were ordered to fan out in a crescent-shaped "curve." Two hundred and fifty cavalrymen were stationed in the center behind the infantry as a reserve.

The advance, marching four hundred yards in front, consisted of artillerymen with muskets, two companies of riflemen, and one company of spies. Commanded by Colonel William Carroll, the inspector general, they were given orders to press forward, engage the enemy, and then fall back to the center so as to draw the hostiles after them. The mounted troops on the left and right flanks would then encircle the hostiles by uniting the front of their respective columns, keeping their rear solidly anchored on the infantry. They were "to face and press inwards" toward the center so as to leave no possibility of escape.[7]

At 8:00 A.M. the advance came within eighty yards of the enemy, who were concealed in the thick shrubbery. They peppered the Red Sticks with grape and received a heavy fire in return. Following Jackson's orders, they then retreated toward the center of the line with the Indians, "now screaming and yelling hideously," rushing forward into the trap. But three companies of the militia, frightened by the war whoops and the number of Red Sticks racing toward them, fled at the first fire. It was a moment of near panic. But Jackson responded instantly. To fill the gap he ordered the reserve to dismount and meet the enemy head-on. At this point the retreating militiamen, seeing their places taken by the reserves and making a "spirited stand," rallied and resumed their former position on the line.

The action now became general. A thousand Red Sticks were sealed inside the curved arms of Jackson's army, and the troops started shooting them at point-blank range. Within fifteen minutes the Indians were "seen flying in every direction." On the left the mounted riflemen gunned them down like so many tenpins, but on the right a hole opened up between the infantry and cavalry because of the failure of the regiment of volunteers to move up fast enough and get into position. A great number of Indians poured through the gap to escape the withering fire coming at them from all sides. They were pursued "with great slaughter" until they reached the mountains, a distance of three miles.

Jackson estimated that the total attacking force of Red Sticks approximated 1,080. Despite the unfortunate break in his line, some three hundred Indians lay dead on the battleground. Many others were killed in flight, and in fact, according to Major John Reid, the general's aide and secretary, probably few escaped unhurt. Still, Jackson had missed the opportunity of wiping out the hostiles entirely. "Had there been no departure from the original order of battle," he informed Governor Blount, "not an Indian would have escaped." The general's own losses amounted to fifteen dead and eighty-five wounded, two of whom later died of their wounds. "Too much praise cannot be bestowed upon the advance, led on by colo Carrol for the spirited maner in which they commenced and sustained the attack, nor upon the Reserve . . . for the gallantry with which they met and repulsed the enemy. In a word the officers of every grade, as well as the privates realised the high expectations I had formed of them and merit the gratitude of their country."[8]

Having collected his dead and wounded, Jackson advanced to the Talladega fort and lifted the siege. These friendly Creeks welcomed him with "manifestations of joy for their deliverance," for they knew that on that very day their stronghold would have been assaulted and "every soul within the fort [would] have perished." To show their appreciation they sold Jackson all the provisions they could spare; he purchased them with his own money and then distributed them to his soldiers, who were "almost destitute." Without enough provisions to continue the war—and since General White had failed to reinforce Fort Strother with men and supplies, as expected—Jackson was forced to turn around and retrace his steps to the fort, giving the Red Sticks time to reassemble their forces. It is quite probable that had Old Hickory been able to hunt down the remaining hostiles from the Talladega battle he might well have broken the back of the Creek uprising and ended the war.[9]

The probability of a quick end to the war was reinforced by the decision of the Hillabee and Fish Pond Indians, possibly the most fierce of the Creek hostiles, to abandon the fighting and make peace. A flag arrived accompanied by a letter from Robert Grierson, a Scot married to an Indian and living at a Hillabee town as a licensed trader. Grierson informed Jackson that because of the Talladega victory the Hillabees were "panic struck," with "no amunition nor resources of any kind" and were prepared "to sue for peace . . . [and] lay down their arms" on any terms he might propose. If Jackson would march his army to "Saccapatae," an abandoned Creek village thirty-five miles south of Fort Strother, and build a fort there, said Grierson, he would "be in the centre to act against all the hostile Indians, and will conquer them in two weeks."

Jackson was delighted with this development, but before agreeing to a cessation of hostilities against the Hillabees he insisted that they "must furnish me indubitable proof of their sincerity." They must, he said in his reply to Grierson, restore all property and prisoners taken from "the whites" or friendly Creeks, deliver up the instigators of the war, furnish his army with provisions, and join him in prosecuting the war against the remaining hostiles. "The terms upon which a final peace will be granted them will greatly depend upon their conduct in the meantime." He could not say with absolute certainty when he would arrive at Saccapatae but he expected to resume his march against the remaining Red Sticks in a few days. Tell the Hillabees, he concluded, that the prophets and those who instigated the war will be punished severely. "Long shall they remember Fr. Mims in bitterness & tears."[10]

The Hillabees bowed to the terms listed in the general's letter and prepared to carry them out. Jackson then wrote to General Cocke, who commanded the eastern Tennessee army, and informed him of what had happened and that he had made peace with the Hillabees. Under the circumstances, he requested that Cocke detail six hundred men from his army and send them to Fort Strother "with as little delay as possible, & with as full a supply as you can obtain."[11]

But the very day Jackson wrote this letter, General White, acting under orders from Cocke, attacked and destroyed several Hillabee towns, burning one village of thirty houses and another of ninety. He spared a few towns as they "might possibly be of use at some future period." At the principal Hillabee town, the one that had appealed to Jackson for peace terms, he killed sixty-four warriors and seized 256 prisoners, twenty-nine of whom were warriors, the rest women and children. He then burned the town.[12]

To the Indians this was overwhelming proof of white treachery. Convinced they had been betrayed by the duplicitous Jackson, the Hillabees swore they would continue the war and repay treachery with blood. They would fight to the death. Indeed, to the end of the war they fought with heightened fury and determination.

Cocke wrote to Jackson on November 27 and informed him of the victory. An early and most reliable biographer, James Parton, claims that Jackson expressed "grief and rage" when he received news of this catastrophe, that he was conscious of the fact that before "the Indian world he stood condemned as a violator of his written word," a man who through trickery and deceit parlayed with a beaten and discouraged enemy in order to strike an "exterminating blow." Despite Parton's statement, the extant documentary evidence does not support it. On the contrary, Jackson nowhere indicates great concern about the attack on the Hillabees, and in his letter of reply to Cocke on December 6 he did not condemn the action.[13] Such behavior is distinctly unlike Jackson's usual practice of protecting his friends, no matter who they were. That he did not speak up for the Hillabees against Cocke in this instance defies understanding, and as it stands, this aberration from his normal behavior does not speak well of him. It seems his hatred for the Creeks had become an obsession.

Old Hickory swung his army back to Fort Strother, hoping to find much-needed supplies and reinforcements. But he found nothing. Days passed. His troops were starving and growing restless and angry. The general himself was suffering from dysentery and the lingering effects of his gunfight with the Benton brothers.

Even Governor Blount advised him to turn around and march back to Tennessee. In a word, retreat. But that only infuriated the crusty general. You want me to retreat, he responded. "What! retrograde under such circumstances! I will perish first. No, I will do my duty: I will hold the posts I have established . . . or die in the struggle."

But what can be done? "I'll tell you what," Governor Blount. "You have only to act with the energy and decision the crisis demands, and all will be well. Send me a force engaged for six months, and I will answer for the results."[14]

With starvation facing them, a large number of Jackson's troops, whose enlistments had expired, decided on their own to return home, with or without their commander's approval. Were they expected to sit at the fort and starve to death when hot food and a warm bed at home awaited them? So they packed their gear and started north.

Jackson's army consisted of two brigades of one-year volunteers and one brigade of militia. It was the latter that decamped first, but they did not get far. Jackson deployed the volunteers in front of them and forced them to return to their quarters, grumbling and swearing to run away at the first opportunity. The next day the situation was reversed. The volunteers headed home and the militia blocked their path. Madness seemed to reign at Fort Strother.

In desperation, Jackson appealed to his field and platoon officers. "I have no wish to starve you—none to deceive you." Large supplies have arrived at Fort Deposit, he assured them, and wagons are about to bring them here. Any number of beeves are in the neighborhood and detachments will shortly bring them in. "Stay contentedly; and if supplies do not arrive in two days, we will all march back together, and throw the blame of our failure where it should properly lie."

It was a stirring appeal, and the officers and men agreed to wait another two days.

Two days passed. Nothing arrived. And the men now insisted that he keep his word and march them home.

Jackson suddenly let out a cry of desperation. "If only two men will remain with me, I will never abandon this post." A Captain Gordeon of the company of spies immediately responded, "You have one, general, let us look if we can't find another. . . ." The remark may have been intended as a joke or a way of embarrassing Jackson so that he would realize the hopelessness of their situation. But then the unexpected happened. One hundred and nine men stepped forward and agreed to remain and protect the post.[15] Heartened by this show of support, Jackson thanked these men and ordered them to guard Fort Strother while he and the remainder of the army marched to Fort Deposit, where he expected to meet the supply train. After that he intended to march his men back to Fort Strother to renew the campaign against the Red Sticks.

On November 17, 1813, the order was given and the bedraggled, half-starved, and weary army broke camp and headed toward Fort Deposit, no doubt hoping with each step that no supply train awaited them and that they could then march back home. But to their dismay and Jackson's great relief they met 150 beeves and nine wagons of flour not twelve miles from camp. The troops gorged themselves. Then, their hunger appeased, they were ordered back to Fort Strother.

They hesitated. They did not respond to the order. They just stared at their commander and grumbled their defiance. Indeed, without saying another word, one company started moving toward Tennessee. In an instant Jackson mounted his horse and detoured ahead of them. About a quarter of a mile ahead of these troops, Jackson met General Coffee with a small detachment of his cavalry. Forming these soldiers across the road, Old Hickory ordered them to shoot any mutineer who refused to turn back. Then he positioned himself in front of them.

As the deserters moved toward him, Jackson never flinched. Stretched high on the saddle of his horse, jaw set and eyes ablaze, Jackson roared a threat to kill any man who disobeyed his order. The look on his face, the cold, fierce determination that sat astride his mount convinced the troops that he meant what he said. Within moments the company gave ground and slowly, grudgingly, turned around.

But the situation was worse than the commander realized. When he returned to the encampment he found a much more extensive mutiny in progress. An entire brigade was poised to desert. Here was the supreme challenge to his leadership.

Still hobbled by his gunshot wound and unable to use his left arm effectively, Jackson seized a musket, rested it on the neck of his horse, and rode out in front of the column. Again came the threats, this time with greater intensity. He swore he would shoot the first man who moved forward. The brigade halted in its tracks. There followed a long period of silence. Then General Coffee and Major John Reid took up positions on either side of the general. Everyone remained perfectly still.

At that critical moment a few loyal companies formed themselves behind Jackson. They raised their muskets in imitation of their commander. There could be no doubt that they would fire on the first man who moved forward toward Tennessee. And that action brought the mutiny to an end. Recognizing they would never reach their homes again if they persisted in their effort to leave, the deserters slowly turned around and returned to their posts. Said one observer: "It is very certain, that, but for the firmness of the general, at this critical moment, the campaign would for the present have been broken up, and would probably never have been re-commenced."[16]

Later it was discovered that Jackson's musket was defective and could not be fired. Had the soldiers dared to risk disobeying him they might have gotten away with it.[17]

But the resentment among the troops did not wane. If anything it grew worse. For many of them, their one-year enlistments would officially end on December 10, 1813, and they began making plans about how they might execute their "escape." Then, on December 9, General William Hall went to Jackson's tent and informed him that his brigade of volunteers planned to silently slip away during the night.

The general sighed. There seemed to be no end to this rebellion. After a moment in which he vented his exasperation he issued an order commanding the volunteers to parade on the west side of the fort. Simultaneously he posted the artillery company with two small fieldpieces to the front and rear of the brigade and strung the militia along an "eminence" commanding the road to Tennessee. Then Jackson rode in front of the volunteers and in a "strain of impassioned eloquence" reminded the volunteers of the dangers they had faced together, of the disgrace that would surely befall them and their families if they deserted, and of the undoubted fact that they would never leave except over his dead body. He said he expected reinforcements at any moment. And until then they could not leave. Once the reinforcements showed up, then they could return home. He ended his plea with the words "I have done with intreaty,—it has been used long enough.—I will attempt it no more."

With that Jackson turned to the artillery gunners and ordered them to light their matches, he himself remaining in front of the brigade and in the line of fire. Unquestionably he would not hesitate a moment to give the order to fire. He knew it and the volunteers knew it. Minutes passed and suddenly there were whispers running up and down the line of men.

"Let us return," could be heard. Let us get out of danger. Better to return to duty than have an artillery piece discharge in your face.

Officers of the brigade stepped forward and pledged themselves for their men, who either nodded or openly said they would return to their quarters. And so the moment of "greatest peril" passed. But Jackson was deeply grieved by their conduct. His volunteers, he sadly informed his wife, had sunk from the "highest elevation of patriots—to mere, wining, complaining, Sedioners and mutineers—to keep whom from open acts of mutiny I have been compelled to point my cannon against, with a lighted match to destroy them. This was a grating moment of my life."

What made it worse was his own deepening depression over the state of his health. "The wound in my arm & the want of rest," plus the dreadful winter weather, he wrote, was nearly overwhelming. His shoulder continuously throbbed and he still could not get his left arm into the sleeve of his jacket without considerable effort. It was the lowest point of his military career.[18]

Then, on December 12, to the commander's total surprise and delight, General Cocke and fifteen hundred men arrived at Fort Strother. Under the circumstances, Jackson had no choice but to keep his promise and allow the first brigade to return home. By this time he was just as anxious to get rid of them as they were to go. They served no other purpose than to keep discontent alive in the camp. So he directed Hall to march them to Nashville and place them at the disposal of the governor.[19]

Unfortunately, as it turned out, the greater part of Cocke's men would be eligible for discharge in a few days and the remainder in a few weeks. Disgusted, Jackson ordered Cocke to march his men back to Tennessee and discharge them, although he begged the men to reenlist when they reached home. On top of that disaster, he received a report from General Coffee that the cavalry had deserted.

So all that was left to Jackson was the second brigade, consisting of militiamen enlisted for three months under a resolution of the Tennessee legislature. And these men expected to be released on the assigned date: January 4, 1814. Nothing he said could dissuade them. Even the governor agreed with the troops. At length he recommended that Jackson retreat to the Tennessee frontier.

When the day arrived for their release and these militiamen prepared to depart, Old Hickory cursed them and wished them each "a smoke tail in their teeth, with a Peticoat as a coat of mail to hand down to their offspring."[20]

Thus, by the beginning of the new year the fort was virtually deserted. Only one regiment separated the indomitable Jackson from the Red Sticks. And in just a matter of days the enlistments for these remaining troops would expire. If that happened he vowed to stay at his post alone.

These hammer blows might have crushed lesser men. Not Jackson. He seemed to gain inner strength from adversity. On the night of December 29 he wrote a letter to Blount in an attempt to shame him into summoning a new levy of troops. "Are you my Dear friend," he asked, "sitting with yr. arms folded under the present situation of the campaign recommending me to retrograde to please the whims of the populace. . . . Let me tell you it imperiously lies upon both you and me to do our duty regardless of consequences or the opinions of these fireside patriots, those fawning sycophants or cowardly poltroons who after all their boasted ardor, would rush home or remain at those fireside and let thousands fall victims to my retrograde."[21]

It was just at this moment of deepest gloom that a miracle occurred. Suddenly, without warning, 850 raw recruits marched into the fort on January 14, 1814, sent by Governor Blount. Jackson could scarcely believe what he saw, but he did not question it or wait to learn how skillful or competent these recruits might be. Nor would he wait while these men discovered the hazards of life in the wilderness or the danger of fighting Indians. Instead he immediately marched them into Creek territory to face the Red Sticks. He foolishly decided to head directly for the important and heavily fortified encampment of Tohopeka (the fort), or the Horseshoe Bend, at the Tallapoosa River. It was a bad mistake.

On January 21 he rested at Emuckfaw Creek, just three miles from the encampment. Not surprisingly, the Red Sticks charged out of their fort and attacked him at dawn the next day. The Creeks peppered the Americans with "quick irregular firing, from behind logs, trees, shrubbery, and whatever could afford concealment." Eventually they were driven off. Jackson and his army barely escaped being cut to pieces, so he wisely began a retreat to Fort Strother. As he pulled back, the Red Sticks stealthily followed, and when he reached Enotachopco Creek and started across the stream, the Indians pounced. They started firing at the moment the artillery entered the water behind the front guard and the flank column.

Instantly alert to what was happening, Jackson ordered the rear guard to engage the enemy at the same time he summoned the left and right columns to wheel around, recross the creek on either side of the Red Sticks, and surround them—in imitation of the Talladega strategy. "But to my astonishment and mortification," Jackson later reported, ". . . I beheld . . . the rear guard precipitately give way. This shameful retreat was disastrous in the extreme." The raw troops scurried for cover in a desperate effort to escape the flashing and roaring hell before them. Jackson managed to re-form his columns and hit the Indians hard. Other detachments of troops were hurried across the creek in strength, and after many minutes of intense fighting the Red Sticks withdrew.[22]

During the turmoil Jackson was described as a "rallying point," even for the brave. "Firm and energetic . . . his example and his authority alike contributed to arrest the flying, and give confidence to those who maintained their ground. . . . In the midst of a shower of balls . . . he was seen . . . rallying the alarmed, halting them in their flight, forming his columns, and inspiriting them by his example." About twenty Americans were killed in the engagement and seventy-five wounded, a good number of whom later died. Approximately two hundred dead Indians were counted in the creek and on the ground.[23]

Jackson proved to be a gallant, resourceful, and skillful commander. Without any appreciable military training worthy of the name he had emerged in the past few months as a highly competent general, indeed an outstanding one. Even the British, later on, admitted that he had extraordinary talents in the art of defense and offense. And in this instance he learned an important lesson about subjecting raw recruits to the savagery of determined hostiles. He wisely retreated to Fort Strother and spent the next several weeks drilling and training his troops into an efficient fighting unit. He imposed the strictest discipline and inflicted the harshest punishment on anyone who disobeyed an order or attempted to desert. He forbade the importation of whiskey and put his men to improving the road between Forts Strother and Deposit.

A hard and determined disciplinarian was forged during the Creek War; but it served his military purpose and need. Here was the Old Hickory of future legend. His very physical appearance announced his character and personality. His face was long and narrow, his frame gaunt, indeed emaciated. But his manner radiated confidence, enormous energy, and steely determination. It bespoke a spirit that willed mastery over his damaged body. His presence signaled immense authority.

During these weeks at Fort Strother, Jackson became a relentless, driving, indefatigable force intent on a single purpose: the destruction of the Creek Nation as a potential threat to the safety of the United States. And during that time he forged for himself an army that was as devoted to Creek destruction as he was. The arrival of the 39th Regiment of U.S. Infantry contributed to the good work so that by late winter, with the appearance of additional volunteers from Tennessee sent by Blount, he had nearly five thousand reasonably well trained and disciplined men with which to annihilate the Red Sticks.

His army now at maximum strength and highly motivated, Jackson planned to move down along the Coosa River, then eastward toward Emuckfaw near Horseshoe Bend. He would destroy the Creeks at the Bend and then march to the Holy Ground (called Ecunchate by the Indians) at the junction of the Coosa and Tallapoosa rivers, which was the sacred meeting place of the tribe. Superstitious Creeks believed the Holy Ground was protected by the Great Spirit and that no white man could violate it and live. Andrew Jackson believed he was just the man to trample over that superstition.[24]

On March 14, 1814, Jackson and his army wheeled out of Fort Strother and headed directly for the heavy entrenchment of Red Sticks at Horseshoe Bend. Leaving behind a portion of his troops to protect the fort, he sallied forth with about two thousand infantry, seven hundred cavalry and mounted riflemen, and six hundred Indians, of whom five hundred were Cherokees and one hundred friendly Creeks. According to Jackson's spies, there were one thousand Red Sticks and nearly three hundred women and children living inside the Bend.[25]

Horseshoe Bend, a heavily wooded peninsula, was almost completely enclosed by the looping action of the Tallapoosa River. At the river end of the peninsula a bluff protected the fort; at the other end a stout breastwork made of timber and trunks of trees "laid horizontally on each other, leaving but a single place of entrance," ran across its narrow 350-yard neck. The height of the breastwork varied from five to eight feet. It had a double row of portholes "artfully arranged" to give the defenders "complete direction of their fire." Because the Indians had constructed the breastwork to form a curved zigzag, attackers could not advance upon it without exposing themselves to a deadly crossfire. Defenders, on the other hand, were well protected and could not be enfiladed. It was "a place well formed by Nature for defence & rendered more secure by Art," admitted Jackson. Within the fort a superb gathering of strength from the hostile towns of Oakfuskee, New Youka, Oakchays, Hillabee, the Fish Ponds, and Eufala had been assembled.[26] Prophet Monahee was the Principal Chief in the fort but Menewa (Great Warrior), a mixed-blood, commanded the fighting.

Old Hickory and his energized army arrived at the Bend at approximately ten o'clock on the morning of March 27, 1814. In this approaching "hour of battle," he told his men, "you must be cool and collected. . . . you must execute commands with deliberation and aim. *let every shot tell.*" But be warned: "Any officer or soldier who flies before the enemy without being compelled to do so by superior force and actual necessity—shall suffer death."

When he saw what faced him the general stopped dead in his tracks. He communicated his astonishment to General Thomas Pinckney. "It is impossible to conceive a situation more eligible for defence than the one they had chosen," he wrote, "and the skill which they manifested in their breast work, was really astonishing." But as he thought about it and calculated his strategy, Jackson soon took a more positive attitude. They have "penned themselves up for slaughter," he reportedly said. To block any escape route he ordered Coffee with his cavalry, numbering seven hundred men, along with the five hundred Cherokees and one hundred friendly Creeks, to cross the Tallapoosa and occupy the opposite side of the river from the Bend, thereby surrounding the peninsula, so that the hostiles were completely confined. Without a means of escape the fortification now became a virtual prison and the setting for the Red Sticks' last-ditch stand.[27]

Facing the barricade, which constituted the focus of the main attack, Jackson stationed his artillery, one six-pounder and one three-pounder (not a particularly powerful battery), on a small eminence about eighty yards from the nearest and 250 yards from the farthest points of the breastwork. At 10:30 A.M. he opened fire.

The Indians inside the fortification began beating their war drums and screaming their defiance. With only a few short interruptions, Jackson kept up "a very brisk fire" for two hours, blasting the hostiles with musketry and rifles whenever they showed themselves above their works or ventured out of the enclosure. Then, without warning and apparently without specific orders from the general, the friendly Creeks, part of the Cherokee force, and the company of spies guarding the other side of the Tallapoosa crossed the river in canoes and set fire to buildings near the shore. They then mounted the bluff and attacked the Red Sticks from the rear. This sudden and unexpected maneuver gave Jackson the diversion he needed, and he seized it.[28]

"Charge!" he screamed.

His order was instantly greeted with "joy" by his soldiers. "Never were men more eager to be led to a charge than both regulars and militia," reported Jackson to Pinckney. "They had been waiting with impatience to receive the order, and hailed it with acclamation." It "was a sure augury of the success which was to follow."

The troops rushed forward under an unrelenting hail of Indian bullets and arrows. The 39th Regiment reached the barrier first and thrust their rifles through the portholes, firing at point-blank range. For a time it was muzzle-to-muzzle shooting "in which many of the enemy's balls were welded to the bayonets of our musquets." Major Lemuel P. Montgomery leaped onto the top of the breastwork and commanded his men to follow. His words had hardly been spoken when a bullet struck him in the head and he fell lifeless to the ground. Ensign Sam Houston immediately took Montgomery's place and repeated the command, whereupon an arrow pierced his thigh. Disregarding the wound, he jumped into the compound, followed by a large contingent of regulars. Within moments the breastwork was breached and the army scaled the rampart in force.[29]

With the capture of the breastwork and the mass arrival of troops within the compound, the end of the Red Sticks was at hand. The infantry rushed forward while the friendly Indians and spies advanced from the rear. The Red Sticks found themselves caught in this crushing pincer. They could not escape. They ducked into the thick brush that covered the ground to seek shelter, but they were flushed out and shot at close range. The killing became savage.

Desperate, frightened, and overwhelmed, the defenders fought furiously, but were "at length entirely routed and cut to pieces." No quarter was given, none asked. "Arrows, and spears, and balls were flying; swords and tomahawks were gleaming in the sun and the whole Peninsula rang with the yell of the savages, and the groans of the dying."

In the midst of this mayhem a frightened, confused, and lost Indian boy of five or six wandered into a group of soldiers, and one of them struck the child on the head and killed him with his musket. An officer reprimanded the recruit for committing such a barbarous act. The soldier simply replied that if the boy had lived he would have grown into a warrior and wreaked revenge on innocent whites.

Once the troops gained the upper hand they set the village on fire. During the conflagration another soldier came upon an old noncombatant Indian sitting on the ground pounding corn with a mortar. The old man may have been senile, for he seemed unaware of the savagery taking place around him. Without giving it another thought the soldier calmly and deliberately shot him dead so that he could return home and boast that he had killed an Indian. As Jackson later told his wife, Rachel, "the *carnage* was *dreadful*."[30] Indeed it was hideous.

In their pell-mell rush to escape the horror surrounding them, many Red Sticks headed for their canoes in the river, only to run smack into Coffee's troops and another blast of deadly fire. Others barreled down the bluff overlooking the river and concealed themselves among the cliffs, which were covered with fallen trees and brush. For the next several hours the American troops hunted down these desperate defenders, flushing them from their hiding places and shooting them on the spot. Only women and children were to be taken captive, although a few of them were "accidentally" killed. By this time the Red Sticks were racing madly about not knowing what to do or where to hide. The remaining warriors in the compound were systematically slaughtered.

Monahee, the principal prophet, was later found dead, shot in the mouth by grapeshot. It was "as if Heaven designed to chastise his impostures by an appropriate punishment," commented Jackson. "Two other prophets were also killed." Menewa, the great chieftain, was wounded at least seven times. He lay unconscious among the heap of dead, but after dark he regained consciousness and crawled to the river, where he found a canoe and made his escape.[31]

For five hours, Horseshoe Bend was a killing field, "but the firing and the slaughter continued until it was suspended by the darkness of the night," reported Jackson. "It was dark before we finished killing them."[32]

As the sun went down it also set on the great and proud Creek Nation. The mangled and painted bodies strewn everywhere and the smoking remains of the once mighty stronghold marked a tragic end to the grand Indian dream of driving the white man back into the sea. For the Americans the victory came at the most opportune time. That part of the Creek Nation that had responded to Tecumseh's call to destroy the American nation was crushed just when the British were about to land troops along the Gulf and provide the Indians with additional support. No one can say what might have happened had the Creek War been delayed and synchronized with the landing of the British troops. They might well have overcome Jackson's army and gone on to capture New Orleans as planned, and then establish a buffer state in the Mississippi Valley to prevent further expansion by the United States.

The next morning the killing was resumed. Sixteen hostiles were found concealed "under the banks" and promptly dispatched. Unfortunately, the barbarity did not abate with the end of the fighting. Tennessee soldiers were observed cutting long strips of skin from the bodies of the dead Indians to make bridle reins of them. The friendly Indians scalped their victims.

Jackson ordered a body count of the hostiles and his own troops. There were hundreds of dead Red Sticks everywhere within the compound, and to prevent counting any of them twice the tip of each hostile's nose was cut off as soon as the count was made. It appalled some observers who watched the ghoulish operation. "The Indians," they reported, "take off the scalps. These soldiers took off the nose."

The total count of Indian dead on the battlefield came to 557. In addition, according to the report of General Coffee and other officers, not less than 300 Red Sticks died in the river and could not be counted. All told, said Jackson, 850 hostiles were slain. Perhaps 20, maybe more, made their escape at night.

Some 26 American soldiers died, Jackson reported, and another 107 were wounded. Among Cherokees, 18 were killed and 36 wounded; in addition, 5 friendly Creeks died and 11 were wounded. The 39th Regiment, which led the charge against the breastworks, suffered the greatest casualties with 17 killed and 55 wounded. Three hundred fifty women and children and three warriors were captured and turned over to the friendly Creeks and Cherokees.[33]

Jackson made a point of extolling the heroism and patriotism of his officers and men. "There never was more heroism or roman courage displayed," he declared. He singled out Major Montgomery, the 39th Regiment with its commander Colonel John Williams, and the militia for special mention. And, he declared, the mixed-blood Creek chieftain Major William McIntoch "greatly distinguished himself." Also, she would be happy to know, Jackson told Rachel, that her nephew, Jack Caffery, "reallised all my expectations. he fought bravely—and killed an indian."[34]

Although the power and will of the Red Sticks was totally shattered, Jackson was not certain whether the hostiles would capitulate. "Having destroyed at Tohopeka, three of their princip[a]l prophets leaving but two in their nation—having tread their holy ground as the[y] termed it, and destroyed all their chiefs and warriors on the Tallapoosee river above the big bend, it is probable they may now sue for peace. Should they not . . . I will give them, with the permission of heaven the final stroke at the hickory ground."[35]

Chapter 5

Sharp Knife

A s far as Jackson was concerned, the Battle of Horseshoe Bend ended the Creek War. About three thousand Creeks, estimated at approximately 15 percent of the entire Nation, lost their lives in the conflict. The Upper Creek country was devastated, with any number of towns destroyed, along with an abundance of foodstuffs. The prophets had directed and supervised the slaughter of all the cattle and hogs they could find; no fields were planted during the war, and whatever stored grain existed was confiscated. The Creek people were starving, making continuation of the war unthinkable. "They are already nearly starved to death," General Coffee told his wife, "having eat up all their provisions." He ordered 23,000 rations to be furnished them and another 14,000 distributed among the equally starving friendly Cherokees.[1]

Jackson buried his dead in the river to prevent their being disinterred and scalped. He had learned that the Indians frequently dug up dead soldiers and stripped, mutilated, and scalped them. As a matter of fact, a number of Red Sticks at Horseshoe Bend were wearing the clothing of those soldiers who had been killed and buried at Emuckfaw.

Having safely disposed of his dead, or so he hoped, Jackson then collected his wounded and marched to Fort Williams to obtain fresh supplies. He continued his scorched-earth policy, with no mercy shown the suffering populations of the communities he traversed. He burned Indian villages as he went and destroyed whatever provisions they might contain. At "my approach," he told Rachel, "the Indians fled in all directions. . . . I have burnt the Verse Town, this day that has been the hot bed of the war, and has regained all the Scalps, taken at Fort Mims."

Because of the severity of the fighting and the reprisals inflicted on them the Indians conferred a special name on their conqueror: Sharp Knife or Pointed Arrow. But those who had developed a special hatred for Sharp Knife referred to him as "Old Mad Jackson."[2]

At Fort Williams the conquering general summoned his army on parade and published an address, extolling their heroism and the importance of their victory. They had destroyed, he said, the "fiends of the Tallapoosa." Never again would they "murder our women and children." Never again would their "midnight flambeaux" illuminate their council house "or shine upon the victims of their infernal orgies. . . . By their yells, they had hoped to frighten us, and with their wooden fortifications to oppose us. Stupid mortals! their yells but designated their situation the more certainly; whilst their walls became a snare for their own destruction. So will it ever be, when presumption and ignorance contend against bravery and prudence."[3]

After allowing his troops a short respite, Sharp Knife set out for the Hickory Ground at the juncture of the Coosa and Tallapoosa rivers on April 5. As he advanced south he burned the towns and villages he ran across. Every day a village was destroyed, sometimes two or three, depending on the army's rate of speed. The Upper Creek country became a scarred and devastated ruin. "We have fully enforced the lex taliones," Jackson boasted.

Totally beaten and cowed, many Red Stick chiefs came to the commander's camp with a flag of truce, assuring him of their desire for peace. Sharp Knife coldly informed them that they must retire to the north of his army above Fort Williams so that they would be cut off from all aid from the British and Spanish in Florida. After they had relocated he would dictate the terms for ending the war.[4]

Once he reached the fork of the Coosa and Tallapoosa rivers he raised the American flag on April 17, 1814, over the old Toulouse French Fort, which was rebuilt and renamed Fort Jackson. From this position he sent out detachments of troops to search for hostiles and destroy their towns. But they found no Red Sticks, most of whom, like Peter McQueen,[5] Josiah Francis, and other "instigators of the war," had already fled to Pensacola to seek sanctuary with the Spanish and to continue their war against the Americans. For them the war had not ended. It would never end.

The friendly Creek chiefs tried to help in bringing peace to the Creek Nation, and they urged the hostiles in Pensacola to surrender. But these Red Sticks stubbornly refused. "I have now friends and arms," read a message sent by Tustunnuggee Haujo to Big Warrior and Little Prince. "You compelled me to fly and if you attempt to trace me up I will spill your blood."[6]

Jackson was particularly anxious to get his hands on William Weatherford (Red Eagle), the Red Stick chief who had led the assault on Fort Mims. That "murderous fiend" had to be apprehended. Of every Creek who surrendered, Sharp Knife asked about the whereabouts of Red Eagle. In response he was told that Weatherford might have fled to Pensacola like Peter McQueen and Josiah Francis. But no one could say for sure. Jackson told them that if they wished to prove their desire for peace, they must bring Weatherford to the camp tied as a prisoner so that he might be punished as he deserved.

Several chiefs who actually knew Weatherford's whereabouts conveyed Jackson's command and eventually prevailed upon him to surrender voluntarily so that the war could be ended. Red Eagle was told that unless he surrendered, Sharp Knife would give no terms to the Creeks by which the starving women and children could be saved. A brave and courageous man, Weatherford realized his duty and although it meant he might forfeit his life he consented.

Without being recognized, he gained access to Jackson's camp. Silently he moved to the general's tent. At its entrance sat Big Warrior, who upon seeing Red Eagle exclaimed, "Ah! Bill Weatherford, have we got you at last?"

"You —— traitor," stormed Red Eagle, "if you give me any insolence I will blow a ball through your cowardly heart."

At that Jackson came running out of his tent. "How dare you, sir, to ride up to my tent after having murdered the women and children at Fort Mims?"

The chief drew himself up to his full height and replied: "General Jackson, I am not afraid of you. I fear no man, for I am a Creek warrior."

He paused, as though suddenly conscious of his precarious situation. "I am in your power. Do with me what you please. I am a soldier still."

Jackson stared at the Indian in amazement.

"I have done the white people all the harm I could," Weatherford continued. "I have fought them, and fought them bravely. If I had an army, I would fight them still. But I have none! My people are no more!! Nothing is left me but to weep over the misfortunes of my country."

"Kill him! Kill him! Kill him!" shouted several soldiers who had heard the commotion and had surrounded the tent.

Silence! Jackson commanded. "Any man who would kill as brave a man as this would rob the dead." After a few moments he turned to Red Eagle and said, "I had directed that you should be brought to me confined; had you appeared in this way, I should have known how to have treated you." Then he again spelled out the same terms of surrender that he had dictated to the other chiefs and the consequences of continuing the war.

Red Eagle answered that he desired peace and the end of the suffering his people had endured. He had no other choice. He could no longer wage war. "Once I could animate my warriors to battle; but I cannot animate the dead. My warriors can no longer hear my voice: their bones are at Talladega, Tallushatchee, Emuckfaw, and Tohopeka."

Staring intently at his conqueror he then "sternly demanded" the same protection that had been extended to other chiefs. You are a brave man, he told the general, and "I rely upon your generosity." If I go to my people and they refuse to listen to the terms for peace offered to them, "you will find me amongst the sternest enforcers of obedience." He acknowledged that the Creeks must go north of Fort Williams to be safe. "This is a good talk," he said, "and my nation ought to listen to it. They shall listen to it."[7]

Literally stunned by the courage and audacity of a man "who so richly deserved punishment," Jackson could not conceal his admiration for this dignified, proud, and boldly independent chief. Nor could he deny the power of Red Eagle's "talk" to bring about an end to the war. Rather than kill or imprison Weatherford, the general agreed to let him go and, together with a small party, search the forest for his followers and friends and persuade them to surrender too. Jackson knew that only Red Eagle could convince holdouts to lay down their arms. Still, before releasing the captive, he issued a sharp warning. "If you choose to try the fate of arms once more, and I take you prisoner, your life shall pay the forfeit of your crimes. But if you really wish for peace, stay where you are and I will protect you."[8] With that, Chief Red Eagle departed.

For the next several days, Jackson continued mopping-up operations. "Every hour brings in more [hostiles]," he said, "all thankful to be received upon unconditional submission." A number of slaves taken at Fort Mims were also recovered, along with one white woman, Polly Jones, and her three children. In addition, Jackson found 150 scalps, "the greater part of which were females supposed to be taken at Fort Mimms."

Since the war appeared to be over, Secretary of War John Armstrong on March 17 appointed General Pinckney and Benjamin Hawkins as commissioners to arrange a peace treaty with the Creek Nation. They were instructed to obtain an indemnity sufficient to pay for the cost of the war. In addition they were told to stipulate that all trade and communication with the Spanish in Florida must be terminated; the right of the United States to build roads, forts, and trading posts in Creek territory must be acknowledged; and all prophets and other instigators of the war must be surrendered. These very generous terms were then communicated to the Indians by Hawkins, who told the friendly chiefs that the United States would reward their loyalty by respecting their land claims, and that those chiefs who had distinguished themselves in battle would receive remuneration in the form of additional land. A few days later, Armstrong decided that the treaty should take the form of a military capitulation and therefore notified Pinckney that he alone would undertake the negotiations, but added that Hawkins could be usefully employed.[9]

Westerners reacted angrily to Armstrong's arrangements, especially Tennesseans, who felt that their state should be represented in making a treaty. Brigadier General George Doherty and eight other officers wrote to their congressman, George W. Campbell, and protested the oversight. They also vehemently disapproved the appointments of Pinckney and Hawkins and the conditions for a peace treaty, as did Jackson. Hawkins was regarded as a devoted friend of the Indians and could be expected to treat them with leniency. And Pinckney was hardly better. There was so much valuable Creek land that they feared their great opportunity to seize it would be lost if Pinckney and Hawkins had sole responsibility for writing the terms of the peace treaty.

Jackson probably expected to be appointed a commissioner and felt keen disappointment in being shunted to one side. After all, he alone had won the war. He also believed that stern measures needed to be taken against the Creeks, particularly in demanding a large land indemnity. And he had very definite ideas of what should be done. He wanted a sizable slice of Alabama and Georgia territory stripped from both friendly and hostile Creeks in order to ensure the complete separation of the tribe from the Spanish in Florida. In fact he felt that *all* the land "we have conquered" should be forfeited. Although justice to the friendly Creeks to the north required that they should be left in "the peaceable enjoyment of their towns and villages," he wrote, ". . . still the grand policy of the government ought to be to connect" American settlements in Georgia with those in the Creek territory and Tennessee in order to form "a bulwark against foreign invasion" and stop British and Spanish influence from corrupting the Indians and instigating frontier warfare. But that meant taking land from hostiles and friendly Creeks alike. To accomplish this object, Jackson proposed to run a line one and a half miles above Fort Williams, starting from the Georgia line and going due west to the Coosa River, then up the eastern bank of the Coosa to the Cherokee boundary, thence west to the Chickasaw boundary. By such a cession the Creeks would be completely isolated from foreign interference. Then, said Jackson, the government should "adopt every means to populate speedily this section of the Union." He suggested that preference be given to "those who have conquered it," allowing them to acquire 320 acres at $2 an acre. "It would be settled by a hardy race that would defend it," he said. Finally he wanted the government to extinguish all Cherokee and Chickasaw claims within the state of Tennessee. It was essential, he continued, that "our settlements" extend to the Mississippi River, for which the Indians should be compensated either with land or money. "Our national security require it and *their* [the Indians'] security require it: the happiness and security of the whole require this salutary arrangement."[10]

Here, in effect, was Jackson's policy for the removal of the Indians west of the Mississippi, a policy he would pursue for the next twenty years and bring to a successful conclusion after he was elected President. National security was at the heart of his proposal. Whether the Indians were friendly or unfriendly, they had to be moved out of any area—but particularly along the Gulf—where they could endanger the safety of the United States. Such a scheme would allow American settlers to occupy this choice land and, at the same time, better protect the nation against foreign invasion.

On April 18, General Pinckney arrived at Fort Jackson to take command of the area and begin negotiations with the Indians. Since the war seemed to be over, he ordered Jackson to conduct his army back to Tennessee, leaving a sufficient force for the garrisoning and protection of the posts already established. Within two hours of the receipt of this order, Old Hickory assembled the troops and marched them back to Fort Williams; there detachments were assigned to disperse any hostiles still in the area and General Doherty was ordered to garrison the several posts and keep open the lines of communication with Fort Jackson.

Before marching the remainder of the army back to Tennessee, Jackson again addressed his troops and commended them for their bravery and valor. "Your vengeance has been glutted. Whenever these infuriated allies of our arch enemy assembled for battle, you pursued and dispersed them. The rapidity of your movements and the brilliancy of your achievements . . . will long be cherished in the memory of your general." Then he notified Pinckney that he and his troops were on their way to Fayetteville, "where I shall discharge them: after which, I shall no longer consider myself accountable for the manner in which the posts may be defended, or the line of communication kept open."[11]

Jackson himself returned to his home outside Nashville, where he received an ecstatic welcome from a near-frenzied mob of friends and neighbors. And he reveled in every moment of it. Throughout his life it meant a great deal to him that his achievements in fighting for his country were properly acknowledged by both his superiors and the general public.

His great victory at Horseshoe Bend naturally won the notice of the administration in Washington, which earlier had resisted granting this supposed backwoodsman a suitable command. But the situation was now radically altered and it had no choice but to offer him the rank of brigadier general in the United States Army with the brevet of major general and the command of the Seventh Military District. This command included Louisiana, Tennessee, the Mississippi Territory, and the Creek Nation.

But the offer disappointed Jackson—and he was not reluctant about voicing his disappointment. He expected a higher rank, at least that of major general, the rank he held in the Tennessee militia. Secretary of War John Armstrong assured him that no disrespect or lack of appreciation was intended. It was simply the fact that no other rank was available. Then, suddenly, the problem was satisfactorily resolved. After a long dispute with the administration, General William Henry Harrison resigned his commission in disgust, and Armstrong promptly offered Harrison's rank of major general to Jackson, who greedily accepted it.[12]

Having achieved the exalted rank of major general in the United States Army, the proud commander immediately assumed all the trappings of high office, such as a glittering uniform. He also informed his wife that "you are now a Major Generals lady—in the service of the U.S. and as such you must appear, elegant and plain, not extravagant—but in such stile as strangers expect to see you."[13]

At the same time the commission was delivered, another order arrived from the War Department. Armstrong informed Jackson that President Madison wished him to proceed to Fort Jackson without delay and, as Pinckney's replacement, negotiate the treaty with the Creeks along the same guidelines that had been issued to Pinckney the previous March. No doubt Pinckney was superseded because of the enormous political pressure exerted by many leading Tennesseans. In addition, the news that the British were massing troops for an invasion of the Gulf probably convinced the administration that Jackson should be given a free hand throughout this region, particularly since he now commanded the Seventh U.S. Military District. Armstrong's letter assured the general that he would be the sole commissioner.[14]

The general did not receive this message until late June, and what with the many problems he encountered with transportation he did not arrive back at Fort Jackson until July 10. Along the route he witnessed the terrible plight of the Creek people. "It is anough to make Humanity shuddar to see the distressed situation of the Indians," he wrote his wife. Not that their suffering would change his intended course of action toward them one whit.

He also learned that Peter McQueen, Josiah Francis, and other prophets had been "received with great attention by the Spanish Governor" in Florida and that they had been furnished arms and ammunition by the British to continue their war against the United States. That was bad enough, but he was particularly annoyed with Hawkins when he heard what the agent had led the Indians to expect in agreeing to a peace treaty. Weeks earlier the general had informed Hawkins of the precise boundary lines he had assigned the Indians. "I am truly astonished that [he] is permitting the Indians to settle down on their former habitations," he fumed to Pinckney. They cannot be permitted to live south of the Alabama River. They must be cleared out. The "strenght" of the frontier depends on "thick and wealthy inhabitants, unmixed by indians."[15]

What Jackson planned to do was call a general convention of the chiefs of the entire Creek Nation—both friendly and hostile—to take place on August 1, 1814, at Fort Jackson and there set down the final terms of surrender. He wanted Hawkins to be present as well and to use his considerable influence with the Indians to get them to obey his summons. "Destruction will attend a failure to comply with those orders," he threatened. This dire warning was repeated in a letter written on July 17 to his good friend General Coffee. "If they do not come in and submit, against the day appointed which is the first of next month, a sudden and well directed stroke may be made that will at once reduce them to unconditional submission." As far as Jackson was concerned the treaty would be a "capitulation of submission" by both the friendly and hostile Creeks.[16]

The chiefs knew better than to defy Sharp Knife. But they wondered why he had adopted such an angry tone toward them, especially those who were his friends. Why threaten them with destruction? And why had they not been consulted about the terms of the treaty? Still, they appreciated Sharp Knife's mood and intended to comply fully with his command. Without question they would appear at the convention.

On August 1, the appointed day, the Creeks stood before a stony-faced commander to hear his "talk." They had been instructed to stand together, friend and foe alike—not that any foes appeared. There was no ceremony, no festivity, no pomp. This cold, desolate scene simply revealed a broken nation prostrate before its conqueror.

Despite appearances, the friendly chiefs naturally expected to be rewarded with gifts for their invaluable military aid in ending the Creek War. They expected to be publicly praised for their loyalty. They expected remuneration in the form of land for their valor and sacrifice. Unfortunately, they soon learned the terrible truth, and the awful dimension of Sharp Knife's vindictiveness.

"Friends & Brothers," General Jackson called out in his reedy voice as he began this convention, hear what "your father the President of the United States" requires of you. "Brothers, listen," we wish to save our friends, protect and support them. *"We will destroy our enemies because we love our friends & ourselves."* To accomplish this a treaty has been written for you to examine. "Our friends will sign the treaty . . . our enemies must depart." Your signatures will prove your friendship. "Consult—and this evening let me see & know who will sign it and who will not. I do not wish to force any of you—act as you think proper."

The treaty was read aloud, and many of the chiefs cried out their dismay when they heard the terms that Sharp Knife had laid down. They were certainly different from those Pinckney had relayed to them through Hawkins. What about the promise that the claims of the friendly Creeks would be respected? What about the promise that those who had distinguished themselves in battle would receive remuneration in the form of additional land? The chiefs were confused. How could identical instructions to Pinckney and Jackson bring such different requirements of them?

True to his belief that a proper surrender involved breaking the back of Creek power, Jackson demanded some 23 million acres of land, which constituted about half of all the land held by the Creek Nation. It was roughly three-fifths of the present state of Alabama and one-fifth of Georgia! It extended from Georgia to the Mississippi Territory, much of it from the region of Jackson's Indian friends and allies. In addition, Sharp Knife wanted four million acres of Cherokee land worth about $40 million and a strip along the Florida line from the Perdido River to the Pearl River. "No tribe was untouched by the seizure," reckons one historian.[17]

The shock of this betrayal, the severity of the terms imposed, and the callous dismissal of what had been promised to the friendly Creeks for their loyalty stupefied the chiefs. They were paralyzed with anger and disgust. And they must "sign or depart" or renew the war.

The Speaker for the Nation, Big Warrior, tried to reason with Jackson, but his arguments, his pleas, his demand for justice made little impression. Sharp Knife decreed that both the Upper and Lower Creeks must sacrifice land so that the United States could be better protected against its enemies. "The United States," he declared, "would have been justified by the Great Spirit, had they taken all the lands of the nation merely for keeping" secret Tecumseh's appearance before them when he urged them to spill the blood of Americans. They should have reported it to their Great Father, the President. The entire Nation was therefore guilty of breaking treaties by maintaining silence and must pay for this failure.

The Speaker protested. The friendly Creeks, he said, had not listened to Tecumseh. They had not waged war against the United States. They had done what was right.

No, responded Jackson. They had not. Had they done right the Creeks would have seized Tecumseh the moment he stepped foot in their village and sent him as a prisoner to their Great Father. "Or," he stormed, "have cut his throat."

Sharp Knife's chilling words visibly horrified the assembled chiefs. Moments passed as he let his words sink in before continuing. "The truth is," he said, "the great body of the creek chiefs & warriors did not respect the power of the United States—they thought we were an insignificant Nation—that we would be overpowered by the British." Well, they had thought wrong. The Red Sticks had sided with Tecumseh; they had murdered and obtained arms and ammunition from the British. "They were fat with eating beef—listen, they wanted flogging . . . they were mad."

The Speaker persisted. He agreed that an indemnity was just and necessary, but he insisted that the treaty terms were premature because many warriors had fled to Florida and with British help intended to continue the struggle. Besides, the indemnity was excessive and would reduce the entire Creek Nation, not simply the Red Sticks, to starvation. "The president, our father," the Speaker concluded, "advises us to honesty and fairness, and promises that justice shall be done: I hope and trust it will be!"[18]

Shelocta spoke next. This chief had joined the American troops at the commencement of the war and fought with them in all the battles against the hostiles. Moreover, he had won Jackson's confidence and respect. When he finally spoke he seemed burdened by a terrible need to save his people from an undeserved fate. He began by reminding the general of his great regard for his white brothers and how he had tried desperately to preserve the peace. He had taken up arms against his own country. He had fought his own people. He did not oppose yielding the lands lying on the Alabama, since it would cut off access to the Spanish and help prevent foreign invasion. But to take the country west of the Coosa would be a crippling blow to women and children and to the men who had fought by Jackson's side.

Shelocta looked directly at the commander and "appealed to his feelings," to the dangers they had faced together, to the trying scenes they had undergone, and to "his faithfulness."

Sharp Knife's icy-blue eyes showed that not a word of Shelocta's appeal made a particle of difference to him. And no one had a greater claim than this Indian on Jackson's generosity and forbearance. But the general would not budge; he would not yield a single acre of the land he demanded as indemnity.

As always, Jackson was expressing the prejudices, fears, mistrust, and hatred of white people living on the frontier toward all Native Americans. Westerners knew only one thing: the Indian was a threat to their lives, and that danger must be eliminated—permanently.

When Shelocta ended his talk, Jackson responded. As he spoke it hardly seemed that he was talking to his friend and brother.

"You know," he said, "that the part you desire to retain is that through which the intruders and mischief-makers from the lakes reached you, and urged your nation to those acts of violence, that have involved your people in wretchedness, and your country in ruin." It was down this road that Tecumseh came to preach his poison. "That path must be stopped." And until this is done, "your Nation cannot expect to find happiness, nor mine security."

Sign the treaty, Sharp Knife commanded. Those who will not sign can go to the British for relief and comfort. But "then I would persue and drive them and the British into the sea." Again he paused so that his threat would be distinctly understood. "Your rejecting the treaty will show you to be the enemies of the United States—enemies even to yourselves."[19]

The chiefs withdrew and counseled among themselves. Much bitterness was expressed, but they knew that no appeal could move this determined conqueror and that they must surrender. "He threatened us," said Big Warrior, "and made us comply with his talk. . . . I found the General had great power to destroy me." Even Hawkins understood that it was hopeless to argue with Sharp Knife. "He marked his line, and demanded their acquiescence," he told General Pinckney. Hawkins then advised the chiefs to capitulate.[20]

The following day the chiefs assembled at the square and sent for Jackson and Hawkins. Again Big Warrior acted as Speaker.

He stepped forward and addressed his words directly to the general. "We are a poor distressed people," he began, "involved in ruin which we have brought on ourselves. It is not caused by any foreign people among us, but of our own color, of our own land, and speak our tongue. They rose against us to destroy us, and we could not help ourselves." We called on our brothers, the Cherokees, Chickasaws, and Choctaws, to aid us, but they did not come. We then called on our white friends and brothers to help, "and you came."

General Jackson, he continued, "you have seen our red and white brothers mix their blood in battle; you have risked your life for us, and came here; and here we meet." We have "put our heads together, and counselled on it" and have decided to give you three miles square of land to be chosen by you from what we must give up. "We give you this in remembrance of the important services you have done us, and our token of the gratitude of the nation."[21]

Was this meant to be a bribe? Did the chiefs really believe that they could win him over by giving him a huge slice of valuable land? That would be the most obvious interpretation. But one historian suggests it was actually an expression of intense disgust and contempt, a practical joke, so to speak, a typical Native American demonstration of humor. It was their way of laughing in the face of disaster. But under the laughter they revealed a sense of fierce pride and a belief in their own innate superiority.[22]

A bribe or a gesture of contempt? Could it be both?

A similar gift was offered to Hawkins for "helping us, and doing good for our nation." Smaller amounts were also provided for George Mayfield and Alexander Cornells, the interpreters.

Jackson was obviously pleased with this token "of their regard for him," although it changed nothing. But he said he would accept it only if the gift was approved by the President and only on condition that in return the Creeks receive its equivalent value in clothing for their "naked women and children."[23]

That evening at 8:00 P.M. the chiefs told Hawkins that they did not give the land to Jackson to receive it back in the form of clothing and "other things." They wanted him to live on the land and when he died "his family would inherit it so that it may always be known what the nation gave it to him for."

In one last attempt the chiefs restated their rights, knowing it would be recorded in official documents. They concluded by declaring that they would sign the treaty the following day, even though no Red Stick chief would be present to sign along with them.[24]

And so the Creeks capitulated to Sharp Knife's vengeance. At 2:00 P.M. on August 9, 1814, they signed the treaty establishing the boundary lines around the Creek Nation as dictated by General Andrew Jackson.[25] They ceded more land than any other southeastern tribe had ever surrendered to the United States. In the treaty the chiefs declared their continued loyalty to the United States "in peace and war." They also stated that in establishing boundaries around the Creek Nation, General Jackson "found it necessary, for political motives and purposes, to run a line . . . through our lands," the lands of the friends of the United States, and left to the defeated Red Sticks lands between the Coosa and Tallapoosa rivers. "We do not deem the exchange an equivalent . . . [and] rely on the justice of the United States to cause justice to be done us."[26]

After signing, the chiefs withdrew from the fort to carry the word of their disgrace and ruin to the other members of their Nation. For his part, Jackson took great pride in what he had accomplished. As he explained to General Coffee, the treaty provided a "free settlement" for the United States "from Georgia to Mobile" and cut off all foreign influence on the Indians. "Added to this in my oppinion the best unsettled country in america—This place perhaps one of the healthiest in the U.S." Once the lines of the boundaries were drawn by survey, he continued, and the "country sectioned & prepared for sale," it would attract many settlers and become very valuable. He told Rachel that he could foresee the time when "the Banks of the allabama will present a beutifull view of elegant mansions, and extensive rich & productive farms and will add greatly to the wealth as well as the security of our Southern frontier." But, he admitted, he had had a devil of a time getting the Indians to agree, because of what Pinckney had directed Hawkins to do and what the agent had said to the Indians. Even so, he admitted that in the end Hawkins had been "of great service" in bringing this convention with the Indians to a successful conclusion.[27]

As the chiefs departed the fort, Jackson looked at these proud warriors with a sense of pity. "Could you only see the misery and wretchedness of those creatures," he wrote to Rachel, "perishing from want of food and Picking up the grains of corn scattered from the mouths of the horses and troden in the earth—

I know your humanity would feel for them, notwithstanding all the causes you have to feel hatred and revenge against."[28]

But he was talking about his allies, his comrades in arms, such as William McIntosh, Big Warrior, and Shelocta. These were not the hostiles. What he had done was sign a peace treaty with his friends and in the process deprive them of their means of survival. He had converted the Creek civil war into an enormous land grab and ensured the ultimate destruction of the entire Creek Nation.

But he had no time to think about that. The War of 1812 still raged, and the British were about to launch a massive invasion of the United States from the Gulf of Mexico with the intention of seizing New Orleans. Major General Andrew Jackson needed to move quickly and prevent it at all costs.

Chapter 6

"Brothers, Listen . . .
I Am Your Friend and Brother"

As part of their invasion plan, it had been the clear intention of the British to establish an Indian buffer zone along the Gulf Coast to block further expansion by the United States and provide protection for their Spanish allies in Florida. The invasion was aimed ultimately at New Orleans, and as it developed, Vice Admiral Sir Alexander Cochrane, who commanded the operation, dispatched Captain Hugh Pigot to the mouth of the Apalachicola River near Pensacola in May 1814 to open negotiations with the Creeks in an effort to gain their assistance in the coming invasion. Pigot carried with him two thousand stands of arms and 300,000 ball cartridges. He later reported that more than three thousand Creeks and Seminoles had agreed to join in raids against the Americans. His report also included a letter from Red Stick chiefs affirming their willingness to support a British invasion and drive the Americans from the coastal area. Obviously the chiefs did not consider their war with Jackson to have ended.[1]

On receiving the report, Cochrane sent Lieutenant Colonel Edward Nicholls to Pensacola with two naval vessels, the *Hermes* and *Carron,* plus a small force of one hundred troops and a supply of arms and ammunition, to begin training the Indians. And Nicholls achieved notable success in carrying out his mission. He armed more than four thousand Creek and Seminole warriors with a thousand pistols, a thousand carbines, five hundred rifles, and more than a million rounds of ammunition.[2] He also promised them that the King of England would protect their interests after the war.

In June 1814, Jackson learned of the British activity in Florida through his spies, and he immediately requested permission from Washington to invade the

Spanish province and bring "retaliatory vengeance" on both the English and Spanish. He told his wife that in conjunction with Spain, the English were "arming the hostile Indians to butcher our women & children."[3] Without waiting for permission to proceed, Jackson invaded and temporarily seized Spanish Pensacola on November 7, 1814, thereby blocking any possible invasion route by the English from that quarter. His skillful action completely disrupted Cochrane's initial plan of entering the continent by way of Mobile or Pensacola and then arching over to New Orleans. He was now forced to invade New Orleans directly from the Gulf, a very difficult and ultimately disastrous operation.

Meanwhile Jackson marched his army to New Orleans, erected a line of defense ten miles south of the city, and shattered an invading British army of five thousand on January 8, 1815. More than two thousand veterans of Wellington's army were killed, wounded, or captured in the action, while Jackson suffered only a little over a dozen casualties.[4] It was a magnificent victory that raised the general to the pinnacle of national popularity and admiration. Thereafter he was known around the country as the "Hero of New Orleans." Old Hickory had become a legend who had proved that the country could defend itself against the most powerful nation of Europe, and the American people could not do enough to show their gratitude and respect. Even Benjamin Hawkins, the Creek agent, congratulated him: "You have my dear friend immortalised yourself and army. You have proved that the first and best disciplined troops in Europe flushed with and accustomed to Victory they are but secondary in America."[5]

The Treaty of Ghent, which ended the War of 1812, was negotiated and signed on December 24, 1814. The British government, as promised, had insisted that it include an article safeguarding the rights of Native Americans. And they succeeded in their demand. Article IX of the document stated that the United States must agree to end hostilities with the Indians and "forthwith to restore to such tribes . . . all possessions . . . which they have enjoyed or been entitled to in one thousand eight hundred and eleven previous to such hostilities."[6] This article automatically nullified the Treaty of Fort Jackson.

But not if Sharp Knife had anything to say about it. That was his treaty, and as far as he was concerned the Creeks had agreed to it and signed it; therefore Article IX did not apply to them. Because "great opposition seemed to exist against" the Treaty of Fort Jackson in the U.S. Senate, the two Tennessee members of the upper house, Joseph Anderson and Jesse Wharton, deliberately stalled any action on it "until it was certain it would carry. The western people

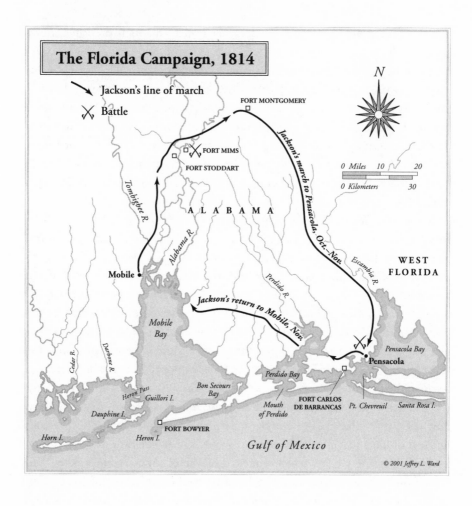

The Florida Campaign, 1814

↘ Jackson's line of march

✗ Battle

FORT MONTGOMERY

FORT MIMS

FORT STODDART

Tombigbee R.

A L A B A M A

Alabama R.

Jackson's march to Pensacola, Oct.–Nov.

Escambia R.

WEST FLORIDA

Mobile

Perdido R.

Jackson's return to Mobile, Nov.

0 Miles 10 20
0 Kilometers 30

Mobile Bay

Pensacola Bay

Pensacola

Cedar R.

Darbone R.

Heron Pass

Guillori I.

Bon Secours Bay

Perdido Bay

Mouth of Perdido

FORT CARLOS DE BARRANCAS

Pt. Chevreuil

Santa Rosa I.

Dauphine I.

FORT BOWYER

Horn I.

Heron I.

Gulf of Mexico

© 2001 Jeffrey L. Ward

were too much interested in that treaty, to hazard any thing in relation to it." Then came the news of the victory at New Orleans, and the two men rushed the Treaty of Fort Jackson to the Senate floor, where it was ratified unanimously on February 16, 1815.[7]

To Jackson such ratification by the Senate placed the treaty outside the terms of the peace treaty signed with Great Britain. Nevertheless he was notified by the secretary of war that commissioners had been appointed to make overtures of peace to the hostile Indians "in pursuance of the stipulations of the 9th article of the treaty of Ghent. . . . The President . . . is confident that you will cooperate with all means in your power to conciliate the Indians, upon the principles of our agreement with Great Britain."[8]

Not on your life. Jackson simply dismissed the directive. In his mind, and the mind of "the western people," the Indians from any one of the southern tribes might momentarily renew hostilities. Several bands of "outlaws," one of which was led by Paddy Welch, had robbed and murdered along the Georgia frontier. In addition, some Creeks refused to abide by the Treaty of Fort Jackson and at the urging of those British officers still in Florida, like Nicholls, demanded the return of their land as required under the Treaty of Ghent. Indeed, General Edmund Pendleton Gaines, in command at Fort Jackson, informed the Hero that chiefs and warriors in his locale told him that Nicholls had advised them "to kill any American they find passing through their country, and not to suffer the lands lately ceded to the United States to be taken possession of by us."[9] Nicholls had remained at Apalachicola, where the Negro Fort had been built by the British at the junction of the Flint and Chattahoochee rivers inside Florida as a supply depot for their Indian allies. Runaway slaves from the north naturally congregated at the fort for protection, so that in time there were several hundred of them armed with guns, cannons, and a large amount of ammunition. The fort was located about sixty miles from the U.S. border and constituted a distinct threat to the lives and property of American citizens.

And the Spanish did nothing about it. Actually they had little control over Florida and were powerless to intervene in any way. The situation got so bad that Jackson finally had to threaten the governor of the colony in Pensacola. The conduct of the slaves who have been "enticed away from the service of their masters" and now occupy the Negro Fort, he told the governor, "will not be tolerated by our government, and if not put down by Spanish Authority will compel us in self Defence to destroy them."[10] But the threat achieved nothing, and in time the Hero was certain that open hostilities would ensue between Spain and the United States over the issue.

However, once the War of 1812 ended, the American army was reduced to ten thousand men commanded by two major generals: General Jacob Brown commanding in the north, and Andrew Jackson commanding in the south. Secretary of War Alexander J. Dallas notified Jackson of his appointment on May 22, 1815, and declared that the Division of the South included the southern states and most of the northwest. The administration, he continued, wished to undertake a policy of "civilizing the Indians, by the establishment of competent posts on a lower route, from Chicago along the Illinois river, to St. Louis . . .

[and] is committed to your special care, as falling within the duties of your command."[11]

By this time Jackson had returned to the Hermitage, his home outside Nashville, where he set up headquarters for the Southern Division and received regular reports of Indian incursions from subordinate officers as well as from commanding generals along the northern frontier. Since the west had been committed to his "special care," he also communicated with the territorial governors of Illinois and Missouri, Ninian Edwards and William Clark, who at the time were serving as commissioners negotiating with the Indians along the Mississippi River. He informed them that not until the tribes "are made to smart by our arms, and taught to disregard the *talks* of bad men, agents of British mercenaries" will we have "peace, tranquility and perfect security." And if these "deluded wretches," these "ruthless Mauraders" reject "the proposals of Peace" that you offer them, "I am authorized to call for an auxiliary force from the Militia" to handle the situation. "Keep me well advised of the Disposition of the Indians on your frontier."[12]

———

Old Hickory fully expected a renewal of an Indian war in the west, and, as he said repeatedly, he was "ready to march at a moments warning" if any attacks on white settlements by marauding Indians occurred. At the same time he did not believe, he said, that "any considerable body of the Creeks" would attempt to renew the war in the south.[13] To ensure their compliance, Jackson continued his efforts to run the new boundary line between Creek territory and U.S. territory as established by the Treaty of Fort Jackson. Those Creeks living on the U.S. side of the line had to remove. Three commissioners had been appointed to meet with the Indians to survey the line, but a number of changes in personnel caused by death, illness, and a resignation unduly delayed the running of the boundary. In addition, the Cherokees, Chickasaws, and Choctaws contested the proposed line, arguing that it trespassed into their territory.

Months later, when the final members of the commission were chosen, Jackson saw to it that his old friend General John Coffee was included among the three. Coffee was an alternate for Benjamin Hawkins, who was too ill to serve, and he proceeded without the other commissioners to survey the northern boundary of the ceded land, an action that was highly questionable but one Jackson fully approved. The other two commissioners, Captain William Barnet and General E. P. Gaines, met the Indians at the confluence of the Flint and Chattahoochee rivers with a large contingent of regular soldiers. And thanks to

Jackson's decision to send the armed force as a guard and thereby "remove any apprehension or danger in the execution of their task," they proceeded without interference to run the southern part of the line. Old Hickory made his position very clear to the secretary of war: "I have no hesitation in believing that it is all important to the tranquility of the south that the line should be run without delay."[14]

Thus, with Jackson refusing to honor the provisions of the peace treaty with Great Britain and steadily enforcing his own treaty, with the government unwilling to take any action against a war hero in defense of Indians, and with Britain unable or unwilling to demand U.S. fulfillment of its promise to return Indian property, the systematic despoliation of the Creek Nation commenced.

A number of friendly Creeks, led by William McIntosh, then reached an agreement with Cherokees by which they conceded to the Cherokees a large portion of land now claimed by the United States under the Treaty of Fort Jackson. But other friendly Creeks, led by Big Warrior, repudiated this agreement in the vain hope of retaining more of the land that Jackson had taken from them.

Edward Nicholls in Florida wrote to Benjamin Hawkins, who passed the letter along to Jackson, protesting what he called a clear and "complete breach of the 9th Article" of the Treaty of Ghent and reminding him of the warning given "by the Indian chiefs through me to your Citizens . . . [that] if your Citizens break through the laws of a free and independent [Creek] Nation guaranteed as such by my Sovereign it must be at their peril."[15]

The letter infuriated Sharp Knife. "Nothing ever surpassed or equaled the bare-faced effrontery of Col Nichol," he stormed. "Nichol" ought to be seized and punished. "The Creek line *must* be run, and with as little delay as possible." Jackson also understood that there was some disagreement between Creeks and Cherokees over ownership of the land on the west side of the Coosa River. But he reckoned it a despicable Indian ploy to keep the United States from running the boundary line, and he had no intention of allowing the Creeks to get away with it.[16]

At this point the chiefs of the Cherokees, Chickasaws, Choctaws, and Creeks held a "grat talk" at Tuckabatchie, the town where the Upper Creeks met to conduct national affairs, to press their claims against the United States. Big Warrior, the Speaker at the Treaty of Fort Jackson, now claimed "that it was no treaty, that he was threatened and compelled to sign it," and that the Creek War had not ended. He therefore would not appoint any of his chiefs to accompany the commissioners in surveying the boundary. Hostile Creeks had crossed the border into Florida, he told Jackson, and "were not Completely cowed & that they would be yet killing of us." A number of friendly Creeks, out of fear for their lives, he went on, "said let us follow them & kill them." To which Sharp Knife replied, "if you kill them I will kill you, let them alone the war is ended with the Indians."[17]

By this time Jackson could no longer abide the tactics of the Creeks in attempting to thwart his will, and he decided once more to threaten them. He sent a "talk" to the tribe and spelled out the consequences of continued opposition to accepting the new boundary line.

"*Friends and Brothers,*" he called out to them. "You know me to be your friend." (Such a comment by Sharp Knife must have elicited astonishment, if not outright laughter.) You remember what happened when you listened to the advice of bad men and became "crasy by the prophcies of your, wicked prophets." You remember how I destroyed your enemies, executed "those wicked prophets," and gave you peace by the "Capitulation and Treaty of Fort Jackson." Remember?

"*Friends and Brothers* I hear with sorrow that some of your people has been listening to the wicked Talks of Colo Nicholls again, and that he has directed you to oppose the running of the line agreeable to the Treaty of Fort Jackson.

"*Brothers* Listen, did I not feed you by the orders of your father the President of the U. States and save you and your nation from starving, have I not by the orders of your father the President sent goods into the nations, to cloath you and your naked woman and children.

"Brothers . . . Listen I now tell you that line must and will be run, and the least opposition brings down instant destruction on the heads of the opposers." If you listen to the "lying talk of Colo Nicholls you will bring down upon you innevitable ruin."

I send you this "true Talk." I have never deceived or lied to you. Justice will be done by the President of the United States, "to all his red children." Listen to my talk. Do as I direct. "I am your friend and Brother."[18]

General Gaines, more suspicious of the Indians than Jackson, if that was possible, kept worrying about a renewed Indian war. Nicholls, he reported, had abandoned Florida in disgust and returned to England. But before leaving he placed his interpreter, Lieutenant William Hambly, in charge at Apalachicola, and Hambly kept promising the Indians that the British would soon return to help them. Gaines wanted to call on the governors of South Carolina and Tennessee to send their militias to create an enhanced force on the southern frontier so that the boundary line could be drawn without opposition and the Seminoles in Florida given "that wholesome correction, by which alone, as long experience proves, savage enemies can ever be made friendly or harmless."

But despite "all the excitement" and Indian rage over what was happening to them, Jackson did not think they "have the temerity to do any acts of Hostility"; still he assured Gaines that "on the event of war with the Indians, every white-man or negroe found in arms with the enemy must be put to the sword."[19]

In the fall of 1815, Jackson decided to travel to Washington to attend to a number of official matters, including some related to Native Americans. He and Rachel and their entourage left Nashville on October 8 and arrived in Washington on November 16. Their route occasioned many dinners, receptions, and other celebrations to honor the "Hero of New Orleans."

The day following his arrival in the capital he went to pay his respects to President Madison and the several members of his cabinet, especially William H. Crawford, the new secretary of war. At the President's residence Jackson was treated with great deference. And Madison noticed that whenever the conversation "flaged" Jackson was seen staring out the window "with a melancholy air . . . on the ruins of our publick buildings" that had been burnt by the British in August 1814 when they invaded from the Chesapeake during the late war.[20] This spread-eagle patriot and nationalist was deeply offended by any enemy action that injured or demeaned his country. In his mind, the British, like the Indians, remained perpetual enemies to the peace, harmony, and security of the United States.

During his stay in Washington he had an opportunity to talk at length with Secretary Crawford. Among other things he urged upon him the building of a "chain" of forts from Mobile to the Georgia border so as to prevent "foreign influence upon the natives, & by offering a strong inducement for the speedy settlement of that section of the country by our own citizens." It should be done, he added, as "soon as the running of the Indian line will allow it," thereby making clear to Crawford that the line would and must be run.

By this time Jackson had become fixated on the idea that the south would never have peace and security until the Indians were removed from the area and replaced, firmly and permanently, "by our own citizens." Otherwise "foreign influence" would constantly incite the Indians to attack American settlements in order to keep the United States weak and vulnerable. Security and removal, therefore, were linked in his mind as the only solution to the problem, and he devoted the rest of his life toward achieving it.

In speaking with Crawford he also insisted that a military road must to be built from Nashville to New Orleans to facilitate the passage of men and arms in case of "any great emergency," such as another invasion or another Indian uprising. He assured the secretary that the road would not cross any land "in which the Indian title has not been extinguished."[21]

An elaborate ball was held in Jackson's honor in Washington on December 7, and there he met many more congressmen and leading figures in the nation's capital. But he was not well, and his arm acted up and added to his discomfort. It was reported that he was too ill to leave his room, and his aide, John Reid, told his wife that "the general's life has been almost dispaired of."[22] Fortunately he recovered and then slowly made his way home. It was a tedious journey made worse because of bad roads and inclement weather.

When he arrived back at the Hermitage, Jackson had both good and bad news waiting for him. The good was that Coffee had taken up his recent appointment as Indian commissioner and without further consultation with the other two commissioners had begun the task of running the northern boundary line. "I am aware of the importance and necessity of finishing this business," he explained to Jackson, "and as such, have determined to act, alone, if I am not joined by the other Comrs. delay with me at this late date is inadmissable." He succeeded in extending the line to the Cherokee boundary and was about to run it to the Chickasaw and Choctaw lines.

Jackson was delighted. He urged his friend to speed through the completion of his task, although he warned him that because of his prompt action it might create jealousy and therefore he ought to obtain the "approbation" of the other commissioners for his work. Just remember, he went on, that Indians "will claim every thing and any thing" so just proceed on "the best information you have."[23]

Coffee provided additional good news when he said that he had met with several Creek chiefs and headmen who affirmed that the Creek land ceded to the United States under Jackson's treaty in truth belonged to them, not to the Cherokees who claimed it. They told him that years ago the Cherokees had applied to the Creeks for land to live on after being driven out of their own country by General Sevier and his men, and that their request was granted. The land in question, the chiefs told Coffee, "was only loaned to the Cherokees, and that the said lands were always considered the property of the creek nation." Any settlement made by the Cherokees, the chiefs went on, involving Creek land was done "without the Consent of the creek nation."[24]

This was very encouraging news indeed, and in Jackson's mind completely demolished the contention by Cherokees that some of the land taken from the Creeks in the Treaty of Fort Jackson actually belonged to them. Now Sharp

Knife had "irrefutable" evidence that the land had been loaned. It had belonged to the Creeks, and it now belonged to the United States.

Still the problem was complicated because the Creeks had ceded all their lands west of the Coosa River. These overlapped with Cherokee and Chickasaw claims to land south of the Tennessee River and overlapped with Choctaw claims to land east of the Tombigbee River. A final settlement of the boundary lines could not be arrived at until all these conflicts were ironed out.

The bad news to greet Jackson on his return home was twofold: first, Coffee informed him that the Chickasaws had threatened to stop him from running the line into what they regarded as their land. Immediately upon hearing this, Jackson wrote to George Colbert, a Chickasaw chief, and warned that if "your people" interfere with Coffee's operation they "will bring down immediate punishment upon them." The only land being taken belongs to the Creeks and has been surrendered to the United States, he said. If the Chickasaws can produce evidence that the land is theirs, it will be surrendered to them. Be assured, however, that "the President of the U States loves his red children, & will do justice to them; but he will punish his red children when they attempt by force to do wrong."[25]

Colbert responded promptly and assured Sharp Knife that his people knew nothing about the running of the line. He would show them Jackson's letter, which he felt would make them "rejoice at your friendly advice."[26]

The second piece of bad news—and it was really bad—came from Secretary of War William H. Crawford. A Cherokee delegation had come to Washington and argued that the execution of the Creek treaty violated their property rights. In the treaty, Jackson had claimed that the Creeks owned the land as far north as the Tennessee River and as far west as the Tombigbee. That was the land that the Creek chiefs had told Coffee had been loaned to the Cherokees. In addition, Crawford declared that the Chickasaws and Choctaws had refused to accept the Tombigbee River as their eastern border. As a result of the Cherokee protest and after examining the various conventions that the United States had held in the past with the tribe, the administration had gone ahead and signed a new treaty with the Cherokees on March 22, 1816, in which a fifty-mile-wide strip in the northwestern part of the Creek cession from the Coosa to the Mississippi line was awarded them. Furthermore, they were also promised $25,500 to pay for the damages by the Tennessee militia during the Creek War. As for the other two tribes, "these difficulties," Crawford told Jackson, "will make it necessary to form conventions with the Choctaw and Chickasaw tribes."

Jackson exploded, not only because it surrendered land that "rightfully" belonged to the United States but it presumed that Jackson's army had stolen property (cows, hogs, horses) belonging to the Cherokees and therefore ruled that $25,500 by way of compensation was due them. Westerners were particularly outraged by this latest treaty, and a formal "Protestation" from distinguished Tennesseans was sent to President Madison denouncing it—both the land and spoliation provisions. On June 21 and again on July 6 the citizens of Nashville and surrounding counties held public meetings in which they condemned the Cherokee treaty and demanded that President Madison extinguish all Indian claims within the state of Tennessee—and do it *now*. Crawford was roundly criticized for creating these problems.[27]

Jackson sent his personal protest to James Monroe, the secretary of state and former secretary of war,[28] declaring that the March 22 treaty with the Cherokees had inflamed the west and would have dire consequences. The disputed land contained from four to five million acres over which the Cherokees "never had the least semblance of claim," he wrote. "This Territory ceded was of incalculable Vallue to the U States, as it opened a free communication to the lower country," strengthened the frontier, cut off all "communication & intercourse between the southern & northwestern tribes," and guaranteed access and supplies in the Gulf area for our "hardy soldiers to meet an invading enemy at the threshold." The people here fought for this land, Jackson argued, and if the treaty takes it away the "exertions of those very citizens" will be destroyed. "And if there services are again wanted will have a banefull effect upon their former spirit of patriotism."

Monroe was sympathetic to the Cherokee claim, but he also acknowledged the demands of the Tennesseans (he intended to run for the presidency in 1816) and particularly the nation's outstanding hero. Perhaps, he suggested, a "double purchase" could be worked out. It was certainly "preferable to the risks of doing injustice or creating hostile dispositions." By all means he felt the government should "endeavor to accomodate the reasonable wishes of our Citizens," but "humanity and policy" also needed to be taken into consideration.[29]

The clamor provoked in the west by the March 22 treaty, and the danger of antagonizing the Hero of New Orleans, convinced the politician in Crawford to turn the matter over to another group of treaty commissioners. Since he too planned to seek the presidency in the election of 1816 and had assiduously built a political organization to assist him in gaining the nomination, it made no sense to antagonize a large contingency in the west. So he announced the suspension of Coffee's survey until conventions could be held with the Cherokees,

Chickasaws, and Choctaws to settle the conflicting claims. Then he did two things: he appointed Coffee, Colonel John McKee, the Choctaw agent, and Congressman John Rhea of Tennessee to treat with the Choctaws; and he appointed Jackson, General David Meriwether of Georgia, and Jesse Franklin of North Carolina as the three commissioners to meet with the Cherokees and Chickasaws. In his letter to Jackson the secretary went out of his way to tell him that the general's opinion of the March 22 treaty had "not in any degree changed the opinions of the President upon that subject." It was an unnecessary bit of provocation that, along with the treaty itself, provided the genesis of bad feelings between Secretary Crawford and General Jackson.

A month later, Crawford added to Jackson's rancor when he reminded the general that the March 22 treaty had been "approved by the Senate and House of Representatives, and is the supreme law of the land. Submission to it is a duty which will not be neglected."

Not to be put down by a "pettifogging politician," such as Crawford, Jackson replied that the militia would not aid in surrendering the land to the Cherokees. And he made no apology for his statement. "Political discussion," he said, "is not the province of a military officer. As a man, I am entitled to my opinion, and have given it freely."[30]

Jackson was clearly insubordinate when he spoke about what the militia would or would not do, but the number and length of the letters with which he bombarded the secretary on this subject—writing him virtually every day and sometimes twice a day—shows how determined he was to have his position upheld by the government. "The people of the west will never suffer any Indian to inhabit this country again." What he said was the truth, he argued, and the Cherokees, Chickasaws, and Choctaws were liars if they disputed it. In his rage he often swore that this "hasty and iniquitious" treaty could lead "to the destruction of the whole cherokee nation, and of course to a civill war."

Why, he asked, is it so difficult for the government to understand that "the real Indians, the natives of the forest are little concerned" about the appropriation of this land? It is the "designing half-breeds and renegade white men" among them who protest our actions. It was one of Jackson's stratagems to fault half-breeds and renegade white men whenever his demands were challenged.[31]

Crawford could only restate the fact that the March 22 treaty was the law of the land and Jackson, as "Commanding General of the Southern division," had better enforce it. Then he subtly suggested that this treaty could be "extinguished" legally if the two groups of commissioners scheduled to meet with the Cherokees, Chickasaws, and Choctaws got them to sign a new treaty by which they relinquished their previous claims.[32]

The suggestion was not lost on Jackson. And, as it subsequently developed, it was quite simple for him to control the two groups of commissioners: his own, and through Coffee the group meeting with the Choctaws. Jackson wrote to his old friend and expressed his own strong feelings and opinions. In a series of letters he suggested a plan by which they could persuade all three tribes to accept the demands made upon them. It was a plan he himself would follow when treating with the Cherokees and Chickasaws.

First, said Jackson, hold an interview with some of the principal chiefs and get them to realize that the "Whites having settled on this land" are not going to surrender it. Tell them, too, that the number of whites will constantly increase. Then impress on them that they can now obtain from the United States government "a fair consideration for this doubtful claim of theirs in money." That money will provide schools to educate their children; it will provide "money to buy negroes to work there land." By agreeing to this settlement they will live in peace. Assure them, too, that "there is no game on this land." Then, if they refuse to take this "fair consideration" for their claim, they must be prepared to "abide by the consequence"—and the Indians knew what that meant.

But be sure to offer a "just compensation," he added. That is the only way we can "get clear of this thing." As it stands the March 22 treaty with the Cherokees is the "supreme law and must be executed." Therefore you must make "every exertion" to extinguish "this hateful instrument."[33]

What added to this "hateful instrument" was the fact that Congress appropriated $28,600 for the depredations of the Tennessee militia during the Creek War, something Jackson fiercely opposed and spent a good part of the summer of 1816 trying to block. When he saw the list of supposed depredations charged against "my army" for 607 head of cattle, 770 head of hogs, and "sundry horses," he raged, calling it a fraud. "It exceeds all corruption, that ever came to my knowledge," he fumed.

In a follow-up letter to Coffee he asked him to meet with Pathkiller, the Principal Chief of the Cherokees, Major Ridge, who had led Cherokee warriors in the Creek War, and Brown Lowry, another Cherokee chief who also aided Jackson in the Creek War, and get from them "a declaration that they will resign all claim for a very small sum[;] they know they never had any right and they will be glad as I believe to swindle the U States out of a few thousand dollars, and bury the claim, if persisted in, which they know might bury them and there nation." In other words, bribe them.

Jackson insisted that the "hight of my diplomatic ambition" was merely the restoration of the land "fairly & Justly ceded by the creeks" that "we fought & bled for." Both he and Coffee could achieve it, he said, if they worked together. Therefore, he urged Coffee to visit him immediately. "I must see you before I go on to the treaty. . . . The public interest requires that I should see you, and have a conference with you."[34]

Thus, in preparing for the conventions with the three Indian tribes, Jackson held long discussions with Coffee, and he continued to write him regularly after they parted. Together they worked out the arguments and tactics to convince or bully the Indians into agreeing with their demands. The arguments included the following: the tribes were a menace to the security of the United States as proved by the Creek War and the subsequent invasion by the British at New Orleans; they must be replaced by white settlers as soon as possible to provide the necessary peace and security to the southern frontier; the land in question had belonged to the Creeks (not the Cherokees, Chickasaws, or Choctaws), who upon their defeat had ceded it to the United States; therefore the recent treaty with the Cherokees had to be abrogated. As to tactics, Jackson told Coffee that a first condition to be remembered at all times was that "an Indian is fickle, and you have to take the same firm stand and support it." Do not waver, do not hedge, do not compromise. Stand firm "and you are sure of success."

But Jackson used other tactics as well at his convention with the Cherokees and Chickasaws. First, fear. "No influence with them is equal to that bottomed on fear or that which proceeds from a military man." Both he and Coffee were generals and would wear their resplendent uniforms at the conventions surrounded by U.S. troops. Second, bribery. The chiefs have to be "conditioned" into accepting the terms offered them, he told Coffee. Bribery invariably determines the outcome of all negotiations with "savages." Finally, the threat of violence when demands for their land are rejected. Such tactics, said Old Hickory, usually bring the proceedings to a "happy" conclusion.

In the next several months Sharp Knife used all of these arguments and tactics with stunning success. The poor Indians never had a chance.[35]

Chapter 7

The Indian Commissioner

Thus armed with the precepts he had carefully worked out himself, Jackson set forth to negotiate with the Chickasaw and Cherokee tribes. As instructed by Crawford, he, David Meriwether, and Jesse Franklin were told to meet on September 1 with the chiefs at the Chickasaw Council House, which was the home of Chief George Colbert. On August 20, General Jackson left Nashville and joined General Meriwether at Campbell's Station. Together they proceeded immediately to the Chickasaw Council House, which they reached on August 29. The third commissioner, Colonel Franklin, was delayed by the illness of his son and did not arrive until September 13.

Throughout the negotiations, Jackson had no trouble in dominating Meriwether and later pronounced him "a fine old fellow." When Franklin finally arrived he gave Jackson some trouble by "Butting at every thing," but the Hero stood his ground and Franklin's "horns" began to get "sore" and he finally became "docile & Butt no more."[1]

The Cherokee delegates did not arrive "as early as expected"—they did not appear until September 6—and the Chickasaws therefore asked for a postponement, since they wished to consult with the Cherokees before the convention got underway, insisting they were not prepared to engage in the negotiations. The commissioners agreed, and not until September 8 did the convention finally open. But it soon became clear that the Cherokee delegates had "positive instructions to dispose of no lands."

The chiefs gathered together and faced the commissioners, not knowing what to expect except a demand most probably that they accept Sharp Knife's definition of the Creek boundary lines. Would the commissioners threaten them with violence if they refused the demand? Would they threaten to with-hold their annuities?

Jackson rose and addressed them. "Friends & Brethren," the President of the United States has sent General Merriwether and me "to meet you here this day, shake you by the hand, brighten the chain of Friendship & greet you with the pleasing tidings that Peace & Friendship exists between the People of the U States & their red Brethren."

It was an appropriate beginning, and the chiefs and headmen of the two Na-tions welcomed his encouraging words. Then Jackson's mood and language turned darker as he recited recent history to them. "When the Creek Nation lis-tened to the tongues of lying Prophets, became crazy & raised the hatchet and stained it with the blood of our innocent women & children," your Father, the President, directed "his warriors" to march against and subdue them. "The or-ders of your Father the President of the U States were obeyed." The hostile Creeks were "conquered" and forced to pay a heavy price for their wickedness. The lands they surrendered now belong to the United States and so you, the chiefs of the Cherokee and Chickasaw Nations, have been assembled to obtain an acceptance of this cession by treaty.[2]

The chiefs and delegates stood passively as Sharp Knife spoke, but they soon made it clear that they had no intention of doing as he asked. Certain lands ceded by the Creeks did not belong to them; they belonged to the Chickasaws and Cherokees and Choctaws. The Chickasaws were particularly adamant about surrendering their country and insisted that every member of "the whole nation" had to be consulted about the matter before any treaty could be con-cluded. Then they handed him a "Charter," signed by President George Wash-ington on July 21, 1794, which guaranteed their property rights.

Jackson bristled. He had not expected to run into such determined opposi-tion at the outset of the negotiation. And he knew where to lay the blame. In a letter to Secretary Crawford he first faulted the Chickasaw agent, William Cocke, who "seemed more anxious" to maintain his popularity among Indians "than promote the views of the Government." And the chiefs were hardly bet-ter. They too worried about their popularity and "not the best interests of the Nation they ruled." And Crawford was also responsible, Jackson charged. "Much embarrassment was occasioned by your letter of the 16th of April to the agent" in which you stated that previous treaties did not negate Chickasaw claims for the area bounded by the Tennessee River and running east of Coffee's survey line. Furthermore, you directed Agent Cocke to obtain evidence supporting Chickasaw claims. Then you urged him to poll the Chickasaws and discover whether they would be willing to cede their claim in return for an indemnity. Your letter was read and interpreted to the Chickasaws by Cocke prior to our arrival and set in motion their determination to resist our efforts to obtain a treaty. To make matters worse, the so-called "Charter" from President Washington that guaranteed Chickasaw territory was presented to prove their claims. And this "Charter" was "recognized" by another treaty in 1801 when it provided a right-of-way through Chickasaw land for a road between Nashville and Natchez. All of which makes our efforts infinitely more difficult.

At this point the commissioners and the other whites in attendance withdrew and left the Indians to council among themselves. Livid, Jackson turned to Cocke, who was not a participant in the convention but a spectator, and charged him with failing in his duty, failing to point out to the Indians the special advantages that would accrue to them if they agreed to the terms offered them.

Cocke shot right back at Sharp Knife. "Advice, when asked for," he said, "was better received, more respected, and generally more relied on," by Indians, "than opinions given before [they are] sought."[3]

Over the next few days the commissioners prepared an address, which was read to the assembled delegates of the two Nations on September 12. In it they said they had come bearing "a peace offering" from their Father the President to his red children. To "his Chickasaw children" the great father proposed a $10,000 per annum annuity for ten years, "amounting to One hundred Thousand Dollars and will make liberal presents to their Chiefs as a Testimony of his individual Friendship & esteem," provided they relinquished all claims to lands included in Coffee's survey. To "his Cherokee children" he proposed an amount of $8,000 per annum for ten years and "generous rewards to their chiefs."

"Friends & Brethren," the commissioners continued, "you must lay aside all ideas of hunting, you cannot support your Families by it; the Game is destroyed—you must cultivate the Earth like your white Brethren & your women like their white sisters must learn to spin & weave." In other words, if they wished to remain in their present location they must become cultural white men and women, whether they liked it or not. And that meant submitting to the laws of the states in which they lived.

The chiefs and headmen let out a groan when they heard that last remark.

The lands the President wants, the commissioners contended, "are of no value to you—That part of your claim will only be a fruitful source of Bloodshed & strife—That he loves his children & wishes to see them live in harmony & peace; No more wars, but all striving for the same end."[4]

The commissioners rejected the arguments of both the Cherokee and Chickasaw chiefs about their claims and reaffirmed the argument that the land belonged to the Creeks and had been ceded to the United States in the Treaty of Fort Jackson.

It took two days and small "presents"[5] (so small they could hardly be called bribes) to eight of the leading Cherokee chiefs to persuade them to sign a provisional treaty on September 14. Each one received $50, except for three chiefs and Thomas Wilson and Alexander McCoy, the two interpreters, who received $100. Although the Cherokees refused to yield any land on the north side of the Tennessee, they agreed to cede their claim to the disputed territory to the south of the river. Because the delegation was concerned about the reaction of the Cherokee National Council of Thirteen, particularly since they had "positive instructions to dispose of no land," they insisted that any treaty must be ratified by the council before it could become final. And that may have been the reason they signed in the first place. The commissioners agreed to the condition and promised to meet with the council at Turkey Town on September 28.[6]

But the Chickasaws proved more intractable, and it took nearly a week of further negotiations to bring them around. They resented what had been offered the Cherokees, claiming the Cherokees had never held any land south of the Tennessee, and in ceding it they had ceded what they did not own. They were alarmed and irritated, according to Jackson, and the sudden death of The Factor, a Principal Chief, "appeared to distract their counsels; Confusion amongst them was visible." Levi Colbert addressed the commissioners and said that his people wished to do what was right but wanted "to know what was legally their own before they could sell."[7] The Chickasaw chiefs also begged for time to consider the commissioners' proposals. At this point Jackson realized that a "favourable result to the negotiation" was not possible unless he addressed "the predominant & governing passions of all Indian Tribes, ie. Their avarice or Fear." Our instructions "pointed to the former & forbid the latter." We were therefore compelled, he informed Crawford, "not from choice but from instructions to apply the sole remedy in our power."

Bribery! This attitude by the three commissioners reveals not only their individual thinking about Native Americans and how best to deal with them, but the government's attitude as well. The secretary had authorized bribes to obtain land, and the commissioners did precisely that. "It was applied & presents offered to the Influential Chiefs amounting to Four Thousand five hundred Dollars," most of which went to the Colbert brothers, George, Levi, William, and James, and Tishomingo, the Speaker of the Chickasaw Nation. On September 20 the treaty with the Chickasaws was signed and witnessed.

Offering bribes really disgusted Jackson. It was not his style. As he said over and over, he much preferred the government to simply impose its authority on the Nations and instruct them on what they must do. But since the government had no intention of following his advice and since the acquisition of the lands in question was essential, he was forced to resort to bribery. He knew the chiefs would take the bribes and he knew they would work.

The commissioners immediately reported their success. We have done well, they assured the secretary. From the Chickasaws they had obtained title to all the land south of the Tennessee River to the west bank of the Tombigbee River, thereby providing the government with "a free & uninterrupted intercourse with the low country," the free use and navigation of the Coosa, Black Warrior, and Tombigbee rivers, and "a rich . . . body of land to the U. States . . . of incalculable political advantage." Even more important, they continued, we probably prevented the outbreak of civil war and have secured the "affections" and "confidence" of "the [white] Population of the south & west to the present administration." If the annuity we gave was larger than usual—and it was—"it is not more than proportionate to the benefits obtained."[8]

The commissioners had also been instructed if possible to obtain title to Chickasaw land in western Kentucky, but in view of the problems they encountered in these negotiations they decided not to raise the issue. But it was not forgotten.[9]

Jackson wrote to his wife and told her about the "long and disagreable time" he had had, but how he regained "by tribute, what I fairly, & hardly purchased with the sword." All this trouble and time and expense, he added, "has been occasioned by the rashness, folly, & ignorance of a great little man." Who could that have been? Jackson did not say.[10] Could it have been Secretary Crawford? But Crawford was six feet three inches tall and weighed over two hundred pounds.[11] More likely the "great little man" was President James Madison, but that is only a wild guess.

All along Jackson had been obsessed with gaining undisputed title to the Creek territory he had "fairly . . . purchased with the sword" so that the frontier could be better protected. He wrote to James Monroe, the sole candidate for the presidency in the election of 1816 after Crawford foolishly withdrew his name from contention in the hope of having a clear field in 1824, and spelled out the "political benefits" of the acquisition. "The sooner . . . this country can be brought into market the better," he declared. It should be divided into two districts by a line drawn due east from the mouth of the Black Warrior to the Coosa River. The northern district should be surveyed, preferably by General Coffee, and readied for sale by next June. If this is done it "will ensure the Treasury an immense sum of money" and provide the government with a populated area "capable of defending that frontier." The invasion of New Orleans by the British immediately after the Creek War proved how vulnerable the southern frontier was to attack by a foreign power, especially "an Enemy possessing a superiority on the Ocean," like Great Britain. And if Indians remain in the area they will surely become tools of such an enemy. Jackson was particularly worried about what he called "the defenceless situation of New Orleans Mobile and their dependencies."

Jackson's obsession—and surely it had become that—centered on replacing red with white men in order to "give to that section of the country a strong and permanent settlement of American citizens, competent to its defence." Such a settlement would provide safety and peace along the frontier and lessen the possibility of foreign invasion augmented with Indian warriors. For General Jackson it was never his paramount wish to take the land from the Indians because of its intrinsic economic value, although he conceded it would bring vast sums to the government. National security was always his primary concern.[12]

Buoyed by their outstanding success with the Chickasaws, Jackson and Meriwether headed for Turkey Town on September 21 to meet with the National Council of Thirteen and win ratification of the treaty signed on September 14 with the Cherokee delegates. They arrived on September 28.

It proved to be a stormy gathering. The commissioners began by addressing the assembled council and saying that they had come "to shake you by the hand of Friendship & receive your sanction" of the treaty. That treaty "is virtually ratified" but we do not wish "to take any advantage of our Red Brethren" and therefore have come here knowing that you "cannot withhold your assent to the stipulations of the Treaty" which you can readily see will "promote the best interests of your nation."[13]

The Principal Chiefs, Pathkiller and Charles Hicks, were outraged by the action of the delegates at the Chickasaw Council House and repeated much of the evidence substantiating Cherokee claims to the disputed land. They were adamant and refused to yield. So, after repeated and unsuccessful appeals by the commissioners, it became clear what had to be done. Again bribery—corrupting a few chiefs who constituted the National Council. And the bribes rarely failed of success as long as they were accomplished surreptitiously and as long as they were of sufficient size to make it worthwhile. Although he hated to do it, Sharp Knife never hesitated in bringing bribes into play as a final means of winning success.

Jackson also learned something valuable from his meetings with the Cherokees and Chickasaws. The secretary of war had suggested that the annuities be stretched over a period of time, but the general discovered that it was impossible to explain such an arrangement to the Indians. "We found that the Indians were more influenced by round numbers, by stipends that would administer to their immediate wants than by distant prospects of wealth & comfort," and therefore decided that the payments should be limited to as short a period as possible.[14]

Once the chiefs signed the document, Jackson and Meriwether reported to Washington that "after a long conference & tedious consultations" the "treaty received a formal ratification from the whole Cherokee Nation in Council assembled."

But that was not true. Pathkiller, Charles Hicks, and sixteen other chiefs later—much later—denied the report. The entire Nation had not consented to the treaty, they said. According to the evidence presented by these chiefs to the secretary of war, but not mentioned in the journal of the commissioners, on the night of October 4, between the hours of nine and ten, "that fatal treaty" was confirmed by the chiefs of only four towns "and not by the whole Cherokee nation." Moreover, "there were six or seven headmen present" at that meeting "who objected to the ratification of the treaty." Under these circumstances, Pathkiller, Hicks, and the other chiefs requested that the matter be investigated "as an act of justice." Of course they failed to mention the bribes they had taken. Unfortunately this protest was presented on September 19, 1817, nearly a full year after the treaty had been signed.[15] The administration simply ignored it.

Had the commissioners really falsified their report? It is impossible to say. They may have thought they had the consent of the entire Nation. But had they known otherwise, Jackson was more likely to threaten the chiefs than lie to the government.

In reporting to the secretary of war the success of their mission, the commissioners also raised an intriguing possibility about how additional land might be obtained. They stated that several chiefs had come to them and "intimated . . .

a strong disposition" among many "Individuals of the nation to emigrate to the west of the Mississippi." They wished to know whether "in the event of a national removal" it was practical to effect an exchange of territory with the government in which the Cherokees would surrender "Territory in this neighbourhood for a like extent in the vicinity of White River" in Arkansas.

Removal! Sending the entire Cherokee tribe across the Mississippi where they could no longer pose a danger to the country! Jackson firmly believed this was the only solution to their problem without resorting to further bloodshed. But this was not a novel idea. President Thomas Jefferson undoubtedly originated it. He had declared that if the Indians could not be civilized, then "we shall be obliged to drive them, with the beasts of the forests into the Stony [Rocky] mountains." The idea of driving or encouraging all the southern tribes to vacate their present location and move west won widespread support along the frontier, and Andrew Jackson was one of its most ardent advocates.[16]

In 1808, Jefferson suggested to leaders of the dissident Chickamaugans living in the Lower Towns that if they did not care to live in the same neighborhood with their countrymen of the Upper Towns they could remove to Arkansas. Led by Chief Tahlonteskee, some 1,023 Chickamaugans, including 386 men and 637 women and children, accepted the offer, exchanged lands, and headed west in 1809, calling themselves "Cherokees West" or "Old Settlers." The Cherokees of the Upper Towns denounced the action and claimed that the dissidents had acted without the approval of the Cherokee Nation. They had no authority to give away tribal land. Soon other Cherokees followed the Old Settlers to Arkansas but without yielding any of their land on the east side of the Mississippi.[17]

So a policy of removal had already begun seven years earlier. Now in 1816, with the Cherokee chiefs raising the possibility of relocation to the west, Jackson and Meriwether responded enthusiastically. They unhesitatingly "encouraged a belief" that what the chiefs had suggested was most certainly "feasible." They also advised that when the Nation had come to a definite conclusion on the subject, delegates be appointed with full authority to negotiate a treaty of exchange and be dispatched to Washington.[18]

Thus removal of the Indians did not begin with President Andrew Jackson in 1830. It began with President Jefferson in 1809 and was vigorously followed by President Monroe. Even President John Quincy Adams, who succeeded Monroe, approved removal, and in 1826 directed Indian agents to attempt the relocation of the Cherokees, Chickasaws, and Choctaws.

Removal began early in the century by presidential action and continued over twenty years without congressional involvement, except when the Senate ratified the treaties. What Jackson did as President was regularize it and give it added legality by having Congress pass the necessary legislation by which all the southern tribes could exchange their land in the east for land in the west. Instead of removal being an executive action alone, it would be a legislative one as well.[19]

Although the negotiations with the Cherokees and Chickasaws in 1816 had been long and tedious, Jackson was delighted with the results, especially after he learned that the Choctaws had also yielded to the demands of John Coffee, John Rhea, and John McKee, the three commissioners sent to negotiate with them, and ceded their land east of the Tombigbee River in return for $16,000 for twenty years and $10,000 in merchandise.[20] What Sharp Knife and the other commissioners obtained constituted a veritable empire, running hundreds of miles east and west, north and south, and encompassing land from Kentucky and Tennessee to Georgia and Alabama.

What a prize to offer the nation for sale to white settlers! Such rich fertile land would prove very attractive to enterprising Americans, and Jackson himself later invested in property at the foot of Muscle Shoals. Jackson wrote to the interim secretary of war, George Graham,[21] and stressed the importance of putting this land on sale immediately. "Nothing," he said, "can promote the wellfare of the United States, and particularly the southwestern frontier so much as bringing into market, at an early date, the whole of this fertile country."[22] Settlement would have the added effect of making possible the building of a military road from Tennessee to the Gulf so that troops could be moved swiftly to halt a foreign invasion, something he had mentioned earlier to Crawford. Once such a road had been built, the security of the country would be immeasurably enhanced. Already he spoke of "Spanish insolence" in Florida and the possibility of "war with Spain." Our national rights, he told Edward Livingston, must "not be trampled on with impunity." Tell the people along the Gulf and "my Neworleans friends that I am wide awake to their security & defence—and only await the sound of war to be with them."[23]

Secretary Monroe, recently elected President, would take office on March 4, 1817, and he agreed with Jackson that the treaties were "incalculable." They would extend "our settlements, along the mississippi, and towards the mobile, whereby, great strength will be added to our union, in quarters where it is the most wanted." As soon as "our population gains a decided preponderance in those regions, Florida, will hardly be considered by Spain, as a part of her dominions. . . . Our attitude, will daily become more imposing on all the Spanish dominions, and indeed on those of other powers in the neighbouring islands." Here was one of the earliest indications that Jackson received from Monroe that Florida and the "neighbouring islands" were targets of the administration's expansionist policy.[24]

The President-elect, in forming his cabinet, decided to offer Jackson the post of secretary of war in view of the general's reputation and success in dealing with the Indians and acquiring their lands. But after careful thought, Jackson rejected the offer and authorized Congressman George W. Campbell, who was heading for Washington, to explain his reasons. He felt not only unfit to take on a purely administrative post but uncomfortable at the thought of residing in the capital the year round. Besides, he enjoyed his present position as General of the Army of the South, since it allowed him to reside at home and tend to his affairs as planter and farmer. Moreover, he worried over the presence of the Spanish in Florida and constantly sounded alarms as to their intentions along the frontier. He repeatedly expressed his fears that the Spanish would provoke a war with the United States. Finally there was the never-ending problem of the Indians, the danger of uprisings, the continued collision between white and red men, and the need to bring peace to the frontier.

All things considered, it made no sense to abandon an important job that he loved and performed expertly for a desk job in Washington. He explained to Monroe that once the "defence of the frontier is caried into effect, by completing those fortifications, that have & may be selected," erecting foundries and armories, and finishing the military road, "then *we will have peace*, for then we will be prepared for war—every man having a gun in his hand, all urope combined cannot hurt us—Then all the world will be anxious to be at peace with us—because all will see we wish peace with all—but are prepared for defence against those (all) who may attempt, to infringe our national rights."[25]

Of immediate moment was the building of a military road, and within a year he and Coffee laid out plans for its construction, with Coffee surveying one hundred townships by July 1817. The road itself was actually built under Jackson's supervision between June 1817 and January 1819, and he selected the points where military posts should be established. Ultimately the road extended 483 miles from Nashville to Madisonville on Lake Pontchartrain, thereby facilitating the rapid movement of troops in the southwest as well as shortening mail service between Washington and New Orleans to seventeen days.[26]

Although Monroe favored Jackson's ideas, especially his plea for the immediate sale of the land taken from the Indians, another member of his cabinet, Secretary of the Treasury William H. Crawford, opposed it. He reportedly felt "it would glutt the markett." At least that is what he said. But "Mr C has a better reason than this," declared Jackson, "he does not like us, wishes at the hazard of the safety of the union to cramp our growing greatness and wishes to prevent the population of Georgia [Crawford's home state] to be reduced by the emigration to this new country, and he oposes it because I have recommended it." Jackson later wrote that he had "obtained the hatred & hidden enmity of Mr. Crawford, about the cherokee treaty, and the Presidential election" in which he had supported Monroe. "I know he is my enemy—& I also know he is a base man."

Be that as it may, Jackson had every intention of removing all "intruders" from the ceded area and making it available for the speedy replacement of Indians with white settlers, thereby adding to the safety of the Union. Once this was accomplished, he said, "all urope will cease to look at it with an eye to conquest. There is no other point of the union (american united) that combined urope can expect to invade with success."[27]

To forestall any attempt by Crawford to block his plans, Jackson wrote to the new President on the day he took office, and not only reargued his position about populating the southwest with white settlers but urgently recommended that the lands on the Ohio River and the east bank of the Mississippi River within Kentucky be obtained from the Chickasaws. It would not only "consolidate our settlements" and "cut off all intercourse between the Northern Indians, and the Chickasaws and Choctaws," but it would also ensure the safety of "our commerce" on the two rivers and strengthen the defenses of the western frontier. And how shall we obtain this land? "I will answer, and I beg you will not be astonished at the ground I assume until you examine it well."

First off, he wrote, whenever "the safety, interest or defence of the country" is involved Congress has the right "to occupy and possess" any part of Indian territory. After all, the Indian Nations are not independent with the rights and privileges of a sovereign state. If they were in fact sovereign, then it would be "right and proper" to conclude treaties with them. "But this is not the fact." They are dependent. To sign treaties with them as we do with foreign powers makes no sense. "I have long viewed treaties with the Indians an absurdity not to be reconciled to the principles of our Government." They are subjects of the United States, like everyone else, living on U.S. land and "acknowledging its sovereignty." Congress has as much right to legislate on Indian concerns as it has in dealing with territorial affairs. The only difference is, Indians are not citizens with the rights of citizens. They are subjects. "I would therefore contend that the Legislature of the Union have the right to prescribe their bounds at pleasure" and when the government needs Indian hunting ground it has "the right to take it and dispose of it." "Hence I conclude that Congress has full power, by law, to regulate all the concerns of the Indians." Of course, when property is taken from inhabitants for public use there ought to be just compensation. That goes without saying.

Indians can no longer live by the bow and arrow, he continued. The game has been destroyed. They must lay aside these weapons and till the soil. "In short they must be civilized." And to do that, their "territorial boundary must be curtailed." As long as we allow them to roam over great distances in search of game "they will retain their savage manners, and customs." And eventually they will all perish. So, said Jackson, my advice is this: by law "circumscribe their bounds— put into their hands, the utensils of husbandry—yield them protection, and enforce obedience to those just laws provided for their benefit." That will civilize them.

It is "too true that avarice and fear are the predominant passions that govern the Indian—and money, is the weapon, in the hand of the commissioner, wielded to corrupt a few of their leaders, and induce them to adopt the plans embraced by the views of the Government." In that way the "poor of the Nation" who receive only a little by way of compensation are influenced by their chiefs, who have been "thus managed by corruption" to give their consent to what then is proposed to them. "Honor justice and humanity," he concluded his letter, require us to follow these basic precepts.[28]

Monroe responded several months later and said that Jackson's ideas were "new but very deserving of attention." He agreed that unless the Indians "become civilized, that they will decline, & become extinct." Although it has been customary to purchase title of Indian land, he continued, perhaps "a compulsory process seems to be necessary, to break their habits, & to civilize them, & . . . to preserve them." Monroe also agreed that Jackson's arguments for "promoting the rapid settlement of the alabama country," for erecting a foundry on the Tennessee River near Muscle Shoals, "and for the extinguishment of the title of the chickasaws, on the Eastern bank of the Mississippi, have great weight."[29] Jackson could take comfort from that, although it was obvious that the President had no intention of adopting the Hero's suggestions.

But of mounting concern to Old Hickory was the situation along the southeastern frontier between the United States and Spanish Florida. Regularly he received reports from his officers stationed along the frontier of the dangers that still existed. One came from General Edmund Pendleton Gaines about "another outrage of uncommon cruelty and barbarism" that had been "perpetrated on the southern frontier of Georgia." It seems that a party of Seminoles from Florida had attacked "a defenceless family and massaccred a woman (Mrs. Garrot) and her two children—the woman and eldest child were scalped, the house robbed and set on fire." The Indians then retreated to the safety of their homes in Spanish Florida. Gaines documented the report with letters, one of which was signed by Alexander Arbuthnot, a British trader from the West Indies, who, said Gaines, was "one of those *self-styled Philanthropists* who have long infested our neighboring Indian villages, in the character of British agents—fomenting a spirit of discord, (calculated to work the destruction of the deluded savages) and endeavoring by pretended care and kindness, to effect the destruction of these wretched savages."

This was the sort of information that truly alarmed Jackson and roused his fears for the safety of Americans living along the frontier. It annoyed him that foreign busybodies like Arbuthnot interfered in the lives of Indians and white settlers for their own nefarious purposes and endangered the peace that he was trying to establish in the region. He had no patience with these meddlers and deemed them worse than the "wretched savages." In fact he called them "fiends" who "ought to feel the keeness of the scalping knife."[30]

All the more reason to bring about a general removal of every tribe along the frontier and send them west of the Mississippi through a land exchange. He kept urging the government to undertake this task, and in 1817 he was given another opportunity to advance it.

Over the years the idea of a land exchange had been gaining support in Congress, and on January 9, 1817, a committee on public land in the United States Senate submitted a resolution to the upper house that would permit a land exchange with any of the tribes east of the Mississippi for land west of that river. The resolution passed on January 14.[31] Anticipating this action, the interim secretary of war, George Graham, wrote to Jackson on January 13 and informed him that the President had authorized the general to "extinguish the Indian title to the two reservations" made by the first article of a convention held with the Cherokees on January 7, 1806. Those reservations included land around the Muscle Shoals and another tract two miles wide on the north side of the Ten-

nessee River. Since the President had deemed it advisable "to enter into a negotiation as soon as practicable," Graham recommended that Jackson and two
other commissioners, General Meriwether (whom Old Hickory requested because "we unite perfectly in our ideas") and Governor Joseph McMinn of Tennessee, meet with the Cherokees on June 20. At that time, said the secretary, the
Indian agent, Return J. Meigs, would have the annuities and money already
owed to the tribe, which could be used as a bargaining chip.

The lands the government proposed to give in exchange were located along
the Arkansas River, immediately adjoining "the Osage boundary line and . . .
presently occupied by a part of that nation." The lands on which the Cherokees
presently reside in the east, said Graham, no longer afford support for the families of the Indians, while those we offer in exchange provide "the means of subsistence" that are "easily attainable in that mode which is most congenial to their
habits," a fallacious argument that Jackson himself had used and would use in
the future in arguing for the exchange. In addition, money for transportation
would be provided along with arms, blankets, and any other articles that he,
Jackson, felt were "expedient or necessary." Any Indian who had property and
wished to remain in the east would enjoy "the rights and immunities of a citizen
of the United States and in the protection of the laws of the particular State or
Territory in which they may respectively reside." Obviously these Indians would
be expected to live and behave like white settlers and be subject to state and local
law.[32]

The commissioners would also meet with those Cherokees who had removed
earlier to the Arkansas and had yet to provide an exchange of land in the east. At
present, according to the government, they occupied land for which they had
no title.

Jackson arrived at the Cherokee Agency in Highwassee on June 18. Three
days later, the appointed day for the start of the convention, none of the eastern
chiefs had appeared. Only the chiefs and delegation from the Arkansas Cherokees were present, along with John D. Chisholm and James Rogers, who were
authorized to negotiate with the commissioners on their behalf. Their attitude
and demeanor pleased the general greatly. They "appear verry solicitous for an
exchange," he reported.

But there could be a problem. The Eastern Cherokee Reform Council at
Amohee had recently adopted a constitution in which unanimous consent by
the Nation was required for the disposal of land, and it explicitly disinherited
those Cherokees who had emigrated from the Nation. Jackson feared that the

Arkansas Cherokees could be "overawed by the council of some whitemen and half breeds, who have been and are fattening upon the annuities . . . & who believe, that their income would be destroyed by the removal of the Indians." These "miscreants" reminded him of "some of our bawling politicians, who loudly exclaim we are the friends of the people, but who . . . care no more for the happiness or wellfare of the people than the Devil does." But Meriwether and he would be on their guard, he said, "& clearly explain, the true interests of the natives." He sincerely believed that at least half the Eastern Cherokees would agree to emigrate.[33]

Still he had been warned that a great number of Indians and whites would be present at the convention and "liquor will be plenty." Without a doubt, "there will be disorders unless restrained by the presence of a few troops," that is, regular troops in uniform, not militiamen. Some "overbearing characters," wrote Return J. Meigs, the agent, to Jackson, "still retaining their ancient barbarous habits and customs," have threatened those Indians who favored exchange and do not realize that the only way they can "retain their ancient customs, so dear to them" is by removal. They do not recognize that they are being constantly surrounded by whites who are ever increasing in number. The pressure on all sides is "incessant" and could eventually squeeze them into oblivion.[34]

Needless to say, Jackson made certain that perfect order was maintained throughout the negotiations, "to preserve respect on such an Occasion." But he had to wait day after day for the arrival of the Eastern Cherokees. Not until June 28 did the chiefs, headmen, and other delegates from the east arrive. Then at nine o'clock in the morning the convention began with an address by General Jackson.

He commenced his "talk" with his usual opening. "Friends and brothers, we shake you by the hand with the cordiality of sincere regards." Other complimentary words followed, and then Jackson got down to the business at hand. The "first Object," he said, was to arrange an exchange of lands as President Jefferson had first announced some nine years before. In detail he explained how the chiefs had gone to Washington and how Jefferson had made the offer of an exchange, which had been accepted. In the ensuing years, 3,700 Cherokees had removed to the Arkansas, said the general, and more were expected. Now it was time for the United States to receive by formal treaty eastern land in return. Those agreeing to emigrate could send an exploring party to the Arkansas and White rivers to reconnoiter the country. When they had found a suitable site for the emigrants not claimed by other tribes they would be given a "just portion" for the country they had left.

"Go where game is plentiful & corn is plenty," where you will be free to follow your ancient customs. Go to a place where you can support your families and where you will be protected. Supplies of all kinds will be sent by your Father the President, including a rifle, ammunition, one blanket and one brass kettle or beaver trap. In addition, a factory will be established where you can exchange your peltries for what you need and want. Flat-bottomed boats with provisions will be provided for the removal, and improvements on the lands given in the exchange will be paid for. "We shall still consider you our children . . . and always hold you firmly by the hand." Those who remain where they are and become citizens, who educate their children and "enjoy a civilized life," can be assured of "our patronage, our aid and our good neighborhood." They will also receive 640 acres of land, which they will hold in fee simple. As for the annuities, they would be shared equally by the Arkansas and Eastern Cherokees.

"Friends & Brothers Listen; let the whole nation hear. Is there one that can say this is not justice to all; has not every man among you a free choice to go or stay and has not the poor indian as well as the rich a right to make a choice; is not the poor Indian as free as the rich and his welfare as much concerned. As free men," he concluded, "you have now to make a choice."[35]

This talk was written up and handed to Charles Hicks, a Principal Chief and former translator, and to Thomas Wilson, clerk to the National Council of Thirteen. They were asked to "read and explain" it to the assembled chiefs and headmen and to invite John D. Chisholm and the other delegates of the Arkansas Cherokees "to attend and erange with them in friendship the whole business they were called on to settle."

The following day the Eastern Cherokees in a written document responded to the request that they admit John Chisholm and the Arkansas Cherokees to their council. And it struck Sharp Knife right between the eyes. "It is inconsistent with the dignity of the nation," the document haughtily began, "to meet in council or hold conferences with a character at once uniting all the base qualities of the human heart. Mr Chisholms General character is too generally known to admit of vindication." Besides, he is white and therefore cannot be part of "the internal police of our nation." However, we will meet with "the bona fide chiefs from Arkansas." As for your talk, General Jackson, it is well understood. "Even the women have become histerical and the nation in general begin to have forebodings of distress."

Reading this, Jackson's face must have dropped in astonishment. He and the other two commissioners were so incensed by this statement that they deemed it "insolent" and directed the secretary not to include it as part of the convention's journal.

Later the commissioners learned that their talk had not been read or explained to the assembled Cherokees as Jackson had asked and that the Arkansas Cherokees were not invited to attend the council. "From private sources that could be relied on," Jackson told Secretary Graham, the commissioners learned that Colonel Gideon Morgan, Jr., through management of the Committee of Thirteen, had concealed the talk from the people and provided no explanation of its contents except to convey ideas which would "sour the mind of the ignorant, inflame the nation by false impressions, and induce them to break up in confusion without doing any thing as they had done before." This Morgan, himself white and married to a mixed-blood Cherokee woman, no longer wished to live under U.S. law. He preferred Cherokee law. And he and his allies had been "agrandizing themselves from the annuities and hard earnings of the poor." For a "large reservation and iron works," the general sneered, they would sell out the entire Cherokee Nation.[36]

The insolence and contempt the Eastern Cherokees had shown the commissioners was in marked contrast to the response of the Arkansas chiefs, who said they were happy that their Father the President had not forgotten his promise that he would give to them a country of their choice for the lands they had left in the east. "Friends & Brothers," they told the commissioners, "We are Cherokees, we wish to preserve our existence as a nation," and are therefore prepared "to sign a relinquishment of our just proportion of our [eastern] country in exchange" for land on the Arkansas. We are sorry to hear that our brothers in the east declare that we are "not entitled to any land or any part of the annuities. . . . They now want to throw us off, do injustice by us, destroy us and destroy the name of the Cherokee Nation. . . . We call upon our father the President to do us justice, fulfill his promise, protect our rights, protect us from such a cruel and unjust an attempt of our Brothers, our Fathers and the Cherokees here. We hope your children will not call in vain."[37]

That sentiment was precisely what Jackson wished to hear, and he applauded it. But the Eastern Cherokees, led by the National Council, now dared to dispute Jackson's interpretation of what took place in Washington when President Jefferson offered to exchange land. The delegates who met Jefferson, they insisted, "were not authorized to transact any business as respects the division of the nation." They were there to take leave of the President, since he was about to retire to private life. And the delegates from the Upper Towns did not know that the delegates from the Lower Towns planned a division of the Cherokee Nation.

To buttress their argument they had John Walker and John McIntosh, two chiefs who had been part of the delegation in Washington, come forward and give witness to the truth of this interpretation. Both these chiefs stated that their sole purpose in visiting Jefferson had been to bid him farewell, that they had no power from the towns to exchange land, and that if any talk was held about such an action that it was "not by their consent."

Again Sharp Knife had to face obdurate Indians, and he was outraged. Their testimony, he reported, was a deliberate "falsehood." He turned and glared at the chiefs, his anger clearly showing in his blazing eyes. To respond to this "wicked deceit," he called on Tochelar, a Principal Chief of the Nation and a member of the National Council of Thirteen, and who also served as a delegate with Walker and McIntosh, to step forward and explain what *really* happened when they met with President Jefferson.

Tochelar was "a virtuous and independent man," the general later reported, and he also knew better than to disagree with Sharp Knife. He stood before the entire council and declared that he had "full powers from the lower towns" to ask for an exchange, that he had spoken directly with Jefferson, and that everything Jackson had said about the President's response was true.

Now it was the Eastern Cherokees' turn to express outrage. Such treachery by Tochelar against his own people was so abhorrent to them that they "broke and turned [him] out of council" and selected Richard Ruly, "a young half breed," to replace him. They also made Tochelar sign a document, intended as a response to Jackson's initial talk, that clearly agreed with the arguments of the Eastern Cherokees and totally contradicted his recent testimony.

The following day, July 4, when the convention reconvened, the document was read and then handed to the commissioners. It was signed by sixty-seven chiefs.

"Brothers," it said: "We Wish to remain on our land, and hold it fast. We appeal to our father the President of the United States to do us justice. We look to him for protection in the hour of distress. We are now distressed with the alternative proposal to remove from this country to the Arkansas, or stay and become citizens of the United States."

The truth is, they continued, "we are not yet civilized enough to become citizens." Nor do we wish to be compelled against our will to remove. We know that if we move "we would, in the course of a few years, return to the same savage state of life that we were in before the United States, our white brothers, extended their fostering care towards us, and brought us out of a savage state into a state similar to theirs."

The Cherokees had a point. If the whites wanted to see their Indian brothers civilized, why send them into the wilderness beyond the Mississippi, where they would surely revert to their "savage" ways? It made no sense. The policy, if such it could be called, was contradictory.

They then pointed out that those Cherokees from the Lower Towns who emigrated to the Arkansas did so without the consent of the chiefs and headmen of the Nation. No exchange of land had been authorized, and no exchange had taken place because the Nation had not legally agreed to it.

General Jackson, you tell us to make a choice. Very well, "our choice is to remain on our lands, and follow the pursuits of agriculture and civilization. . . . We therefore request that you will press the subject no further . . . but suffer us to remain in peaceable possession of this our country."[38]

Jackson exploded—as usual. He could scarcely believe that they would dare contest what he had said to them. The intrigue of "base and designing white men . . . and half breeds," he raged, had "turned out" the old chiefs who wanted to remove and were now "ruled by a committee of thirteen members, the greater part young quarterroon whitemen" under the evil influence of Colonel Morgan.

Jackson stared at the document and the names affixed to it. Then he turned to the assembled chiefs and growled that he wanted them "to hear and understand" that their statement "gave their father the P. the lye, it gave us the lye." He demanded to know how many of the chiefs were prepared to give the President the "lye," and give him and the other commissioners the "lye." Did they wish to be regarded as wayward children who defied their Father and forced him to send his soldiers into the territory to guarantee his rights? "The promise of the President to the arkansas, must be full filled," he stormed. And it *will* be fulfilled. "Look around you," he shouted, "and recollect what had happened to their brothers the Creeks."

The implication was obvious.

Before calling on all of the chiefs to say whether they were prepared to give the President the "lye," he first asked Tochelar to step forward. He and the other commissioners had heard, he said, that Tochelar had been forced "from threats and chicanery" to sign this document. Was that true? Give your answer, Tochelar, he commanded. Quietly Tochelar responded that he did not know what was in the document when he signed it and "he would not give the President the lye, or us." The "answer read was not his answer." He did in fact go to Washington and asked for an exchange of land. He wished only justice for the Arkansas Cherokees and for everyone to have a "free choice to go or stay."

Jackson turned next to The Glass, another Lower Town chief who expressed a wish to relocate to the Arkansas. He too repudiated the document and swore he would not give the President the "lye." Whereupon Jackson went from chief to chief, demanding their answers and proceeding, he said, until "this base attempt of fraud and deception" had been "compleatly exposed" and that "Justice" was done "the cherokees on the arkansas." The chiefs then "asked permission" to reconsider their position. Jackson insisted that they take the Arkansas Cherokees into their council and "be friendly one with another," each having a choice, "the poor as well as the rich, the fool as well as the wiseman." With that the convention adjourned for the day.[39]

On July 5 the chiefs remained "in council to themselves" and no meeting with the commissioners took place. But on July 6 the commissioners sent the chiefs "a rough draft of their final terms and directed a meeting tomorrow morning for the purpose of promulgation & more fully explaining their views."[40]

Jackson had used a threat of violence to begin the process of forcing the Indians to his will. Now he and the other commissioners resorted to bribery. By a "private article" they paid certain "Individuals of this nation the sum of four thousand two hundred and Twenty five dollars" before "they could give their consent that the chiefs should cede the national right." Thousands of dollars were promised, and these bribes included Arkansas Cherokees as well as Eastern Cherokees. Charles Hicks, one of the Principal Chiefs, and Major John Walker received $3,425, while John D. Chisholm obtained $1,000. As Jackson said, "we were compelled to promise John D. Chisholm the sum of one thousand dollars to stop his mouth & obtain his consent." Yet the commissioners had the gall to inform Graham that "the corruption that rules here—flows from a few corrupt whitemen, and half breeds, who by undue means has got into the council of this nation . . . who fatten on corruption."[41]

When the chiefs returned to meet with the commissioners on the evening of July 7 they announced that they would accept the terms offered to them. According to the treaty that "the chiefs, headmen, and warriors of the whole Cherokee nation" formally signed the following day, the U.S. government would give to the Arkansas Cherokees as much land west of the Mississippi as it received east of that river "acre for acre as the just proportion due" these Indians.

In return the government received a little over two million acres of land in Georgia, Alabama, and Tennessee. A census would be taken in June 1818 of the Eastern and Arkansas Cherokees to determine the number of those who chose to remove or intended to remove or had already removed. The annuity due from the United States to the entire Cherokee Nation would be divided between the two groups in proportion to their numbers and would continue to be divided thereafter. Those who moved to the Arkansas would receive a rifle with ammunition, one blanket, and either a brass kettle or a beaver trap. They would also receive compensation for any improvements on the land they were leaving that added real value, the amount to be determined by a commissioner appointed by the President. The government would also provide flatboats and provisions for the removal. Those who chose to remain in the east and who wished to become citizens of the United States would receive a 640-acre homestead "in which they will have a life estate, with a reversion in fee-simple to their children."[42]

Jackson was tremendously excited about what he and the other two commissioners had accomplished. As he repeatedly said in letters to friends and members of the administration, "the cession of land obtained is not important." What was important was "the Principle" that an exchange had established. "The security of all is laid by this treaty [and] makes those who are prepared here for civill life happy." In less than two years, he calculated, "it will give us the whole country," for he was convinced that in establishing the principal the remainder of Cherokees in the east—with the exception of "those prepared for agricultural persuits, civil life, & a government of laws"—would remove.[43]

It took seventeen weary days, Jackson complained, to bring the Indians to an acceptance of the treaty, and "we had to take stronger ground than was taken by the commissioners last year." But it had been well worth the effort. The commissioners informed Graham of the success of their mission, and he immediately ordered sixty flatboats to be delivered to Return J. Meigs, the Cherokee agent, between November 1 and January 1, along with "the necessary quantity of meat and flour." In addition, one hundred long rifles with four pounds of powder and twelve pounds of lead for each rifle would also be sent. Graham told the commissioners he was "fully impressed" by what they had done and was certain the Senate would be too. Most probably some members of the upper house would oppose the treaty, he declared, because they were in opposition "to the general policy of removing the Indians to the west of the Mississippi." Also, there would be some who would contest it because it did not receive "the unbiassed sanction of a majority" of those Cherokees living on the east side of the river. In addition, they would claim that the right of the United States to Indian land based on what took place in January 1809 with President Jefferson did not give the government a "right to any portion of the Cherokee lands" and was "too strongly enforced by the commissioners." Nevertheless, despite these objections, it was Graham's opinion that the treaty would be ratified, as indeed it was on December 11, 1817, by a unanimous vote.[44]

As Jackson had said, this treaty established a "Principal." If no place else, that principal established itself deep within Sharp Knife's consciousness. Henceforth, if he ever had the authority and power he was determined to implement the principal and remove all five southern tribes—Cherokees, Choctaws, Creeks, Chickasaws, and Seminoles—beyond the Mississippi River.

Chapter 8

To Seize Florida

Jackson returned to his home outside Nashville when the treaty negotiations terminated, and he threw himself into overseeing the building of the military road, the selection of town sites in the areas ceded by the Indians, and the arrangements of land sales for new settlers. As "soon as the lands are sold," he told Coffee, "the Legislative authority will have the right to lay off counties, Establish Towns &c &c." In addition to everything else he was also attentive to the actions of intruders who squatted within Indian territory. He used his soldiers to take them into custody and haul them before the civil authorities.[1]

Jackson also received disturbing news from General Edmund P. Gaines about the activities of the Indians along the Florida border. Earlier, in the spring of 1816, when Madison was still President, Jackson had been forced to contend with the presence of the Negro Fort in Spanish-held Florida at the junction of the Chattahoochee and Flint rivers. This fort was a beacon for runaway slaves throughout the entire southeast. It was built in a square and extended over two acres; its ramparts and parapets were made of hewn timber filled with dirt, and it mounted nine to twelve pieces of cannon, several of which were very large, along with mortars and howitzers. Inside there were several large stone houses and "Comfortable barracks." According to Gaines, three hundred "negroes" lived in the fort, wore red coats, and had been supplied with "a large quantity of British muskets, Powder and other supplies."[2]

The British again. Their interference on the frontier never seemed to end. Jackson ordered the construction of fortifications just above the Georgia-Florida border and requested permission from the secretary of war to attack and destroy the Negro Fort. The reply was typical of the Madison administration: try diplomacy. Call attention to the problem by notifying the governor of Florida, Mauricio de Zúñiga. "The principles of good neighbourhood," wrote William Crawford, the then secretary of war, require that Zúñiga be invited "to put an end to an evil of so serious a nature." If he failed to act on the suggestion it would then be up to the President to decide what further action should be taken.

To Jackson this meant do nothing, which was galling. Nevertheless he followed the directions and wrote to Zúñiga and told him quite frankly that the fort had to be leveled. Failure to do so "will compel us in self Defence to destroy" it and the "Banditti" within it. Zúñiga responded by admitting his concern over the problem and assuring Jackson he would have his full cooperation. Thus, if the renowned General "Andres" Jackson would like to assist in the reduction of the fort he would be proud to serve under him![3]

Under the circumstances, Jackson decided to give General Gaines discretionary authority to invade Florida and attack the Negro Fort. In actuality he gave him a clear signal that he wanted it eliminated. "If the fort harbours the Negroes of our citizens or friendly Indians living within our Territory," he told Gaines, "or hold out Inducements to the Slaves of our Citizens to desert from their owner's service, this fort must be destroyed." He stressed that "you possess the power of acting on your Discretion, which I hope you will exorcised on this."[4]

Gaines needed little encouragement. He constructed Fort Scott near the mouth of the Flint River north of the Florida boundary, as Jackson had directed, and sent out an expedition to destroy the Negro Fort. A naval contingent out of New Orleans reached the mouth of the Apalachicola on July 10, 1816, and provided support for the land operation. On July 27 the gunboats came within range of the fort and opened fire, using hot shot. On the very first volley they hit the fort's magazine. Suddenly there was an enormous explosion that killed 270 persons and wounded sixty-one. Several of the black leaders were later turned over to the Indians and subjected to a long and painful death.[5]

So much for the "negro menace." But there still remained the danger of marauding Red Sticks harassing the frontier from their safe sanctuary in Florida and drawing upon an enormous amount of help from their kinsmen the Seminoles. The Seminoles were actually part of the Creek confederation. They were Hitchitee people and got their name from the Creek Muskogees, who called them "Seminoles," which roughly means "frontiersmen." In a real sense the Seminole Nation was not a single tribe but an alliance of remnants of earlier tribes such as the Apalachicolas, Yamasees, and Uchees, along with newer groups like the Tallahassees, Oconees, and Mikasukis. Many settlers from the Upper Creek towns had migrated into Florida and spoke the Creek tongue, Muskhogean. Americans lumped them all together and called them Seminoles, probably out of convenience in negotiating treaties.[6]

These Seminoles, said Gaines, appeared to have "taken the advice of the man who calls himself A. Arbuthnot," a British agent and "the prime director on the part of the seminola Indians in the adjustment of our affairs." Arbuthnot, a trader from the West Indies and a self-promoting meddler who has "long infested our neighboring Indian villages," had arrogantly presumed to plead the case of the notorious Red Stick prophet Peter McQueen, one of the prime instigators of the Creek War and a man Jackson itched to capture and execute. McQueen claimed that his property in slaves and cattle had been wrongly seized by Americans, and he wanted them returned. Indeed, Arbuthnot further argued that the land ceded by the Creeks in the Treaty of Fort Jackson should also be returned because Article IX of the Treaty of Ghent, which concluded the War of 1812, specifically required the restoration of "all possessions" held by the Indians as of 1811. Accordingly, in a letter written May 3, 1817, he asked the commanding officer at Fort Gaines "why American settlers are descending the Chattahouchy driving the poor Indian from his habitation and taking possession of his home and cultivated fields." This was a violation, he protested. Article IX respecting Indian rights "has been infringed upon" by Americans, and the commandant should "represent to them their improper Conduct, and prevent its continuence." All of this was duly reported to an exasperated General Jackson.[7]

As the months passed, the Seminole Indians inside the Florida border, especially those living on Okolokne Sound at the mouth of the Apalachicola, just east of Pensacola, continued to cause trouble. Not only did they welcome the Creeks who fled from Jackson after the defeat at Horseshoe Bend but they were accused of killing white settlers within Georgia. When General Gaines demanded that the murderers be surrendered to American authorities, the Indians replied that they were only seeking "satisfaction" for murders committed by Americans. They acknowledged killing Mrs. Obediah Garrett and her two children, explaining that when they entered her home and found a kettle belonging to several Indians who had been killed they concluded that her husband was the culprit and therefore killed her and her children. Worse, Neamathla, the chief of Fowltown, located just north of the Florida border on land claimed by the United States under the Treaty of Fort Jackson, informed Major David E.

Twiggs, the commanding officer at Fort Scott, that "the Flint river was the dividing line between us." Twiggs was dumbfounded. He reported that Neamathla also said that "I must not cut another stick of timber on the opposite side from this, the land was his and he was directed by the Powers above to protect and defend it." Obviously, Twiggs added, "talking could not frighten him."[8]

That did it. Gaines communicated all this to Jackson and told him he had decided to take action and destroy Fowltown. "I am convinced," he wrote, "that nothing but the application of force, will be sufficient to ensure a permanent adjustment of this affair." Accordingly, he directed Twiggs and 250 men of the 1st Brigade from Fort Scott to arrest Neamathla and his warriors and bring them before Gaines. If the Indians resisted they were to be treated "as Enemies."

The troops arrived at Fowltown early in the morning of November 21, 1817, and were "instantly fired upon." The fire was returned and the Indians fled, leaving behind one dead woman, four dead warriors, and several others who were wounded. The soldiers finished their work by burning the town. Among items found in Neamathla's house before it was set on fire were a British coat with gold epaulettes and a certificate signed by a captain of marines stating that Neamathla was a "faithfull friend to the British."[9]

In interrogating several natives, Gaines learned that there were approximately two thousand Red Sticks and Seminoles and four hundred runaway slaves from Georgia in the area and that they had been promised British help by Captain George Woodbine in New Providence. Clearly something had to be done to prevent these combustible materials from exploding into another Indian war by Creeks and Seminoles.[10]

The destruction of Fowltown was later regarded as the first military action by the American army in precipitating the First Seminole War. But the killing did not end with this engagement. Nine days later a "very considerable" number of Seminoles strung out about 150 yards along the shore of the Apalachicola River, a mile below the juncture of the Flint and Chattahoochee rivers that forms the Apalachicola, took their revenge by ambushing a boat conveying forty soldiers, seven women, and four children commanded by Lieutenant Richard W. Scott. They killed all but six soldiers, who escaped, four of them wounded. The seven women, wives of the soldiers, were either killed or taken prisoner. When the Indians captured the vessel they seized the children by their heels and dashed out their brains against the sides of the boat.[11]

Jackson forwarded this information to the newly appointed secretary of war, John C. Calhoun of South Carolina, the noted War Hawk who helped drive

President Madison into asking Congress for a declaration of war against Great Britain in 1812. The general pointed out to Calhoun that Spain was required by treaties to restrain the Indians from invading U.S. territory. Obviously the Spanish government could not keep the peace. Therefore, if the Indians continued to use Florida as a "sanctuary," we must "follow the marauders and punish them in their retreat"—after giving Spain "due notice," of course. "The War Hatchet having been raised . . . [the] frontier cannot be protected without entering their country."[12]

The response from Washington came quickly enough. On December 26, 1817, Secretary Calhoun officially ordered Jackson to proceed immediately to Fort Scott in Georgia and take command of American forces in that district, where a reported 2,700 Seminoles regularly threatened the frontier. In the interim General Gaines was told that it was the President's wish that he consider himself "at liberty to march across the Florida line" if he felt he had adequate forces "and to attack them [the Seminoles] within its limits, should it be found necessary, unless they shelter themselves under a Spanish fort. In the last instance, you will immediately notify this department." In replacing Gaines in command of the American forces, Jackson was instructed by Calhoun to "adopt the necessary measures to terminate a conflict" President Monroe had wished to avoid "but which is now made necessary" by the "Settled hostilities" of the Seminoles.[13]

These orders arrived just as Jackson was passing through an extremely unpleasant controversy with the administration that almost precipitated his resignation from the army. It seems that Major Stephen H. Long, a topographical officer, had been ordered by the War Department to depart Jackson's army and take up his duties with the northern division—without clearing it with Jackson first or even notifying him. The general was justifiably outraged. He had been bypassed, an act in his mind, he told President Monroe, that was "a violation of military etiquette and subversive of every principle of subordination." Because of his anger he then did something incredibly stupid—and improper. He issued a division order on April 22, 1817, forbidding "the obedience of any order emanating from the Department of War" unless it came through the commanding general "as the proper organ of communication."[14]

Needless to say, the order, when broadcast around the country, created an uproar, and Jackson was accused of insubordination. Here was the origin of the real fears any number of officials felt about the Hero, namely that he was a "military chieftain," a potential "man on horseback," and as such a danger to the Republic. Anyone who had any dealings with Old Hickory knew he could act violently, precipitately and uncontrollably if crossed, contradicted, or insulted. His superiors certainly understood how prone he was to take offense, how quick to suspect conspiracy in any action he regarded as offensive. Years earlier, Thomas Jefferson remembered Jackson's anger. "His passions are terrible," Jefferson said. "When I was President of the Senate, he was Senator, and he could never speak on account of the rashness of his feelings. I have seen him attempt it repeatedly, and as often choke with rage. His passions are, no doubt, cooler now; he has been much tried since I knew him, but he is a dangerous man."[15]

A dangerous man. Some politicians, certainly Henry Clay, probably William H. Crawford and others, began to wonder if a possible Napoleon had arisen in their midst who would undermine the rule of law and destroy the very foundation of American freedom.

When the present charges of insubordination erupted in Congress, Jackson threatened to resign his commission. But the administration had no wish to antagonize its popular (the masses absolutely idolized him) and successful general—or lose him. Still, it could not allow him to dismiss and supersede civil authority at will. But how to do it without alienating him?

It took months before everything was smoothed out. Monroe wrote several letters to mollify the general. "My earnest desire is, to terminate this unpleasant affair in the most honorable manner for you," he assured Jackson. You cannot imagine how painful this is for me, "the most painful that could have occurred . . . on a point, involving such serious consequences and on which it is my indispensible duty to decide." And the point, as Jackson should have known, involved the authority of the chief executive over the officers of the army. In such cases, said Monroe, the War Department cannot be separated from the President. The orders of the department are my orders, the orders of the chief executive. No officer of the army can rightfully disobey an order of the President who is by virtue of the Constitution the commander in chief of the armed forces.

Monroe continued at length to lecture him on something Jackson should have known and understood without question. But it was necessary to speak at length because he was addressing a hypersensitive officer who was unaccustomed to being bypassed in the chain of command. In essence the President agreed with Jackson that the order should have come through him, not around him, and that in the future it would constitute the "general rule," which was what Jackson demanded. The only exception to the rule, cautioned Monroe, would involve cases of "urgency" about "which, the dept. should be the judge. The reasons which you urge, have in this view, great weight." And because of their weight a general rule would be adopted.

The President wrote again on December 2, repeating that he hoped the affair would be terminated "with perfect delicacy to you."[16]

It worked. The general rule "fully meets my approbation," the Hero responded, "for I see in it that magnanimity of conduct only to be met with in great & good minds." Monroe's soothing words and his repeated affirmations of his "great respect and sincere regards" apparently overcame the resentment Jackson had harbored for months. It was like him to be quick to anger, even quicker to retaliate, but he always stood ready to overlook a quarrel if he felt proper amends had been offered and his sense of honor placated. This Monroe had done. Nevertheless Jackson reminded the President that "I can never abandon principle, be the personal consequences what they may." He also said that he believed cases of necessity created their own rule and formed exceptions from the general rule. "I have never complained of any order being issued in cases of necessity, when I was immediately advised thereof—nor is it a source of real complaint." He admitted that he had intended to resign over the incident, "but I have determined, since the receipt of your letter not to resign," at least not now.[17]

The general rule was adopted, and Calhoun issued an order on December 29 in which he affirmed that the War Department would not issue directives to subordinate commanders except in emergency situations where "the public interest may require it," and that a copy would be transmitted to the general of the division for his information. Furthermore, he wrote to Jackson himself and confirmed that "the orders accord substantially with your view." He also said that he honored the Hero "with feelings of respect, which any lover of his country has towards you." He ended with a wish that the country would continue to be "benefited by your military services."[18]

Another reason Jackson willingly accepted Monroe's mollifying words and plea that he not resign were letters from John Rhea, a Tennessee congressman and one of the general's friends. On November 27, 1817, Rhea informed Jackson of "a conversation respecting you" that he had had with the President. Be assured, he told the general, that "the President entertains and has for you undiminished every degree of friendship he ever had." His confidence in you is unimpaired. He is your friend, and he opposes every idea of your resigning or retiring "from the service of your country." So does Secretary Calhoun and even "Mr. W[illiam] H. C[rawford]."[19]

It was at this moment that Calhoun ordered Jackson to assume command of the Seminole operation, and it immediately crossed the general's mind that Rhea could be very useful to him in executing his designs on Florida. For some time he had been pressing the administration to end the problems in the south by ousting Spain from its possessions along the Gulf. West Florida had already been seized by the Madison administration on the presumption that it was part of the Louisiana Purchase. But that did not satisfy Jackson. He felt, and repeatedly argued, that the remainder of the Florida peninsula should also be acquired by the United States. In his mind it was the only way of terminating the danger of Indian attacks and ultimately preventing foreign invasion from the Gulf region. Already General Gaines, acting on orders, had captured Amelia Island on December 23 from pirates and slave traders who had seized it earlier in the year. Now Jackson had been ordered into Florida to end the menace of Seminole attacks along the frontier. How much easier it would be for him to snatch Florida outright in a quick military action and force Spain into relinquishing it, thereby solving the problem of Seminole raids into Georgia once and for all.

And that was exactly what he decided to do. Such action would end the Indian menace and complete security measures by which easy invasion by foreign powers through the Gulf could be terminated. So he wrote directly to Monroe (bypassing Calhoun in the process) and laid it on the line. Since the administration, he said, had already authorized the invasion of Amelia Island, we could complete the operation by seizing "simultaneously the whole of East Florida" and holding it as indemnity "for the outrages of Spain upon the property of our citizens." It would also "save us from a War with Great Britain" or any other European power intent on attacking us.

Since Jackson also recognized the diplomatic and international furor such an action would cause if the administration officially authorized it, he suggested to the President that his plan could be activated without "implicating the Government." Just "let it be signifyed to me," he wrote, "though any channel, (say Mr. J. Rhea) that the possession of the Floridas would be desirable to the United States, & in sixty days it will be accomplished."[20]

That letter should have caused Monroe to sit bolt upright when he read it. Knowing Jackson as he did, and the problems the general could cause if not controlled, he should have responded immediately if he intended to prevent him from executing the seizure. He was being asked to authorize an illegal action with international repercussions. This was a matter for his immediate personal attention; Jackson had to be halted before the passage of another day. And knowing from past experience that Jackson could and probably would disregard instructions from the secretary of war if he felt the good of the country required it, Monroe should have realized that he himself had to write a direct order to the general and warn him against any move that would constitute a veritable declaration of war against Spain.

But Monroe did nothing of the kind. Instead, on January 30, he directed Secretary Calhoun to instruct Jackson "not to attack any post occupied by Spanish troops, from the possibility, that it might bring the allied powers on us."[21] Undoubtedly Monroe had received Jackson's letter when he acted in this circuitous manner. Knowing how Jackson had invaded Florida without authority in 1814, did he for a moment think his directive to the secretary absolved him from his responsibility to halt this intended action? If so he was incredibly stupid or naive. At the very least he should have assured himself that Calhoun had obeyed his directive and instructed Jackson against a seizure. But he did not. And Calhoun never sent the order!

Under the circumstances and understanding Monroe's past desire to take Florida, is it not likely that the President really wanted Jackson to seize Florida but not with even the slightest hint that it had executive authorization? He later claimed he was ill and after showing Jackson's letter to Calhoun and Crawford forgot about it until after the invasion had occurred. How could he forget such an important matter? On reading the letter, both Calhoun and Crawford told him it was about Florida and required an answer, and yet Monroe claimed he forgot about it.

Jackson later insisted that he did in fact receive a response from Rhea, who told him that he had Monroe's approval. Rhea's response was received by Jackson in mid-February and destroyed a year later at the President's request, a request conveyed through Rhea—or so the general claimed.[22] However, in the Jackson papers there is a letter by Rhea dated January 12, 1818 (obviously written before Monroe had received Jackson's request), in which he says, "I expected you would receive the letter you allude to, and it gives me pleasure to know you have it, for I was certain it would be satisfactory to you. you see by it the sentiments of the President respecting you are the same."[23] Just what Rhea is alluding to can be and has been disputed, but it surely helped convince Jackson, if he needed convincing, that on the matter of Florida he and Monroe entertained similar views. Even more convincing was a letter the general received from the President himself, dated December 28, which said, "This days mail will convey to you an order to repair to the command of the troops now acting against the Seminoles," an obvious reference to Calhoun's letter of December 26. These Indians,

Monroe continued, have "long violated our rights & insulted our national character. The mov'ment will bring you, on a theatre, when possibly you may have other services to perform depending on the conduct of the banditti at Amelia Island, and Galvestown."

Inasmuch as the invasion had already been approved, what "other services" did Monroe have in mind if not the seizure of Florida? From his earlier correspondence with the President, Jackson knew how Monroe felt about the need to take Florida. If he required any further proof of the President's intentions it came with the concluding part of the letter. "This is not a time for you to think of repose. Great interests are at issue, and until our course is carried through triumphantly & every species of danger to which it is exposed is settled on the most solid foundation, you ought not to withdraw your active support from it."[24]

The fact that Calhoun never sent any order to the general forbidding an attack on Spanish posts as Monroe claimed is exceedingly strange. The secretary was an excellent administrator and it is unlikely that he forgot about it or would countermand instructions from his superior. Of course, he might have presumed that the orders given previously were sufficient; but is it not also possible that he really knew Monroe's true intentions and therefore withheld sending the order? This assumption about Monroe's real intentions takes on added validity in the light of a letter Calhoun wrote to Jackson on February 6 in which he said, "I have the honor . . . to acquaint you with the entire approbation of the President of *all the measures* which you have adopted to terminate the rupture with the Indians. The honor of our arms, as well as the interest of our country requires, that it should be as speedily terminated as practicable; and the confidence reposed in your skill and promptitude assures us that peace will be restored on such conditions as will make it honorable and permanent."[25]

From the beginning of Jackson's direct involvement in the Creek War and the War of 1812 he had steadfastly insisted that the only way to bring about a "permanent" peace in the south was to drive foreigners from the Gulf Coast. And that is what the President and the secretary wanted him to do, employing all the measures necessary to end the Indian war. Surely he had more than enough indication that his recommendation about the seizure of the peninsula had been approved at the highest level.

Even the Spanish understood the administration's true intentions. Luis de Onís, the Spanish minister to the United States, complained that the Madison/Monroe policy of seizure began in 1810 and 1812 when West Florida, including

Mobile and the district of Baton Rouge, was claimed by the United States as part of the Louisiana Purchase. The President declared, Onís wrote in his *Memoirs,* "that as all these territories belonged to the United States as an integral part of Louisiana, he considered it expedient to occupy them." Then, "to these publick acts of aggression and violence were afterwards added General Jackson's march . . . into East Florida. . . . I protested in the name of the king, against all and each of these excesses; but the cabinet in Washington refused to reply to me, and inflexibly adhered to their system of policy."[26]

When the inevitable international storm broke over Jackson's seizure of Florida and Old Hickory was threatened with censure, Rhea took to the floor of the House of Representatives and insisted that the general had informed Calhoun of his intended actions and had received a reply on February 6 "acquainting him of the entire approbation of the President of all the measures he had adopted to terminate the war."[27] Clearly that is what Jackson believed and so communicated it to Rhea, who relayed it to the other members of the House of Representatives.

The dispute raged on for over a dozen years without coming to any resolution, but Jackson remained convinced to the end of his life that the administration had initiated and approved the taking of Florida.

Jackson compounded his brazen suggestion by calling on a group of eight officers who had served with him in the Creek War to assemble a corps of Tennessee volunteers to join his army and march with him into Florida. "The Seminole Indians have raised the war hatchet," he told them. "They have stained our land with the blood of our Citizens; their war spirit must be put down; and they taught to know that their safety depends upon the friendship and protection of the U. States." To do this he wanted a thousand mounted "Gun men" armed and equipped to serve for the duration of the campaign. "Your General who led you to victory on the plains of Talledega, Emuckfau, and Tahopek, asks you to accompany him to the heart of the Seminole Towns, and there aid in giving peace and safety to the Southern Frontier."[28]

Another explosion of outrage occurred among the members of Congress when they heard about this invitation. Jackson, they said, had usurped their authority by raising an army without authorization. No one had given him leave to call for volunteers. No one in Congress even knew about it until word leaked out from one of the eight officers who received the call. Here was another example, they said, of Jackson's contempt for lawful authority and readiness to take the law into his own hands.

Abner Lacock of Pennsylvania in the Senate and Henry R. Storrs of New York in the House brought in reports from their respective committees recommending that some appropriate action be taken to rein in this rampaging general. As soon as he heard about these reports, Jackson fired off a response in which he argued that he had done nothing improper. After all, volunteers were the equivalent of militia and were raised in accordance with state laws and standard military practice. He took this action, he said, in the interest of saving time, since he felt it was an emergency situation. Besides, to add to the eight hundred regulars and one thousand Georgia militiamen that Jackson had been told would make up his command, Calhoun in his letter of December 26 had authorized Jackson to call on neighboring governors for additional militia if he needed them.[29]

Jackson left the Hermitage on Thursday, January 22, 1818, and headed for Fort Scott. As he traveled though Tennessee he was delighted to find that "Volunteers were flocking to the standard of their Country" so that he anticipated at least two regiments of mounted "Gun men" who would be mustered into service at Fayetteville by February 1. He himself arrived in Huntsville on January 26 and immediately reported to Calhoun. In his letter he strongly recommended the building of "a national Depot, with an Armory, Foundery, & every facility for fabricating of Weapons of War . . . adequate to the supply of our South Western states . . . without being dependant upon foreign or Atlantic work shops."[30]

Moving on as best he could through heavy rains that turned roads into quagmires and played havoc with the progress of baggage wagons, he reached Hartford, Georgia, on February 12. There he met General Gaines, recently arrived from his seizure of Amelia Island, and learned about the wretched condition of the soldiers guarding Fort Scott, who were faced with dwindling supplies and low morale.[31] Almost without pause, Jackson continued his march but again faced a hazardous terrain that slowed his progress. Nothing but "bad roads, high waters, &c constant rain," he complained to Rachel. When he reached Fort Early he expected to obtain supplies, which he badly needed; but instead "I found half a pint of corn & half a pint of flower pr man." He pressed on "through a wilderness of sixty miles, with various large water courses unusually high to pass," reminding him of the Israelites starving in the wilderness. From several dispatches he learned from the commander of Fort Scott that unless supplies reached him in a matter of days he would be forced to abandon his post.

In all it took Jackson forty-six days to traverse 450 miles from his home in

Tennessee to Fort Scott. He finally arrived at 7:00 P.M. on March 9, 1818, and he took pride in the fact that he had not lost a single man due to sickness or casualty. When he reached the fort he could tell that the situation was desperate. "The idea of starvation had spread far & wide," he wrote, "and a panic was every where." With what little beef and pork he had, added to one quart of corn per man, he had only rations for three days. Appeals for help had already gone out, and several supply ships from New Orleans were said to be on their way. As a matter of fact, two such ships were anchored in the bay at the mouth of the Apalachicola River inside the Florida border.[32]

Without a moment's hesitation, Jackson decided to head directly for the ships. On the morning of March 10, hardly a day after arriving at Fort Scott, he distributed among his soldiers what little food and provisions remained and then struck out for Florida and the supply ships. His army now consisted of three thousand troops, both regulars and volunteers, and an additional force of two thousand Indian allies, most of them friendly Creeks.[33]

The invasion of Florida had begun.

Chapter 9

The First Seminole War

Jackson's route to the supply ships took him along the east side of the Apalachicola River, while William McIntosh, the mixed-blood general commanding the friendly Creeks, marched down the western bank. Without firing a shot, McIntosh reported that his men captured Red Ground, an Indian village, and a party of 180 women and children and fifty-three warriors. But the chief of the town, along with thirty warriors, escaped. Jackson himself did not encounter the enemy and on March 15 reached the site of the former Negro Fort, where he met a boatload of food ascending the Apalachicola River. His situation had now completely changed, "and the prospect of plenty is ours."[1]

Jackson ordered the fort rebuilt and placed Lieutenant Gadsden of the engineering corps in charge. Gadsden did such an excellent job that the general renamed the site Fort Gadsden. He notified Calhoun of his presence at the fortification and said he was headed for St. Marks. "I have no doubt but that St. Marks is in possession of the Indians. . . . I shall take possession of the garrison as a depot for my supples," and since Spain has acknowledged "incompentency" to "keep her Indians at peace with us . . . I will possess it, for the benefit of the United States, as a necessary position for me to hold, to give peace and security to this frontier, and put a final end to Indian warfare in the South."[2]

In Jackson's mind, obviously, the only way to end the war and bring peace to the frontier, as he had been ordered to do, was by occupying posts held by the Spanish, the very thing that Monroe claimed he wished to prevent.

The Seminoles sought help from both the Spanish and British and had been seeking help ever since the Americans began their "lawless incursions to drive us from our lands." Several chiefs wrote to the Bahamian governor, Charles Cameron, and pleaded for assistance. "Our brethren are now fighting for the lands

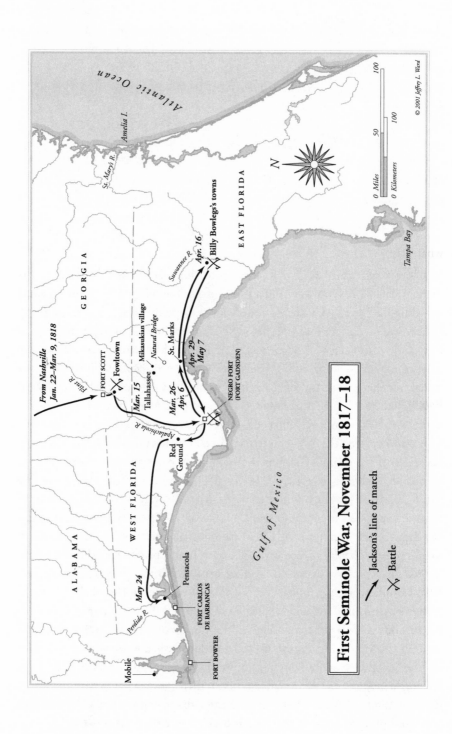

First Seminole War, November 1817–18

→ Jackson's line of march
✗ Battle

Atlantic Ocean

Amelia I.

St. Marys R.

GEORGIA

From Nashville
Jan. 22–Mar. 9, 1818

Flint R.

FORT SCOTT
Fowltown

Mar. 15
Tallahassee

Mikasukian village
Natural Bridge

St. Marks

Mar. 26–
Apr. 6

Suwannee R.

Apr. 16
Billy Bowlegs's towns

Apr. 29
May 7

EAST FLORIDA

NEGRO FORT
(FORT GADSDEN)

Apalachicola R.

Red
Ground

WEST FLORIDA

ALABAMA

May 24

Pensacola

FORT CARLOS
DE BARRANCAS

Perdido R.

Mobile

FORT BOWYER

Gulf of Mexico

Tampa Bay

N

0 Miles   50   100
0 Kilometers   100

© 2001 Jeffrey L. Ward

they inherited from their forefathers, for their families and friends," they wrote. "But what will our exertions do, without assistance." The American troops and settlers are killing our people and stealing our food. "To whom can we look up to for protection and support, but to those friends who have at former times held forth their hands to uphold us, and who have sworn in their late treaty [of Ghent] with the Americans, to see our just right and privileges respected and protected from insult and aggression."

But look what has happened. Look at our situation. "We now call on your excellency," they wrote Cameron, "as the representatives of our good father, King George, to send us such aid in ammunition, as we are absolutely in want of; and as our brother chief, Hillisajo, was informed, when in England, that when ammunition was wanting . . . that your excellency would supply us with what was necessary. We have applied to the Spanish officer at the fort of St. Marks; but his small supply prevented his being able to assist us." We must, therefore, depend on your excellency, and we pray that you will not only send ammunition but "an officer, or person to lead us right."[3]

On this last point the chiefs "in full council assembled" appealed directly to King George and asked "that British officers should be constantly kept among us" so that we shall not "be driven to the desert sands of the sea, from the fertile fields of our forefathers." As "our good father, king George" knows, "we have fought and bled for him against the Americans, by which we have made them our bitter enemies." Surely, then, he will "not forget the suffering of his once happy children here. We therefore rely on his future protection and his fatherly kindness." It is our hope that he will "continue his protection; famine is now devouring up ourselves and our children."[4]

The Scot trader Alexander Arbuthnot tried to lend the natives his assistance. He was seventy years of age and had come to the Suwannee in Florida from the Bahamas in the spring of 1817 to trade with the Indians, and he genuinely sought to help them. He exchanged blankets, beads, paints, rum, knives, tomahawks, guns, and powder for skins, beeswax, and corn. He got along so well with Native Americans that the Seminoles sought his counsel and the Creeks gave him the power of attorney to act on their behalf. With him came two other Englishmen: Captain George Woodbine of the Royal Marines, who had helped organize Indian attacks on Americans in Florida during the War of 1812, and Robert C. Ambrister, a rather dashing young officer of the Royal Marines who had lost his commission because of an illegal duel and had come to Florida with Woodbine in the hope of finding adventure and a way back into the service.

When the Americans began their so-called "depredations" in Florida, Ambrister applied to British military officers for aid. He wrote regularly to Colonel Edward Nicholls, whom Admiral Cochrane had sent to Pensacola in 1814 and who had armed more than four thousand Creek and Seminole warriors. Nicholls had also promised these Indians that the King of England would protect their interests after the war. Now Arbuthnot asked him to make good his pledge. Unlike Nicholls and Woodbine, both of whom operated solely to advance English imperial ambitions, Arbuthnot cared about Indian interests and believed that both the British and Americans treated them badly. So he complained to both the U.S. Creek agent in Georgia and to his own government. In his letter to Nicholls he informed the officer that the Americans had encroached on Indian territory, had burned their towns, and had made "fields where their houses stood." The Indians had appealed for help, he added, but "they complain of the English government neglecting them, after having drawn them into a war with America; that you, sir, have not kept your promise, in sending people to reside among them; and that if they have not some person or persons, resident in the nation to watch over their interest, they will soon be driven to the extremity of the peninsula."[5]

Here was proof, Jackson later claimed when he saw these documents, that the British and Spanish were culprits in perpetuating warfare along the frontier. They encouraged Indian attacks, supplied the natives with arms and ammunition, and promised them continued aid. He felt totally justified in carrying the war into Florida.

Once his army had feasted on the supplies provided by the ships on the Apalachicola, Jackson ordered them into formation and commenced active operations to penetrate the center of the Seminole country. He left Fort Gadsden on March 26 and headed northeast in the general direction of St. Marks. Five days later he was joined by McIntosh and the Creek allies, along with a detachment of Tennessee volunteers. The Red Sticks had a special hatred for McIntosh. He had "caused much blood to be spilt, for which," said an assembled council of Muskogee chiefs, "we denounce him to the whole nation, and will give the usual reward of the brave, to any one who may kill him." But McIntosh had a grievance of his own against the Red Sticks. During the civil war he had suffered heavy property losses at their hands.[6]

To protect a flotilla of ships carrying provisions for one of Jackson's garrisons—which he had ordered up from New Orleans via Pensacola—the general wrote to Colonel José Masot, the Spanish governor in Pensacola, and informed him of its approach and warned him against any interruption in its free passage across Spanish territory. In the present contest "against our mutual enemies, the Seminole Indians," he said, I expect your cooperation. Anything less will be judged by me "as a hostile act on your part." It is interesting that here Jackson regarded the Spanish as American "allies" in the war against the Seminoles.

The letter had all the arrogance and insolence of Andrew Jackson at his worst. But Masot chose not to take offense. Still he took a firm stand. He declared that he would permit passage of the transports this one time, provided the usual custom duties were paid; but in the future he insisted that Jackson apply to the proper authorities for permission to enter and transit across Spanish territory.[7]

As Jackson and his army headed northeast from Fort Gadsden toward a hostile Mikasukian village, his advanced spy company ran into and attacked a small party of Indians, who put up a spirited fight. Jackson immediately extended his flank columns so as to encircle the party. Realizing what was happening, the hostiles quickly retreated. Old Hickory pressed forward and occupied a number of Mikasukian towns. The next day he scoured the countryside to secure whatever supplies were available, at the same time reducing to ashes all the villages he captured. He estimated that nearly three hundred houses were destroyed, while his men confiscated "the greatest abundance of corn cattle &c brought in." He also destroyed all the Negro plantations he found along the Apalachicola.

In the "Council houses" of the "King" of the Mikasukians he discovered more than fifty scalps; "and in the center of the public square, the old red stick's standard, *A Red Pole,* was erected, crowned with scalps, recognized by the hair, as torn from the heads of the unfortunate companions of [Lieutenant Richard W.] Scott," who had commanded the boat the Indians had ambushed along the shore of the Apalachicola River.[8]

The presence of "A Red Pole" was a clear indication that the hostiles who had fled to Florida, following their defeat at Horseshoe Bend, believed that they were continuing their war against the Americans. As far as they were concerned, they had joined the Seminoles to carry on the war. To them what whites called the First Seminole War was actually the second part of the ongoing Creek War.

Such quibbles did not concern Jackson. Whatever the war was called, he was intent on pacifying the southern frontier by subduing the Indians and expelling the Spanish. But a problem arose because there were both friendly and hostile Creeks living along the frontier, and this situation made it almost impossible to distinguish between them. Consequently, the mere "sight of an Indian," wrote the governor of Alabama, William Bibb, "creates among the [white] women and children the most frightful apprehensions." And such apprehensions usually produced bloodshed.[9]

Another matter of concern was the presence of runaway slaves who had escaped their masters and found refuge with the Seminoles and aided them in their attacks on white settlers. They even infiltrated Spanish towns, Jackson said, especially St. Marks. Which was another reason why he directed his army toward that fortress.

After sloughing through a wet and swampy terrain, he arrived at St. Marks on the evening of April 6 and immediately wrote to Don Francisco Caso y Luengo, the commandant of its fort, informing him that he had invaded Florida at the President's direction, and had "penetrated to the Mekasukian towns & reduced them to ashes." These "Barbarians" have fled to your fortress for protection, he charged, and I have reliable evidence from the governor of Pensacola that they demanded ammunition from you with a threat of taking possession of the fort if you refused; that, in fact, because of "your defenceless state, they were already in possession of St. Marks." In addition, Jackson said he had captured the wife of Chief Chennabee of Fowltown, who assured him that in the past the "Indians & Negroes" had obtained their ammunition from St. Marks. "To prevent the recurrance of so gross a violation of neutrality & to exclude our savage Enemies from so strong a hold as St Marks, I deem it expedient to garrison that fortress with American troops, until the close of the present war." This can be justified, he said, "on that immutable principal of self defence." Under the circumstances Jackson wanted it understood that he expected "that every facility will be afforded by the Agents of the King of Spain to chastise these lawless & inhuman savages. . . . I came not as the Enemy but as the Friend of Spain. Spanish rights, and property will be respected." He needed St. Marks, he added, as a depot to ensure the success of his operations. Later their two governments could work out the problem of his occupation and resolve whatever difficulties arose over his actions.

To give Jackson his due, he certainly knew how to put a legal face on illegal actions. He kept up the charade that Spain and the United States were allied in their war against the Seminoles and he presumed that Spain would do whatever was necessary to help him defeat their common foe.

Since "our mutual savage enemies" were concentrating their forces "near or on the Suwaney," he wrote, a prompt answer, with an English translation ("as neither myself nor staff are acquainted with the Spanish") was requested. Jackson ended this incredible letter by asking the commandant for the loan of a "small vessel" so he could communicate with three schooners carrying supplies for his army that had arrived in the Bay of St. Marks on April 2.[10]

Luengo responded in an extremely cordial manner, maintaining the pretense that he and Jackson were somehow allies. He congratulated the general on his recent victories over the Indians and assured him of his good wishes on the ultimate success of his mission. But he emphatically contradicted the testimony of Chief Chennabee's wife. The Indians and Negroes, he said, had not received ammunition from his fort, nor had they taken possession of it. As for Jackson occupying his fort, the commandant explained his concern about the difficulties he would face with his government if he complied without proper authorization. To obviate those difficulties, "I shall immediately solicit" that permission. Until he received it he hoped "your excellency will desist from your intention." Rather, he added, such troops as Jackson thought convenient to leave in this vicinity could assist him in the defense of the fort, all accomplished with "good faith and harmony" without the necessity of formal occupation. "Most excellent sir," he concluded, "I kiss your excellency's hands."[11]

Jackson's response to this reply was brusque and to the point. "The occupation of St. Marks is essential to the accomplishment of my campaign." The Indians and Negroes are planning to take the fort the moment my army moves from this vicinity; and the retaking of the fort would "cost me more American blood than I am disposed should be shed. Success to my operations requires despatch; you will excuse me, therefore, in refusing your request" to wait until you obtain permission from your government. St. Marks must "be immediately occupied by American troops."[12]

Jackson had allowed this "negotiation" to take place in the hope that the commandant would yield without question to his demand. Convinced now that the Spaniard was stalling, "I hesitated" no longer, "and as I could not be received in friendship, I entered the fort by violence." On April 7, two light companies of the 7th Regiment and one of the 4th were "ordered to advance, lower the Spanish colors, and hoist the star-spangled banner on the ramparts of Fort St. Marks." The Spanish garrison offered no resistance and the order was promptly executed.

On entering St. Marks, Jackson later reported, he found "evidence of the duplicity & unfriendly feelings of the commandant." He also found that "savage Enemies of the U.States" had been permitted entrance into the town and that the chiefs had held councils in the commandant's own quarters. In addition, he discovered "that the Spanish Store Houses had been appropriated to the use & were then filled with goods belonging to the hostile party—That Cattle knowingly plundered from the Citizens of the U. States had been contracted for & purchased by the Officers of the Garrison from the Spanish theieves—That foreign agents had free access within the wall of St. Marks."[13]

Once in command of the town, Jackson ordered an inventory of Spanish property "taken and receipted for," after which he assured the commandant that his rights and private property would be respected. Transports were obtained and Luengo and his "family and command" were dispatched to Pensacola. "Sodom and Gomorrow are destroyed," Jackson informed his wife.[14]

Jackson was disappointed to find St. Marks empty of hostiles, but he did discover and arrest that "noted Scotch villain Arbuthnot who has not only excited but fomented a continuance of the war." Worse, he was "an inmate of the family of the Spanish Commandant." Here was another example of Spanish "duplicity."

What was he doing in this country? Arbuthnot was asked. What was he doing as "an inmate in the commandants family"? What were his relations with the hostiles?

Whatever the old man's response, it justified "a suspicion that his views were not honest," and so Jackson clapped him in irons "untill evidence of his guilt" could be gathered. Obviously poor Arbuthnot was already judged to be guilty and all Old Hickory needed was physical evidence of his guilt before hanging him.

Another important capture resulted on April 3 when Captain Isaac McKeever, a U.S. naval commander cruising the coast at Jackson's request, lured two important Red Sticks aboard his ship by flying the British flag: the prophet, Josiah Francis (or Hillis Hadjo), and Himollemico, who had reputedly led the attack on Lieutenant Richard W. Scott's boat. Josiah Francis carried on his person a commission as brigadier general in the British army, a rifle, and a snuffbox presented by the Prince Regent. The two hostiles thought they had found allies when they boarded the ship and expected to obtain ammunition and powder. Instead they found a rope. Sharp Knife hanged them on April 8.[15]

After they were cut down, the general was asked about disposing of the bodies. "Shall they be thrown into the river?" he was asked.

"No," Jackson replied, "they have ceased to be enemies, let them be buried as decently as our means will admit of. See that it is done."[16]

Jackson had also hoped to get his hands on Peter McQueen, one of the most daring and intrepid leaders of the hostile Creeks who had been captured at Tallapoosa back in April 1814 but had managed to escape. Once more, however,

McQueen eluded Jackson, so the general decided to head for Bowlegs Towns on the Suwannee River, approximately one hundred miles to the east.

The warrior leader Chief Bowlegs, a Hitchitee, was a brother of King Payne, who had been killed in 1812, and the uncle of such later chiefs as Billy Bowlegs and Micanopy. He had moved the Indians from the Alachua area around present-day Gainesville to the Suwannee at the end of the Patriot War of 1812–1813 when Americans from Georgia attempted to seize east Florida. Jackson understood that Bowlegs was the recognized chief of the towns along the Suwannee River and that these towns sheltered many runaway slaves, along with a large contingent of Indians who belonged to the powerful Alachua branch of the Seminole alliance. But the route to the towns led through a flat and swampy wilderness.

On the morning of April 9, Jackson swung his army out of St. Marks with only eight days' rations, and on the following day he was joined by more Tennessee volunteers and the Creeks under McIntosh, whom he had left to scour the countryside around the Mikasukian area. Although the weather was dry and pleasant, the army still had to wade through sheets of water that soaked them to the skin. This plus the depth of the swamps and the shortage of forage "occasioned the horses to give out daily in great numbers."

On the morning of April 12 at a place called Natural Bridge on the Ecofina River, they came upon a party of Indians along the rim of a swamp. McIntosh and his Indian allies, plus about fifty Tennesseans, attacked and routed the Seminoles, killing thirty-seven warriors and capturing six men and ninety-seven women and children. A white woman who had been taken prisoner "at the massacre of Scott" was also found in the group. In addition, McIntosh's Creeks captured some horses and about five hundred head of cattle that had belonged to Peter McQueen. But once more, the wily prophet eluded Jackson and disappeared into the swamps.

The general's disappointment at failing to capture McQueen prompted an old Indian woman to offer to exchange the prophet for the right of allowing her people to be "carried to the upper tribes of the Creek nation, and there provisioned until they could raise their own crops." If Jackson would agree, the woman declared, McQueen would be "tied and carried to the commandant of St. Marks." Without a moment's hesitation, Sharp Knife agreed, and, he said, she appeared "much pleased with these terms." He set her free with written instructions to the commandant of St. Marks concerning the agreement. "Having received no further intelligence from McQueen, I am induced to believe the old woman has complied with her part of the obligation," he wrote. Actually she was never heard from again, and McQueen avoided capture and probably died around 1820.[17]

But the Bowlegs Towns were still Jackson's immediate objective, and he pressed forward, despite the swamps and "the continued sheets of water" that hampered his progress. On the morning of April 15 his scouts surprised a small party of Seminoles and killed one warrior and captured a man, a woman, and two children. He was approximately twelve miles from his objective.

That night he encamped and issued a general order to his troops. The order accompanied his plan for the "attack on the negroes and Bowlegs Towns," and he wanted every man to act as a soldier and not willfully kill women and children but "to recollect we war with savages who have without mercy torn the locks from the head of the aged matron down to the infant babe. These are the wretches who should feel the avenging rod." Also the soldiers were forbidden to "touch any of the supplies in the enemy's towns" until after the attack had ended.[18]

Early the next morning the army set out for the Bowlegs Towns with the expectation that they would reach their objective by 1:00 P.M. But much to Jackson's regret, after marching sixteen miles they reached a "remarkable pond" at 3:00 P.M. that was still six miles from the Towns. He would have camped for the night had not six mounted Indians discovered his presence, escaped capture, and presumably rushed away to inform other hostiles of his presence. So he hurried forward by forced marches to complete his mission. Around sunset he reached his objective, formed his lines, and put them in motion. His left flank, consisting of the 2nd Regiment of Tennessee volunteers commanded by Colonel Thomas Williamson and a portion of friendly Creeks under Colonel Noble Kennard, who was a Hitchitee chief and had signed the Treaty of Fort Jackson, commenced the attack. At the center, which Jackson himself commanded, he stationed the Georgia militia, regulars, and the volunteer Kentucky and Tennessee guards. The right column consisted of the 1st Regiment of Tennessee volunteers under Colonel Robert H. Dyer and part of the friendly Indians under McIntosh, who were expected to cut off the hostiles' retreat at the western side of the river.

Several hundred Negro warriors put up a stiff resistance but could not match the Americans' firepower and finally retreated and crossed the river. Jackson guessed that Dyer and the friendly Creeks "did them considerable injury." The following day, nine Negroes and two Indians were found dead, and two other Negroes were captured.

The remaining Seminoles vanished into the wilderness, and although Jackson sent Gaines with a strong detachment of men across the river in pursuit, the enemy completely disappeared. Their flight had been so precipitous, Jackson reported, that a "great quantity of goods, corn &c." was discovered strewn through the swamps. In all, the army gathered a large quantity of corn, about thirty head of cattle, and many horses.[19]

Old Hickory scoured the swamps for six miles beyond the Suwannee River without locating the main body of hostiles. Most probably the Indians divided into small parties and hid in remote areas. Eventually they retreated to the Alachua country, the lakes in north central Forida, or to Tampa Bay. For the next several days the Americans looted and burned what was probably Suwannee Old Town on the west bank of the river. They burned more than three hundred houses.[20]

On the evening of April 18, while the troops gathered around campfires and exchanged gossip about the likelihood of their returning home now that the war seemed to be over, the swaggering former marine Robert C. Ambrister, together with Peter B. Cook, a recently dismissed employee of Arbuthnot's, and several others, but not including Woodbine, strode into the town, totally unaware that their Seminole friends had decamped and that General Andrew Jackson and his army now occupied the site. They were instantly seized. On the person of one of the prisoners was found a letter from Arbuthnot to his son, John, who worked at his father's store on the river, warning him of Jackson's approach. Now Sharp Knife understood how the Seminoles had managed to escape his grasp and how they had succeeded in taking their families and much of their supplies with them. He erupted in anger.

Both Ambrister and Cook soon realized the seriousness of their situation and decided to cooperate with their captors in the hope of winning clemency. They revealed that Arbuthnot's schooner, *Chance,* was moored at the mouth of the Suwannee River preparing to sail for Tampa Bay. At the suggestion of his aide, Lieutenant Gadsden, the general quickly agreed to send him with a detachment of soldiers down the river to seize the ship, thereby providing needed transport to St. Marks for his sick and wounded soldiers.

Without appreciable difficulty, Gadsden captured the *Chance,* where he discovered additional documents that convinced Jackson, when he read them, that both Arbuthnot and Ambrister were involved in "corrupt transactions" and should be tried for their "crimes" by a "Special Court of Select officers."[21] The documents also "involved the british Government in the Agency."

Jackson promptly informed Secretary Calhoun of this evidence. "I hope the execution of these two unprincipled villains," he wrote, "will prove an awfull example to the world." As for Great Britain, he would leave that matter to the administration and would forward the incriminating papers to the secretary as soon as practicable.[22]

For Jackson the Seminole War was over "for the present." He had destroyed the Bowlegs Towns along the Suwannee; burned the Mikasuki village near Tallahassee, which was perhaps the largest Seminole settlement in Florida, along with hundreds of other Indian dwellings; "confiscated" their food supplies and driven them into the swamps, where he believed they would starve; captured Arbuthnot and Ambrister; executed Josiah Francis and Himollemico; and taken possession of St. Marks, which he called "the hot bed" of the war and the source of foreign interference in frontier affairs. What more was necessary to end the war? Should it be renewed, he told Calhoun, it would take only "a small party to put it down promptly." He therefore intended to turn around and head back to the Apalachicola, where he would clear out a group of Red Sticks who he had heard had assembled west of the river and were being "fed and supplied by the Governor of Pensacola." Thereafter, if the government did not require anything further from him, he would return home to Nashville "to regain my health." Like his troops he felt quite ill and in desperate need of rest. Already he had ordered the Georgia troops back to Hartford, where they would be mustered, paid, and discharged.[23]

Indeed, it had been an exhausting and frustrating tour of duty, and Jackson was anxious to quit Florida before the onset of what he called "the sickly season." It was now early May, and already the weather was becoming unbearably hot and humid.

So Jackson and his army departed the Bowlegs Towns and headed west for St. Marks, which he reached in five days, a distance of 107 miles. After further assessing his situation he sent out a detachment of troops to scour the area where the Red Sticks had reportedly assembled. He ordered that the Indians be received "as Friends if disposed to surrender, or inflict merited chastisement if still hostile."[24]

Of immediate concern were the two British prisoners, Alexander A. Arbuthnot and Robert C. Ambrister, and he wasted little time in turning them over for trial to a special court of thirteen officers, presided over by General Gaines. The court convened on April 26 and heard three charges against Arbuthnot: "exciting and stirring up the Creek Indians to war against the United States"; acting as a spy for the Indians and supplying them with arms; and "exciting the Indians to murder two American traders, William Hambly and Edmund Doyle." The court denied its jurisdiction on the third charge and it was dropped. As to the other two charges, documentary evidence was presented that counted heavily against the defendant. Straightaway Arbuthnot's letter to his son, John, was submitted. In it the trader declared that Jackson with an army of over three thousand men was headed for the Suwannee towns and he wanted his son to cross the river and save as many skins, books, and other goods as possible but to abandon the corn. "Tell my friend Bowleck that it is throwing away his people to attempt to resist such a powerful force."[25] As far as the court was concerned, this letter alone proved that Arbuthnot had assisted the Seminoles in their escape from Jackson's approaching army.

Other evidence was presented indicating that Arbuthnot had advised the Creek chief Little Prince not to comply with the Treaty of Fort Jackson, that he had supplied the Indians with arms, and that he had corresponded with British officials as the agent of the Indians, having received their power of attorney.

Arbuthnot spoke in his own defense. The evidence that he advised Little Prince was hearsay, he argued, and his letter to his son was meant to get him out of harm's way. However, he did admit to selling kegs of powder to Bowlegs, but insisted they were meant to aid the Indians in obtaining food, not killing Americans. He was calm and dignified, and he ended his argument with the hope that the court would "lean on the side of mercy."[26]

There were two charges against Ambrister: "aiding, abetting, and comforting the enemy, supplying them with means of war"; and "leading and commanding the Lower Creeks in carrying on a war against the United States." Again, documentary evidence was submitted. In a letter to Governor Cameron, Ambrister had said that Josiah Francis and "all the Indian chiefs" had asked him to tell the Prince Regent in England "that they are at war with the Americans" and "ask for his assistance." They "beg your excellency will be as expeditious as possible. Your excellency is the only dependence they have, and who the Prince Regent told them would give them every assistance that lay in your power." In another letter, written in his own hand, Ambrister acknowledged that he had sent a party of Indians to attack the invading American army.

To these charges Ambrister pleaded not guilty to the first, and "guilty and justification" to the second. Then he threw himself on the "mercy of this honorable court."

Several witnesses testified, and after a short deliberation verdicts were returned on April 28. By a two-thirds vote the court found Arbuthnot guilty and ordered that between the hours of eight and nine o'clock in the morning he be "suspended by the neck, with a rope, until he is *dead.*" Ambrister was also found guilty and it was ordered that he "be shot to *death*" at the same hour.[27]

Then one of the members of the court requested a reconsideration of the vote on Ambrister, with the result that they changed the punishment to "fifty stripes on his bare back" and confinement "with a ball and chain to hard labor for twelve calendar months." And with that the court adjourned.

On the evening of the same day the Hero of New Orleans approved the sentence of Arbuthnot and the first sentence of Ambrister. They were both to be executed. Jackson believed without question that Ambrister was the "successor" of George Woodbine, "that unfeeling monster" who was responsible for the deaths of many innocent women and children; also that he had participated in a war against the United States and had thereby forfeited his allegiance to his country. He was nothing but an outlaw and pirate and deserved to be shot. At the appointed hour on April 29 the executions of both men took place.[28]

Jackson's behavior in this situation reflects frontier fears, bigotry, and hatred at their worst. The Seminole War was over, or so he said, and he was dealing with two foreign nationals whose fate was really not up to him to decide, and certainly not by a "special court." And the case against the two men was weak. Although Ambrister had pleaded guilty to one charge, the court had decided to let him off with twelve months of hard labor and fifty lashes. What gave Jackson the right to reverse it? That question was asked again and again in the succeeding months.

By right the entire matter should have been referred to Washington. Jackson as commanding general of American forces might have at least consulted with his superiors. But no; he in his usual arbitrary manner had decided that these men were guilty of unspeakable crimes in inciting the "Negroes & Indians in East Florida to war against the U States," and that their punishment was fully merited. "The proceedings of the Court martial in this case," he informed Calhoun, ". . . presents scenes of wickedness, corruption, and barbarity at which the heart sickens." He said he hoped the executions would "convince the Government of Great Britain as well as her subjects that certain, if slow retribution awaits those unchristian wretches who by false promises delude and excite a Indian tribe to all the horrid deeds of savage war."[29]

The execution of two British subjects on foreign soil by a seemingly out-of-control military chieftain raised once again the fear that another "Napoleon" had arrived in the New World to extinguish liberty and ride roughshod over the rights of American citizens. As a matter of fact, the Spanish called Jackson "the Napoleon of the woods." It certainly seemed that the general knew no law but his own. Both houses of Congress agreed to look into the matter and formed the usual committees to investigate and report their findings.[30]

Still Jackson believed he had more than enough evidence to confirm that the British not only incited Indians to make war on the United States but supplied them with munitions. Thus, the two British "miscreants" who were parties to this violation of American sovereignty deserved what he had meted out.

And the Spanish were equally guilty. They did nothing—they were really helpless—to police Florida, and because of their inattention to their treaty obligations allowed the "savages" to acquire supplies within their towns to carry on their war against the United States. As long as Florida remained in Spanish hands, and as long as the British had free access to the peninsula, Jackson felt, the United States was subject to constant Indian warfare and possible invasion. He therefore declared, "by the immutable laws of self defence," that he was justified in executing Arbuthnot and Ambrister and seizing St. Marks.

Old Hickory soon gave his critics even more evidence of his frightening arrogance. He had initially decided to return to Nashville to recover his health now that the Seminole War had ended and had so informed the secretary of war. But he changed his mind. It was fully four months since he had suggested to the President that he seize Florida, which he knew to be Monroe's real objective, and in all that time he had not received a single hint that the administration disapproved such a plan. In fact he said he had positive if indirect evidence that his idea had been approved. In all the fighting and burning of villages and killing of "Negroes & Indians," Spanish authority still existed in East Florida. True, St. Marks had been taken, but the Spanish governor of Florida remained in Pensacola waiting to reassert what little control he had over the entire province once the American army recrossed the border.

Jackson decided to act. Prior to his expedition to the Bowlegs Towns he had communicated with the governor, Colonel José Masot, asking permission for American supply ships from New Orleans to pass freely up the Escambia River to Fort Crawford, and Masot had refused. If you want supplies, the governor said, you can obtain a Spanish vessel in Pensacola and pay the required duties, just like everyone else.[31] That response was not what Jackson wished to hear, and it no doubt infuriated him. It didn't help his frame of mind that there were rumors that Indians had "free access" to Pensacola, that they were kept advised of all Jackson's movements, that they were regularly supplied "with ammunition & munitions of war," and that large numbers of them were presently congre-

gating in the town and staging raiding parties into Alabama where "eighteen settlers fell by the tomahawk."[32]

If the Spanish remained in Florida, thought Jackson, the Indians would again
raise "the War hatchet" the moment he and his army left for Tennessee. Under
the circumstances Jackson decided he had no choice but to seize Pensacola and
completely extinguish Spanish rule in Florida.

At daybreak on April 29, the very day the two British subjects were executed,
Old Hickory swung out of St. Marks with an army of twelve hundred regulars
and volunteers, leaving two hundred men to garrison the fort, and headed for
Fort Gadsden. He had gone hardly a half-dozen miles when he received a letter
from General Thomas Glascock of the Georgia militia that convulsed him with
anger.

It seems that Governors William W. Bibb of Alabama and William Rabun of
Georgia had ordered out soldiers to protect their respective frontiers, and Rabun
had given Captain Obed Wright command of an expedition against the reputedly hostile villages of Chiefs Hopony and Phelemme near the Flint River.
Learning that Hopony had moved to a Chehaw village, Wright led his troops to
the village on April 22, massacred women and children and a chief named
Howard who was an uncle of General William McIntosh, and burned the town,
without knowing that the Chehaws were Jackson's allies and under his protection. In addition these Indians had fed Old Hickory's half-starved soldiers on
their march from Tennessee through Georgia, and many of the young warriors
from the village had enlisted in his army.[33]

Little Prince immediately complained to the Indian agent and described
what had happened. "The white people came and killed one of the head men,
and five men and a woman, and burnt all their houses. All our young men have
gone to war with General Jackson, and there is only a few left to guard the town,
and they have come and served us this way. As you are our friend and father, I
hope you will try and find out, and get us satisfaction for it. . . . Men do not get
up and do this mischief without there is some one at the head of it, and we want
you to try and find them out."[34]

The explosion that erupted out of Jackson when he read the letter ricocheted
around the country. Here the Chehaws had fed his men, given their warriors to
help him defeat the hostiles, and accepted Sharp Knife's protection against their
enemies, and what was their reward? American soldiers had rained destruction
on them and their village and proved once again the treachery of the white man.

Jackson felt dishonored, betrayed. He immediately ordered the arrest of

Wright and sent a company of Tennesseans to apprehend him and convey him in chains to Fort Hawkins, where he was to be kept in close confinement until a court-martial could be assembled. At the same time the general fired off a blistering letter to Rabun that must have scorched the governor's eyeballs when he read it. In it he called the attack "base, cowardly and inhuman." The warriors of that village were "with me, fighting the battles of our *country* against the common enemy." Only "a cowardly monster in human Shape" could kill Chief Howard, "a Superanuated Indian chief worn down with age" who carried the flag of truce. That a governor of a state would presume to wage war against an Indian tribe at peace and under the protection of the United States is monstrous. "I trust you will be able to excuse to the Government of the U. States, to which you will have to answer. . . . This act will to the last ages fix a Stain upon the character of Georgia."[35]

Realizing the Chehaws might imitate what occurred with the Hillabees in the Creek War and bring a fresh outbreak of violence along the frontier, Jackson sent them a "talk," explaining how grief-stricken he was on hearing the news of their betrayal and what he intended to do about it.

"Friends and Brothers," he wrote, the "news fills my heart with regret, and my eyes with tears. . . . I promised you protection; I promised you the protection and fostering friendship of the United States. . . . I did not suppose there was any American so base as not to respect a flag, but I find I was mistaken. . . . I have ordered Captain Wright to be arrested and put in iron" until the President "makes known his will.

"Friends and Brothers: Return to your village; there you shall be protected." Wright will be punished and "you shall also be paid for your houses and other property that have been destroyed; but you must not attempt to take satisfaction yourselves." Do not permit your people to kill any whites, he warned. That will only bring down destruction on you. "Justice shall be done to you; you must remain in peace and friendship with the United States. . . . I am your friend and brother, Andrew Jackson."[36]

Wright was duly apprehended, but in the long hassle over jurisdiction between military and civilian authorities in the case he managed to flee the country and reach Havana, Cuba. The Indians received an indemnity of $8,000 as compensation for the destruction of their homes and property. As for the dispute between Jackson and Rabun, the Monroe administration, as usual, ducked away from the problem and eventually it faded away.

Jackson continued his march toward Pensacola as he fired off these orders and letters and talks, wading through water that brought on coughing spasms, he said, but did not slow the pace of his advance. He boasted that he was able to walk twenty-five miles a day even though he was emaciated and in desperate need of rest.[37]

He also peppered José Masot with letters, listing the complaints he had recited to Calhoun. Masot either denied the charges or explained them away. The supplies provided to Indian women and children consist of wood, fish, and "other trifling objects," he contended, certainly not weapons of war. As for the "few unarmed and miserable" Indians in Pensacola, they are not hostile toward the United States, as proved by the fact that Americans live among them without being "insulted or molested." With respect to supplies being carried up to Fort Crawford "there will, in future, be no difficulty."[38]

Jackson rejected the response, repeated his charges, and warned Masot of the consequences if he did not allow him free access into the city. This is the third time American troops have had occasion to enter Pensacola, he wrote, and "this time it must be held until Spain has the power or will to maintain her neutrality." Understand me, he continued; "my resolution is fixed—& I have strength enough to enforce it."

Masot roared back at him. "I protest, as an infringement and insult offered" to His Catholic Majesty, and I order you to "leave the boundaries." You have "violated the Spanish territory," and if you proceed, "I will repulse you force to force" and the "effusion of blood" that will result will be on your head. "You will therefore be responsible before God & Man for the consequences."

Why do you persist in your resistance to my demands, Jackson replied, when you do not have the military strength to protect yourself and the people of the town against my army of thousands? If you surrender peaceably all Spanish persons and property will be protected. "If the peacable surrender be refused, I shall enter Pensacola by violence and assume the Government." The blood that will be shed "will rest on your head. Before God & man you will be responsible."[39]

"I protest before God and man that my conduct is blameless," Masot screamed back at him. Those "who resist aggressions, can never be considered an aggressor."[40]

Jackson had had enough of this senseless bickering, and on May 24 he and his army arrived at Pensacola and swept aside the token effort at resistance made by the Spanish. Masot had already retreated to Fort Carlos de Barrancas outside Pensacola, so Jackson sent a note to Luis Piernas, who now commanded the town, and told him that he had been informed that Piernas had orders to fire upon his troops seeking to obtain supplies from an American ship anchored in the bay. "I wish you to understand distinctly," he wrote, "that if such orders are carried into effect, I will put to death every man found in arms."[41]

The town was easily occupied, the Spanish flag hauled down, and Spanish authority extinguished. Again Jackson called on Masot to surrender Barrancas, and when the Spaniard refused the general fired on it with a nine-pounder and an eight-inch howitzer battery. A spirited fire was kept up throughout the morning of May 27 and intermittently during the afternoon. By that time Jackson was prepared to mount the walls and had his ladders ready. The garrison saw what was happening, and, fearful of a night attack, decided to surrender. A white flag suddenly broke out over the fort, and the governor and the garrison capitulated. The terms of the surrender amounted "to a complete cession to the u states of that portion of the Floridas hitherto under the government of Don Josse Massot."

Old Hickory found three hundred men guarding the fort. "This number of americans," he later boasted, "could have kept it from combined Urope."[42]

He then issued a proclamation to the inhabitants of the town and assured them that the seizure of the province did not emanate from any desire to extend the territory of the United States or out of any hatred toward the Spanish government. This was a war to end "the horrors of savage massacre." The United States felt compelled to take possession of those parts of Florida where Spanish authority could not be maintained. He reaffirmed his pledge to the people that their property would be respected and protected. Spanish laws would continue to operate with respect to property and "free toleration to all religions guaranteed." Then he announced the establishment of a provisional government with Colonel William King as civil and military governor of Pensacola with authority to enforce U.S. revenue laws. Captain Gadsden would act as collector. Finally, the archives of the province would be brought under American custody.[43]

With the capture of the old Negro Fort (now Fort Gadsden) and Fort St. Marks and Fort Carlos de Barrancas, the destruction of many Indian villages, the killing of a number of important chiefs, the executions of the foreign agitators Arbuthnot and Ambrister, the destruction of Spanish authority in Florida, and the establishment of a provisional government, Jackson was convinced that he had fulfilled his obligations to his country and completed his assignment as commanding general. East Florida, as he had promised, was now an American possession. "I view the Possession of the Floridas," he told the President, "Essential to the peace & security of the frontier, and the future wellfare of our country."

One thing more, he said. Fort St. Augustine, the only vestige of the Spanish presence in Florida, and Cuba are also essential to "the security of our southern frontier and to our commerce in a state of war, and can be taken by a Coup de' Main whenever thought necessary." Give me the 5th Infantry and a twenty-two-gun brig and I will take Fort St. Augustine in short order. Give me another regiment and a frigate and "I will insure you cuba in a few days."[44]

Having gotten that off his chest, he then reported his military operations to Secretary Calhoun. "The Seminole War," he said, "may now be considered at a close."[45]

Chapter 10

Despoiling the Chickasaws

As the general headed for home he wrote to his wife and told her that he was emaciated, had a bad cough from "so much exposed wading waters" and traveling on foot some twenty-five miles each day, and was utterly exhausted. But he boasted that his troops were very healthy, that in the entire campaign only three men had been lost in battle, one more from sickness, two by drowning, and one by accidental shooting. When he reached Columbia, Tennessee, on June 26 he discharged the Tennessee volunteers. He himself arrived home in Nashville on June 28 amid wild celebrations.

The American people had never before had a hero like Andrew Jackson. He continually brought glory to his country by demonstrating its military might. England and Spain had been toppled once again by the sons of freedom led by an all-conquering hero. "I have destroyed the babylon of the South," he trumpeted.[1]

Actually he did more than that. He caused an international incident that could have resulted in a war with England or Spain or both. His high-handed dealings with Spanish and English nationals, according to several critical newspapers, were outrageous. What right did a "military chieftain" have to execute two men without proper legal authorization? What right did he have to seize Florida, establish a government, and install military officers to run the operation? Killing Indians was one thing, but jeopardizing the peace of this nation was something else again.

The British minister to the United States, Charles Bagot, informed Secretary of State John Quincy Adams that his government would have a formal response over the executions of its nationals and requested the proceedings of the trial.

He could not imagine any "possible circumstance which would warrant their execution" but was willing to withhold comment until he read the transcripts. Adams assured the minister that the United States government had not authorized the trial, that it was totally "unexpected."[2]

Luis de Onís, the Spanish minister, was not so easily put off. Starting on June 17, he peppered Adams with protests over Jackson's actions. He told the secretary that his country had seriously considered signing a treaty with the United States that would have relinquished East Florida, but not now. Not when the honor of Spain had been so deeply offended by this most "unfortunate incident." Even the French minister, Hyde de Neuville, called on the secretary and "in a very grave tone, shaking his head," said, "it was a very disagreeable affair."[3]

Monroe had no stomach for this kind of unpleasantness. He was caught between a highly sensitive and very popular general who was quick to take offense at any criticism of his actions and foreign governments who would demand an explanation, if not an apology and compensation, for what had happened in Florida. So he ducked away from the dilemma by departing for his farm in Loudoun County, Virginia, and did not return until mid-July.

Secretary of War Calhoun was "extremely dissatisfied with General Jackson's proceedings in Florida," according to Adams. He believed that Old Hickory hoped to start a war with Spain and then command "an expedition against Mexico." Something had to be done to put the general in his place and remind him that civil, not military, authority ran the country. He wanted Jackson censured, and he had considerable support among the other members of the cabinet.[4]

Except for John Quincy Adams. Adams defended the action, and when the full cabinet met to address the problem, he argued in the general's favor. What resulted from the meeting was a recommendation that Monroe either return Florida and censure Jackson or retain the country and defend his general.

But Monroe preferred a third way. He would refuse to defend Jackson or take responsibility for what had happened, and at the same time he would assure the Spanish that his administration had not authorized the action but that military circumstances necessitated the seizure of St. Marks and Pensacola because of Spain's inability to police its colony and prevent Indian depredations along the frontier.

At this juncture, Monroe finally communicated with Jackson. Six months had elapsed since the general had suggested using Rhea as a conduit for authorization to seize Florida. Now, on July 19, he undertook the sensitive task of speaking to a man whose pride, temper, and inflated sense of his rights as a citizen and general had to be scrupulously observed with soothing words of support and appreciation. And Monroe failed miserably. He opened his remarks by declaring that in his position he must take "a comprehensive view of the whole subject," examine all the circumstances and all the "dangers to which this measure is exposed . . . and all the good" that might result from it. "In transcending the limit prescribed by [your] orders," he wrote, "you acted on your own responsibility." In attacking Spanish posts you in effect declared war, a power reserved exclusively to Congress under the Constitution.[5]

Jackson chose not to take offense. He had no problem with accepting responsibility. "Responsibility is not feared by me if the General good requires its assumption. I never have shrunk from it, and never will." But in his reply to Monroe he denied that he had transcended orders. The order of December 26, 1817, was comprehensive, he said, and provided him with the fullest authority in conducting the campaign. You ought to know, he sarcastically added, that "*all the acts* of the inferior are the acts of the Superior—and in no way, can the subordinate officer be impeached for his measures." Jackson seemed to be repeating what Monroe's enemies had said so many times in the past, namely that the President sometimes acted as though he "hasn't got brains enough to hold his hat on."

What Monroe did not seem to understand, and something Jackson repeated again and again to him, as well as to the secretary of war and to others, was the fact that American citizens on the frontier were being massacred and would continue to be massacred unless United States troops were present to protect them. Once the troops were "withdrawn we will soon see our frontier again deluged in blood, and Penssa. garrisoned by British troops, conjointly with Spanish, and to regain it will cost much blood and treasure." Florida must remain in U.S. hands, he insisted, and the Indians be made aware that we will destroy them and burn their villages if they continue to attack American settlements. Common sense and the "immutable laws of self defence" dictate this policy.[6]

For his part, Calhoun wrote to Jackson and admitted that a war with Spain "would be nothing"; but such a war would in a short time become "an English war. In such a war, I would not fear for the fate of our country; but certainly, if it can be prudently and honorably avoided for the present, it ought to be." We need time, he said, time to grow, perfect our fortifications, enlarge our navy, and pay our debts. Surely the general understood what he meant.[7]

From the secretary's letters and his subsequent behavior, Jackson assumed that Calhoun supported his position and defended his actions. In fact, the secretary wrote him in early September stating that "I concur in the view which you have taken in relation to the importance of Florida to the effectual peace and security of our Southern frontier, and such, I believe, is the opinion of every member of the administration." He assured the general that St. Marks would be retained until Spain could garrison it with sufficient troops. Fort Gadsden "and any other position in East or West Florida within the Indian Country" would be retained, he said, "so long as there is any danger" or risk to U.S. security. Not until years later did Jackson learn of Calhoun's real feelings about his actions. As for Monroe, Jackson said he had no desire "to injure" the President "unless impelled in my own defence." But "when my country is deprived of all the benefits resulting from my acts I will not consent to bear . . . responsibility that ought to be those of another. My situation is . . . delicate, I must for the present be silent."[8]

A wise decision. He had more to gain by keeping his mouth shut. Already the American people were beginning to show "a general display of approbation" for his actions in Florida.[9] Wherever he traveled there were celebrations to honor his presence. Ordinary citizens seemed determined to show by their demonstrations how much they admired and revered him, how much they appreciated what he had done for them. In countless cities the toasts raised on July 4 saluted his heroism and service to the country. Surely the administration and Congress would get the message sooner or later.[10]

Indeed, thanks in large measure to the efforts of John Quincy Adams, the Spanish understood their predicament and the likely consequences if they retained their troublesome colony, and on February 22, 1819, agreed to cede to the United States all the territories east of the Mississippi River known as East and West Florida for $5 million in assumed claims against Spain. It took two more years to win ratification of the treaty, during which time Pensacola and St. Marks were returned to Spain, but this was accomplished by both countries on February 22, 1821.[11]

As for the British, they were so anxious to cultivate the friendship of the United States and exploit the ever-growing American market, and they were so convinced by the evidence Richard Rush, the U.S. minister in London, submitted to Lord Castlereagh concerning the guilt of Arbuthnot and Ambrister, that they lodged no protest, nor did they demand satisfaction over the executions of the two men.

But on the home front a number of congressmen took exception to Jackson's "irresponsible" and unconstitutional actions, and the Speaker of the House, Henry Clay, tried to win a censure of the general in the lower chamber. The debate began when the House Committee on Military Affairs brought out a report on January 12, 1819, condemning the executions of Arbuthnot and Ambrister. In one of Clay's more glorious efforts, his voice soaring with sarcasm, he went so far as to accuse Jackson of killing Indian prophets so as to deny the tribe their own religion and force them to convert to Christianity. "Spare them their prophets!" he begged in mocking tones. "Spare their delusions! Spare their prejudices and superstitions! Spare them even their religion, such as it is, from open and cruel violence."

Having returned from Europe, where he helped negotiate the treaty that ended the War of 1812, Clay felt he had a good sense of European attitudes toward Americans. In a more thoughtful and sober statement he told his colleagues in the House that there were two topics that Europeans constantly referred to when criticizing the United States. The first "is an inordinate spirit of aggrandizement—of coveting other people's goods. The other is the treatment which we extend to the Indians."

Clay warned about the dangers of allowing an uncontrolled general to declare war and kill foreign nationals on his own with impunity. He realized, he said, that the public applauded the feats of their hero, but he reminded his colleagues that they were elected to act honestly, independently, intelligently, and with due regard to constitutional procedures, not according to the passing whims of an uncomprehending public. You may disregard what I am saying, he said, you may "even vote the general the public thanks; they may carry him triumphantly through this House. But, if they do, in my humble judgment, it will be a triumph of the principle of insubordination—a triumph of the military over the civil authority—a triumph over the power of this house—a triumph over the constitution of the land. And I pray most devoutly to Heaven that it may not prove, in its ultimate effects and consequences, a triumph over the liberties of the people."[12]

From that moment on, Andrew Jackson harbored a devastating hatred for Henry Clay that continued for the rest of his life. And he did everything in his considerable power to block the Speaker's one great ambition: to become President of the United States.

On February 8 the House, in a series of votes, overwhelming refused to condemn the seizure of Florida or disapprove the executions of the two British nationals; and, by a vote of 107 to 100, it rejected a resolution of censure against Jackson. It also declined, by a vote of 70 to 100, to characterize the seizure of Florida as unconstitutional.[13]

Jackson felt exalted—and completely vindicated. The electorate did too. "Among the people," one newspaper reported, ". . . his popularity is unbounded—old and young speak of him with rapture."[14]

But the report of the Senate investigating committee also condemned the general. Unfortunately it was issued so late in the legislative season that the members voted to table it so they could adjourn on March 4. Besides, they, too, understood the mood of the people. A new era in American politics seemed on the rise.

The Florida affair achieved the first of two very important goals that Jackson espoused: the first was the expulsion of any foreign presence in the south; but the second goal remained, namely the removal of the southern tribes west of the Mississippi River. The secretary of state, by his diplomacy and Jackson's essential help, had succeeded in achieving the first goal. Now Sharp Knife would resume his efforts with the second.

In late June 1818, while still recuperating at home from his physical debilities, Jackson received a letter dated May 2 from the secretary of war enclosing a commission to treat with the Chickasaw Nation and extinguish its title for the remaining portions of its land in Kentucky and Tennessee. "The President is very anxious to remove the Indians on this side to the west of the Mississippi, and if the Chickasaws could be brought to an exchange of territory, it would be preferred." General Isaac Shelby, a Revolutionary War veteran and a former governor of Kentucky, would also serve as first commissioner out of respect for his age and service in the Revolution. Because of their "knowledge of the Indians" and their "weight of character," the President "anticipates . . . that the object in view will be effected."[15] But, because of Shelby's age and docility, Jackson was expected to dominate the negotiations and make the important decisions.

Thus, once again, removal by executive decision was set in motion. The Chickasaw land in question, which lay between the Ohio and Yazoo rivers, was one of the most fertile and desirable in the entire west, and white settlers had set up a clamor in both Kentucky and Tennessee to take the necessary steps to extinguish the Indian title. Many of these settlers claimed ownership going back to the 1780s when North Carolina and Virginia sold the land to pay their Revolutionary War debt. The legislatures of both states repeatedly memorialized Congress to no avail. Finally, in the spring of 1818, the President acted.

On June 27, Shelby contacted Jackson and asked him to make the arrangements for holding the meetings, adding that because of "the infirmities of old age" he could not travel farther south than Nashville. Jackson responded that he too suffered from bad health and that he would try to "fix the period for the meeting, as early as possible."[16]

At the same time Sharp Knife wrote to James Colbert, the half brother of the three leaders of the Nation, and asked the Indian to meet him with the Speaker, Tishomingo, on July 22 to arrange a time and place for the treaty negotiations to begin, preferably near Nashville. But he was told that the Colbert brothers, William, George, and Levi, were decidedly opposed to "holding any meeting or talk, and have declared that they would loose every drop of bl[oo]d in their veins, before they will yield to the United States another acre of land."

That would undoubtedly cause trouble, Jackson explained to Shelby, and knowing the influence the Colberts exerted over the Nation it would be necessary to silence their opposition, along with that of the Speaker, before any treaty could be negotiated. Unfortunately, Calhoun's letter to the commissioners stated that Congress had appropriated $53,000 for talks with the Chickasaws and Quapaws, but only $4,500 for "moneyed presents . . . to the chiefs." That small amount also had to cover compensation for the secretary and interpreters. An additional $6,500 worth of goods was forwarded to Chickasaw Bluffs (present-day Memphis) "to be distributed under your orders," but these goods "can not be converted to any beneficial use," Jackson sighed, since they were so far away. Why the government would transport the goods to such a distant place was unfathomable. As for the money payments, obviously such a puny amount would not do. The Chickasaws had set a very high price on their salt licks and would not exchange them for anything but hard cash. The salt licks in the territory were the most valuable and prized of the Chickasaw land. Something more than $4,500 had to "be applied to their senses," Jackson insisted, "and the small sum to which we are confined at once tells me, that without more ample powers & means nothing can be accomplished."

Jackson urged Shelby to write to the President and ask him to allow them to draw whatever sums were necessary to effect a worthwhile treaty. After all, what was $20,000 or $30,000 compared to "this tract of country which is important not only to the growing greatness of the west, but also the strength & defence of the United States?"[17]

James Colbert replied on July 17 and informed Jackson that a council had been held in his house on July 13 and "it was determined by the chiefs then present that the Chickasaw nation had no land to sell or exchange whatever." In addition the $12,000 annuity for ten years guaranteed by the Chickasaw treaty of 1816, which Jackson himself had negotiated, had not been paid, "and the nation are daily looking anxiously for it." Nevertheless, the Nation would be "very happy to meet you, and hear what you have to say to them"; but the place of the meeting must "be somewhere in the centre of the nation, as the warriors would not like any treaty to be held on the frontier."[18]

It must have been very frustrating to Jackson to hear that the annuity had not been paid. The administration had regularly failed to meet its treaty obligations, and the general had previously warned that such actions defeated any effort to gain additional land from the Indians. This was money promised and owed them. "Indeed it is my opinion that, until these arrearages are paid, even to name the subject, would tend to frustrate the object of the Government."[19]

Calhoun regretted the delay in paying the annuity and blamed it on the new agent, who had not gotten to his post in time to receive the money. He told Jackson he had directed that the entire annuity be paid at once "unless directed otherwise by you or Governor Shelby." Then he had a suggestion which he thought might help the negotiations. "It is possible that the payment of so large an amount at the time of negotiating the treaty, might be turned to some account"—like temporarily postponing it until after a treaty was signed. He was sure Jackson would catch his drift. He also said that his original instructions were not intended to put "any limitations on the powers of the commissioners as to the terms on which the land should be acquired." The goods and money specified when he commissioned the two men to undertake the mission "were intended to be used at your discretion in bringing about the treaty, by presents to the principal chiefs, or otherwise." In other words they were to be used to bribe the chiefs. "Should a larger sum be necessary in that way, you are authorized to draw for it, provided it does not exceed $5,000. The treaty itself you will, of course, make on such terms as you may judge proper."[20]

By the time Calhoun's letter reached him, Jackson had already told Colbert that the annuity had been deposited in a Nashville bank "many months past" and that he had ordered the agent to distribute it "forthwith." But Calhoun's suggestion about holding off the annuities as a means of "bringing about a treaty" gave Jackson an idea. So he wrote to the agent and instructed him to postpone the payment of the annuity to October 1. "This will ensure us a full delegation from the Nation." It was a rather cruel action on Jackson's part, because the money belonged to the Indians and many of them were in desperate need of it. But Sharp Knife was not thinking about Indian need. Uppermost in his mind was the need of his country.[21]

Genuinely concerned about the willingness of the Chickasaws to meet with him and Shelby, Jackson wrote to James Colbert and explained the necessity of holding a convention. This land, he declared, belongs to white men who bought it thirty-five years ago and they are "pressing your father the President for Possession of their land." He can no longer keep them from occupying it and he knows that Congress, when they reconvene in December, will pass a law permitting them to take possession. The Treaty of Hopewell gave Congress the right "to regulate all the concerns of the nation." That is why the President has sent General Shelby and me to meet with you and "give you a Just compensation" for this land, either "in land west of the Mississippi, or in money." If you refuse to meet with us then you will have "to depend on the Justice of congress, and receive such compensation as congress may think proper to give you."[22]

It was a form of blackmail, and it was not lost on Colbert. As Jackson later explained to Shelby, an "open council by treaty" would mean "greater liberallity will be extended to them than they can expect from congress." And the blackmail worked. The Chickasaw Nation agreed to meet the commissioners on October 1 at the Old Town of the Chickasaws. Then Colbert sarcastically informed Jackson that the Indians would "part with their lands for the price the u. states gets for theirs." That last remark brought Jackson up short. "These are high toned sentiment for an Indian," he sniffed, "and they must be taught to know that they do not Possess sovereignity, with the right of domain."

Embedded in every action was the assumption of many Americans at the time, especially westerners and southerners, that the Indian Nations were not sovereign, but subject to the laws of the United States, an assumption later confirmed by John Marshall, the Chief Justice of the United States. And the implicit racism of Jackson's remark is still another fact of frontier life, if not American life, in the early nineteenth century. Indians were distinctly inferior to whites, and for them to presume an equality with their "betters" was offensive and intolerable.

Jackson also told Colbert that the Chickasaws had lived on the land for the past thirty-five years and had enjoyed "the benefit of the game, by hunting thereon—[and] that now the game is destroyed, and it is of no further use to the Indians, the Individual who has Bought & paid for it demand possession." It was the old dodge and lie about how the land no longer provided for the needs of the Indians because they did not farm like whites and only lived from hunting game.

The value of the Chickasaw land was such that Old Hickory was determined to succeed in this mission of removal. And the first thing he did was instruct

Shelby on the strategy that they had to follow. We must, he said, "take a high and firm ground" in dealing with the Indians, "or we will fail in success, we must speak to them in the language of truth—and endeavour to put to rest the oposition of the Colberts, by touching their interest, and feeding their avarice."[23]

It was the old technique. Once again Jackson, following the lead suggested by Calhoun, planned to corrupt the chiefs and headmen with money, a policy long practiced and endorsed by the administration and implemented by Sharp Knife at every opportunity. It was disgraceful on all sides, and it certainly dishonored the nation that allowed and encouraged it. And because flagrant bribery would be the very fiber and core of the negotiations, Jackson always did it surreptitiously. "Secrecy is necessary, or the influence of the Chiefs would be destroyed," he declared.[24]

Since the Chickasaws insisted that the talks take place in the center of their Nation, Jackson suggested to Shelby that he travel first to the Hermitage and recuperate from the trip before they both started out together for the Indian country. "I shall expect you at my house about the middle of September."[25]

In due course, Shelby arrived at the Hermitage and spent several days resting and listening to Jackson expound on how they would conduct the negotiations. He felt that two or three companies of militia ought to accompany them on their trip in order "to give weight and force to our proposals." Indeed, the two men took a small army with them, including Colonel Robert Butler, one of Jackson's many wards, to serve as secretary; William B. Lewis, Jackson's close friend, confident, and neighbor, to act as commissary; plus soldiers, land speculators, and other hangers-on.[26]

In mid-September this grand display of American land-jobbers set out for the Chickasaw meeting ground. The "commissioners and suite" arrived at their destination on the evening of Tuesday, September 29, and to their annoyance "found everything wrong." The Indian agent, Henry Sherburne, had not yet arrived. He was supposed to bring the annuities and provisions needed to conduct the negotiations. The talks could not begin until these supplies became available. It later turned out that he was "unacquainted" with the Indians as well as ignorant of the geography of the country or why his presence was required. In addition, the interpreter, James Colbert, had not arrived, and "not half the nation notified" of the time or place of the meeting. Runners had to be sent out to all parts of the Nation to bring them in so the convention could begin.

The next morning the commissioners appeared at the treaty ground at nine o'clock sharp and waited until noon for the agent to show up. By this time a number of chiefs and warriors had begun to arrive and were dismayed not to find their annuities or provisions. In desperation, Captain Carter, the quartermaster, was sent to locate the agent and haul him before the commissioners.

"The agent was not coming to the treaty," intoned George Colbert, one of the principal chiefs, in a solemn voice. He said he would not come.

But Carter found Sherburne twenty-four miles from the camp on his way to the talks. Unfortunately the agent had no money to pay the annuities. But he did have "a draft in his possession on the Branch Bank of New Orleans for $19,950—for several weeks unnegotiated." Carter raced ahead to give the commissioners this information and assure them that Sherburne would arrive for breakfast the following morning.

On Friday, October 2, many more chiefs began to assemble at the camp. They looked "very distant and gloomy," noted the secretary, Robert Butler. In the harshest language possible they registered their complaint that "their annuities were withheld and when they expected money, goods were offered them." Was this how they were to be treated?[27]

Jackson fumed. At 10:00 A.M. Sherburne arrived. He had nothing in his pocket but the unnegotiated draft of annuities owed the Chickasaws for 1817. At the first sight of Sherburne, the general tongue-lashed him, while the Indians listened and watched, their faces registering their dismay. It was a particularly bad beginning.

But Jackson reacted promptly. He dispatched Benjamin Smith to Nashville with "special instructions" to his friend and business agent, James Jackson, to have the draft negotiated. James Jackson was not related to Old Hickory, but he was a financial adviser and frequently made land purchases for his client. The general also sent a Mr. Winchester to Chickasaw Bluffs to see about the goods sent to the commissioners by Calhoun to be used as presents for the chiefs.

As Smith and Winchester took off, Jackson explained to the chiefs what he had done and asked them to be patient. It was an action, recorded the secretary, "which seems to have worked a happy change in the countenances of the natives. Nothing decisive is contemplated by the commissioners until the arrival of the funds, but their unremitting attention seems given to prepare the minds of the chiefs for the ultimate object of their mission."[28]

On Saturday the interpreter, James Colbert, appeared. A few chiefs waited on the commissioners, but nothing official was attempted. Sunday and Monday were also barren of progress. By Tuesday the commissioners began to realize that the Nation would disperse if the talks did not commence very soon. At this point a Mr. Alexander arrived from Nashville with a book containing copies of the North Carolina land grants to white settlers. The commissioners then asked William B. Lewis, the commissary chief, to provide an exact amount of the land claimed by the Chickasaws in Kentucky and Tennessee. From maps in his possession, Lewis estimated that 5,644,800 acres constituted their land in western Tennessee, of which 1,373,918 acres had been granted by North Carolina, leaving a balance of 4,270,882 acres "vacant and unappropriated." As for Kentucky, Lewis said he could not provide an exact figure but thought 825,600 acres were involved. However, he did not know to what degree North Carolina and Virginia had disposed of this land.[29]

Jackson and Shelby then began to prepare their first official "talk" to the Chickasaws while Sherburne started making a list of claims preparatory to the distribution of the annuities once the money arrived.

One day followed the next without any sign of Smith. Then Winchester returned from his trip to the Chickasaw Bluffs and on Monday, October 12, presented a written report on what he had found. There were seventeen packages in the first arrival for the commissioners, he said, which were "in good order and carefully deposited in a secure building" under the supervision of the factor, M. P. Ballio. But the last arrival of fifteen packages "had been opened and exposed for the purpose of drying *indiscriminately* with the *Annuity goods.*" Much of these goods were water-damaged and too damp to repack. Winchester next provided an inventory of the goods and their condition. These included saddles "of very inferior quality"; bridles of "good quality" but badly damaged in shipment, as were rugs; powder, half of which "may be fit for use"; lead; hats "but little injured"; blue cloth of good color "not rotten"; "shirting weak stained"; swan skins; plaids "ruined"; sashes "colors injured"; fishing lines and hooks but "rusted very much"; thimbles; cotton balls; box combs; scissors "very much rusted" and needles "ruined"; mirrors "every one injured"; blankets most "in good order" but "some of them stained"; and rifles "a good deal rusted."[30]

Much of what the commissioners had to distribute was hardly more than junk, but they had little choice given the importance of their mission and the growing sense that the Chickasaws would not exchange their land for an equal amount across the Mississippi. Only money and goods would be acceptable.

Finally, Smith returned to the campsite on the morning of Monday, October 12, with $37,550 to pay the annuities, almost double the amount of the draft.

WILLIAM BLOUNT,
territorial governor and future
U.S. senator, who helped
advance Andrew Jackson's
early political career.

BENJAMIN HAWKINS,
U.S. agent to the Creek Nation.

*TECUMSEH,
the great Shawnee chief
whose oratory and
dream of an Indian
confederation stirred an
uprising within the
Creek Nation.*

*This picture of the Cherokees attacking a frontier station in Tennessee vividly depicts
what the settlers faced around the time Jackson moved to Nashville.*

Shortly after Jackson's election to the Tennessee superior court, he faced down and arrested Russel Bean, who had successfully defied the sheriff and his entire posse.

The massacre at Fort Mims by Red Sticks on August 30, 1813, set in motion Jackson's successful campaign in the Creek War.

During the Creek War some of the volunteers and militiamen of the west Tennessee army attempted to desert, but Jackson, with only token help, halted them in their tracks.

The conventions Jackson held with the southern tribes frequently ended with a ball play, a forerunner of lacrosse. Here Choctaws vie with one another to throw or carry a ball, cradled in a webbed racket, between goalposts.

*This scene depicts Jackson's invasion of Florida in 1818 as he
headed toward Pensacola during the First Seminole War.*

*This broadside provided excellent propaganda about Great Britain's practice of
rewarding Indians who supplied it with American scalps.*

War and Pestilence!

HORRIBLE AND UNPARALELLED
MASSACRE!

Women and Children
FALLING VICTIMS TO THE
INDIAN'S TOMAHAWK.

While many of our most populous cities have been visited by that dreadful disease, the Cholera, and to which thousands have fallen victims, the merciless Savages have been as fatally engaged in the work of death on the frontiers; where great numbers (including women and children) have fallen victims to the bloody tomahawk.

This broadside appeared as late as 1832 and was based on a true story about the murder of women and children on the frontier. Many best-selling books at the time involved Indian kidnapping and murder.

WILLIAM MCINTOSH,
*a Creek chief who allied himself
with Jackson in the Creek War.*

MENAWA (Great Warrior)
*led the Creeks against Jackson in the
Battle of Horseshoe Bend and
managed to escape.*

SHELOCTA,
another Jackson ally
during the Creek War,
argued unsuccessfully
against the Treaty of
Fort Jackson.

PUSHMATAHA,
a Choctaw chief who fought
with Jackson at the Battle of
New Orleans and tried to
prevent the despoiling of
his Nation.

CHIEF BLACK HAWK
led the Sac and Fox Indians in
the Black Hawk War during
Jackson's administration.

NEAMATHLA,
a Red Stick chief who acted
as spokesman for the
Seminoles in negotiations
with Governor Jackson.

MAJOR RIDGE,
a Cherokee chief and
leader of the Treaty Party
who agreed to removal and
was later assassinated.

JOHN ROSS,
Principal Chief of the Cherokees,
who valiantly resisted removal.

OSCEOLA,
leader of the Seminoles in
the Second Seminole War,
in a lithograph by George Catlin.

ANDREW JACKSON in his fancy
uniform as major general of the
U.S. Army, around the time of the
Battle of New Orleans.

*GENERAL JOHN COFFEE,
Jackson's close friend and commander
of the cavalry during the Creek War.*

*MAJOR JAMES C. GADSDEN rebuilt the Negro Fort, which was
renamed Fort Gadsden during the First Seminole War.*

JAMES MONROE served as secretary of state and of war and as president during Jackson's career as a major general in the U.S. Army and Indian commissioner.

WILLIAM H. CRAWFORD, as secretary of war and of the treasury, pursued policies Jackson found abominable.

JOHN C. CALHOUN,
as secretary of war,
argued in favor of censuring Jackson
for seizing Florida during the
First Seminole War.

JOHN QUINCY ADAMS,
as secretary of state,
defended Jackson's seizing Florida
and convinced the Spanish
government to sell it to the
United States.

JOHN H. EATON,
Jackson's ward and military aide,
was appointed secretary of war and
supervised the implementation of
the Indian Removal Act.

This Albert Newsam
lithograph, although
not one of the better-
known portraits of
Jackson, was executed
at approximately the
time he signed the
Indian Removal Act.

This portrait of the "Great Father" and his Indian "children" represents the attitudes and prejudices of citizens toward Native Americans. On the wall can be seen a picture of Columbia standing over a prostrate Great Britain.

Now the talks could begin. The chiefs and warriors were assembled, and at 11:00 A.M. the first talk began with Bentley McGee acting as interpreter.

"Friends & Brothers," Jackson began. "We have been chosen by your father the President of the United States to meet you in council, and brighten the chain of friendship, by shaking hands and greeting you as his children. We come to see that the sums due your nation be equally distributed among the poor & the sick to benefit all & make you happy."

There is no question that in all his dealings with whites and Indians, slaves and free men of color, Jackson always had a deep concern for the "poor & the sick." This regard for the less fortunate was a constant factor in his life and greatly influenced his presidency years later.

"Brothers," he continued, the land in Kentucky and Tennessee which you claim and which was sold by North Carolina and Virginia thirty-five years ago to pay off their Revolutionary War debts is demanded by those whites who paid for it. The President has kept them away from it so that his "red children might hunt on it." But the game is gone and "his white children claim it now from him."

"Friends & Brothers, your father the President must do justice to all his children," red and white, and prevent ill will between them. He wants to "have your lives finally settled" and will exchange "land over the Mississippi for this country." Or, if you are unwilling to exchange, he will "give you a fair and reasonable price for your claim . . . which will not interfere with the settlement or arrangement of your nation. You will then have more land left than your nation can cultivate for six hundred years." If you refuse, Congress will act and then "you cannot look to him for redress."

After this long and necessary prelude, Jackson turned grim and spoke in a sharp, clear, and forceful tone. "Friends & Brothers: We hear that bad men in your nation threaten your chiefs with death if they surrender this land." If this happens, he promised, "your father the President he will put them to death for it."

"Listen," he exhorted them. "We must speak plain & tell you the truth." If you refuse this offer, the land "will be taken possession of by your white brethren" and the President "will look on your conduct as acts of ill will & ingratitude. . . .

"Friends & Brothers, We have given you our talk and have nothing more to say until we get your answer; take our talk with you and think well; and let us have your answer as soon as you can."[31]

The chiefs and headmen withdrew and during the following three days met in council at George Colbert's house. Day followed day without a decision. By October 15 it had become clear that there was a great deal of opposition among the Chickasaws toward either exchanging or selling their land. There was also constant fear that any move to despoil the Chickasaw Nation would result in the deaths of many chiefs. The commissioners then realized that it had become "absolutely necessary" to feed "the avarice of the Chiefs." And do it immediately.

No two ways about it, said Jackson, corrupting the chiefs by bribery was the only path to a successful mission. But since the "sum authorized [was] entirely too small" the commissioners quickly formulated a plan to get around it. In the Chickasaw Treaty of 1816, which Jackson had negotiated, reservations had been set aside for George and Levi Colbert. It was now proposed to give them those reservations in fee simple and a conveyance taken for the benefit of the government if the President accepted it; but in order "to render the thing perfectly secret to secure the chiefs," the reservations would be leased to a citizen of the United States. General Jackson and William B. Lewis would hold the property in escrow until the government exercised its option.

The amount of money originally proposed for these reservations was $10,000, but the Colbert brothers rejected it and said they would send a deputation to the President "remonstrating against selling or exchanging their land." So the sum was raised to $17,000, "which made them listen," but after a long discussion the council decided that if a "doceur" of $3,000 could be added a treaty might be acceptable. At that point the commissioners made it clear that this offer was final and if the chiefs refused it then "the white people would certainly move on their lands by the thousands and all the evils which their father the President was trying to avert would ensue."

The chiefs agreed. A deed was drawn up in the name of James Jackson, and a bond given for $20,000 in cash or merchandize as the Indians desired it. If the government exercised its option it would pay $8,500 each to the principal chiefs, George Colbert and Levi Colbert; $1,666.66 to James Colbert, the interpreter; $666.66 to Captain Sealy, a mixed-blood officer; and $666.66 to Captain William McGillvery, a mixed-blood who had served as a lieutenant of a Chickasaw contingent in the Creek War. If the government refused the option, the reservations would be delivered over to private speculators.[32]

It was quite a subterfuge the commissioners devised to wiggle around the financial limitation placed on them by Calhoun, but it did the job. "The adoption of this course," said the confidential journal, was the only one possible to "secure the grand object" and protect "the lives of the chiefs."[33]

On Sunday, October 18, the commissioners were informed by Levi Colbert that the chiefs had rejected the offer of an exchange of land, since they were not born in the country beyond the Mississippi and did not know it. But if they let the President have their land *"they wanted what he had* in exchange and that was mony."

How much? Colbert asked the commissioners to be generous, and Jackson assured him that he and Shelby "would be liberal," just as the President had instructed them.

Jackson offered $20,000 each year for twelve years. This the chiefs "sternly refused remarking that they loved mony well but they loved their land much better."

Jackson then offered to add one year but this too was rejected. Finally "to make all hearts straight" he said he would agree to fourteen years. And that was his last offer.

Colbert replied that the chiefs would consider it, and the meeting adjourned for a few hours. When they reconvened, Colbert asked if one cent could be added. Jackson refused. They had gone to their limit. Surely, said Colbert, one cent was nothing to a nation "as strong as iron, great rich and strong" as the United States.

Would "one solitary cent" satisfy the Chickasaw Nation, Jackson asked?

It would, replied Colbert. Whereupon the general and the chief shook hands.

Later the interpreter said that they had shaken hands on a fifteen-year annuity "which was not the understanding of the commissioners," and there the matter rested until the council reassembled to sign the treaty.

Jackson was particularly pleased at their success, even though he did not get the Chickasaws to remove. The prospect of adding so much valuable property to the country was intoxicating to both commissioners, and they looked forward to getting it in writing the following day.

On Monday, October 19, the chiefs arrived around 11:00 A.M. Right off, Jackson tried to explain that he had not agreed to fifteen years, that one cent did not mean an additional year. The Indians just stared at him. "They could not nor would not understand it in any other light, but that his meaning was an additional annuity on which they shook hands & that they had come prepared to sign the treaty as agreed upon." They had not come to sign some "new" agreement dreamed up by the commissioners.

Jackson could have threatened them, but he was a very practical man. He had to consider what was the "prudent" thing to do. Should he risk the convention when he already had in his hands a magnificent slice of Chickasaw territory just waiting for his signature? Why jeopardize "the grand object for the pittance of $20,000 to be paid fifteen years hence"? That made no sense. Besides, threatening them could be risky. Chickasaws were a very warlike tribe. They were among the bravest and most intrepid and courageous of southern tribes. Threatening them could be and likely would be a mistake.

So he agreed. The words "fifteen years" were inserted in the blank time line in the treaty. Then it was read and explained "in the presence of a large gathering of young warriors." It was necessary to interpret the treaty to the rank and file of Chickasaws because of suspicions that their chiefs would be coerced into dismembering their Nation and sending them all westward into a foreign land. Once this necessary step had been taken, the document was "duly signed and solemnly executed and attested."[34]

At last. The United States had obtained clear title to all the Chickasaw land north of the southern boundary of Tennessee (the 35th parallel), a veritable empire of prime real estate.[35] The negotiations had required bribery (Jackson, like many others, called the bribe a "doceur"), the deliberate and unconscionable withholding of annuities, and false statements of fact, but Jackson had become used to such practices, much as it offended his sense of what constituted the proper manner of treating natives. And it had taken time, days and days of waiting and talking and finding ways of keeping the negotiations on track. Shelby later complained that "the Indians have been very litigious and slow in the decisions; the business which might have been done in two or three days, it has taken twenty days to effect."[36]

Once the treaty was signed, the annuities were promptly distributed by Sherburne to the heads of families, who were agreeably surprised by the apportionment they received. Heretofore they had never gotten anywhere near as much. "It made the poor much more happy and comfortable hereafter." Other sums were doled out to particular chiefs and favored individuals for their services.

One other dishonorable aspect of this convention was the fact that the journal of the proceedings was kept secret to protect the lives of the chiefs who had been bribed. In later years the Chickasaws felt anger, bitterness, and frustration over what had been done to them by the American government and by their own chiefs.

Some members of the U.S. Senate also resented Jackson's actions, especially the reservations of the salt licks. "I have been secretly slandered in the Senate," declared the general a year later, "and the same Junto continues it in the papers." It was a "notorious fact," he said, that when we appeared at the treaty ground no one "believed we would succeed" and every warrior and chief was determined "not to give us a foot of land." But we did succeed. We succeeded because "I [took] upon myself the risque and responsibility of sending to Nashville for the money and gave [it] to the agent a responsible receipt for his Post note and drafts. . . . It was well known without this and other funds we could not succeed. We created funds out of the property of the Indians, that obtained the cession."[37]

Jackson and Shelby were anxious to return home once the administrative details were completed, but they first attended "a Ball play which the Natives" provided them and their suite. With the conclusion of the "Ball play" (a ball game), the commissioners and their entourage immediately "set out in the evening leaving the Nation more happy & contented than it ever was known to be & Levi Colbert took occasion to remark we have made a good treaty—observing we are now safe from the claims of our white brothers and we can live in peace and friendship."[38]

All that remained of the once vast holdings of the Chickasaws was their territory in northeastern Mississippi and a tract of half a million acres in northwestern Alabama. But in time Sharp Knife fully intended to dispossess them from this last vestige of their homeland and send them all into the wilderness beyond the Mississippi River.[39]

Chapter 11

Despoiling the Choctaws

On their way home, both Shelby and Jackson sent a bill to the secretary of war for $2,303.15 for their expenses to and from the treaty ground and for other "disbursements while there." Jackson himself took personal advantage of the riches he had brought to his country by purchasing a section of land south of the Tennessee River on the military road. No one bid against him, so he obtained the land for $2 an acre even though poorer land in the area sold for as much as $83 per acre. It was another mark of his enormous popularity with the public. "I am compelled to say," he wrote, that it was as "gratifying as it was an approval of my official acts."[1]

There is no doubt that Jackson personally benefited to an extraordinary degree from the land wrenched from Native Americans. And he encouraged his friends and others to follow his example and purchase this valuable real estate. But the idea behind stripping the Indians of their property had little to do with material gain as far as Jackson was concerned. His main purpose was to increase the number of white settlers along the southern frontier to better secure the area against foreign invasion. As long as Indians remained in residence, they would be prey to the wiles of foreign intrigue to the detriment of U.S. interests. As he said repeatedly, "it is the denseness of our population that gives strength and security to our frontier." Of secondary importance for him was a personal financial killing.

The documentation involved in Jackson's own land purchases is almost nonexistent, because he frequently operated through his agent, James Jackson, or such friends as John Coffee and John Overton. Like so many other Americans at the time he regularly speculated in land, for that was the quickest method of gaining wealth.

The general arrived home on November 12, and a week later the people of Nashville gave him and his staff a splendid "Ball in commemoration" of having cleared away all Chickasaw claim to Tennessee land. His friend the banker John Overton speaking for the welcoming committee, assured the general of the community's undying support and appreciation for what he had accomplished. Now it was up to the President and Congress to accept and ratify the treaty.

Jackson wrote to Monroe and expressed some fear that there might be a problem. "I trust the price given will be viewed as a mere drop in the buckett, compared to the advantage of this cession." Think of the "vast sum that it will bring into the treasury of the u states." And all this for $20,000 for fifteen years.

There was indeed some strong opposition to the treaty in the Senate, particularly to the reservations given in fee simple to the Colberts. The objection centered on the fact that it would set a precedent for all future treaties. Despite these criticisms the Chickasaw treaty was submitted to the upper house on November 30 and won easy ratification on January 6, 1819. The Hero also received a letter from Calhoun conveying his own and the President's enthusiastic approval and congratulations on the success of the mission.[2]

Indeed the government had particular reason to be pleased with the acquisition, especially since a similar mission to the Choctaws had ended in failure. In May 1818, John McKee and Daniel Burnet were commissioned to negotiate for Choctaw lands in Mississippi. They met the Indians in October but could not persuade them to part with their land. Obviously the enterprise needed Sharp Knife's strong hand.

And it just so happened that early in December 1818, while Jackson was recuperating at home, "James Pitchlynn a half breed son to John Pitchlynn interpreter for the Choctaw nation" visited the general and offered to help in an exchange of Choctaw land for lands west of the Mississippi. He said that he, along with the entire Choctaw Nation, had been compelled to "give a decided negative to the demands" of Commissioners McKee and Burnet. But this denial, he insisted, was not to be considered "as expressing a decided determination on part of the nation not to exchange their country for lands westwards of the Mississippi; the failure of the treaty was owing to other causes." For one thing, McKee was unpopular because of his part in forcing the Choctaws into relinquishing their claims east of the Tombigbee; for another, Burnet was "totally unqualified for the business in which he was engaged." Moreover, said Pitchlynn, it would not do to exchange a small part of Choctaw land. It must be the whole thing or nothing. And, to make the deal, the Nation must be "liber-

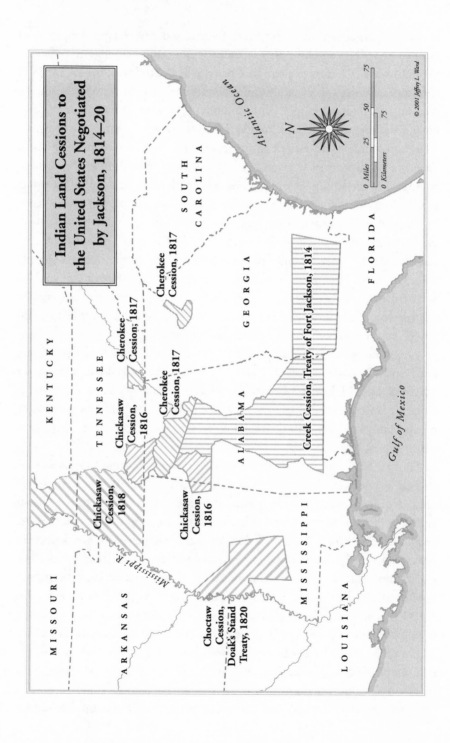

Indian Land Cessions to the United States Negotiated by Jackson, 1814–20

MISSOURI

KENTUCKY

Chickasaw Cession, 1818

Mississippi R.

ARKANSAS

Choctaw Cession, Doak's Stand Treaty, 1820

TENNESSEE

Chickasaw Cession, 1816

Cherokee Cession, 1817

Cherokee Cession, 1817

Chickasaw Cession, 1816

Cherokee Cession, 1817

Cherokee Cession, 1817

SOUTH CAROLINA

GEORGIA

ALABAMA

Creek Cession, Treaty of Fort Jackson, 1814

MISSISSIPPI

LOUISIANA

FLORIDA

Gulf of Mexico

Atlantic Ocean

N

0 Miles   25   50   75

0 Kilometers   75

© 2001 Jeffrey L. Ward

ally paid for their farms and improvements" according to their value. "A liberal remuneration in this respect," Pitchlynn declared, "will have a greater effect on the minds of the Indians, than the same reward bestowed in any other way." The "half breeds and Chiefs who have the most valuable farms and stocks have the greatest influence in treaties." There would be no exchange "at any time, without a provision on this head." Of course, Jackson knew exactly what that meant.

In the exchange process the removal of stock must also be paid for, Pitchlynn added, and he suggested $3 per head for cattle and $6 for horses as an acceptable amount. Also there must be provisions, ammunition, and a few other minor considerations, which he enumerated, after which Jackson invited him to write them up as an address, which he would forward to the secretary of war for consideration.

In his conversation with the general, Pitchlynn claimed that upward of three hundred warriors and their families had already crossed the Mississippi under the command of a Choctaw chief by the name of Captain White. "Those coctaws with their friends in the nation," he said, "are all anxious for an Exchange." He then queried Jackson about what he thought the United States would offer in return. The general refused to be specific, but he did feel that the President would offer as much land in the west as the Choctaw Nation now held in the east and allow a fair consideration for all improvements that added value to the land, with "the poor of the nation" receiving full compensation. In addition the usual gun with powder and lead to last a year, a blanket, and a trap or kettle plus provisions until the Choctaws could raise a crop would be provided—or so Jackson believed. And transportation would most assuredly be made available to conduct the families and stock across the river. However, Jackson said very pointedly, those Indians who chose to remain in the east would be subject to the laws of the United States. And he told Pitchlynn that if the Indians refused an exchange, Congress was more than likely prepared to pass a law that would prohibit the Choctaws from hunting west of the Mississippi. Such a bill was actually introduced in the House of Representatives by George Poindexter of Mississippi on November 20, 1818, but it failed of passage.

In forwarding Pitchlynn's address to Calhoun, Jackson accompanied it with a letter of his own in which he said he was convinced that if half the Choctaws removed, the whole Nation would go. Only those making money who lived along the Natchez Trace, running through their territory in northern Mississippi, would oppose the exchange.[3]

Not surprisingly, on March 29, 1819, Calhoun responded to this information by commissioning Jackson, along with John McKee and Daniel Burnet, to renew negotiations with the Choctaws. The general would be paid $8 a day as compensation "for the time actually employed."[4]

Shortly thereafter the general wrote to McKee, the Choctaw agent, and offered some advice. McKee had been told by the government to get a sense of the Nation on whether or not "they were disposed" to meet with the new commissioners to work out an exchange. The Nation was divided into three districts, called the Lower Towns, Six Towns, and Upper Towns, each comprising around eight thousand people, and led by the Three Medal Chiefs or Principal Chiefs. The Three Medal Chiefs were called Mingos, or kings, and were elected every four years. Currently the three were Pushmataha, Mushulatubbee, and Puckshenubbee, who ruled the southern, northeastern, and western districts of the Nation respectively.[5] The system of Medal Chiefs had been instituted by the French in an effort to create a hierarchy as a more convenient means of dealing with the tribe. Each district was subdivided into kindred clans or Iksas, and each had generals and captains—titles conveniently borrowed from whites.[6]

"Permit me to suggest the propriety of making the following statement to the Chiefs of the nation by way of preparing them for the Cession," Jackson wrote to McKee. The Indians must be told that Congress, at its next session, will surely require those Choctaws who have already departed for the west to return to the east if the entire Nation does not agree to an exchange. If this happens it "will place the Nation in an unpleasant Situation." They will not be able to provide for themselves by hunting. The Six Towns will separate and some warriors will join one group and some another until "they will become extinct, and lost as a Nation." Worse, if they refuse the western land offered to them, the whites will soon hear about it and they will "immediately Settle on it and the U States will be compelled to make Sail of it." Make no mistake, "it is a fact and ought not to be withheld from them, as it will bring to their view their true Situation and open their Eyes to their own benefit and happiness."

Tell the chiefs, he concluded, that we have been instructed not only "to be liberal to the Nation but to them individually." Have Pitchlynn speak to them. He has offered his services to me and he will be "amply rewarded."[7]

There seemed to be a good chance of cajoling the Choctaws into surrendering their land in Mississippi, although Jackson's poor health and the constant bombardment of criticism he heard from Washington politicians almost caused him to resign his commission as general and retire to his farm outside Nashville. By 1819, when he received this latest commission, he had endured such physical and emotional pain over the past few years that he really did feel it was time for him to retire from public life and tell the administration to find someone else to do the dirty business of despoiling the Indians.

Andrew Jackson frequently indulged in self-pity and often told Monroe of his desire to resign. "I am weared with public life," he wrote. "I have risqued my life for public good, I have met privations and fatigue to promote the true interests of my country. I have worn out my constitution to preserve her rights and procure her safety, and when her security, permitted me to retire from the scenes of war, I have been assailed by the *drones of the hive,* I have been accused of acts I never committed, of crimes I never thought of, and secretly slandered in the Senate, by some of its unworthy members, and charged of doing acts in my official capacity to promote my private Views, and enhance my own interest."

True enough. He had indeed risked his health and his life repeatedly for his country and for his country's benefit. He had fought and won the Creek War; repelled the British invasion at New Orleans and brought the nation its first great military victory; proved for all time that this nation could successfully defend its independence and republican form of government; made the people proud to call themselves Americans; subdued the Seminoles and won Florida; guarded the country along the frontier; acquired millions of acres of land from Native Americans so that whites could live on it peacefully without fear of violence and bloodshed—and his reward, as he said, was a "worn out" constitution and the unrelenting physical ills he suffered on account of living for months and years in the wilderness and swamps. He had done these things and achieved these things because he was a patriot with an intense love of his country. And yet he was repeatedly and everlastingly lashed by politicians and hostile newspapers for immoral acts and wicked designs on the fabric of American law and government. As he said, he was accused publicly of crimes he never thought of, much less committed. And it never ceased. Even today, Andrew Jackson is remembered more by some for the supposed "evil" he did and not the good he rendered his country. Actually Americans owe him a great debt, the south particularly.

"When I see such corruption in the members of our Senate," he went on in his letter to Monroe, "I dispair of a perpetuation of our happy constitution, and have a wish to retire to private life." What preyed on his mind at this time was the assaults on his character for his capture of Pensacola. He was accused of seizing the town because of his own and his friends' interest in land speculation. In addition, the reservation of a salt lick on the Big Sandy branch of the Tennessee

River in the Chickasaw treaty was leased to Jackson's close friend and neighbor William B. Lewis, in a transaction that smelled of corruption. Jackson knew nothing about the lease, but Senator John Williams claimed that the lick was intended for the general himself or one of his close relatives. Eventually the lick had to be renegotiated, and not until 1834 was it finally ceded to the United States.

But the more the general was attacked, the more he rose to his own defense. And although he railed against the unfair criticism he constantly faced and threatened to walk away from public life, he nevertheless felt a deep obligation to serve his country. "Sir," he told Monroe, "you know my Services is my country, [and] as long as I can render any that may be serviceable to her" I shall do so. "I cannot bare the idea of abandoning you, so long as you may think my services may be necessary for my country—and this I will never do."[8]

So he agreed to undertake the Choctaw mission, difficult though it might be, since the Choctaws continued to refuse to part with their land despite repeated efforts to get them to recognize the precariousness of their situation. McKee responded to Jackson's suggestion about eliciting a sense of their wishes with respect to an exchange. "I had the fullest confidence before the council convened that the Six Towns at last would accede to the wishes of the Government," he told the general. John Pitchlynn and several others were present and expressed an "unequivocal desire to cross the Mississippi." But "a few halfbreeds with but little claim to distinction" worked assiduously on the chiefs and convinced them that the country on the Red River where they would relocate had "neither soil water nor game." This information alarmed even those Indians who were disposed to migrate, and so the Council refused to meet with the commissioners, thus aborting a possible treaty negotiation. Instead the Choctaws decided to send a delegation to Washington consisting of the Three Medal Chiefs; Jesse Brashears, Alexander Hamilton, Levi Perry, all mixed-bloods; and David Folsom, who later became a Medal Chief when he deposed Mushulatubbee. Pitchlynn and his friends "exerted themselves with zeal and industry" to convince the Nation to exchange, McKee reported, "and are sorely mortified at the failure."[9]

For Jackson, it was just as well. He was really relieved that the proposed mission was aborted. He wanted nothing more to do with Indian treaties, since they seemed to bring him nothing but complaints and accusations of venality. He told William B. Lewis he had been "very wantonly assailed" because of the salt lick reservation and had been forced to make a report about it to the Tennessee legislature, which he submitted on September 23, 1819. If this was his thanks for clearing title to some of the best land in the state, then "I had determined never to have anything to do again in Indian treaties."

The legislature formed a committee to investigate the matter and ended up by commending him on his career, especially his actions in Florida, and his clearing title to all Indian lands in Tennessee. They therefore awarded him a sword of honor. Thomas Jefferson, of all unlikely people, wrote and congratulated him on his many successes, assuring him of the lasting "gratitude of his country for former achievements" and "these new proofs of the salutary energies of their great benefactor." He saluted the general "with assurances of his constant & affectionate attachment & high respect."[10]

Over the next several months, when not defending himself with written statements or personal appearances, Jackson tried to keep the peace between Indians and white squatters by issuing warnings to whites that unless they had authorization they were forbidden to enter those areas reserved by treaty to Native Americans. The problem was particularly acute in Cherokee country. Inform these intruders, Jackson wrote to the agent, Return J. Meigs, that they and their stock will be removed by "military authority." They will be arrested and turned over to the courts "to be dealt with as the law directs. I will thank you to give this publicity throughout the nation, it may have the effect of inducing all to remove without military coercion."

Accordingly, a notice was posted, dated at "Shallow Ford, Chatehootchy, Georgia May 29, 1820," which read:

> Intruders on the cherokee lands beware, I am required to remove all whitemen found trespassing on the cherokee land not having a written permit from the agent Colo R J Meiggs, this duty I am about to perform—The Regulars & Indian lighthorse will be employed in performing service, and any opposition will be promptly punished. All whitemen with their stock found tresspassing on the Indian land will be arrested, and handed over to the civil authority of the United States to be dealt with as the law directs, their families removed to the United States land, there crops, houses and fences destroyed. . . . Andrew Jackson, Major Genl comdg Division of the South.[11]

When white intruders squatted on Indian land, they frequently made "large improvements" and sometimes banded together to defend "their property" when troops appeared. Or they fled only to reappear and reclaim "their property" when the troops departed. It was a difficult job, but Jackson was determined to honor the commitments he had made, even though several officers complained of the burden that had been placed on them. "I fear General," wrote General Richard Keith Call, "it will be extremely inconvenient for the regular Troops under my command to march in to the Creek Country after performing their duties in the Cherokee Nation. Their services will be required at all points." It was virtually an impossible job, he said.[12]

In this matter Old Hickory was very even-handed in his treatment of Indians and whites. Citizens did not receive preferential treatment if they broke the law. He understood implicitly that the only way to prevent bloodshed along the frontier was to be just as severe with them if they violated treaty agreements as he was with the Indians. He told Calhoun that it would "take him nearly three months" to clear the Cherokee country of white settlers. "Three times I had the stock of intruders driven from the Cherokee land," he said, "their houses and improvements destroyed. But this availed nothing; the troops would no sooner leave the country, than the Intruders would return." By this time Jackson had become convinced that using force and threats to keep intruders out permanently was a hopeless task. It was like trying to rid a house of termites or other destructive pests, he said. The only answer, as far as he was concerned, was removal of the tribes. But the secretary assured him that he was "well satisfied with your measures for the removal of the intruders." Just try to be lenient when you deal with them, Calhoun added.

In the spring of 1820, Jackson's Military Road from Florence, Alabama, to Gulf ports near New Orleans was completed and the general, who had long urged its construction as essential to national defense, set out on a tour both to inspect it and "to take such further measures for its improvement as seem to be necessary on an examin[ation] of its present state." He found it a truly magnificent creation. It was eighty feet wide in most places and had been cleared of all logs and trees and underbrush, although he discovered that "Certain Bridges and Cosways" already needed repair. All the low places had been "causwayed and all the creeks and rivers requiring it bridged in a substantial manner." Many of the bridges were 450 feet long or longer and made of solid oak. Built by soldiers, it was certain, commented Jackson, to prove "beneficial both to the people of the country and to the government."[13]

It also proved beneficial to some Indians, especially mixed-bloods, who found that their associations with whites along the road in establishing service stations of one kind or another brought unexpected wealth. But this very fact made them implacable foes to Indian removal. Why abandon such newfound prosperity to relocate to the wilderness beyond the Mississippi?

After completing his inspection, Jackson continued his tour through the southern sections of the Cherokee and Creek Nations in Alabama and Georgia and dispatched a detachment of troops to clear out squatters in the Cherokee lands. He was absent on this mission for several weeks, after which he returned to Nashville on June 18 exhausted and not a little disheartened.

The constant intrusion of white settlers on Indian lands and the failure of the government to carry out the promises of their treaties with the tribes were problems that Jackson faced almost daily. Throughout the spring and summer of 1820 he oversaw the operation of removing squatters from Cherokee property where they had made the greatest inroads.[14] He used threats and military force to expel them and regularly bombarded the administration with pleas to honor its commitments. But it was an unending struggle. He had virtually reached the point where he felt he could not turn back the white tide that was engulfing the southern tribes, nor get the administration to fulfill its treaty obligations.

John Rodgers, an influential Englishman among Cherokees who had married a mixed-blood and had removed to Arkansas under the treaty signed in 1817 at the Cherokee Agency at Highwassee, complained to Jackson about conditions resulting from the removal when promises were broken and whites continually settled on their land. There were approximately five thousand men, women, and children now residing on the Arkansas River. "We were promised bread for the first year after our arrival here," Rodgers said, "—we came calculating to find it—but there was none—The sufferings and privations we had to contend with in consequence of this failure are better felt than described— hunger, sickness, and in some instances death has been the fatal consequence." What is worse, "we were promised that the white intruders on our land Should be removed by the government—but Our Agent has stated he had no orders from Government to removed them." We were told that no whites would settle between the Arkansas and White rivers to the west of us, but "White people have, and Still are Settling there. I can not suppose Sir these things are to be attributed to You," but I must "Soliscit the favour to be informed whether you think the promises made at Highwassee will be complied with." These promises were the reason I came here. "Until those promises are complied with, I can not ask or recommend my friends to follow me."

Such information drove Jackson to distraction. How could he in conscience urge—nay, demand—that the tribes move west if everything promised them went unfulfilled? Jackson forwarded the letter to the President with his endorsement, adding that "the Arkansas cherokees complain of injustice done them by the last treaty & are dissatisfied with it." And to Calhoun he added that this feeling was prevalent among all the Cherokee people.[15]

Further injustice was visited on the Indians, the Choctaws in particular, because of renewed pressure from the Mississippi congressional delegation to send them westward to the Arkansas Territory, which had been established in 1819, two years after the admission of Mississippi as a state in the Union. The delegation was responding to the demands of whites that the Choctaws be relocated now that the Arkansas Territory had been created, one with a territorial government that could see to their needs. Since the Indians had previously expressed a keen interest in an exchange of land and a number of them had already removed, the congressional delegation insisted that the entire Nation be relocated at once. The people of Mississippi, the governor and the legislature, said the *Mississippi State Gazette,* were "grossly annoyed" over the Indian problem and demanded the removal of the Choctaws from the lands "which they hold to the great detriment of this state. . . ." And, as commissioners for this task, they wanted Jackson to head the mission, a sentiment "unanimously" endorsed by the congressional delegation.[16]

There was also pressure from James Pitchlynn, who told Monroe that Head Chief Red Foot and the senior captains of the Six Towns wished to exchange their land on condition that they receive just compensation for their improvements. But he warned that they were "rich white men people living in the nation" who gave "bad talks to the Indians" and "tell them not to exchange lands." Pitchlynn claimed that he and some of his friends had argued for removal and thought a good one-third or half of the Nation would move. "Some of the Indians," he said, "has threatened to knock me in the head on this account."[17]

Responding to the pressure coming at him from all angles and anxious to rectify the mistakes of the previous negotiations, Calhoun decided to try again with another mission, and he wrote Jackson telling him that "the President is very desirous to employ you upon this duty." He added that if Jackson accepted, he, as first commissioner, and General Thomas Hinds of Mississippi, could choose the time, place, and manner of conducting the negotiations.

Although he "had determined never to have anything to do again in Indian treaties," Jackson replied that "I never can withhold my services when requested by old Monroe." Moreover he owed a debt of gratitude to the people of Mississippi for the support they had rendered when he defended New Orleans from the British. "I feel it a duty therefore, to endeavour to serve them, when they by their representatives believe I have it in my power." He said he would be happy to serve with Hinds, who, after all, had led the Mississippi Dragoons at the Battle of New Orleans and in whom he had great confidence. He conveniently forgot to mention his obligation to the Choctaw Indians, who also assisted him in that battle.[18]

Jackson then suggested to the secretary that in sending the instructions for the mission he include the bounds of the land in Arkansas to be exchanged with the Choctaws. At present the Indians are scattered and "wandering over a great space of [the western] Country." The chiefs are anxious "to perpetuate the existence of their Nation by concentrating the whole in a country that will support them as a Nation. . . . The pride of a real Indian is in the strength of his Nation and this is a chord I mean to touch to obtain the object in view." When I speak with them I wish to point out the lands and describe its limits where they will be sent. Then I can say to them, this land will "perpetuate them as a nation and thereby make his children happy."[19]

To the President, he declared once again that "it is still my duty as a patriot to make my private interests and views subservient to my country's good." He implicitly believed that he acted out of a sense of his "country's good." Bad as it was at times, he never thought he acted contrary to the safety, the honor, and the integrity of the United States.[20]

Calhoun responded to his request by stating that he was not "sufficiently acquainted" with the area west of the Mississippi to provide boundaries but supposed that the farther south and west the Choctaws were sent "the better." Just be sure the territory is part of the United States territory as purchased from the Quapaws in the Arkansas district and not occupied by Cherokees, Quapaws, or any other tribe. As for the terms of the proposed Choctaw cession, Calhoun left it "entirely to your sound discretion."[21]

That sounded like carte blanche, and that was exactly what Jackson believed it to be. He was in complete charge and intended to remove as many Choctaws as possible. Unfortunately, Calhoun gave him only $20,000 to cover all expenses of the negotiations, including the pay of the commissioners and secretary, which was hardly enough to meet these costs, much less provide the "doceurs" needed for bribery. Calhoun added that this sum did not include money to be paid the Indians as stipulated in the treaty. In other words, what was expended on the Choctaws proper would have to be part of the treaty document itself.

Jackson immediately set to work. He wrote Hinds and asked when he could attend the negotiations, suggesting that the 20th of September to the 1st of October might be a good time since supplies of corn would be available. He also wrote to McKee, the Choctaw agent, and asked him to calculate how much rations would be needed daily for the convention. He planned to liquor and feed the natives with a very liberal supply of rations to put them in a receptive mood.

He then notified Calhoun that the instructions did not mention reservations and "it strikes me that reservations will have to be made to some of the half breeds who have a wish to remain, before their consent can be obtained." If we do grant reservations, he said, it should only last as long as the individuals reside on the land. Otherwise it should revert to the United States. "Fee simple ought not to be granted."

The department replied that it preferred no mention of reservations in the treaty if it could be avoided. But if the success of the negotiation hinged on providing them "to some of the half-breeds," then let the reservations be "restricted as you propose." Just remember that the Senate will not accept reservations in fee-simple. Do what "you judge best for the interest of the United States."

As finally worked out, the commissioners agreed to begin negotiations on the first Monday in October. Jackson also asked that the $20,000 allotted for the negotiations be drawn on the Natchez bank, since its notes were redeemable in specie, which the Indians invariably requested. As for the rations, the contract for providing them was awarded to Jackson's friends William Eastin, who was married to Rachel Jackson's niece, and William B. Lewis. These men saw to it that each Indian received a daily ration of one and a half pounds of beef, one pint of corn, and one quart of salt, "plus free access to liquor."

To what extent liquor played a part in the negotiations with the Indians cannot be precisely evaluated. It was not like an outright bribe. But undoubtedly it helped smooth the way over difficult hurdles in the talks, and it frequently brought signatures from Native Americans who had no idea what they were signing.

For each ration, Lewis and Eastin received a commission of nine cents, and they put up a bond of $10,000. Local merchants received the contracts for liquor and tents and a few other provisions. But another friend, Samuel R. Overton, was appointed secretary and received a per diem allowance of $5. Both Jackson and Hinds received $8 per day.[22]

As the time drew near to head for the treaty ground, Jackson decided to lecture the administration once again on what he thought its policy toward the Indians should be. Because of the increasing trouble he was having in expelling intruders from Cherokee territory, he used that problem as a point of reference, starting with John Rodgers's letter of June 7 about his removal to the Arkansas Territory.

It was Jackson's opinion that the entire Cherokee Nation wished to go west if it had the means. Why not, he suggested, institute an entirely new policy and appoint a "confidential agent" to go among them and enroll those who wish to relocate; and when they enroll "take their relinquishment of all their claim to land where they now live"? Then let Congress pass the necessary legislation establishing the exchange. "There can be no question but Congress has the right to legislate on this subject." From experience I know that more justice can be done to Indians by legislation than by treaties. Forget treaties. It is virtually impossible to get a treaty "without corrupting their Chiefs. This is so inconsistent with the principles of our Government that it is high time" for a change. "Treat them humanely and Liberally but put an end to treating with them, and obtaining their Country by corrupting their Chiefs." We now have the military strength, the will, and the need to enforce any law Congress may deem advisable. Heretofore the United States lacked that strength and was too weak to execute its laws regulating Indian affairs. "The American arm is now sufficiently strong to carry into effect every regulation which the wisdom, humanity and justice of its Government may adopt with regard to these unfortunate People." Now is the time to reverse the policy, said Jackson, especially if it is determined that the Cherokees "are ripe for emigration." It will also fulfill the pledge given to Georgia in 1802 when that state ceded her western lands to the central government on condition that all Indian land claims would be extinguished within Georgia's boundaries.[23]

If this policy was not adopted, Jackson predicted, whites would continue to occupy Indian lands, bloodshed would result, and the army would be kept in perpetual motion going from one area of tribal residence to the next trying to reestablish peace. And no sooner would the army move on than the whites would reappear and the cycle would begin all over again. The administration, if it was wise, would initiate a policy of total removal. In time all the tribes would be transported to the Arkansas Territory and an exchange of land would be enacted by Congress, and the army, if necessary, would enforce it.

Here in faint outline was what Jackson would later institute as President. As general, as commissioner, as policeman of the southern district, he knew from experience that the Indian problem would never be solved by continuing the policy first established by President Washington. Times had changed. The country had grown in strength and size and population. The industrial revolution had begun, along with a market revolution. An independent domestic economy had been established; manufactures flourished. Roads, bridges, turnpikes, and canals now stretched across much of the nation. It was time, as Jackson said, to reverse course and adopt a different policy that would address all these new circumstances. If such a change was not adopted, he believed that the southern Nations would in time disappear, just like the Yamasees, Delawares, and Mohegans.

Although Calhoun agreed with Jackson and said so many months later—"I entirely concur with you that it is perfectly absurd to hold treaties with those within our limits, as they neither are or can be independent of our government"[24]—the administration was in no mood to inaugurate such a revolutionary and potentially explosive policy. For one thing, a presidential election was in the offing, although Monroe had no difficulty in winning reelection. For another, Congress had already expressed a wish to reduce the army from ten thousand to six thousand men, and a new Indian policy, such as Jackson proposed, might require large expenditures of men and money.

In the meantime, Jackson left Nashville on September 14 headed for the Choctaw Treaty Ground, near a place where a man by the name of Josiah Doak operated a tavern (Doak's Stand), on a flat, grassy area alongside the Natchez Trace near the Pearl River, and accessible from any part of the Choctaw Nation. The general and his sizable "suite," which now included his ward and nephew Andrew Jackson Donelson, a graduate of West Point who served as aide-de-camp, arrived at Doak's Stand on September 28 and were joined a day later by General Hinds with seventeen Mississippi militiamen and the Choctaw Indian agent, Colonel John McKee. On October 2 they all moved together to the treaty ground, which was about a mile below Doak's Stand.

To Jackson's annoyance and concern, another white man showed up: Colonel Silas Dinsmore, a former Choctaw agent whose ruling on passports had stirred a lively controversy with the general back in 1812. It was reported that Dinsmore had said that "the policy of our government towards the Indian tribes was a harsh one," a remark that Jackson instantly interpreted to mean that he had come to counsel the Indians against signing a treaty. A collision between the two men would have been unavoidable had Hinds not learned that the real reason for Dinsmore's appearance was a promise he had received years before from the Choctaw chiefs that he would be compensated for the loss of livestock and other property destroyed by "some turbulent young Choctaws" when he was absent from the agency. He had therefore come to the treaty ground with the expectation that in the final treaty he would be granted a reservation of land as reimbursement for his loss. Hinds explained this to Jackson, and a potentially violent meeting was averted.

The two men passed each other many times during the convention but never spoke. Finally Dinsmore decided to attempt a reconciliation and on a late afternoon approached the general, who was sitting on a long bench in front of the commissioners' tent and engaged in a light conversation with several members of his entourage. Since Congress was expected to debate the admission of Missouri into the Union in the coming session, Dinsmore thought he would mention it by way of starting a conversation with the general. He looked directly at Jackson and in a particularly friendly manner asked whether Jackson intended to go to Washington once the treaty was completed. Surely he would want to attend the opening session of Congress.

As he spoke, Sharp Knife turned and faced Dinsmore. He gave him one of his famous stares of contempt and anger. Then he let the poor man have it.

"No, sir," he barked. "I never go where I have no business."

Dead silence. The group dispersed. The possibility of Dinsmore's receiving a reservation of land in the treaty totally vanished.[25] Had he really wanted to make amends, he should have begun the conversation with an apology or confession of guilt. That was his only recourse if he expected to undo the past.

Not until late in the evening of October 2 did the headmen and warriors of the Choctaws begin to arrive. Little Leader and ten of his men and a boy appeared and drew their rations. They were joined by seven or eight of Puckshenubbee's men. They agreed to accept the rations but on orders from their chief refused provisions.

On October 3, the two Mingos, Puckshenubbee and Pushmataha, arrived with about seventy or eighty men. Puckshenubbee was a tall man, quite thin and bony, with a religious or "superstitution cast of mind." He was a good man and much beloved by his people, and was thought to be quite an intellectual. He always looked glum, and his taciturn demeanor hid his thoughts, even from his own people. Pushmataha, on the other hand, was the great man of the Nation, known from tribe to tribe. He had fought with Jackson against the Creeks and Spanish and British. He was about five feet ten inches tall and stood very erect. He had broad shoulders, a full chest, a prominent forehead, high cheekbones and thick lips. His mouth was very large, and he was a magnificent orator. Jackson had conferred on him the title of "General." Wherever the chief went, people turned and stared at him and wondered who he was.[26]

Sharp Knife stepped forward and greeted the chiefs, inquiring of Puck-shenubbee why he had ordered his men not to accept the provisions provided them by the government. The chief drew himself up and in a stern voice replied that he had no intention of accepting favors from "his father the President, and did not wish to subject him to any expense."

That was a bad sign. Right at the outset, Jackson knew the negotiations would be rough going, and he did not try to hide his annoyance and disappointment. And it certainly did not help when he declared that the chief's attitude was "disrespectful" and would be so considered by the President. Then he asked if the Mingo knew why he had come. Puckshenubbee shook his head. To give the Nation a "talk," Jackson informed him, "relative to their common good." We are here to make you people "happy."[27]

To each group of Choctaw headmen who arrived, the general praised their courage and assured them that although he had learned "with much pain" the "many threats" that had been made by "bad men" who promised to put to death any who attended the treaty or consented to sell or exchange any part of Choctaw territory, they should not be afraid. "Fear not those threats," he cried. "The arm of your father the President is strong, and will protect the poor Indian from the threats of white men and half-breeds, who are growing rich by their labor." They make "slaves of the poor Indians, and are indifferent to their happiness. They care not whether the poor perish, or are lost to the nation, if they can grow rich by their labor, and by living on the main roads through the country."[28]

Once again he pounded out his concern for the poor and his opposition to the rich who used their influence and power to advance their selfish goals. These were themes he would repeat most tellingly when he later became President of the United States.

In view of the attitudes he had encountered among the Principal Chiefs and what he had heard since arriving at Doak's Stand, Jackson had now come to the realization that the total removal of the Choctaw Nation was not going to happen—at least not now. All he could do at present was obtain as much of the eastern land as they were willing to sell or exchange. So he sent runners out with his "talk" to encourage the absent headmen and warriors to attend the convention. The President "invites you to come forward, and tell him your mind freely, and without fear. You shall not be injured. He will protect you." Then, in a major shift of direction, he said that those who wished to stay where they were and "cultivate the earth" might do so; and those who removed "will receive there a good country for a small part of their lands here."

Whatever your choice, he said, the President wishes that you make it "freely, and all be happy." As soon as you assemble, he concluded, I will deliver the Great Father's friendly talk. If you refuse to come, "he may never speak to you again."[29]

Over the next several days, additional headmen and warriors appeared at the treaty ground. Eighty of them showed up on October 4, and Red Foot, a chief of the Six Towns, arrived with eighty more men the following day. The Reverend Cyrus Kingsbury, a Presbyterian minister and a very influential voice among the Choctaws who had steadfastly opposed any exchange, also came and spoke privately with the commissioners. He had not heard of the Pitchlynn letter to Jackson, and when it was shown him and when the President's purposes in calling the convention were explained he withdrew his objections to holding the treaty talks.

A white man by the name of Welch also appeared. He was a deserter from the U.S. Army who had married Puckshenubbee's granddaughter. Immediately recognized, he was arrested. As soon as the chief heard what had happened, "he and his clan" expressed a wish that Welch be released provided a substitute could be offered in his stead. At first Jackson refused, knowing its effect on other members of the army, "but being advised that it would greatly soften the temper of the chief, and knowing that much good would result from it, should the great chief be thereby brought to hear and adopt our talk," he agreed, on condition that a "young healthy and stout" substitute was made available. One was accordingly produced, examined, and found acceptable. Welch was released, and this, Jackson told Calhoun, "made the old chief very friendly—and he has been intimate and friendly ever since."[30]

The following day Mushulatubbee arrived, but only two headmen from his district accompanied him. Mushulatubbee was the Principal Chief of the Three Medal Chiefs and had held the title many years. A handsome man, he stood six feet tall and was quite heavy. He indulged frequently and was known for his lively and cheerful disposition. He was not much of an orator and so delegated Pushmataha to speak in his place. On arrival he explained to Jackson that a number of his warriors were on the road and would soon join him at the treaty ground.

That evening, Puckshenubbee informed the commissioners that he was prepared to hear the President's talk; Jackson assured him that as soon as Mushulatubbee's headmen and warriors arrived, he and they would hear it. The Mingo nodded. He said that in two days, that is, Monday, October 9, there would be "a great ball-play" at which all those men belonging to his district would be present. Very well, replied Jackson, I will give the Great Father's talk on Tuesday.

By this time it really looked as if a treaty might be secured. It had taken many days to accomplish, but the initial resistance had been overcome. The rest was up to the commissioners, Jackson in particular. He had to make the Choctaws understand that their future happiness—and even their existence—depended on their agreeing to an exchange.

On Sunday more warriors arrived. Then, on Monday, as promised, "the principal chiefs gave us a ball-play," which ended "with a dance in the evening. All the Indians seemed to be in a good humor, and, as far as we could judge from appearances," reported the secretary, "in a favorable temper for negotiation."[31]

The following day, Jackson and Hinds appeared before all the chiefs, headmen, and warriors of the Choctaw Nation in council. Jackson said that this same talk would be delivered to late-arriving Indians at a future date. Then he began.

"Friends and Brothers," many of your brothers have gone west, and the President has heard that a large portion of his Choctaw children still living in the east "are in a distressed condition, and require his friendly assistance. They live upon poor land, and are not willing to cultivate it. The game is destroyed, and many of them are often reduced almost to starvation." They have wandered into Alabama and Louisiana; they are scattered over the country from Tennessee to New Orleans. "Many have become beggars and drunkards, and are dying in wretchedness and want. Humanity requires that something should be done for them."

The President begs you to help them in providing for your friends and brothers. "You cannot refuse it." Some of you live well but others have not the means of "supporting their squaws and children." The President is anxious to make "all his Choctaw children happy," so he has sent me and General Hinds to come here and shake you by the hand and assure you of his friendship. He wants you to listen to his talk and he has directed me to point out the land beyond the Mississippi where his other Choctaw children now reside and are happy and where you may also "live and be happy."

Why stay here? "Without a change in your situation, the Choctaw nation must dwindle to nothing. This is what every good and wise chief will endeavor to prevent."

If you stay, Jackson warned them, in time you will be Choctaws no longer. You will become like white men. "You must cultivate the earth like your white brothers," because the game is gone. "You must also, in time, become citizens of the United States, and subject to its laws." Tribal laws, religion, and society cannot survive in the east. Only through removal can tribal identity be preserved.

Achieving a small degree of equality with whites might sound like a great idea to a few Native Americans, but most Indians at that time had no burning desire to become cultural white men. They knew their identity and wished to preserve it. The threat, therefore, thoroughly alarmed them.

And because he was a racist like most Americans of his age, Jackson did not really believe that either black or red men could ever receive total equality with their "white brothers." That was another reason why he begged them to go west, where they could live as Choctaws. "The fish, fowl, and game are plenty," he assured them. There you can farm or fish or hunt.

If you stay where you are, white men will inevitably settle on your land. And you know what happens after that. Your father the President "does not wish to drive you from your land by force; nor does he ask you to sell it, or give it away." Just exchange it. "He has not sent us here to cheat or to threaten you."

Calhoun had left the terms of the Choctaw session up to the commissioners, and they decided to ask for what Jackson called "a small slip of your land here," for which the Indians would get double the amount in the west.

"A small slip of your land." But that "slip" represented more than five million acres, nearly half of the remaining Choctaw land in Mississippi, in exchange for which they would receive thirteen million acres in Arkansas and the future Indian Territory.

We need this land, Jackson continued, because "the people of Mississippi are much exposed to the invasion of foreign enemies. The Choctaw nation is equally exposed. A cession of part of your country is necessary for your defence."

This argument about national security may have been all-important to Jackson and white men around the country, but it probably had little effect on the Choctaws.

Jackson then brought up the subject of their school, and assured the chiefs that the President had "every wish to educate and civilize his Choctaw children." Funds and land would be made available to establish schools in the west. "No loss or injury shall be suffered by the change." But in offering to "civilize" Indians, the Monroe administration was following a contradictory policy. Here it was trying to send the natives to the west at the same time it was educating them for life in the east. It made little sense.

If you say no to this offer, Sharp Knife continued, it can only mean that your minds have been poisoned by the "false statements of white men and half-breeds living amongst you." These bad men wish to keep you in a state of poverty and servitude, and their only object is "riches and power." If you reject the President's offer and desert "the part of your nation" that has already gone west, "the Great Spirit will look down upon it with displeasure." You will no longer be friends and brothers.

Having invoked the Deity and subtly threatened reprisal, Jackson ended by describing the new land beyond the Mississippi as one of "many water courses, rich lands and high grass abounding in game of all kinds—buffalo, bear, elk, deer, antelope, beaver, turkey, honey and fruits of many kinds. . . .

"What say the chiefs and Choctaw people to this great offer?"[32]

There was a long silence. Smoking pipes appeared and were handed around. Then Pushmataha rose and addressed his own people, telling them that General Jackson was a great warrior and deserved a "respectful" reply. He suggested the council adjourn until the middle of the following day. Before they broke up, however, Puckshenubbee asked for a written copy of the talk, which "his half-breeds" would translate "to see that there were no mistakes, and that every thing was well done." The commissioners agreed, and the meeting adjourned with handshakes all around.

The chiefs and headmen held a secret council that evening where they discussed the merits of Jackson's proposal. As the discussion proceeded, it became clear that they needed time to sort out their reactions. The following day they did not meet with the commissioners, nor the day after that, although Jackson felt that appearances continued to be favorable. Nearly a hundred more warriors arrived at the treaty ground; they had not heard of the pending negotiations from their captains until the runners brought them the news. They joined their brothers and were given a summary of the state of the negotiations.

It soon became clear that most of the chiefs and headmen felt that Sharp Knife had misrepresented the facts about the new land he had offered them. They then appointed Pushmataha as their Speaker to convey these thoughts at the next council meeting.

At twelve o'clock the following day, the council reassembled and the commissioners asked if they had come to any conclusion about the proposed treaty. Pushmataha rose, addressed the commissioners, and said that he had been appointed to reply. Then in a most cunning yet deferential manner, describing Jackson as a great man and himself as a miserable fool, he let Sharp Knife have it full blast.

Pushmataha accused the Hero of deception. You speak of "a little slip of land" as though it were nothing, but I know that land and "it is a very considerable tract of country," said the chief. You speak of the land in the west as one of rich and fertile soil, one abounding in game. "I am also well acquainted with that country. I have hunted there often, and chased the Commanchee and the Ovashsashi over those endless plains, and they have sometimes chased me there. I know the country well," and "it is poor and sterile, trackless, sandy deserts, nude of vegetation of any kind."[33]

As he concluded and resumed his place, all eyes turned toward Sharp Knife, who surprisingly kept his temper in tight control. It was a skill he had long developed. He knew when to release an eruption and when to hold himself in tight control. And this was not the time to show his true emotions.

He rose from his place and took the speaker's stand. "Brother Push," he said in a quiet but firm voice, "you have uttered some hard words. You have openly accused me of misrepresentation and indirectly of the desire to defraud the red people in behalf of my government." At that point Jackson allowed a small display of emotion to show through. In an excited rush of words he said, "These are heavy charges, charges of a very serious character. You must explain yourself in a manner that will clear them up or I shall quit you."

"My great friend, General Jackson," replied Pushmataha, "who familiarly calls me brother, whom my inner soul loveth . . . has become excited by some of my remarks." You ask for an explanation, well, the truth is that "the grass is very short [in the western country], and for the game it is not plenty, except buffalo and deer. . . . There are but few beavers, and the honey and fruit are rare things. . . . The rivers are . . . liable to inundation during the spring season, and in summers the rivers and creeks dry up or become so salty that the water is awful for use."

He then excused Jackson from any willful misrepresentation, since he is obviously "ignorant of the geography he is offering to swap." He is ignorant because he even offers land in what belongs to Mexico.

There was a hush throughout the crowd. No one moved. Finally Jackson spoke.

"See here, Brother Push, you must be mistaken," he responded. "Look at this map; it will prove to you at once that you are laboring under a great geographical error yourself." He then spread out a map.

Pushmataha looked at it. "The paper is not true," he declared.

A long argument ensued, and the chief asked about the white settlers already living on the land being offered. Would they "be considered Indians or white people?" Jackson replied that there were only a few and he would have them ordered off the land.

"I beg your pardon," said the chief. "There are a great many of them, many of them substantial, well to do settlers, with good houses and productive farms, and they will not be ordered off."

"I will send my warriors," Sharp Knife stormed, "and by the eternal I'll drive them into the Mississippi or make them leave it."[34]

By this time it was late, and the argument was going nowhere. Both sides agreed to adjourn. And despite what had been said, Jackson was still hopeful about the outcome. Time seemed to be slipping away, and he was concerned that unless he presented formal proposals for a treaty, some of the chiefs might depart, taking their warriors with them.

On October 13 he presented a plan in which the Choctaws would cede the "small slip of your land"[35] to the United States and receive in exchange land from the Arkansas River south to the Red River and west to the headwaters of the Arkansas River. It was all very inexact. Neither the commissioners nor the Indians had any idea what lands were being offered the Choctaws, a situation that would cause monumental problems in the future.[36] But one thing was known at the time: the government was offering nearly triple the amount of land it would receive in return.

Jackson also promised that each man who emigrated would receive a blanket, kettle, rifle, gun, bullet molds and wipers, and ammunition sufficient for hunting and defense. In addition he said that enough corn would be provided to support a family for at least a year and during the time they traveled west. An agent would be appointed with goods to supply the emigrants' wants. And schools and a blacksmith shop would be established.[37]

The chiefs and headmen again went into secret session, but there soon appeared "a considerable want of harmony in council." A committee consisting of the Three Medal Chiefs and six white men and "half-breeds" from each of the three districts was formed to consider the treaty and make a report. For three days they counseled among themselves. Puckshenubbee was particularly opposed to a cession, and at first Pushmataha agreed with him. But as he listened and remembered some of the things that Jackson had said, he slowly realized that the Choctaws had much to lose if they persisted in refusing the terms offered to them. Pushmataha was a realist and decided that it was better to be humiliated than exterminated.[38]

For his part, Jackson knew that the time had come to make a very forceful pitch or jeopardize the successful termination of his mission. On October 17 he summoned the chiefs, headmen, and warriors of the Nation to assemble and hear what he had to say. This time he would pull no punches. If necessary he would resort to outright threats.

"Friends and Brothers," he shouted at them, if you "are so lost to humanity as to abandon those who have gone and settled over the Mississippi," then you leave the President no alternative but to negotiate with your brothers in Arkansas for an exchange of land in the east for the land they now occupy in the west. Your brothers have no legal right to the land they occupy, and therefore the President "will insist upon acre for acre" in an exchange. Which means that "the country here may be cut up" and taken from you. It means that your schools may be disrupted. It means that Congress under the terms of the Treaty of Hopewell "have a right to manage the affairs of this nation; and they will do so, if compelled by the obstinacy of chiefs and the wickedness of your advisers." If you will not listen "you must suffer the consequences." This is the second time the President has met you in council. His patience is exhausted. "You are advised to beware."

The warriors, chiefs, and headmen recognized the threat. But to be sure they understood him fully, Sharp Knife recalled to them what had happened when the British invaded and how he had sent a message to Chief Red Foot and warned him that unless the chief and his warriors joined him against the British, "he should find him and his army in his town in a few days." Red Foot had heeded the warning and joined him, and the British had been defeated.

Over and over he repeated one theme: do not listen to bad men who advise against this treaty. Your father the President "will not be trifled with and put at defiance. A heavy cloud may burst upon you" and you will be without friends and without protection.

"Listen well," he commanded them, "and then determine. Your existence as a nation is in your hands." If you refuse, he warned, "the nation will be destroyed."[39]

At last he had said it. "The nation will be destroyed." Did he mean by force of arms? Or was it the extinction he warned would result from white intrusion? He did not have to elaborate. The end result would be the same.

At the secret council meeting that followed, Puckshenubbee remained adamant. In an outburst directed at many of the headmen and warriors, he declared that he would not consent to an exchange of land and would take no further part in the negotiation. When the commissioners heard about his "insulting conduct" they called the other chiefs, headmen, and warriors together for yet another talk.

We have been sent, Jackson said, to treat with the whole Nation, not just a single chief. We wish to know the will of the majority. Tomorrow the treaty will be presented to you for signature. If it meets the will of the majority of the nation, we can conclude the business at hand. Otherwise we shall depart.

At this point bribes were discreetly distributed to the influential chiefs and "half-breeds," and that action added to the threat of destruction turned things around.

The following day, Wednesday, October 20, the Choctaws and the commissioners reconvened. The articles of the treaty were read and explained to the Indians and then handed to them for their signatures. One by one the chiefs, headmen, and warriors affixed their signatures or their mark to the document. Jackson could now let out a sigh of relief. The Treaty of Doak's Stand was finally done.

In addition to the provisions spelled out on October 13, some $4,674.50 went to twenty-six chiefs, headmen, and "ball-players" as "donations." Even Puckshenubbee received a gift of $500, despite his opposition, although there is some evidence that only whites and "half-breeds" living within the Nation seriously objected to the exchange. The treaty also stipulated that of the tract ceded to the United States, fifty-four sections would be sold to raise a Choctaw school fund.[40]

It was quite an acquisition. In congratulating the commissioners, one Mississippi newspaper called the little "slip of land" as "fine as any in the United States." Another newspaper hailed the treaty as Jackson's greatest accomplishment since his defeat of the British in 1815. So delighted were the people, the governor, and legislature of Mississippi that they named their new capital after Andrew Jackson and the county in which it was located after Thomas Hinds.[41]

The Choctaws ceded nearly one half of their Mississippi land or 5,169,788 acres in exchange for approximately 13,000,000 acres lying in the western section of Arkansas and what is now the southern half of Oklahoma.[42]

In one final bit of business the Choctaws asked that the boundary lines be so marked "as always to remain plain, so much so, that white people may see them, and not clear fields over them, as has been the case on other lines." Jackson obliged them by sending the request directly to Calhoun, urging that the lines of the new Indian boundary be drawn quickly and clearly. As it turned out,

those Indians who removed were pitched into an unknown country already settled by whites ready to dispute Choctaw rights and cheat them of their land.
And those who remained in Mississippi were increasingly subject to white attack. Worse, they found it virtually impossible to obtain justice in the state's
courts. The pressure would continue to mount in the ensuing years for them to
join their brothers in Arkansas.[43]

The Treaty of Doak's Stand was the last of the great Indian treaties that Jackson personally negotiated, and it embodied all his ideas about what to do with
tribes who blocked southern and western expansion and who constituted a
threat to the security of the United States. Over a period of seven years he had
acquired millions of acres of land in North Carolina, Florida, Georgia, Alabama, Mississippi, Tennessee, and Kentucky, land from the Atlantic Ocean to
the Mississippi River, from the Ohio River to the Gulf of Mexico. It was an
enormous haul of prime real estate, which rapidly filled with white settlers and
strengthened the nation's defense against possible invasion from the Gulf.[44]

Many Native Americans still remained in the east, resisting the idea of becoming cultural white men and resisting any further exchange of land. Their removal, as far as Jackson was concerned, must follow. Ten years later it did.

Chapter 12

The Making of a President

Jackson arrived back at the Hermitage on November 10 and collapsed. He had a severe cold and cough and he was spitting up blood. Worse, the bullets in his left breast and shoulder produced "violent pain." He was unable to work or think or conduct his business as general and farmer. He was tired and worn out and sick of chasing white intruders out of Indian lands only to have them return when his back was turned. The Indian question could have been settled so easily, he said, if the government would behave like a modern, civilized nation and ship the "savages" out of harm's way. As he lay prostrate on his bed it became more and more evident that he needed to resign his commission and take care of his health and the needs of his family.[1]

But his country also needed him and prepared to call him again to a new duty. The treaty ceding Florida to the United States was close to final ratification. The Spanish had already agreed to relinquish the province, and King Ferdinand VII had signed the document on October 24, 1820, and returned it to Washington. It was now awaiting ratification by the Senate. No sooner did Monroe receive word of the Spanish action than he wrote to Jackson and asked him to agree to serve as governor of this new territory. "The climate will suit you," he purred, as though the general did not know what the climate of Florida was like. Even though Monroe had offered the post to him back in 1819 after the treaty was signed and had been refused, he tried once again to coax him into accepting. "It will give me pleasure to place you in that trust," he assured the general, knowing that Jackson had a high regard for him personally. Calhoun followed up with a letter about how his "talent and experience" were essential in establishing a government in Florida. "It will require in particular a military eye," he said, "as its defences ought to receive early and prompt attention." Besides, the Hero's name was intimately entwined with Florida and it would be essential "at the outset" to put the government on a "respectable footing."

At first Jackson was inclined to reject the offer. "My fortune and constitution have already been much impaired in the service of my country." Besides, he doubted that he could benefit "the public good." But when he realized that by accepting he could "quicken the organization of the Government and tend to draw to that country a respectable population" whose presence would enhance the security of the nation, he began to waver. Then his friends in Washington and at home begged him to accept and plied him with every conceivable argument about the benefits that would accrue from his acceptance. His Washington friends, led by Senator John H. Eaton, felt the appointment essential to validate his actions when he seized Florida in 1818. That was a telling argument. So Jackson accepted, but on one condition: that "I may resign as soon as the Government is formed and in full operation."[2]

Jackson's acceptance spared Monroe from an embarrassing situation. The country was still feeling the effects of the Panic of 1819 and the government wished to reduce the size of the army, necessitating the demotion of one of its two generals: Jackson and Jacob Brown. Both men were difficult to handle, but Brown had the active support of the secretary of the treasury, William H. Crawford. Getting Old Hickory to accept the Florida post and resign his commission, which he had been threatening to do for years, was the perfect solution to Monroe's dilemma. And when the President assured the Hero of the importance of the position, Jackson agreed to take it. On February 13, 1821, the Adams-Onís Treaty was submitted to the Senate, and six days later it was ratified with only four dissenting votes. Immediately Monroe appointed the Hero of New Orleans governor of East and West Florida with powers of a "captain general and intendant of Cuba and commissioner" to receive the territory from the Spanish. On June 1, Jackson resigned his army commission.

Once he accepted his new post, Calhoun instructed him on current Indian affairs in the Florida Territory, much of which he already knew, and urged him to appoint a special commissioner to negotiate a formal peace with the Seminoles. He also suggested that Jackson attempt to discover the "extent and limits of the country" to which the Seminoles "have a just claim, and to give such information for the guidance of persons who may wish to emigrate or explore the country, as you think proper." The President, he said, feels certain that whatever is done will "promote the public interest."[3]

Upon receiving the instruments of his commission from Secretary of State John Quincy Adams, Jackson asked about the Creek Red Sticks who had fled to Florida after the Creek War. "Are these Indians to be ordered up to the Creek Country, there to settle themselves, or are they to be protected in their new settlement?" He added that by moving the Creeks out of Florida, "greater security will be given to our frontier." And not only would it strengthen the frontier by bringing more whites into the area but it would be easier to prevent smuggling and end the problem of runaway slaves from the states above the Florida border. The matter was passed along to the secretary of war, who referred it to the President. Monroe then decided that "no immediate measure ought to be taken" because it would probably anger the people of Georgia, who feared that such a move would seem to postpone the extinguishment of the Creek title to lands in that state, something the federal government had promised to do years before. Instead the President asked for further information about the number of Creeks who might be involved.[4]

Jackson also wanted the runaway slaves to be transported back across the border; otherwise "scenes of murder and confusion will exist," he told Calhoun. And he felt that a garrison should be established at Tampa Bay "for the safety of the Frontier" and the elimination of smuggling into the Seminole Nation.[5]

On April 14, Jackson, his wife and adopted son, Andrew Jackson, Jr., and several others departed Nashville aboard the steamboat *Cumberland* and headed for New Orleans. From the Crescent City they moved on to Mobile Bay, where they waited more than a month for official instructions to be sent to the Spanish authorities in Pensacola to surrender Florida to him. The delay annoyed the general. Typical Spanish procrastination, he growled. They were obviously dragging their feet to irritate and frustrate him. Not until July 17, 1821, after interminable negotiations with Colonel José Callava, the governor, did he finally enter Pensacola and take possession of Florida.

Despite a tempestuous tenure of only a few months, Jackson performed creditably as territorial governor. He provided a framework for government by organizing East and West Florida into two counties with administrative and judicial offices. In setting up the government he insisted that there be "no distinction between the rich and poor the great and ignoble." Every freeman was to have the vote, he declared. He created civil governments for each county and appointed mayors and aldermen for the principal towns and empowered them to act as town councils. In a letter to Calhoun he modeled the government "so as to give perfect security to Individual rights" and as far as possible maintain a

"Spanish mode" in civil trials; but in criminal proceedings, common law was to be practiced. County courts also served as county governments, and for each court he appointed a clerk, sheriff, and prosecuting attorney.[6]

As for the Creek presence in Florida, Governor Jackson now decided to take action. He summoned both Creek and Seminole chiefs to Pensacola to instruct them about his policy. Among the chiefs were Neamathla, a Red Stick, and the mulatto King. As usual, when the Indians arrived on September 18 he put on a theatrical show for their benefit by surrounding himself with the trophies and symbols of his office. And when he spoke to them his voice was harsh and his demeanor stern, although he assured them that he was their friend and brother, that the hatchet had been buried, and that he wished nothing but their happiness.

"I give to you a plain, straight talk, and do not speak with a forked tongue,"[7] he said after a long introduction about how they had listened to bad men like Peter McQueen, the Prophet Francis, British agents, and Spanish "incendiaries." It is necessary that you be brought together, he continued, "either within the bounds of your old Nation, or at some other point, where your Father the President may be enabled to extend to you his fatherly care and assistance. Those who fled from their Nation and joined in the War against us, must return to their country . . . for they cannot be permitted to settle all over the Floridas and on her Sea Coast. Your White brethren must be settled there, to keep from you bad men and bad talks."

Jackson ended by demanding to know "where the Red people in the Floridas are settled" and how many of them there were so that the President could determine where they would be "collected together." The chiefs fully understood his meaning but said nothing. "Your former disobedience is forgotten," Jackson announced in conclusion, and the President "again receives you as his children."

Neamathla replied that he had heard many rumors about what would happen to them but had received no satisfaction until he had heard Jackson's talk. He thanked the governor for his "straight talk" and agreed to return the next day with the information Jackson requested.

Neamathla served as spokesman when he and the other chiefs reassembled in the executive chambers. He began by promising to carry the governor's talk to his Nation. Then he recited the names of fifteen towns and their locations stretching from the Apalachicola to the Suwannee rivers and estimated there were about two thousand "Souls" in those towns, but of the exact number he was uncertain.

Jackson then asked where the Seminoles (not the Creeks) wished to be "concentrated," and the chiefs replied that they would have to consult together and let him know. Very well, he responded, but tell your people to "remain where they are now, and to take care of their crops, collect all your Chiefs and inform me . . . where those who have been raised in the Floridas wish to be settled." This information would be sent to the President, who would in turn appoint an agent who would "point out where you are to settle and what he will do for you his red children." As for the Upper Creeks, they must return to their Nation, except for those who had been raised in Florida. They would be settled where the President directed. Jackson also promised to write to General McIntosh, the mixed-blood Creek chief, "that he shall not trouble you" when they moved north. He then shook hands with each of the chiefs and gave them a copy of his talk. "They replied they well understood it." The date was September 20, 1821. Less than a month later he resigned as governor and returned to Tennessee.[8]

On balance, Jackson's tenure as territorial governor was more successful than anyone thought possible. True, there were turbulent moments, particularly in his relations with Spanish officials in trying to wrench possession of important documents, like land grants, from their control. But he understood the necessity of establishing a territorial government according to the principles of the Northwest Ordinance of 1787. He certainly understood the need to unite East and West Florida and provide democratic rule as it was understood in the early 1820s. He especially wanted to integrate the territory into the United States, politically and culturally, and attract as many white settlers as possible. Their presence would serve as a guard against smugglers, pirates, slave traders from abroad, and foreign agents—especially foreign agents. As he told President Monroe, "Congress ought to provide an energetic code of law for its government, that may as far as possible . . . Americanize the Floridas."[9]

Jackson's tenure as governor lasted throughout what he called the "sickly season," when the heat and humidity were unbearable. He remained slightly more than eleven weeks in Florida, longer than he ever intended. He officially resigned on November 13, 1821, declaring he had fulfilled his mission and that his health and that of his wife needed the comfort and rest that only his home in Nashville could provide. Actually he left Florida on October 8 and arrived in Nashville on November 5. Monroe accepted his resignation on December 1, 1821.

Two years later the government finally got around to working out a treaty with the Seminoles. When Jackson read about it in the newspaper he immediately wrote to Calhoun with suggestions. "I am well acquainted with the Indian character," he said, "and I have no hesitation in saying that the government will experience some difficulty in concentrating the Florida Indians at the proposed point in the Peninsula" unless troops were sent to Tampa Bay before the talks were held. Such troops "would have a powerful influence upon their mind, and give *great effect* to the Talks of the Commissioners." He further suggested that the Indians be located where whites are in sufficient numbers to "overawe" them. Placing whites between the Indians and the Atlantic Ocean and the Gulf of Mexico, he wrote, "will afford protection & peace to all." Calhoun responded that it was too late to move troops from Baton Rouge to Tampa Bay, but in all other respects the commissioners, William P. DuVal, James Gadsden, and Bernardo Segui, would try to implement all the other points Jackson had raised.[10]

As it turned out the Seminoles were coaxed, bribed, and forced into accepting a reservation in central Florida that was swampy and infertile, although Jackson was told it was "valuable as hunting grounds." This arrangement was codified in the Treaty of Moultrie Creek, signed on September 18, 1823. Conditions on the reservation turned out to be so hideous that many of the Seminoles ran away and moved back to their former homes along the Apalachicola, where they were subsequently accused of stealing cattle and burning houses belonging to whites. The new territorial governor, William DuVal, called out the militia, subdued the Indians, deposed Neamathla, and installed a new head chief who was more amenable to white demands.[11]

When Jackson first arrived home after resigning as governor, several chiefs of the Upper Creeks visited him and poured out their complaints about how the agent, David Mitchell, was in cahoots with Chief McIntosh and was defrauding the poorest Creeks of their annuities, claiming debts owed to merchants that had to be paid first. Totally sympathetic to their complaints, Old Hickory promised to help. He immediately wrote Calhoun and informed him of this fraud. "You will see the hypocrisy of Genl. McIntosh of the Creek Nation. He is a . . . disciple of his late Agent and friend, Mitchel. Had I not sent on my resignation I would give him such a talk as would make him tremble." And indeed Jackson had learned long ago how to make an Indian tremble. The new agent must be instructed, he insisted, not to notice merchants' claims and to distribute the annuity to each family fairly. This "will put it out of their power to create fictitious debts, or to swindle the nation."[12]

It is because the Indians knew that Jackson was eminently fair with respect to the distribution of annuities (especially in protecting the poor) and in carrying out the conditions of treaty agreements that they regularly came to him at the Hermitage or wrote him when they had complaints about the treatment they had received from either agents or the government. They knew he could be severe and harsh, but they also knew he would be fair and protect their rights. And he did not hesitate to demand the arrest and imprisonment of whites who violated treaty agreements.

Indian chiefs were not his only visitors during the months following his return from Florida. Once he was home and retired from the army, various friends and Tennessee politicians began talking to him about his future. Not surprisingly, the local newspaper in Nashville suggested his name as a possible successor to President Monroe, a suggestion quickly repeated by other newspapers in other states. By mid-1822 it was a foregone conclusion that his name would be formally advanced for the presidency, and on June 27, Felix Grundy, a local state representative, wrote and informed him that his many friends in Tennessee wanted to know whether there was any reason or cause which "would render it improper" for them to bring his name forward "for the office of Chief Magistrate of the U States at the approaching Election."[13]

Jackson's position on this subject was one he had long ago adopted. He would remain silent. "The voice of the people I am told would bring me to the Presidential chair," he wrote, "and it is probable, some of the Legislatures may bring my name before the Public. —but I have long since determined to be perfectly Silent—I never have been a candidate for office, I never will." The people, of course, have a right "to call for any mans services in a republican government—and when they do, it is the duty of the individual, to yield his services to that call." That sentiment had always been his belief, even when ill and tired and almost overwhelmed with the criticisms leveled at him for his actions as a general and Indian commissioner. "I will be silent—neither sayi[ng] aye, or nay, altho I have been often solicite[d]." As for the presidency, he would serve if summoned but he would not actively seek the office.[14]

Accordingly, on July 20, the Tennessee legislature formally nominated Andrew Jackson for President of the United States. Simultaneously, there were a number of other developing candidacies aspiring to Monroe's chair, most of whom sat in the cabinet. To start, there was John Quincy Adams, who, as secretary of state, occupied the position that traditionally led straight to the presidency. Then there was William H. Crawford, the secretary of the treasury, who graciously, but foolishly, stepped aside in 1816, expecting Monroe to name him as successor—which of course Monroe did not. Finally, there was John C. Calhoun of South Carolina, the secretary of war. So, sneered the general, there they are, "all up for the Presidency, and he [Monroe] sits and looks on" without saying or doing anything. "Was I President I would Remove all who have come out as candidates for the Presidency—and fill my Cabinet with those whose whole time could be devoted to the duties of their office, and not to intrigue for the Presidency."[15]

Thus began the long process to place General Andrew Jackson in the White House. But it did not come quickly, or with the ease that so many people predicted. The Tennessee legislature might nominate him, but the traditional nominating engine, a congressional caucus, rejected the bid put forward by the general's friends and handed the prize to William H. Crawford. Some men had urged an end to caucus nominations, but they failed to take into account the political astuteness of Senator Martin Van Buren of New York, who succeeded in winning this nomination for Crawford, albeit with a much reduced number of participants in the caucus. Eventually there were five candidates: Adams, Crawford, Calhoun, Jackson, and the distinguished Speaker of the House of Representatives, Henry Clay, a man Old Hickory despised.

Shortly thereafter, Calhoun's candidacy collapsed when Pennsylvania came out in support of Jackson. The secretary needed a strong northern endorsement, and without it he recognized the hopelessness of his candidacy and agreed to stand for the vice presidency instead.

To increase his visibility as a statesman and silence those who contended that the general lacked valid credentials for the presidency, Jackson's friends in Tennessee decided to run him for the office of U.S. senator against the incumbent, John Williams, a very vocal critic of Old Hickory's negotiations with the Chickasaws and his record as territorial governor of Florida. Although it took a great deal of hustling to round up the necessary votes, since Williams had already received a number of pledges of support, the Hero was elected to the U.S. Senate on October 1, 1823, by the narrow vote of 35 to 25 in the state legislature.[16]

The narrowness of the vote rankled, but Jackson took some comfort in the fact that of the twenty-five men who voted against him only three were reelected in the next election. "Every intrigue that could exist," he told his friend John Coffee, "—& indeed corruption was resorted to" by Williams's friends to defeat me. "I am a senator against my wishes & feelings—but from my political creed . . . I am compelled to accept."

Actually his victory was much more significant than he allowed. "No person but *Jackson* could have broken down such a combination" of legislative votes that had been assembled against him, remarked one observer.[17]

A few weeks later, Jackson headed for Washington, and he arrived in the capital on December 3, two days after the start of the first session of the 18th Congress, and took his seat on December 5. His friends regularly urged him to be careful and not lose his temper under any circumstance. One misstep could ruin his presidential candidacy. But he had no fears on that score. "When it becomes necessary to philosophise & be meek," he said, "no man can command his temper better than I." And his appearance in the upper chamber proved to be nothing less than brilliant. The presence and charisma he exuded startled everyone. "The General is calm, dignified and makes as polished a bow as any man I have seen at Court," remarked Sam Houston. "He is much courted by the Great as well as the sovereign folks." Part of the reason was his physical appearance. He stood tall and ramrod-straight with a shock of graying hair that seemed to be standing at attention. His features were ordinary enough, "excepting the eyes which are very piercing & when he is excited resemble those of a chafed lion."

And he went out of his way to impress society. "He is constantly in motion to some Dinner party or other," Senator John H. Eaton informed Rachel, "and tonight stands engaged at a large Dancing party at Genl Browns."

The reaction he created in Congress amused Jackson. "I am told the opinion of those whose minds were prepared to see me with a Tomahawk in one hand, and a scalping knife in the other has greatly changed and I am getting on very smoothly."[18]

Indeed. Washington politicians were awed by his behavior, and Mrs. Daniel Webster said that General Jackson was the most presidential-looking of all the candidates now running in the next election.

Senator Jackson kept his wife informed of his activities and asked her to have their children write to him, "even Lyncoya," his Indian son. He intended "to exhibit" a letter Lyncoya had written to Monroe and Calhoun, "as I mean to try to have him recd. at the military school [West Point] as early as I can." A few days later he wrote his wife again and said he expected his two Andrews to "behave well . . . [and] I shall expect them both to have improved much, and also Lyncoya—I shall expect our son to answer the letter I have wrote him." In several subsequent letters he referred repeatedly to his Indian son. "Tell Lyncoya to read his book and be a good boy and obey you in all things."[19]

Then early in the new year he received the following:

Hermitage December 29, 1823

Dear Father

When the Mad Wolfe & Ogilvie came here from their woods, they said, How do you do, Father? You had not sent them to school as you have me. They could not [speak?] as I can. Their young ears had not known Neither had their war limbs gathered [streng]th from your table, nor rest under [your] roof, yet they called thee Father. [Whe]n as an infant you placed me on your knee [you] Learned me the talk of your Andrews [Jackson's adopted son, Andrew Jackson, Jr., and his ward, Andrew Jackson Hutchins] [and] made me their companion at Home, [their f]ellow in school, and their rival in their duty to you. If the Mad Wolfe & Ogilvie *[page torn]* call thee Father & not the bold, may [not] Lincoyer, & be justified? Yes he answers *[page torn]* he can? and since he is not told that [when?] a big man, he must have the white mans [sk]in, but to be just, to [avoid] only evil actions, to do good, is to be the *bigerest* of men, he hopes to have this stature of the ma[n]. Not to feel a blush, when he is told hereafter, *this is the Indian boy I* [once] *raised.*

Your obliged & grateful

Lincoyer[20]

Lyncoya was ten years old when he penned this letter. He obviously had Indian friends, as did his father. And Lyncoya was raised as Jackson's son. Unfortunately, he never got to West Point. By the time he reached the proper age for admission his father's rivals controlled the government, "which prevented any application for a warrant." Instead the boy chose the saddler's trade, which had been Jackson's occupation as a youth. In 1827, "his education being sufficient," Lyncoya was formally bound to a saddler in Nashville. But he died shortly thereafter of "pulmonary complaints," perhaps pneumonia, at the age of sixteen. Although nursed "with a father's and mother's tenderness," declared a newspaper's account of his death, he succumbed after "very severe sufferings" on June 1, 1828. He "expired under the roof of the hero who had conquered his nation but who followed his remains to a decent grave, and shed a tear as the earth closed over him forever."

Jackson truly loved the boy. "By the general and Mrs. Jackson he was mourned as a favorite son, and they always spoke of him with paternal affection."[21]

The general's early weeks and months as a senator were spent more in making an impression in the Washington social circle than in applying himself to his new duties. His reputation was greatly enhanced when the medal voted to him by Congress on February 27, 1815, for his triumphant victory over the British in New Orleans was formally presented to him by President Monroe in the White House on March 16, 1824, the day following the Hero's birthday. A glittering crowd of notables attended, including cabinet members, congressmen, and a select number of Jackson's friends and supporters. In presenting the medal the President recalled how grateful the nation was to him for rescuing them from one of the darkest moments in the history of the country. With that he placed the medal around Jackson's neck.

"You are aware how disagreable to me these shows of pomp & perade are," Old Hickory wrote his wife that evening, "& how irksome it is for me to speak of myself—still it was necessary; and I with reluctance performed it—not without a tremor which allways seises me on such occasions."

As he turned and faced the audience, Jackson spoke softly and with genuine gratitude. It is not certain whether he then read from a prepared statement or spoke extemporaneously. In any event his remarks were gracious and appropriate for the occasion.

Receiving this medal, he said, brought back memories of how the "Tocsin of war" summoned thousands of "brave yeomanry of our country to support its Eagles & to protect our frontier from the ruthless savage & the inroads of a British foe." In the name of those patriots who suffered "privation & peril" in the victory he accepted "this emblem" that Congress had "conceived me worthy to possess." Against a superior and well-organized army of professional British soldiers intent on "Beauty & Booty" in New Orleans, the heroic Americans who fought with him "preserved it from polution & Ravage." That victory would always be remembered "as one of the proudest moments of my life."[22]

The recollection of that victory and what it meant to Americans was what his supporters emphasized as the presidential contest of 1824 entered its final year. The field had been reduced to four candidates, Jackson, Adams, Crawford and Clay, and almost all the talk around the halls of the Capitol involved the possible outcome of the election. At first Jackson's candidacy was dismissed or minimized because of his singular lack of appropriate credentials. What else had he done besides kill Indians and British soldiers? And while spread-eagle nationalists might delight in such a candidate, most serious voters recognized that that career did not merit occupancy of the White House. But with each passing month it became increasing obvious to Washington observers that the general's popularity was so widespread among the electorate that he had become a real contender and might indeed win election.

A frightening thought, especially to Henry Clay. The Speaker could hardly believe that a quarrelsome, irascible, and difficult-to-control "military chieftain," who disregarded law, the Constitution, the powers of Congress, and the property rights of foreigners in their own country, could be placed at the head of the government. Such a result would surely end in despotism.

And now that frightening man sat in the Senate, saying absolutely nothing and doing nothing as important issues such as the tariff and internal improvement were being debated and legislated. Indeed, the Old Hero was silent. There were, he said, "so many who by their itch for *discoursing,* seem desirous to enlighten and inform the community and their brethren associates." That was not his style. "I am content rather to be a listener, than an actor."[23]

Naturally enough, because of his military experience and knowledge, Jackson was made chairman of the Senate Committee on Military Affairs. And who should he find as a member of that committee but Thomas Hart Benton, the senator from Missouri, who with his brother, Jesse, had tangled with Jackson in a barroom brawl back in 1813 just before the outbreak of the Creek War. Jesse had put the bullet in the general's shoulder that still lay in place, periodically causing Jackson considerable discomfort.

The two senators, both realists, both pragmatists, and both westerners, recognized immediately the value of putting aside their ancient feud and forgetting the past in the interest of advancing their future careers. Benton was a skillful parliamentarian in debate, and his support could be very important. Besides, Jackson was on a determined course of proving to all the Washington potentates that he and his presidential candidacy needed to be taken seriously. All of which struck Senator John H. Eaton as something wonderful and unique, and he shared his delight with Rachel. "It will afford you great pleasure I know," he wrote, "to be informed that all his old quarrels have been settled. . . . He is in harmony and good understanding with every body, a thing I know you will be happy to hear." Jackson himself added a postscript to the letter. It "is all true. . . . It is a pleasing subject to me that I am now at peace with all the world." When he first arrived in Washington everyone expected to meet an uncouth frontiersman, ready to commit "some act of violence." They did not know me. "In this they have much mistaken my character." They believed I was "a most dangerous and terrible man—of savage habits & disposition, and wholly unacquainted with civilised life." They said publicly in the newspapers that "I can break, & trample under foot the constitution of the country, with as much unconcern & careless indifference" as would one of our frontiersmen who might break British game laws if suddenly transported to that country. They even thought I would behave like Sam Houston and dress in Indian clothes and carry a tomahawk, "allways ready to knock down, and scalp any and every person who differed with me in opinion." They did not know the real Andrew Jackson. They did not know the man who long ago learned the important lesson of controlling his temper when necessary and only letting it run free when it suited his purpose. Instead of a war-whooping savage they "found a man of even temper, firm in his opinions advanced, and allways allowing others to enjoy theirs."[24]

And Jackson spoke the truth. His lack of control, his sudden bursts of passion, his emotional tantrums directed at soldiers, Indians, or politicians, were always under his sovereign command.

With Benton, the reconciliation with the Hero came quickly and naturally. Jackson decided he needed the Missouri senator and therefore took the first step and inquired after the health of Benton's wife. Several days later the Hero called at Benton's lodgings and, not finding him home, left his card: "Andrew Jackson for Colonel Benton and lady." Shortly thereafter Benton visited Jackson's boardinghouse and left his card. Finally the two men walked up to each other, shook hands, and smiled away the enmity of ten years.[25]

As chairman of the Military Affairs Committee the general took special interest in the concerns of veterans, especially those who had served with him. And because of his position, his former comrades in arms, on hearing he had "turned politician," wrote to him for help in winning pensions or other financial benefits. Some of their claims were of long standing and "almost obsolete," and the senator felt a special obligation to bring them to a speedy and successful conclusion. "An old soldier, you know, should not in time of peace forget his old associates."[26]

Nor did he forget Native Americans. He still wanted them removed by legislative fiat, but that would obviously have to wait until his election as President. Still, problems relating to the Indians were regularly brought to his attention— land claims involved in the Seminole War for one thing, boundary disputes between whites and Indians for another. Governor McMinn of Tennessee sent along a letter by Chief Black Fox complaining about the amount of land provided the Cherokees who had moved to Arkansas under the terms of the treaty of 1817 that Jackson had negotiated. It "was not near as much as that we relinquished" in Tennessee, the chief protested, and he demanded more territory along the White River area. It was true that the boundaries were not properly drawn—and rarely to the benefit of Indians—and Jackson fully appreciated the problem, knowing full well that unless treaties were "complied with literally and fully," constant discord and even outbreaks of violence ensued. The disputed western areas would continue to create irritating problems, sometimes requiring the renegotiation of treaties.[27]

The Choctaw boundary established by the Treaty of Doak's Stand was one such that required renegotiation, and it undoubtedly caused Jackson some anguish when he learned that Puckshenubbee had been "much beaten by a party of Indians for haveing agreed to the treaty." John Pitchlynn, the interpreter, expressed fears that the chief was "likely to be again maltreated on that account" unless Jackson intervened. "An admonition" from the general "will prevent any attack in future on that good Old man." Unfortunately when Puckshenubbee went to Washington as part of a Choctaw delegation to renegotiate the boundary he stumbled down a steep bluff while taking a walk late one night along a darkened area. He fractured his skull, shoulder blade, and collarbone. After lingering in and out of consciousness for two days, he died in mid-October 1824.[28]

Pushmataha also died in 1824. He too had gone to Washington to attend the treaty negotiations and had come down with the croup. Here was a man who had fought with Old Hickory in the Creek War and at the battle of New Orleans and argued with him at the treaty grounds in 1820. Poor Push. He could eat possum and rabbit on the banks of the Bucatunna without difficulty but the highly seasoned dishes served in Washington brought on a "complication of diseases that resulted in his death on the night of the 23d of December, 1824."

Jackson, along with a number of other officials, gathered at the bedside of the dying Mingo. The general leaned over the sixty-year-old man and asked, "What is the last request of the chief?"

Pushmataha looked up at him and whispered, "Bury me with the big guns firing over the grave." And his request was honored. He was buried in Washington with an artillery salute fired over the gravesite. Several military companies turned out for the funeral, together with marines from the navy yard and two military bands. "It was a great procession." Many congressmen, including Jackson, attended and "treated us with great kindness," said Chief David Folsom. "I can truly say that we have received every mark of friendship and brotherly love from the white people since we have been among them." As another gesture of respect for Pushmataha he was buried with all the honors of a brigadier general.[29]

The deaths of these two great chiefs and the ongoing pressure to exchange their remaining lands in Mississippi prompted the Choctaw warriors and headmen to replace their three full-blood Medal Chiefs with educated mixed-bloods who understood the white man's law and could better prevent the tribe's wholesale removal to the west. And the Choctaws were not alone. The Creeks, Chickasaws, and Cherokees also took a position of vehement opposition to any further sale or exchange of their lands.

As chairman of the Senate Military Affairs Committee, Jackson regularly asked the secretary of war for copies of letters and documents dealing with past Indian treaties, including his own, and the commissioners who had been appointed to conduct them. It was as though the first thing on his agenda if elected President would be to address the entire problem of the Indian and produce a prompt resolution.[30]

For the remainder of the year, as his national popularity kept growing, the presidential election crowded almost everything else from Jackson's mind. He had become a serious contender; indeed only John Quincy Adams approached him in attracting support. Crawford had suffered a severe stroke and there was little his chief manager could do to bolster his campaign. Clay had expected to capture the west and south, but Jackson's candidacy ended that hope. Still the Speaker had enormous influence in the House of Representatives, and if the election went to the House because no candidate received a majority of electoral votes he would in all probability be chosen the next President.

The election took place during the fall of 1824, and when the votes were tabulated it showed that the election would in fact be determined by the House. No one had the constitutionally required majority of electoral votes. Jackson had a plurality of 99, Adams came next with 84, Crawford followed with 41, and Clay brought up the rear with 37. In the popular vote, Jackson again beat out the competition with 152,901 votes against 114,023 for Adams, 47,217 for Clay, and 46,979 for Crawford. There was no problem with the vice presidential race. John C. Calhoun won handily.[31]

As many congressmen had predicted months earlier, the number of candidates in the field precluded an election in which one individual would be a clear-cut winner. Inasmuch as the Twelfth Amendment to the Constitution mandated only the top three contenders to go to the House of Representatives, Henry Clay was automatically eliminated. And because of the high regard in which he was held by his colleagues in the lower chamber, he, more than any one else, would select the next President.

Jackson was philosophical. "Having been supported by the majority of the people," he wrote his friend John Overton, "I can have no feelings on this occasion—If party or intrigue should prevail, and exclude me, I shall retire to my comfortable farm with great pleasure." It is more important, he told Samuel Swartwout, "that our happiness and plain republican institutions should be well maintained" than that any one man "shall take charge of our destinies." Who shall rule is "less important than how he . . . shall govern when in power." "I have risked much for the liberties of my country, and my anxious and sincere prayer is, that they may long endure."[32]

But, as he should have known, once Congress reconvened in December 1824, intrigue and political shenanigans ran rampant. All the managers of the different candidates busied themselves in trying to win over Clay for their candidate. One of the most persistent rumors involved the likelihood that Clay would throw his support to John Quincy Adams in return for appointment as secretary of state. Since that office traditionally led to the presidency, there was increasing talk that the two men had worked out a "bargain & sale" by which they would accommodate each other's ambitions. "I envy not the man who may climb into the presidential chair in any other way, but by the free suffrage of the people," Jackson rumbled.

Clay did indeed have a meeting with Adams on January 9, 1825. "Mr. Clay came at six," Adams recorded in his journal, "and spent the evening with me in a long conversation."[33]

On February 9, 1825, the House of Representatives met to fulfill its constitutional duty of selecting the President, and on the first ballot John Quincy Adams was elected. He received the votes of thirteen states, followed by Jackson with seven and Crawford with four.

"I weep for the Liberty of my country," moaned Jackson. The "rights of the people have been bartered for promises of offices."[34] Or so it seemed, for no sooner was Adams inaugurated than he chose Clay as his secretary of state.

Jackson raged. "So you see, the Judas of the West has closed the contract and will receive the thirty pieces of silver. His end will be the same. Was there ever witnessed such a bare faced corruption in any country before?" Soon other congressmen repeated the charge. A "corrupt bargain" had been struck between Adams and Clay, they contended, to deprive the people of their right to choose the President. Jackson may not have had the majority, but he was certainly the clear favorite of the people. For politicians in Washington to disregard their decision was infamous. "Oh," wailed Jackson, I "shudder for the liberty of my country."[35]

He immediately resigned his office and headed back to Tennessee. At each stop along the way, crowds turned out to welcome him and deplore the criminality that had occurred by corrupt politicians. "Well, general," said one man in West Alexandria, Pennsylvania, "we did all we could for you here, but the rascals at Washington cheated you out of it."

"Indeed, my old friend," rasped the still-seething Jackson, "there was *cheating,* and *corruption,* and *bribery* too."[36]

So ended the presidential election of 1824–1825, but so began the campaign for the presidential election of 1828. And with it the entire political landscape underwent a revolutionary change. Martin Van Buren with his conservative forces abandoned the badly stricken Crawford and joined Calhoun to put together an alliance in support of General Jackson that became the Democratic Republican Party or simply the Democratic Party. The friends of Adams and Clay coalesced to form the National Republican Party. Van Buren toured the south to win support for the new alliance, and a fierce battle began in and out of Congress to win the next election.[37]

And the Indians were not forgotten in this bitter contest. During the Adams administration, Georgia made renewed attempts to get the government to honor its pledge made in 1802 to extinguish Indian claims within Georgia's borders. The new secretary of war, James Barbour, suggested setting up a territory in the west and relocating individual Indians, rather than entire tribes, to this area. But Georgia objected. According to the Treaty of Indian Springs, which the Monroe administration had negotiated in 1821, the Creek Indians ceded additional land in Georgia, except for a strip west of the Chattahoochee River, and they were required to remove by September 1, 1826. The governor of the state, George M. Troup, wanted to hurry the process along and opened talks with the Creek chiefs in order to run the new boundary line. As expected, there were disagreements and the Indians protested. Adams called for an investigation which when completed indicated that the Treaty of Indian Springs had not been duly approved by the Creek Nation. At a cabinet meeting, Barbour adopted the Jackson position by arguing against making treaties with the Indians and insisting that they were "altogether subject to our laws." Adams questioned the constitutionality of such an interpretation, at which point Secretary of State Clay ventured to say that Indians were "inferior" and that there never was a "full-blooded Indian who took to civilization." He predicted that they were destined to extinction and that "their disappearance from the human family will be no great loss to the world."

None of the other members of the cabinet objected or showed any surprise at this blatant contempt for a so-called "inferior race," an attitude, recorded

Adams, for which "I fear there is too much foundation."[38] The widespread denigration and outright slander of Native Americans crossed party lines, crossed sectional lines, and crossed social and economic lines. It was a near-universal attitude that most Americans accepted as commonplace.

Adams called a halt to the survey and ordered a renegotiation of the treaty. In an agreement reached on January 24, 1826, the Treaty of Indian Springs was declared "null and void." Troup strenuously objected and threatened to call out the militia to sustain Georgia's territorial rights. Adams responded by vowing to employ "all means under his control to maintain the faith of the nation." Meanwhile the anti-administration Senate appointed a committee headed by Thomas Hart Benton to look into the dispute. Not surprisingly, the committee faulted the government for interfering in the internal affairs of a state and applauded everything that Troup had done to protect Georgia's interests. Once this report was published, John Quincy Adams was politically finished in the south. That report alone constituted a "recommendation of Jackson to the voice" of the entire region. In fact, in Georgia both sets of electors in the 1828 presidential contest pledged themselves to Old Hickory.[39]

At one point the administration did make an effort to treat with the Chickasaws and Choctaws to get them to agree to another cession of land. It appointed three commissioners to undertake the negotiations: Thomas Hinds, Jackson's colleague in the Treaty of Doak's Stand; John Coffee; and William Clark, former governor of the Missouri Territory, who had in the past participated in a number of boundary talks with the Indians. In addition, John D. Terrill was also appointed as special agent to prepare the Chickasaws for the negotiation. Terrill and Coffee immediately contacted Jackson for advice, and Hinds came to see the general at his home outside Nashville.

Jackson was shown the instructions to the commissioners from the secretary of war and discussed the matter at length with Hinds. His recommendation followed the main lines of the policy he had embraced years before, but there were additions. He told Terrill that from his knowledge of the Chickasaws they would not under any circumstances sell a portion of their land. It will be easier, he said, to work toward an exchange of their *entire* country. But be honest with them. Tell them frankly that the whites will continue to migrate into their lands and they will harass the President with demands that the Indian titles be extinguished. Use the example of the Cherokees and Creeks in Georgia, he said. It will "furnish a striking example." Then say that their father the President will give them a country of equal extent in the west from which they will never be moved. "You must be prepared to give assurance of permanency of title, and dwell upon the idea that they will never be asked to surrender an acre more."

Jackson also suggested that Terrill intimate that a union among the Choctaws, Creeks, and Chickasaws might result from a general migration of these tribes, which would create "a great, powerful and happy people" so that when their children were educated they might become members "of the United States, as Alabama and Mississippi are." It is an interesting commentary that Andrew Jackson fully expected the Indians to become citizens and participate in civil government, once they were educated and transformed into cultural white men.

Above all, he concluded, do not make promises you cannot "religiously perform." If you do and you cannot deliver, "they will say to you, you lye too much. nothing will defeat a negotiation with Indians so soon as the discovery of an attempt to deceive them."[40]

To Coffee he again advised that they go the distance and get both tribes to move en masse. "You must get the whole territory or none," he counseled. And do not haggle over the price. Your instructions do not stipulate any restrictions over what is to be paid. Let the President and the Senate worry about that. And when it comes to money, insist that it be "an annuity for a term of years *only*." From experience I know that "you will have to pay them *well*." Just keep in mind that "the chickasaw and choctaw country are of great importance to us in the defence of the lower country, a white population instead of the Indian, would strengthen our own defence much."

If the tribes protest that they do not know the country beyond the Mississippi, Jackson continued, agree to letting them see it; but appoint an agent to accompany the inspection team, and stipulate that they will have just so many months to decide. "Unless the Indians are acquainted with the country you propose giving them in exchange, they will not, nay, ought not, to enter into a final treaty before they obtain this information." And always remind them that the treaty is not final until approved by the President and Senate.[41]

Despite all this advice and the conversations Jackson had with Hinds at the Hermitage, the negotiations failed. It was added proof that if the southern tribes were ever to be removed en masse it would require Andrew Jackson's leadership and determination from the White House.

For the remainder of John Quincy Adams's term in office the presidential contest between the two parties raged to an ever fiercer degree. New forms of campaigning were devised and old ones perfected. Democrats planted hickory trees in town squares and wore hickory leaves in their hats to show their allegiance. Hickory brooms, hickory canes, and hickory sticks were distributed everywhere. "Odds nuts and drumsticks!" snorted one National Republican newspaper. "What have hickory trees to do with republicanism and the great contest."

What indeed. But ordinary citizens loved it. "The hurra boys were for Jackson," sighed one man, "and . . . all the noisey *Turbulent Boisterous Politicians* are with him."

Without doubt the election of 1828 was one of the filthiest in American history, with no holds barred. Jackson's wife was labeled a bigamist, his mother a prostitute, and he himself a murderer. And Adams hardly fared better. He was called a pimp for the Czar of Russia and charged with living in kingly splendor in the White House. Other charges of immorality or misbehavior by the two men were invented or distorted. But the one issue that towered over all was the "corrupt bargain" charge, and it sufficed to defeat Adams's bid for reelection.

When the final results of the election were counted, Jackson garnered 647,276 popular and 178 electoral votes to Adams's 508,064 popular and 83 electoral votes. Adams swept New England, New Jersey, and Delaware. He also received a majority of electoral votes in Maryland, sixteen out of New York's thirty-six votes, and a single vote from Illinois. Jackson took all the rest. His "triumphant majority," trumpeted one newspaper, resulted from the "ardor of thousands." It was "the howl of raving Democracy," sneered another.[42]

"Well, for Mr. Jackson's sake, I am glad," said Rachel Jackson, "for my own part, I never wished it."[43] A few weeks later, on December 22, she suffered a massive heart attack and died. She was buried on Christmas Eve in her garden. Over her grave her husband erected a small, round, white-domed roof supported by pillars of white marble resembling a Greek temple. Later a tablet was placed directly over the grave that read in part, "A being so gentle and so virtuous, slander might wound but could not dishonor."

Weeks later the Hero of New Orleans prepared to leave for Washington to take up his duties as President of the United States. "My heart is nearly broke," he wept.[44]

Chapter 13

The Indian Removal Act

From the very start of his administration, President Andrew Jackson knew exactly what he wanted to do. He said he would institute a policy of "reform retrenchment and economy." Convinced the government had become corrupt over the past decade, he promised to cleanse the "Aegean stables," inaugurate a system of rotation in distributing the patronage (his enemies called it a "spoils system"), and practice fiscal conservatism to pay off the national debt. A democrat to the core, he believed his program would "protect liberty," "restore virtue in government," and ensure "obedience to the popular will." The people are sovereign, he declared. Their will must be obeyed. "The majority is to govern."[1]

In his inaugural address, given on a bright and sunny March 4, 1829, President Jackson stood before a cheering crowd estimated at twenty thousand and addressed these goals. He also raised the issue of the Indian. But his remarks masked his true intent. "It will be my sincere and constant desire," he declared, "to observe toward the Indian tribes within our limits a just and liberal policy, and to give that humane and considerate attention to their rights and their wants which is consistent with the habits of our Government and the feelings of our people." Anyone who knew him knew what that meant: removal of the remaining southern tribes beyond the Mississippi River.[2]

Indeed he planned to undertake at long last the task he felt should have been completed years before, namely to involve Congress in what had been the sole action of the President to relocate the Indians in the west, where, he said, "they will always be free from the mercenary influence of White men, and undisturbed by the local authority of the states." Once the relocation was completed, the federal government could then "exercise a parental control over their interests and possibly perpetuate their race."[3]

To ensure proper assistance in his efforts at removal, Jackson appointed his longtime friend and biographer John H. Eaton to serve as secretary of war, knowing that Eaton would execute his directions with all the loyalty and dedication with which he had performed so many other tasks for him in the past. In addition he appointed John M. Branch, a Georgian totally committed to removal, as attorney general. Such a combination of Jackson, Eaton, and Branch virtually guaranteed the speedy relocation of the southern tribes. But the President's main task involved persuading Congress to join his efforts and thereby provide additional legal and moral authority to his plan.

Jackson was anxious to start the process as soon as possible, because events were already developing that could escalate into a dangerous confrontation between the government and the state of Georgia. On December 20, 1828, approximately a month after Jackson's overwhelming election as President (and perhaps because of it), the Georgia legislature, infuriated over the Cherokee presumption in declaring its complete sovereignty after adopting a constitution modeled on the U.S. Constitution, decreed that all Indian residents within the state's boundary lines would fall under its jurisdiction after six months. Once this happened, serious trouble would surely follow. The legislature also acted because it had lost patience with the federal government for its failure to keep the promise it made in 1802 to extinguish Indian land titles within Georgia.

In view of this action and the likelihood that Alabama and Mississippi would follow suit, Jackson dispatched two Tennessee generals, John Coffee and William Carroll, to visit the Creeks and Cherokees and try to persuade them to remove voluntarily. They were instructed to inform the tribes that the President agreed with Georgia's action. Tell them, Jackson directed, that "the President is of opinion that the only mode left for the Indians to escape the effects of such enactments, and consequences more destructive . . . is, *for them to emigrate. . . .* He is sincerely anxious . . . to save these people, and relieve the States." Describe to them "the fine and fertile and abundant country" in the west where the federal government "could and *would* protect them fully in the possession of the soil, and their right of self government." There they will grow "to be our equals in privileges, civil and religious." But if they refuse to remove "they must necessarily entail destruction upon their race."

Obviously Jackson's concern over the likely extinction of Native Americans had grown stronger during the past few years. It behooved him therefore to convince the tribes to remove if they wished to "perpetuate their race." But their possible extinction never dominated his thinking. National security remained his prime concern.

It is also true that in all his dealings with Native Americans he showed genuine feelings of concern for their welfare, particularly the poor among them, and their rights as members of their particular tribes—provided their welfare and rights did not collide with those of the United States. His paternalism was appreciated by many chiefs who regarded him as their friend. They knew he had taken an Indian orphan into his home and had raised him as his son. They also knew that he anticipated Indians' becoming full-fledged citizens of the United States once they adopted the habits of white men. Given the greed of whites for Indian territory and their insatiable demands that would only accelerate in the coming years, and given the fact that the two races could not and would not "intermingle" or live side by side, Jackson felt he had no choice but to insist on removal as the only means of preventing conflict and Indian annihilation. As "hard and cruel," as the policy was, wrote one contemporary a short while later, it "is now universally felt to have been as kind as it was necessary." Indeed many historians today agree with that conclusion.[4]

Which is not to exonerate Sharp Knife of the horrors that followed. Still, to properly understand him and why he behaved as he did, it is necessary to reemphasize that he never intended or imagined the horror that accompanied removal and that he acted out of a fierce nationalism and an overwhelming concern for the nation's security and unity. Quite frankly, Jackson was obsessed over national security, which is quite understandable considering his experiences over the years with the British and Spanish and their involvement with hostile southern tribes.

It is true that he could be a fire-breathing and ruthless opponent if crossed or contradicted. Like most Americans at the time, he was a racist (not that he had the faintest idea what that meant), and he held an assortment of wrongheaded prejudices about Native Americans. But he was not a madman intent on genocide. Nor was he intent on the wholesale punishment of Indian tribes for their alleged past "misconduct." Removal was meant to prevent annihilation, not cause it.

Carroll and Coffee followed Jackson's instructions to the letter. But they did not have his skill in a face-to-face encounter and the chiefs of both tribes absolutely refused to grant the President's request. This was their land; their fathers were buried in it; it was their home. They had no connection with the Arkansas

Territory and had no desire to visit it. Not only would they refuse to emigrate, they told the commissioners, but they would counsel other tribes against emigration.[5]

The resistance of the Indians and what had become mounting opposition by many church groups to any attempt by the government to relocate the southern tribes convinced Jackson that a major political problem was developing that could easily spin out of control. He had to take immediate executive action. So, as a first step, he ordered the army to run off all white intruders in Indian lands and if necessary destroy their cabins and fields. Next he assigned Thomas L. McKenney to undertake the task of molding public opinion in favor of removal. McKenney had served as superintendent of Indian trade and had become the head of the Bureau of Indian Affairs, beginning in 1824. He was hailed as a humanitarian who cared personally and deeply about Native Americans. And although he had supported Adams's reelection, more important, he favored removal. He also recognized that whites, from the beginning of their arrival in North America, had pushed the Indians westward and degraded their cultures until many eastern tribes had vanished. Furthermore, he appreciated the fact that Indians readily acquired the worst vices of the white race. If they were ever to make real progress toward civilization and legal equality with other Americans, they must be removed. Such was his thinking. He therefore proved to be a most effective advocate among church groups in getting them to understand that removal was best for the red people.[6]

Jackson also cautioned key southern leaders against any action that might jeopardize the administration's new policy and generate northern opposition. Then he replaced a number of Indian agents with reliable loyalists whose commitment to removal was above question. When he took office there were twenty such agents and thirty-six subagents. Over the next two years he removed ten agents and nineteen subagents.[7]

The urgency to bring about removal as quickly as possible increased with the discovery of gold in northeastern Georgia in the summer of 1829, bringing with it an avalanche of white squatters into Cherokee territory. And although the invasion brought boisterous demands from church groups to expel the intruders, led by Jeremiah Evarts, the administration saw it as additional proof that the whites were about to overwhelm the Indians in their eastern territory.[8]

"Overwhelm" is hardly the word. The Cherokees were being inundated. And they cried out to their Great Father to protect them. "There are hundreds of whitemen searching and digging for gold within the limits of the nation," they wrote. ". . . The number of these intruders has been variously stated from one to two thousand . . . which we cannot but consider as depriving us of property for which the faith of the Gov't is pledged for our protection. . . . We humbly request that you will consider the subject, as soon as the pressure of business will admit, and if possible grant the wishes of our people."[9]

Not only were Americans invading Indian territory, but the annuities owed to the tribes were frequently handed over by agents to white creditors to pay for outstanding debts. When Jackson heard that the agent for the Creeks had "paid out large sums in discharge of judgements recovered by the white citizens of Alabama," he immediately instructed the secretary of war to investigate the "impropriety" of this action and submit a report. Control of money owed the tribes, he protested, was being taken away from them without their knowledge or consent.[10]

All of the more cordial—that is, nonviolent—relations between the two races that had been developing since the end of the Indian wars over ten years earlier now seemed close to collapsing. "Our white brothers on each side of us appear to have lost all the good feelings which formerly existed," complained several Creek chiefs. "All appear to have turned their hands to crush us." They have no regard for us or our rights as guaranteed by your treaties.[11]

By this time, whites were more brazen and determined to take whatever Indian land was still available within settled states, and they became extremely adept at justifying their actions. A short time later, several white settlers insisted that they had moved into tribal lands with the consent of the agent and the permission of the Indians themselves. They said they had settled in the Cherokee Nation "and pitched their crops for the year." They further declared that they "will not now permit, at this season of the year, their families to be turned out of doors, and their wives and children deprived of the means of subsistence." Not "without making the manly resistance of husbands and fathers in defence of every thing sacred and dear." They had a right to settle in the Nation, they protested, and they expected the state to enforce their right.[12]

One "old and feeble" chief wrote to his Great Father and advised him of the "dreadful consequences" if these conditions persisted. "Your white sons and daughters are moving into my country in abundance and they are spoiling my lands and taking possession of the Red peoples improvements. . . . And your soldiers have refused to prevent it." Your white children "are bringing whiskey and opening drinking houses . . . they steal our property and make false accounts against us [and then] they sue us in your state courts for what we know nothing of." And what has been the result? "My Red children . . . have been compelled to resort to there guns." When that happens "the whites have collected themselves in bodies and hunted up . . . and shot them as if . . . they had been so many wild dogs." "All I want is peace," the old chief begged. Only you my Great Father can help. "With every Respect I have the honor to be your unfortunate old brother."[13]

This was the situation Jackson faced when he became President, and it kept getting worse over the next several years. The collision of the two peoples in the southeast had become increasingly dangerous. The worst in white culture seemed to be destroying what was left of Indian life and civilization. He had to do something. So, as his final action in inaugurating the new Indian policy, he prepared to go to Congress and request appropriate legislation to end the collision, the intrusion, the killing, and the debasement of Indian culture and "save the remaining tribes from extinction." In December 1829, when the two houses reconvened, he formally presented his proposal and provided specific details. Without doubt he fully intended to make Indian removal his administration's first piece of major legislation.

Among the Jackson papers there is a draft of his first annual message in the President's hand. In it he set down his thinking about foreign affairs, rotation, the tariff, internal improvements, the public debt, the national bank, and the Indians. The Native Americans constituted the final topic he dealt with, but the document breaks off just before he reached a conclusion. What he wrote out was a recapitulation of present conditions, particularly how the government had tried to civilize the tribes and encourage them to abandon "their wandering ways." All to no avail, he said. "It will not answer to encourage them to the idea of exclusive self government. It is impracticable." No people can form a government or social compact "until education and intelligence was first introduced." True, each tribe has a few educated and well-informed men, but the great body of southern Indians "are erratic in their habits, and wanting in those endowments, which are suited to a people who would direct themselves and under it be happy and prosperous." And while we have tried to be solicitous and caring in our treatment of them, we have told them that "it cannot be conceded to them to continue their efforts at independence within the limits of any of the states."

With these harsh words the document ends. But the draft message was subsequently turned over to advisers, including Martin Van Buren, Andrew Jackson Donelson, William B. Lewis, Amos Kendall, and James A. Hamilton, the son of

Alexander Hamilton. Together they produced a final version that was delivered to Congress after it reconvened on December 7, 1829, and read aloud by a clerk. It was written in a flat, somber and prosaic style, quite unlike Jackson's unique and forceful form of utterance.

It starts off by describing the current situation and what the President had recently done to correct it. These southern tribes, he said, are surrounded by whites who are destroying the resources the Indians depend on for livelihood and which will therefore doom them to "weakness and decay." Look at what happened to the Mohegans, the Narragansetts, and the Delawares, he continued. They are gone, extinct. And the same fate "is fast overtaking the Choctaw, the Cherokee, and the Creek. . . . Humanity and national honor demand that every effort should be made to avert so great a calamity." It is too late to wonder whether it was just to have included them within the territorial bounds of the United States. That step cannot be retraced. A state cannot be dismembered by Congress without its consent nor restricted in the exercise of its constitutional powers. You are now asked whether it is indeed possible to do something for the Indians that is consistent with the rights of the states and "actuated by feelings of justice and a regard for our national honor . . . to preserve their much-injured race."

As a matter of fact, something can be done. "I suggest for your consideration" the propriety of setting apart an ample area west of the Mississippi, outside the limits of any state or territory now formed, to be guaranteed to the Indian tribes, each tribe having distinct control over the portion of land assigned to it. There they can be Indians, not cultural white men; there they can enjoy their own governments subject to no interference from the United States except when necessary to preserve peace on the frontier and between the several tribes; there they can learn the "arts of civilization" so that the race will be perpetuated and serve as a reminder of the "humanity and justice of this Government."

The emigration should be voluntary, the President declared, for it would be "as cruel as unjust to compel the aborigines to abandon the graves of their fathers and seek a home in a distant land." They should be "distinctly informed" that if they choose to remain where they are within the limits of the states, then "they must be subject to their laws." But if they stay it is surely visionary to expect protection of their claims to land on which they have never dwelt nor made improvements "merely because they have seen them from the mountains or passed them in the chase." By submitting to state law if they stay and receiving protection in their persons and property like other citizens, "they will ere long become merged in the mass of our population."[14]

And that ended the section in the message on the Indians. Since removal would be voluntary, that meant that the Indians had to sign treaties by which they formally gave their consent to emigrate. And that could prove exceedingly difficult.

Indeed, reaction around the country to Jackson's proposal came as a shock to him. A storm of protest directed by the American Board of Commissions for Foreign Affairs, again under the leadership of Jeremiah Evarts, engulfed both Congress and the administration. Cries of outrage came in the form of petitions opposing removal and protesting the betrayal of Native Americans and the many promises given them in the past. How could civilized Christian men thrust "aborigines" into a wasteland and not see the act as evil and contemptible?

But Jackson was not to be denied. To ensure the passage of a removal bill, he actively intervened in Congress to make certain that committees in the House and Senate charged with drawing up the bill were staffed with reliable supporters of his policy. As it turned out, Hugh Lawson White of Tennessee, whom Jackson first considered as a possible secretary of war, chaired the Senate Committee on Indian Affairs, and John Bell, also of Tennessee, headed the House committee. And both committees were dominated by southerners committed to removal. Additional strength for the pro-removal forces was provided by Andrew Stevenson, the Speaker of the House, who could be relied on to break any tie votes that might occur. As it developed, his vote was required on three separate occasions to save the removal bill from defeat.

Congress referred the various parts of the President's message to the appropriate committees, and on February 22, 1830, Senator White reported out a bill from his committee that involved an exchange of land with the eastern tribes. Not surprisingly, the Bell committee in the House reported a similar bill two days later. But the Senate version came up first for a full debate.

It set off a brouhaha of the first order, and it began on April 6. Senator Theodore Frelinghuysen of New Jersey led the opposition and spoke for three days, for a minimum of two hours each day. He was a former president of the American Board of Commissioners for Foreign Missions, a deeply religious man who was nationally known for his record of humanitarian concern for the plight of the Indians. In his address before the Senate he castigated the Democrats for their hypocritical attempt to disguise the fact that they were intent on removing not just the southern tribes, but all the Indians; and if those Native Americans refused, to subject them totally to state control.

Thus, right from the very start, the debate was politicized. "Party spirit now took hold of it," wrote Senator Benton, "and strenuously resisted the passage of the act. It was one of the closest, and most earnestly contested questions of the session."[15]

Frelinghuysen made a point of mentioning the intrusion of the President himself in the proceedings. It was done, he said, "without the slightest consultation with either House of Congress, without any opportunity for counsel or concern, discussion or deliberation, on the part of the coordinate branches of the Government, to despatch the whole subject in a tone and style of decisive construction of our obligations and of Indian rights."

Here was an excellent example of an ongoing problem that Congress would encounter in its relations with the chief executive: his determination to have a voice in the legislative process. He would demonstrate it again most forcefully in his veto message of the Bank bill that came up in 1832 and in his "Protest" message to the Senate in 1834 when that body censured him for removing the government's deposits from the Second National Bank of the United States without the consent of Congress.

"We must," Frelinghuysen thundered, "firmly protest against this Executive disposition of these high interests." He has no business intruding. The Indians deserve our careful, thoughtful, and free discussion of their situation. We have treated them so badly in the past. Must we continue to do so into the future? We call them "brothers" and yet we steal their land. They have yielded millions of acres to us "and yet we crave more. We have crowded the tribes upon a few miserable acres of our Southern frontier: it is all that is left to them of their once boundless forests; and still, like the horse-leech, our insatiable cupidity cries, give! give! give!"[16]

John Forsyth of Georgia came screaming back at Frelinghuysen. And with his speech the debate became sectional as well as political. It is well enough, he stormed, for New York, the New England states, and a great many other northern states to do as they wish with the Indians within their borders, as they have been doing for years, leaving the Indians to their "tender mercies." But when it comes to the southern tribes it is a totally different matter. Now the long "arm of the General Government is to be extended to protect the Choctaws, Chickasaws, Creeks and especially the Cherokees from the anticipated oppressions of Mississippi, Alabama and Georgia." The actions taken by the north over the past decades, without a murmur from anyone, are to be denied to the south.

Robert Adams of Mississippi seconded Forsyth's contention. Any person, be he white, red, black, or whatever, living within the boundaries of a state is subject to its laws, he said. No exceptions. Otherwise chaos results. In our federal system we have national rights and state rights. Are we now to have Indian rights?

Peleg Sprague of Maine answered these attacks and reminded his colleagues of their duty as "solemnly promised" to abide by the terms of the treaties already signed with the tribes. If they simply would honor those promises, much of the problem would be resolved. Can the President be trusted to use whatever money the Congress assigns to the bill for proper purposes? Or will he use it to bribe and intimidate the Indians into signing removal treaties, as has been done in the past?[17]

In light of this argument some senators were disposed to insist on an amendment that would somehow guarantee legitimate negotiations; another amendment was proposed to delay action until it was determined whether the western lands were adequate to the needs of the tribes. Both amendments were voted down by the Democratic majority. Other objections were swiftly turned aside, and on April 26, 1830, the Senate bill passed on a strict party-line vote of 28 to 19.[18]

The Bell bill in the House had not yet come up for debate when the approved Senate bill arrived for consideration. Bell then agreed to allow the White bill to take precedence, and on May 15 the debate in the House began.

Henry R. Storrs of New York took dead aim at the White House and fired a near-lethal blast. He repeated Frelinghuysen's argument about Jackson's assault on the constitutional system in attempting to control congressional business. "If these encroachments of the Executive Department are not met and repelled in these halls," he stormed, "they will be resisted nowhere. . . . The concentration of power in the hands of the Executive leads to despotism." We need to stop it in its tracks. We need to stop it now.

Other critics pointed out that the administration planned to dump tens of thousands of human beings, including the old, the sick, and the children, into the "Great American Desert," which was unfit for human habitation or cultivation. And because many House members were vulnerable to the strong opposition by their constituents, especially from certain religious groups like Quakers, even loyal Democrats were leery about voting for the measure. Joseph Hemphill of Pennsylvania, for example, was so torn over the question that he suggested a substitute bill that would postpone removal for a year to allow an independent commission to inspect the western country and report back.

Congress likes nothing better than postponing action on contentious issues. But southerners, almost en masse, were determined to force passage of the bill.

Wilson Lumpkin of Georgia, a member of the House Committee on Indian Affairs, insisted that the Senate measure before them had nothing to do with party prejudice and everything to do with preserving the Indians from certain annihilation. Only removal could spare them this tragic fate. Fortunately, he added, President Jackson understands this fact and has acted out of concern for their welfare. "No man entertains kinder feelings toward the Indians than Andrew Jackson," he declared.

Thomas F. Foster, another representative from Georgia, credited Jackson with listening to the Indians and responding to their needs. As a matter of fact, he added, they had come to him and asked for his assistance. What was he to do? Remain silent? Hardly. "Would this have been like Andrew Jackson? Sir, it would have been at variance with every act of his life."[19]

As the arguments mounted and intensified emotionally it became obvious that if the removal bill was to have any hope of passage, the man who entertained such kindly feelings toward the Indians would have to take an even more active role in the House debate. And he did. Throughout the spring, Jackson increased pressure on Democrats to end the debate and get the bill passed. They were reminded that he "staked the success of his administration upon this measure" and would brook no opposition to its passage, including the substitution of the Hemphill bill. The substitution, they were advised, was unrealistic and would mean the ultimate defeat of removal. The President understood these matters a lot better than any Pennsylvania congressman and had declared unequivocally that a commission would never complete its mission within a single year. The substitute measure had to be voted down and the original bill passed.

It was, but it was close. On the Hemphill proposal, ninety-eight representatives voted for it and ninety-eight voted against. Fortunately the administration was prepared. Speaker Stevenson voted against it, and the proposal died. With still added pressure from the White House through John Bell, several Democratic members of the Pennsylvania and Massachusetts delegations were whipped into line, and when the bill came up for a final vote it passed 102 to 97.[20]

It was a close call. Any number of House Democrats voted against the bill. They rightly feared that they too might be removed at the next election. Indeed, it was "one of the severest struggles, that I have ever witnessed in Congress," declared Democratic congressman Pryor Lea of Tennessee. It was "as protracted and excited as any that had ever before taken place," commented Senator Martin Van Buren.[21]

The slightly amended House measure went back to the Senate for approval, at which time Frelinghuysen and Sprague renewed their efforts to scuttle it with amendments to guarantee Indian rights and limit removal to those Indians living in Georgia. But they failed. The bill passed without difficulty, and a grateful President Jackson signed it on May 28, 1830.

Actually the Indian Removal Act did not remove the Indians at all. What it did was empower the President to exchange unorganized public land in the trans-Mississippi west for land held by the Indians in the east. In addition it gave to the Indians who moved perpetual title to the new land and compensation for improvements they had made on the old. The federal government would assume all the costs involved in the removal and provide Indians with "such aid and assistance as may be necessary for their support and subsistence for the first year after their removal." Finally the act authorized an appropriation of $500,000 to carry out these provisions.[22]

This monumental event in American history brought the entire government into the process of expelling the southern Indians from their homeland. Heretofore the early Presidents—many of whom were founding fathers of the Republic—removed Indians by executive initiative. What Jackson did was force the Congress to face up to the Indian issue and address it in the only way possible. And what it did at his direction was harsh, arrogant, racist—and inevitable. There was no way the American people would continue to allow the presence of the tribes in the fertile hills and valleys that they coveted. Sooner or later, white culture and life would engulf them.

The Indian Removal Act did not order the removal of the Indians, even though that was a foregone conclusion once the talks actually began about exchanging land. And, as far as Jackson was concerned, the Indians could refuse to remove and stay where they were; but if they stayed, they had to recognize that they were subject to state law and jurisdiction. No longer could they live under their own laws and practices. Henceforth the laws and practices would be white laws and white practices. But knowing Indians as he did, he understood that few could live under state jurisdiction. It was a hateful alternative. It therefore made sense for them to resettle in the west. That way they could preserve their Indian heritage and way of life.

Unfortunately the President's noble desire to give the Indians a free choice between staying and removing, one devoid of coercion, was disregarded by land-greedy state and federal officials, who practiced fraud and deception to enrich themselves and their friends at the expense of the native tribes. The removal process sullied virtually everyone involved in it.

Where Jackson is particularly culpable is in his insistence on speed and economy in reaching a decision with the several tribes. He wanted action immediately. He lacked patience, and by his pressure to move things along quickly he caused unspeakable cruelties to innocent people who deserved better from a nation that prided itself on its commitment to justice and equality. Removal could not be speeded up; it could not happen overnight. It would take months and years to properly transport and settle people from the country of their birth to a place they knew nothing about.

And $500,000 would not begin to cover the cost of removal. It actually took tens of millions of dollars to complete the process. Jackson wanted a quick ending to the Indian problem, and he achieved it. In his eight years in office some seventy-odd treaties were signed and ratified, adding to the public domain approximately 100 million acres of Indian land in the east at a cost of $68 million and 32 million acres of land west of the Mississippi River. But the cost in human lives and suffering was incalculable.

Eventually most Americans accepted what had happened. And even when the opposition party came to power it pursued the same savage practices against Native Americans as had the Democrats. Within a few years many thought the policy humane and enlightened. They understood the rationale behind removal and approved it. What they and Andrew Jackson failed to realize was that they had betrayed some of their most cherished ideas about American justice and decency.

Chapter 14

"Remove and Be Happy"

Jackson was enormously pleased that the first piece of important legislation to be passed in his administration was the Indian Removal Act, and he acted quickly to get it implemented. What he planned to do was meet personally with the chiefs of all the southern tribes and try to persuade them to accept the idea of an exchange, after which treaties could be negotiated. And because the task would be formidable, he felt that he himself must provide a fitting example of how to go about it. But already there were signs of likely trouble. The Cherokee *Phoenix,* a biweekly newspaper published in New Echota, Georgia, and edited by Elias Boudinot, who had been educated in Connecticut, came out flatly against removal.[1]

For Jackson the period of cajoling and arguing with the Indians had ended. He would give them a simple choice. They could remain under state jurisdiction or remove; there was no other alternative. Then, if they chose to stay and later found that they could not live under the laws of the state, they were on their own. They would have to find "by their own means, a country, and a home." And they could also look elsewhere for protection. The national government would not provide it. A point, insisted Jackson, that needed to be driven forcefully home to them.

Secretary of War Eaton understood it and spelled it out in unmistakable language to agents and other officials involved in Indian relations. "Their great father," he wrote John Donnelly, "is resolved that if they now refuse he will trouble them no more, but leave them to remove or not, as they please, & when they please and at their own expense." This applied particularly to the Choctaws in Mississippi, for in May a treaty proposed by Chief Greenwood LeFlore had been sent to the President. In it the Indians said they would acquiesce to removal for approximately $50 million.

That staggered Jackson. Were they mocking him? The price was absurd. Nevertheless he submitted it to the Senate, but with a recommendation that it be rejected. Such a treaty would set a bad example to the other tribes, he said, who would demand sums so exorbitant that they would bankrupt the government. As expected, the Senate rejected it, and the Choctaws were informed that if they "believe they can live under the laws of Mississippi" the President "is perfectly willing they should do so; but should they find they can not, & become desirous to seek a new home, let them understand, that they must seek it as they can, & in their own way; for no other application will be made to them for a treaty."[2]

Actually Jackson was extremely hopeful that the Choctaws would agree to an exchange. The very fact that they had offered to sell their land convinced him and Eaton that they had already accepted the idea as inevitable. Under the circumstances he was anxious to leave Washington and get back to Tennessee, where he could arrange to meet with the Choctaws and the other southern tribes and obtain their consent to the government's new policy.

Congress finally adjourned on May 31, and Jackson immediately made plans to head home and meet with the southern tribes. But first there was the matter of reconstructing the bureaucracy that handled Indian concerns.

Since 1824 a Bureau of Indian Affairs headed by Thomas L. McKenney had supervised the government's relations with the several tribes. But by 1829 it had become an "enormous quagmire"; several secretaries of war complained about its "perplexing" operations. There was no regularity in the way treaties were administered, and regulations governing agents in the field were haphazard. Now Jackson decided to reconstitute the bureau and replace McKenney, who had been enormously helpful in winning converts to removal but had recently expressed doubts about whether Jackson's plan would be the blessing he had once believed. And his dismissal was brutally executed. While away from Washington he received a notice in August 1830 from the chief clerk of the War Department, Philip G. Randolph (who was Eaton's brother-in-law), that he had been given a furlough until the end of the month, after which his services were no longer needed. When McKenney asked the reason for his dismissal, Randolph replied, "Why, Sir, every body knows your qualifications for the place; but General Jackson has long been satisfied that you are not in harmony with him in his views in regard to the Indians."

Still, it took several more years before Jackson finally obtained the necessary

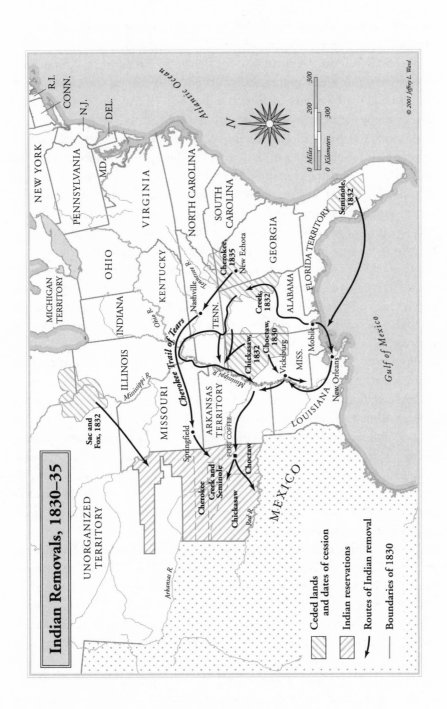

Indian Removals, 1830–35

© 2001 Jeffrey L. Ward

NEW YORK
PENNSYLVANIA
R.I.
CONN.
N.J.
DEL.
MD.
VIRGINIA
OHIO
MICHIGAN TERRITORY
INDIANA
KENTUCKY
NORTH CAROLINA
SOUTH CAROLINA
GEORGIA
ILLINOIS
MISSOURI
TENN.
Nashville
Cherokee, 1835
New Echota
Creek, 1832
Choctaw, 1830
ALABAMA
FLORIDA TERRITORY
Seminole, 1832
Atlantic Ocean

Sac and Fox, 1832
Springfield
ARKANSAS TERRITORY
Chickasaw, 1832
Vicksburg
MISS.
Mobile
New Orleans
Gulf of Mexico
LOUISIANA
FORT COFFEE
Cherokee
Creek and Seminole
Chickasaw
Choctaw

UNORGANIZED TERRITORY
MEXICO
Arkansas R.
Red R.
Mississippi R.
Ohio R.
Tennessee R.
Cherokee Trail of Tears

N

0 Miles 100 200 300
0 Kilometers 100 200 300

Ceded lands and dates of cession
Indian reservations
Routes of Indian removal
Boundaries of 1830

legislation from Congress to establish an Office of Indian Affairs under a permanent commissioner. And this administrative setup, once enacted, remained in place well into the twentieth century. By the act passed in 1834, the reorganized bureau provided a more cohesive system of operation, regularized procedures that had grown out of tradition rather than law, and involved Congress directly in the government's dealings with the Indians.[3]

As soon as he had settled McKenney's fate and done as much as possible to reform the Indian bureaucracy, Jackson headed home. He expected to meet immediately with several chiefs of the southern tribes in Franklin, Tennessee (Eaton's hometown), a short distance from Nashville. Meanwhile Eaton contacted Governor George R. Gilmer of Georgia and assured him of the President's agreement with the action taken by the state but expressed the hope that the governor would "lend whatever facilities may be in your power to restrain the citizens of Georgia from passing into and settling on the lands of those people." He estimated that about six thousand Cherokees, a third of the tribe, had already emigrated to the west "and are doing well." The rest were sure to follow if handled with discretion and not by any state action that could cause controversy.[4]

Once home, Jackson waited for weeks to get a response from the chiefs. Then, when he heard that the Cherokees and Creeks had decided not to attend the meeting but instead take their case directly to the United States Supreme Court, he bristled. They dared to hire William Wirt, a former attorney general in the Monroe and Adams administrations and one of the foremost constitutional lawyers in the country, to plead their cause. Worse, Wirt took the case. "The course of Wirt has been truly wicked," Jackson told his friend William B. Lewis. He has taken a "large fee to protect them in their rights as an independent Nation." So be it. "I leave the poor deluded Creeks and Cherokees to their fate, and their anihilation."[5]

Not until July 21 did Eaton finally arrive at the Hermitage. Meanwhile the President summoned General John Coffee, who had a great deal of experience in negotiating treaties with the Indians, to join him and Eaton on their trip to Franklin. He left his home on July 28 fully expecting to meet the chiefs of the Chickasaw and Choctaw nations around the middle of August. The Chickasaws did show up on August 19, but the Choctaws chose to stay away. Having come to the very edge of agreeing on an exchange, they suddenly backed off. Chief Greenwood LeFlore wrote Eaton and told him that the warriors were violently opposed to meeting him and especially Jackson in Franklin, adding that the lives of the chiefs and headmen would be in great jeopardy if they even proposed a possible sale of their country. They knew the power of Jackson's "talks," and they feared his threats and bribes. Maybe later it would be possible to meet Eaton face to face or some other "good men" whom the President would send "to explain to us the views of the government on the subject of the removal of our people west of the Mississippi." But not now.[6]

Always certain that a conspiracy existed to thwart him, Jackson immediately jumped to the conclusion that Major David W. Haley, who had acted as a special messenger to the Choctaws, was the "tool" of LeFlore and was "acting the double part with the view to obtain large reserves for the Indians, and to participate in them." He also suspected that it was the northern section of the Choctaw Nation that led the "conspiracy." So he decided that if full delegations could be brought from the eastern and southern sections, then he would treat with them "and leave the halfbreeds and wicked white men" in the north to live with the consequences of their evil work.[7]

With the Choctaw pull-out, the President was left with the Chickasaws who were anxious to meet with him to plead for his help. The Mississippi legislature, following the lead of Georgia, had decided to exercise jurisdiction over Chickasaw lands in the northern section of the state. What it did was forbid tribal leaders from exercising the powers of their office and threatening them with a fine of $1,000 and imprisonment if they disobeyed. The state further declared that all the Indians were subject to Mississippi law.

The Chickasaws appealed to Jackson for protection against these clear violations of treaties signed and ratified by the United States. What Mississippi had done was wrong, they argued, and the President had an obligation to enforce federal law. But if they really expected him to heed their plea they were very much mistaken.

Jackson met with the Chickasaw delegation in the Presbyterian Church of Franklin on August 23, 1830. Twenty-one chiefs and their agent, Colonel Benjamin Reynolds, assembled to hear the words of their "Great Father." The President stood before them with all the trappings of his office, intent on over-awing them with his presence and executive power.

He started out in his usual manner of addressing them as "friends and brothers" and telling them how glad he was to meet with them and shake their hands and assure them of his continued good will and friendship. He said he had been empowered by Congress to provide justice to his red children and grant them western lands in exchange for their present country. He added that he would pay the expenses of their removal and support them for a year. I am here "to point you to a course which cannot fail to make you a happy and prosperous people. Hear and deliberate well, and under the exercise of your own reason and matured judgment, determine what may appear to you to be done for the benefit of yourselves and your children."

Then he repeated the same old complaints about how they were surrounded by their white brothers, how states had been created around their land, and how the states "claim a right to govern and control your people as they do their own citizens." You must realize, he continued, that if you stay where you are you will be subject to Mississippi's "civil and criminal codes." Understand one thing: "your great father has not the authority to prevent this state of things."

But what of the treaties that were signed with the United States? the chiefs asked. Are they not the law, and are not the states subject to the law?

"Brothers, listen," Jackson responded. "To these laws, where you are, you must submit;—there is no preventive—no other alternative. Your great father cannot, nor can congress, prevent it. The states only can." It is for you to decide. If you stay can you give up your ancient customs and form of government? If you can do so, then "your great father has nothing to say or to advise." He can only express the hope "that you may be perpetuated and preserved as a nation; and this he believes can only be done and secured in your consent to remove to a country beyond the Mississippi. . . . Where you are, it is not possible you can live contented and happy."

"Father," the chiefs replied in a written document, "We the Chickasaws have occupied the country not only where we now live from time immemorial but a large portion of the rich and fertile lands of Tennessee and Alabama. . . . We have from time to time sold piece after piece of our country to our white brothers . . . untill we have but a small home left that is barely sufficient to subsist upon while living and to bury our bones when we are dead. . . . Father, you call us your children . . . but we humbly" say to you "that we cannot consent to exchange the country where we now live for the one we have never seen."[8]

In reply Jackson spoke very calmly. He said he understood their feelings about leaving the graves of their ancestors and moving to an unknown land, but they had to face the fact that the white man would soon engulf them. Survival as a race necessitated removal. The whites would not compromise. Annihilation was the alternative.

"Old men!" he called to the ancient chiefs. "Arouse to energy and lead your children to a land of promise and of peace before the Great Spirit shall call you to die."

Then he turned to the young warriors. "Young chiefs! Forget the prejudices you feel for the soil of your birth, and go to a land where you can preserve your people as a nation." You will endure "as long as the grass grows or water runs."

Jackson closed his talk with a warning. "Reject this opportunity which is now offered to obtain comfortable homes" and you may never have another opportunity to do so again. If you reject the offer, "call not upon your great father hereafter to relieve you of your troubles. . . ." You will be subject to state control and regulations. And that is final. Then, in a few years, "by becoming amalgamated with the whites your national character will be lost . . . you must disappear and be forgotten."

The words crushed the Chickasaws. Disappear and be forgotten. Just like the Mohegans and Narragansetts, the Delawares and Yamasees. But was this true? Would the Chickasaws and the other southern tribes have disappeared? Was it remotely possible that they could retain their tribal identity if they remained in the east? Jackson thought not. And what is clear is that Native Americans would have had to yield to white law and white culture. They shuddered at the very thought of it. Indian Nations and possibly Indian civilization as such would be obliterated in the process.

A long silence followed. Then, to bring the meeting to an end, the Great Father announced that if they wished to avoid the calamity of extinction and were willing to remove, all they needed to do was simply state their terms and his delegates, Major Eaton and General Coffee, would "act candidly, fairly and liberally towards you."[9]

After hearing this prediction of inevitable doom the Chickasaw chiefs withdrew to council among themselves. At different times they met with Eaton and Coffee, who repeated much of what Jackson had said. The chiefs attempted to bargain with the two men about how much land each head of a family would receive in the west and the amount of annuities that could be granted. But the two men rejected several of the demands as exorbitant and stated that they would only consider "reasonable" proposals.

It took the Chickasaws four days to make their decision. Then, on August 27, they met the President, Eaton, and Coffee at the Masonic Hall. The chiefs formed a square and the President took a seat in the center. One of the chiefs who served as the delegation's secretary approached Eaton and extended his left hand, which held a sheet of paper. He also extended his right hand, which Eaton took and shook. The chief then asked Eaton to read the paper to the President. The major took the sheet, turned to Jackson, and read what had been handed him.

Franklin, August 27, 1830

To our great father the president. Your red children, the chiefs and head men of the Chickasaws, have had under consideration the talk of our father. . . . On the decision we this day make and declare to you and the world, depends our fate as a nation and as a people.

Father, you say that you have travelled a long way to talk to your red children. We have listened—and your words have sunk deep into our hearts. As you are about to set out for Washington city—before we shake our father's hand, perhaps with many of us for the last time—we have requested this meeting to tell you, that after sleeping upon the talk you sent us, and the talk delivered to us by our brothers, major Eaton and gen. Coffee, we are now ready to enter into any treaty based upon the principles communicated to us by major Eaton and gen. Coffee. Your friends and brothers.

(Signed etc.)[10]

The "great father" smiled broadly to show his pleasure and satisfaction. He told them how happy he was that they had listened and heeded his advice. He said he would always remember them, and he expressed his hope that the "Great Spirit above would take care of, bless and preserve them."

Indeed Jackson was deeply moved by what had happened. He rose from his chair and reached out his hands to bid them all an affectionate farewell. One chief was so overcome with the President's own show of emotion that he rushed forward and grasped Sharp Knife with both hands. "God bless you, my great father," he exclaimed. Then he turned away to conceal the expression on his face, so deep was his feeling of affection.

There was dead silence in the room. No one moved or spoke. The emotional level in the room had risen to such a level that they simply stared at one another in recognition of what had just happened: the father casting out his children. Jackson knew too. He surely realized that he was saying goodbye to these pitiful figures forever. But it had to be.

Still they loved him. They really did. He was, said one reporter, "by them so much beloved," and yet they realized he was expelling them from "the land of their youth, where the bones of their fathers reposed." It was without doubt a heart-rending scene and a frightful tragedy, but Jackson never for a moment paused over the human wreckage he left in his wake.[11] He walked away from the meeting fully convinced that he had performed a great service for the Chickasaws and spared them from inevitable destruction.

This Franklin treaty exchanged the remainder of Chickasaw land in the east for an unknown wildness beyond the Mississippi. Each warrior, white man with an Indian family, and widow with a family received a half section of land. Single persons received a quarter section. The Nation was granted an annual annuity of $15,000 for twenty years. And chiefs like Levi Colbert and other tribal leaders received reservations of four sections each. Bribing the chiefs was always an essential part of any treaty, although in this instance Jackson took no part in it, since he could rely on Coffee and Eaton to do what was necessary. Besides, it offended him personally and it would be unseemly for a President to indulge in such tactics. The other terms of the treaty contained all the main points of Jackson's "talk."

Jackson saw this victory as one that had been won against the schemes and wickedness of "bad men." "Thus far we have succeeded, against the most corrupt and secrete combination that ever did exist," he declared, "and we have preserved my Chickasaw friends and red brethren."[12]

Best of all, the treaty started removal off on a very successful note. Unfortunately, a short while later, a Chickasaw delegation explored the western country and returned with the alarming news that what they had seen was totally unacceptable. Only the Mexican lands along the Sabine River met with their approval. If this country could be acquired for the tribe, the Nation would willingly remove. Otherwise they would stay right where they were. So the Franklin treaty had to be renegotiated, since the Senate would not ratify it. In the interim the Chickasaws continued to suffer under Mississippi laws, along with the many squatters, whiskey traders, and peddlers who regularly invaded their land. It got so bad that they finally capitulated and informed their Great Father in 1832 that they would agree to an exchange.[13]

As for the other southern tribes who continued to thwart his wishes, Jackson predicted an unhappy fate, except perhaps for the Choctaws. Although they had refused to meet him in Franklin, they did send him a message on August 16 stating that if he sent some "good men" who would "explain to us the views of the government on the subject of the removal" they would willingly meet them. Apparently they too chafed under Mississippi law. Indeed, they had said and now repeated, "We are distressed. We cannot endure the laws of Mississippi."

That was all the opening Jackson needed. He sent a friendly letter to the chiefs accepting their offer and appointed Eaton and Coffee as commissioners to present his "talk" to them. He made it clear in the talk that he was offering the Indians their last chance for survival. "I feel conscious of having done my duty to my red children," he wrote. "If any failure of my good intention arises, it will be attributable to their wont of duty to themselves, not to me." Once they refuse him, he told James Pitchlynn, "he will interfere no more" but allow them to "go as they can, & at their own expense." He will feel it his duty to report to Congress and say that they have rejected his offer to "remove and be happy" and recommend that "all appropriations be withdrawn & they left to find other new homes as they can."[14]

Coffee and Eaton met the Choctaws between the two prongs of Dancing Rabbit Creek in Noxubee County, Mississippi. The Indians, as directed, assembled on September 15, 1830. They flocked to the spot, but so too did gamblers, saloon keepers, prostitutes, and other undesirables. Missionaries were excluded by order of the two commissioners.

Actual negotiations began at noon on Saturday, September 18, amid what can only be described as a tumultuous gathering of six thousand Mingoes, chiefs, captains, warriors of the Nation (many of them drunk), and women and children who were obviously apprehensive and fearful. The dregs of white society circulated among the Indians to urge them to consent to what the commissioners proposed. Whiskey was brought into the Nation "by dissolute *whites*" in "great abundance." Intemperance, wrote one, "with all its attendant evils, stalks about in every direction."

Greenwood LeFlore, a mixed-blood, showed up in civilian clothes, leading many to suspect that "he was in collusion with the United States Commissioners." Mingo Mushulatubbee wore a new blue military uniform presented to him by General Jackson. Mingo Nittakechi appeared in full Indian garb, with a fringed hunting shirt and leggings, both adorned with beading, a bright colored shawl around his head, silver bracelets on each wrist, and seven crescent-shaped silver "gorgets" hanging from his neck. Little Leader, a prominent figure in the negotiations, was resplendently adorned in "a gorgeous Indian dress, adorned with beadwork and silver ornaments."[15]

Coffee inaugurated the convention and laid out the terms of a proposed treaty. The proceedings progressed so well that it soon appeared that a treaty would be signed without any difficulty whatsoever. He said that the white people would never again ask the Choctaws for more land, whereupon Tushka Mastubbee, an old Choctaw who had attended other conventions, replied: "*I don't believe you. Your tongue is as forked as a chicken's foot.*"[16]

But then, to the surprise and consternation of all the whites assembled, the Choctaws suddenly announced that they had voted almost unanimously to reject the terms presented to them. Eaton and Coffee were dumbstruck. It was a rude awakening. Coffee shouted and berated them, and Eaton addressed them "with brutal roughness" and threatened them with violence. "If they refused to enter into a treaty," he warned, ". . . the President in twenty days would march an army into their country, build forts in all parts of their hunting grounds, extend the authority and laws of the United States over the Choctaw territory and appoint United States judges that would be sent among the Choctaws to maintain and enforce the laws of the United States." And what could the Choctaw Nation do about it? he sneered. Raise their tomahawks? "Should the Choctaws go to war against the United States it would be . . . the ruin of the tribe." If rejection is your will, so be it. We will negotiate no longer, Eaton concluded. If you persist in your defiance we will leave tomorrow and return to Washington.[17]

The Choctaws stared at the two men in a state of shock. They believed what Eaton had said about an army marching through their territory. And with that realization, all resistance drained out of them. They could do nothing but capitulate and accept the inevitable. On Monday, September 27, a treaty was drawn up. It was submitted and explained, and at 1:00 P.M. it was signed. The great Choctaw Nation agreed to cede to the United States all 10,423,130 acres remaining of their land east of the Mississippi. And they agreed to remove to an area west of the Arkansas Territory in three stages: the first in the fall of 1831, the second in 1832, and the last in 1833. Of course, there were bribes. Twelve sections of land were reserved for chiefs along with a small stipend, and twenty sections were awarded captains without stipend. In addition, eighty-four and three-quarters sections were distributed to other favored individuals. An annuity of $20,000 per year for twenty years, donations for schools and a church, and gifts of blankets, axes, looms, hoes, rifles, and ammunition were also provided.[18]

"Intimidation and moral coercion" produced the Treaty of Dancing Rabbit Creek, said one. But there was another operating factor. The Indians felt "a peculiar dread and horror" of having to live "under the white man's laws." They received no justice under those laws, only fines, imprisonment, and sometimes death. It was a powerful weapon in the hands of the commissioners, and no doubt markedly advanced the capitulation of the Choctaw Nation.[19]

Jackson was ecstatic, and as soon as Congress reconvened in early December he sent the treaty to the Senate for ratification. Eaton duly reported that the negotiations had been entirely aboveboard. Persuasion convinced the Indians, he swore, not bribes, nor threats, nor secret agreements. The Senate was delighted to hear it and ratified the treaty on February 25, 1831, by a vote of 35 to 12.

"Our doom is sealed," wrote one chief on learning of the ratification. "There is no other course for us but to turn our faces to our new homes toward the setting sun."[20]

This was the first removal treaty to be signed, ratified, and carried into effect. It marked the beginning of the mass relocation of Native Americans beyond the Mississippi under the Indian Removal Act. It marked the beginning of humiliation and deprivation of a proud race of people. Once gone, they would be out of sight and mind, and presumably out of harm's way.

But from start to finish the operation of the removal policy was a horror. Deliberate fraud, corruption, mismanagement, and theft marked almost every step in the process. The Indians were abused and mistreated. Indifference and exploitation characterized white behavior toward these unfortunate people. The Choctaws requested General George Gibson as their guide to their new location, a man they trusted and admired. Bureaucrats deemed otherwise. Little sympathy was shown for the needs and wishes of these émigrés.

Universal sadness accompanied the first contingent of Choctaws as they left the land of their ancestors. And then the elements added to their agony. The winter of 1831–1832 was a "living hell." The suffering these Indians endured beggars the imagination. Those who watched their torment never forgot it.[21]

Although Jackson reveled in the knowledge that the final migration of southern tribes had begun at last, he was shocked and outraged by the calamity that followed. He realized that a new set of guidelines had to be drawn up to prevent a recurrence of the tragedy, although operating at a distance made it nearly impossible for him or anyone else in Washington to assuage the suffering and prevent fraud and theft.

Still, he believed he had vastly improved the ways the government treated Native Americans. When he became President there were four basic weaknesses in the handling of Indian affairs: lack of uniformity in administering treaties and laws, irregular regulations involving field personnel, lack of a uniform accounting system, and lack of legality sanctioned by Congress.[22] And because removal overloaded the system and forced the secretary of war to spend most of his time attending to Indian affairs, Jackson decided to institute unified operating procedures at all levels.

During the tenure of John Eaton and his successor, Lewis B. Cass, as secretary of war,[23] substantial improvements of these procedures were realized. With respect to removal, Jackson's reform began by transferring the operation from civilians to the military. Then he established the Office of Commissioner of Indian Affairs to coordinate and direct the operation, which included enrolling all the people to be removed and evaluating their property. Superintendents were instructed to discover the number of Native Americans to be removed, how many would travel together, the route to be taken, the quantity of provisions needed for each individual, and the places where depots of provisions could be established along the way. As for payment, each head of a family upon enrollment was presented with a rifle, blanket, kettle, and five pounds of tobacco, as well as a blanket for each member of the family. The superintendents were instructed to make certain that the Indians gave "their own free consent" to removal and that the conditions and circumstances of their relocation were distinctly understood. They were warned against leaving anything unexplained "of which they can eventually complain."

The final phase of the operation involved transportation of the tribes and their subsistence. Here an officer of the army was designated as the person responsible for all purchases and expenditures during the westward trek. These purchases and expenditures were based on the requisitions issued by the superintendents.[24]

Unfortunately, these reforms were invariably executed by men with deeply held prejudices against Native Americans, and their method of implementing the regulations frequently worsened conditions. Fraud, theft, and violence were commonplace, and the victims could do little to protect and defend themselves.

Despite these problems, removal continued without interruption. On March 24, 1832, the Creeks finally gave up their intent to sue in the Supreme Court and yielded all the land they owned east of the Mississippi River. But it was done in a very curious way. It was not a removal treaty as such. Rather it was a clever administrative ploy by which the Creeks were induced to surrender their land in return for a pledge that the land would be allotted to the chiefs and headmen. Those allotments could then be sold to whites, who, upon purchase, expected the Creeks to leave and move west. According to this Treaty of 1832, ratified by the Senate in April 1832, the Creek Nation ceased to exist in the east. They "have no more land to sell as a Nation," said Enoch Parsons, one of the census takers. "The whole of their land is now individual property." Since their situation had become hopeless, they headed west into the unknown.[25]

The Seminoles also agreed to relocate, and they accepted a provisional treaty on May 9, 1832, pending approval of their new site in the west. Meanwhile, the Chickasaws found they could no longer live under Mississippi law, and the presence of such white "trash" as gamblers, prostitutes, saloon keepers, and suchlike made the situation intolerable. Refusing to "submit to this evil," they petitioned their Great Father to send an agent to negotiate an exchange of land. With relatively little trouble, General Coffee completed a treaty with the Chickasaws on October 20, 1832, in which the Indians ceded to the United States all their remaining land east of the Mississippi. In return, each family and single individual received sections of land in the west, with families owning ten or more slaves obtaining an additional section and those with fewer slaves getting a half section.[26]

It was one victory after another for Sharp Knife, and he was delighted. "Surely the religious enthusiasts, or those who have been weeping over the oppression of the Indians," he told Coffee, "will not find fault with it for want of liberality or justice to the Indians." He was especially pleased by the economy involved. "The stipulation that they remove at their own expence and on their own means, is an excellent feature in it. The whole treaty is just, we want them in a state of safety removed from the states and free from colision with the whites; and if the land does this it is well disposed of and freed from being a corrupting source to our Legislature."[27]

Jackson believed what he said. Never mind the suffering it caused. All he could think about was that there would be no more "colision" between whites and Indians and that the Gulf region was now safe—or at least safer than it had been—from foreign invasion.

Meanwhile, western tribes began to feel the pressure created by the emigration of eastern people into their country. For example, the chiefs of the Big and Little Osage Nations appealed to their Great Father and asked to see him and share with him "our wants and grievances." Years ago, they said, "we were a powerful nation." But not now. "Our hunting is destroyed; and we find our country bound on the north, south, and eastern sides, by nations of Indians who have been induced to cross west of the Mississippi by the Government of the United States." We made a treaty in 1825, thinking citizens of the United States would settle on it. But we find Delawares, Shawnees, Creeks, Choctaws, and Cherokees everywhere, and "they take from us our means of subsistence." They steal our stock. "Father we have buried the tomahawk with all nations except the Pawnees" and expect the protection promised us. Moreover, the annuities do not come on time and many of our people are starving. And when they do arrive we are denied a choice of money or merchandise as stipulated in the treaty of 1825. "Father, we wish to speak with you and shake you by the hand and renew our friendship. We wish to come to Washington and ask for your help and guidance."[28]

But the Great Father could not provide the comfort and protection they begged for. The lands beyond the Mississippi were not his immediate concern, but he assured the Osage Nations that when the appropriate surveys had been completed there would be no difficulties between tribes. All would live in peace and find happiness. Or so he fervently believed.

Jackson gave little thought to the consequences of whole tribes moving west and butting up against other tribes who were native to the region. That problem gave him little concern. His immediate problem was relocating the eastern tribes as quickly and as economically as possible. And, by the end of his first administration, the Choctaws, Creeks, Chickasaws, and Seminoles had capitulated to his demand. Of the so-called Five Civilized Nations only the Cherokees held out.

But not for long.

Chapter 15

Andrew Jackson Versus
the Cherokee Nation

The great Cherokee Nation that had fought the young Andrew Jackson on his arrival in Tennessee back in 1788 now faced an even more powerful and determined man who was intent on taking their land. But whereas in the past they had resorted to guns, tomahawks, and scalping knives, now they chose to challenge him in a court of law. They were not called a "civilized nation" for nothing. Many of their leaders were well educated; many more could read and write; they had their own written language, thanks to Sequoyah, a constitution, schools, and their own newspaper. And they had adopted many skills of the white man to improve their living conditions. Why should they be expelled from their lands when they no longer threatened white settlements and could compete with them on many levels? They intended to fight their ouster, and they figured they had many ways to do it. As a last resort they planned to bring suit before the Supreme Court.

They had already sent a delegation to Washington to plead their cause. They had petitioned Congress to protect them against the unjust laws of Georgia that had decreed that they were subject to its sovereignty and under its complete jurisdiction. They even approached the President, but he curtly informed them that there was nothing he could do in their quarrel with the state, a statement that shocked and amazed them.

Next they appealed to the general public through an address drawn up by the Committee and Council of the entire Cherokee Nation. They begged the American people to listen to their cries for justice. "It never occurred to us for a moment, that without any new treaty, without any assent of our rulers and people, without even a pretended compact, and against our vehement and unanimous protestations, we should be delivered over to the discretion of those, who had declared by a legislative act, that they wanted the Cherokee lands and would have them.

"Shall we be compelled by a civilized and Christian people, with whom we have lived in perfect peace for the last forty years, and for whom we have willingly bled in war, to bid a final adieu to our homes, our farms, our streams and our beautiful forests? No. . . . We are sure [the American people] will not fail to . . . sympathize with us in these our trials and sufferings."[1]

The appeal had little real effect, although it did stir the consciences of a number of religious northern groups who read the address. The plight of these oppressed people affected mostly those who lived far from any contact with Native Americans. Those closest to them wanted their land, and were determined to have it.

So the Cherokees hired William Wirt to take their case to the Supreme Court. In the celebrated *Cherokee Nation* v. *Georgia* he instituted suit for an injunction that would permit the Cherokees to remain in Georgia without interference by the state. He argued that they constituted an independent nation and had been so regarded by the United States in its many treaties with them.[2]

Speaking for the majority of the Court, Chief Justice John Marshall handed down his decision on March 18, 1831. Not surprisingly, as a great American nationalist, he rejected Wirt's argument that the Cherokees were a sovereign nation, but he also rejected Jackson's claim that they were subject to state law. The Indians were "domestic dependent nations," he ruled, subject to the United States as a ward to a guardian. Indian territory was part of the United States but not subject to action by individual states.[3]

When the Cherokees read Marshall's decision they honestly believed that the Nation had won the case, that Georgia lacked authority to control their lives and property, and that the courts would protect them. The Supreme Court, the Principal Chief told his people, had decided "in our favor." So they stayed right where they were, and missionaries encouraged them to stand fast.[4]

But they figured without Sharp Knife and the authorities of Georgia. In late December 1830, the state passed another law prohibiting white men from entering Indian country after March 1, 1831, without a license from the state. This move was obviously intended to keep interfering clergymen from inciting the Indians to disobey Georgia law. Eleven such missionaries were arrested for violating the recent statute, nine of whom accepted pardons from the governor in return for a promise that they would cease violating Georgia law. But Samuel A.

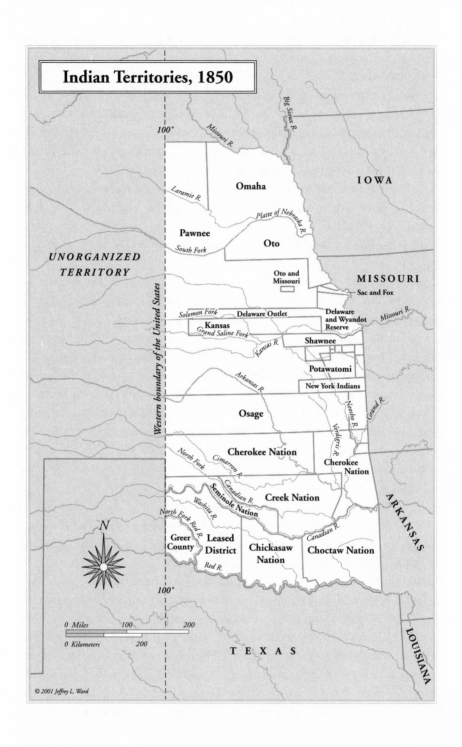

Indian Territories, 1850

100°

Missouri R.

Big Sioux R.

I O W A

Laramie R.

Omaha

Platte of Nebraska R.

Pawnee

Oto

**UNORGANIZED
TERRITORY**

South Fork

Oto and
Missouri

MISSOURI

Sac and Fox

Solomon Fork

Delaware Outlet

Delaware
and Wyandot
Reserve

Missouri R.

Kansas

Grand Saline Fork

Kansas R.

Shawnee

Western boundary of the United States

Potawatomi

Arkansas R.

New York Indians

Osage

Neosho R.

Verdigris R.

Grand R.

Cherokee Nation

Cherokee
Nation

North Fork

Cimarron R.

Canadian R.

Creek Nation

A R K A N S A S

Seminole Nation

Washita R.

North Fork Red R.

Greer
County

Leased
District

Chickasaw
Nation

Canadian R.

Choctaw Nation

N

Red R.

100°

0 Miles   100   200

0 Kilometers   200

T E X A S

LOUISIANA

© 2001 Jeffrey L. Ward

Worcester and Dr. Elizur Butler refused the pardon, and Judge Augustin S. J. Clayton sentenced them to the state penitentiary, "there to endure hard labor for the term of four years." They appealed the verdict and their case came before the Supreme Court.

On March 3, 1832, Marshall again ruled in *Worcester* v. *Georgia*, declaring all the laws of Georgia dealing with the Cherokees unconstitutional, null, void, and of no effect. In addition he issued a formal mandate two days later ordering the state's superior court to reverse its decision and free the two men.[5]

Jackson is reported to have said on hearing the decision, "Well, John Marshall has made his decision: *now let him enforce it!*" Actually Jackson said no such thing. It certainly sounds like him, but he did not say it because there was nothing for him to enforce. The Court had rendered its judgment, directed an action by the state's superior court, and then adjourned. It would not reconvene until January 1833. Neither Georgia nor the state's superior court responded to the order. Not until a response was forthcoming could the Supreme Court issue an order of compliance or a writ of habeas corpus for the release of the two men. Thus Jackson was under no obligation at that time to take action. Why, then, would he refuse what no one asked him to do? Why would he make such a foolish remark? Rather, he said that "the decision of the supreme court has fell still born, and they find that it cannot coerce Georgia to yield to its mandate."[6]

What he did do was maneuver behind the scenes. He was presently involved in a confrontation with South Carolina over the passage of the tariffs of 1828 and 1832. The state had nullified these acts and threatened to secede from the Union if force was used to make it comply with them. The last thing Jackson needed was a confrontation with another state, so he quietly nudged Georgia into obeying the court order and freeing Butler and Worcester. A number of well-placed officials in both the state and national governments lent a hand, and the governor, Wilson Lumpkin, was finally persuaded to accept an arrangement whereby he released the two men on January 14, 1833.[7]

With the annoying problem of the two missionaries out of the way, both Georgia and Jackson continued to lean on the Cherokees to get them to remove. "Some of the most vicious and base characters that the adjoining states can produce" squatted on their land and stole "horses and other property" and formed a link with as many "bad citizens" of the Cherokee Nation "as they can associate into their club." Missionaries decried what was happening to the Cherokees. If only "whites would not molest them," wrote Dr. Elizur Butler in *The Missionary Herald.* They have made remarkable progress in the last dozen years and if left alone they can and will complete the process toward a "civilized life."[8]

But allowing eastern Indians full control of their eastern lands was virtually impossible in the 1830s. There was not army enough or will enough by the American people to bring it about. As Jackson constantly warned, squatters would continue to invade and occupy the land they wanted; then, if they were attacked, they would turn to the state government for protection, which usually ended in violence. All this under the guise of bringing "civilization" to the wilderness.

Even so, the Cherokees had a strong leader who had not yet given up the fight. They were led by the wily, tough, and determined John Ross, a blue-eyed, brown-haired mixed-blood who was only one-eighth Cherokee. Nonetheless he was the Principal Chief, and a most powerful force within the Nation. He was rich, lived in a fine house attended by black slaves, and virtually controlled the annuities paid by the United States to the tribal government for former land cessions. His appearance and lifestyle were distinctly white; in all other respects he was Indian.[9]

From the beginning of Jackson's administration, Ross urged his people to stand their ground and remain united. "Friends," he told his people, "I have great hopes in your firmness and that you will hold fast to the place where you were raised. Friends if you all unite together and be of one mind there is no danger."[10] And the Cherokees cheered his determination. They approved wholeheartedly of his leadership and they took comfort in what he said. So, with the Nation solidly behind him, Ross resolutely resisted any thought of leading his people from their ancient land into a godforsaken wilderness.

By the spring of 1832, removal applied to all the eastern tribes, not simply the southern tribes along the Gulf of Mexico. Earlier treaties—especially the Treaty of Prairie du Chien in 1825—had pretty much cleared a large portion of the Old Northwest around Illinois, Wisconsin, and the Michigan Territory of such tribes as the Chippewas, Sacs and Foxes, Menominis, Iowas, Sioux, Potawatomis, and Winnebagos, who had already settled west of the Mississippi.

But resistance also flared. The Sac and Fox Indians, led by Chief Black Hawk, found their western country unacceptable and decided in the spring of 1832 to leave Iowa and return to their home in Illinois. White settlers in the area regarded the action as an invasion and called on state and federal governments to protect them. Illinois militia proved incapable of expelling the tribe, so federal troops were dispatched and drove Black Hawk and his people north into Wisconsin. There the Indians made a heroic but futile stand against their pursuers. More than three hundred Indians were killed, and Black Hawk himself and some of his chiefs were taken prisoner and held as hostages. A treaty was subsequently signed on September 21, 1832, by which the tribe paid an indemnity for expenses incurred in this Black Hawk War. A buffer zone was also established to keep the Indians from returning to Illinois.[11]

Black Hawk was taken to Washington "for the future good conduct of the late hostile bands" and he met President Jackson in the White House on April 26, 1833. The two old men sized up each other, and Black Hawk was singularly impressed by the Great Father. "He looks as if he had seen as many winters as I have," the seventy-year old chief remarked, "and seems to be a great brave."

Jackson's impression was less complimentary. All the old prejudices against Native Americans rose up within him, and he tongue-lashed the poor defeated Indian for "drenching the frontier in mindless slaughter." Then he said that he had decided to imprison Black Hawk and the other chiefs in Fortress Monroe until he deemed it safe for them to return to their people. Not until he was satisfied that their return would not provoke another clash with white settlers, and not until he learned that the tribe would take them back, would he permit their departure.

Black Hawk objected. He wished to return home to his family and his people. He promised to keep the peace.

"You will go to Fortress Monroe," barked Jackson, "and remain there contented until [I] give [you] permission" to leave. Your captivity is conditional upon the conduct of the Sac and Fox warriors and the diminution of "all the bad feeling which has led to the bloody scenes on the frontier."

The chief said nothing in response. "I concluded," Black Hawk wisely commented, "it was best to obey our Great Father, and say nothing contrary to his wishes."[12]

While in prison the ancient warrior was visited by the distinguished British actress, Fanny Kemble, who was utterly charmed by the chief's dignity and bearing. She described him as a "diminutive, shrivelled looking old man." He wore a blue cloth "surtout," with scarlet leggings, a black silk neckerchief, and earrings. The very thought of him, she wrote, "cooped up the whole horrible day long, in this hot prison-house full of people, made my heart ache."[13]

Black Hawk did not remain long in prison. A month later he was released and paraded around the country. He was sent on an extended tour of eastern states in order to impress on him the superiority of American life and power and the futility of resisting removal. His first stop was Baltimore, but before beginning his grand parade he was hauled once more before the President for final instructions.

The great chief with a small entourage was taken to a hotel in Baltimore where Jackson was beginning his own northern tour following the successful conclusion of the confrontation with South Carolina over nullification. A compromise tariff had been worked out by Henry Clay and John C. Calhoun in 1833 that appeased the state and resulted in a rescinding of the Ordinance of Nullification. The President was now headed north to reassure the American people that the Union was stronger than ever.

Black Hawk stood before the Great Father calmly and with great self-presence. The President again appeared stern and severe. Finally he spoke. "When I saw you in Washington, I told you that you had behaved very badly, in raising the tomahawk against the white people, and killing men, women and children upon the frontier." Jackson's eyes showed his anger as he spoke. "Your conduct last year compelled me to send my warriors against you, and your people were defeated, with great loss, and your men surrendered, to be kept until I should be satisfied that you would not try to do any more injury."

Since our last talk, Jackson continued, the commanding generals on the frontier have approved your return, and the Indian people have requested it. "Your chiefs have pledged themselves for your good conduct, and I have given directions, that you should be taken to your own country."

As always, Black Hawk remained calm and showed not the slightest reaction to this welcome announcement. His innate dignity never left him. And he said nothing.

The Great Father spoke again. "Major Garland will conduct you through some of our towns. You will see the strength of the white people. You will see, that our young men are as numerous, as the leaves in the woods. What can you do against us? You may kill a few women and children, but such a force would be soon sent against you, as would destroy your whole tribe."

The other chiefs in the room stirred when they heard these words. Jackson's voice then took on a hard tone. "We do not wish to injure you. . . . But if you again plunge your knives into the breasts of our people, I shall send a force, which will severely punish you for your cruelties.

"Bury the tomahawk," the Great Father commanded, "and live in peace with the frontier." Heed the councils of Ke-o-kuk and the other friendly chiefs, "and I pray the Great Spirit to give you a smooth path and fair sky to return."

At this point Chief Black Hawk stepped forward and looked squarely at the

President. He spoke quietly, remembering where he was, to whom he was speaking, and what was expected of him, but he never failed to project the aura of a great and proud leader.

"My Father," he began. "My ears are open to your words. I am glad to hear them. I am glad to go back to my people. I want to see my family. I did not behave well last summer. I ought not to have taken up the tomahawk. But my people have suffered a great deal. When I get back, I will remember your words. I won't go to war again. I will live in peace. I shall hold you by the hand."

And so the interview ended. That evening both men attended a performance at the Front Street Theater, and the audience was treated to a spectacle both on and off the stage. The Great Father and the Great Chief sat in splendor with their respective entourages. The audience stared at them in amazement.[14]

A few days later the President left Baltimore for Philadelphia on his national tour, while Black Hawk slowly headed home by way of those towns and cities that could impress him the most. And he created quite a stir. Some Americans had never seen a live Indian before, let alone a warrior who had been defeated and captured. "He appeared melancholy & dejected," wrote one young Irishman, "never smiled, a most dignified look."[15]

For most Indians a look of melancholy and dejection registered their growing awareness that they must leave the land of their birth and the sites of their ancestors' graves and move west, that their Great Father was determined to expel them from their country and that nothing they could say or do would change his mind or prevent their expulsion—not fighting, and certainly not suing in the courts of the United States. The end was closing in on them.

Still the Cherokees held out, although even they had begun to feel the unrelenting pressure. A so-called Treaty Party of chiefs and headmen emerged within the Nation who understood Jackson's inflexible will and had decided to bow to his wishes and try to get the best treaty possible. They were led by very capable, hardheaded, pragmatic men, including the Speaker of the Cherokee National Council, Major Ridge; his son, the educated and politically ambitious John Ridge; the editor of the Cherokee newspaper *Phoenix,* Elias Boudinot; and his brother Stand Watie, as well as John A. Bell, James Starr, and George W. Adair.

John Ridge took a leading role in the emergence of the Treaty Party, for when the *Worcester* decision was first handed down he instantly recognized that Chief Justice Marshall had rendered an opinion that abandoned the Cherokees to their inevitable fate. So he went to Jackson and asked him point-blank whether the power of the United States would be exerted to force Georgia into respecting Indian rights and property. The President assured him that the government would do nothing. He then advised Ridge "most earnestly" to go home and urge his people to remove. Dejected, the chief left the President "with the melancholy conviction that he had been told the truth. From that moment he was convinced that the only alternative to save his people from moral and physical death, was to make the best terms they could with the government and remove out of the limits of the states. This conviction he did not fail to make known to his friends, and hence rose the '*Treaty Party*.'"[16]

The members of this Treaty Party certainly risked their lives in pressing for removal, and indeed all of them were subsequently marked for assassination. Not too many years later, Elias Boudinot and John Ridge were slain with knives and tomahawks in the midst of their families, while Major Ridge was ambushed and shot to death.[17]

John Ross, on the other hand, would not yield. As head of the National Party, which opposed removal, he was shrewd enough to recognize immediately that the President would attempt to play one party off against the other. "The object of the President is unfolded & made too plain to be misunderstood," he told the Nation. "It is to create divisions among ourselves, break down our government, our press & our treasury, that our cries may not be heard abroad; that we may be deprived of the means of sending delegations to Washington City to make known our grievances before Congress . . . and break down the government which you [Cherokees] have, by your own free will & choice, established for the security of your freedom & common welfare." If we permit ourselves to be hauled off "to a barren and inhospitable region" we will face "no other prospect than the degradation, dispersion and ultimate extinction of our race."[18]

Under the circumstances, Ross decided to go to Washington and request a meeting with the President in order to try again to arrange some accommodation that would prevent the mass relocation of his people to what was now the new Indian Territory, which Congress had created in 1834 and which eventually became the state of Oklahoma. He was tormented by the knowledge that his people would be condemned to a "prairie badly watered and only skirted on the margin of water courses and poor ridges with copes of wood." Worse, districts would be laid out for some "fifteen or twenty different tribes, and all speaking different languages, and cherishing a variety of habits and customs, a portion civilized, another half civilized and others uncivilized, and these congregated tribes of Indians to be regulated under the General Government, by no doubt white rulers." The very thought of it sent shivers through Ross's entire body.

Since he had fought with Jackson at the Battle of Horseshoe Bend during the Creek War, he reckoned that his service during that battle would provide him with a degree of leverage in speaking with the President. And, as Principal Chief, he could speak with the duly constituted authority of the Cherokee Nation as established under the Cherokee Constitution of 1827.

He had another reason for requesting the interview. He had heard a rumor that Jackson had commissioned the Reverend John F. Schermerhorn, an ambitious cleric who had assisted in the removal of the Seminoles, to negotiate with Ridge and his associates and see if a deal could be worked out that would result in a treaty. Definitely alarmed, Ross asked to speak with the President, at which time he said he would submit his own proposal for a treaty.[19]

Jackson had never liked Ross. He called him "a great villain." Unlike Ridge and Boudinot, said Jackson, the Principal Chief headed a mixed-blood elite, and was intent on centralizing power in his own hands and diverting the annuities to those who would advance his authority and their economic self-interests. Real Indians were full-blooded Indians, not half-breeds, he declared. They were hunters; they were true warriors who, like Ridge and Boudinot, understood the President's concern for his red children and wished to prevent the calamity of certain annihilation that would ensue if they did not heed his pleas to move west. As for Ross's authority under the Cherokee Constitution, Jackson denied that it existed. He said that this so-called constitution provided for an election in 1832 and it had not been held. Instead the Principal Chief had simply filled the National Council with his henchmen—another indication, claimed Jackson, of an elitist clique who ruled the Nation and disregarded the interests of the majority of the people.

The President did not wish to meet Ross. He knew this interview would only be a repeat of earlier interviews. Whenever he comes to Washington, Jackson declared, the chief "often proposed to make a treaty for mony alone, & not Land." Which showed that he was a greedy rascal, not a true leader. Then, Ross would insist on letting "the Cherokees seek their own country beyond the limits of the United States—to which I always replied we were bound by treaty to keep our Indians within our own limits."[20]

Despite his feelings about the chief, Jackson decided to grant Ross's request for a meeting. Above all else he wanted Cherokee removal, and if that meant seeing this "great villain" and hearing about his proposal for relocating the tribe, then he would do it. As a consummate politician, as Ross realized quite well, Jackson understood the value of playing one party off against another, so when he granted the interview he directed that Schermerhorn suspend his negotiations with the Treaty Party and wait for the outcome of his interview with the Principal Chief.

Actually Jackson and Ross were much alike. They were both wily, tough, determined, obsessed with protecting the interests of their respective peoples, and markedly dignified and polite when they came together in the White House on Wednesday, February 5, 1834. It was exactly noon when the Principal Chief arrived, and the Great Father greeted him with the respect due Ross's position. The chief returned the compliment. For a few minutes their conversation touched on pleasantries, then they got down to the question at hand and began playing a political game that involved the lives of thousands, both Native Americans and white settlers.

Unfortunately, despite his many talents and keen intelligence, Ross was no match for the President. He simply lacked the resources of his adversary.

The Principal Chief opened with an impassioned plea. "Your Cherokee children are in deep distress," he said, ". . . because they are left at the mercy of the white robber and assassin" and receive no redress from the Georgia courts. That state, he declared, has not only "surveyed and lotteried off" Cherokee land to its citizens but legislated as though Cherokees were intruders in their own country.

Jackson just listened. Then the Principal Chief acted imprudently and made impossible demands on the President. To start, he insisted that in any treaty the Cherokee Nation must retain some of its land along the borders of Tennessee, Alabama, and Georgia, land that had already been occupied by white settlers. He even included a small tract in North Carolina. He then required assurances that the United States government would protect the Cherokees with federal troops in the new and old settlements for a period of five years.[21]

Jackson could scarcely believe what was being demanded of him. Under other circumstances he would have acted up a storm in an attempt to frighten and cower the chief. But on this occasion he decided against it. Instead, in a calm and quiet but determined voice, he told Ross that nothing short of an entire removal of the Cherokee Nation from all its land east of the Mississippi would be acceptable.

Having run into a stone wall, Ross headed in another direction. In view of the gold that had recently been discovered in Georgia and North Carolina, he wanted $20 million for the entire Cherokee domain, plus reimbursement for losses sustained by the Nation for violations of former treaties by the United

States. He also asked for indemnities for claims under the 1817 and 1819 Cherokee treaties. The total amount almost equaled the national debt.

On hearing this, Jackson also changed direction. His voice hardened, his intense blue eyes flared, and the muscles in his face tightened and registered his growing displeasure. Obviously the Principal Chief had not caught the President's meaning when he rejected the first demand. He snapped at Ross, rejected the proposal as "preposterous," and warned him that the Great Father was not to be trifled with. If these demands were the best the chief could offer, then there was no point in continuing the discussion.

That brought Ross up short. Completely surprised by Jackson's reaction, he protested his sincerity, and to prove it he offered to accept any award the Senate of the United States might recommend. Apparently the chief was attempting to set up a bidding contest between the upper house and the chief executive. Surprisingly, Jackson accepted the offer and assured Ross that he would "go as far" as the Senate in any award that might be proposed. And on that conciliatory note the interview ended.[22]

In less than a week, Ross received his answer about what the Senate would offer. John P. King of Georgia chaired the Committee on Indian Affairs, which considered the question. That was bad enough. Then the committee came up with an offer of $5 million. The figure shocked the Principal Chief. Jackson probably knew beforehand what would happen and therefore agreed to Ross's suggestion. Now the Indian was faced with rejecting the money outright or accepting this paltry sum and thereby losing credibility with his people. Naturally he chose the former course. He claimed he had been misunderstood, that he could not possibly agree to such an amount, and that his reputation among the Cherokees would be shattered if he consented to it. He left Washington an angry and bitter man.[23]

Actually Jackson thought that $5 million was a generous offer, in view of the estimated federal share from the sale of Cherokee lands.

Having disposed of Ross, Jackson turned back to Schermerhorn and instructed him to renew the negotiations with the Treaty Party. With little difficulty the cleric managed to arrange a draft removal treaty signed on March 14, 1835, by Schermerhorn, John Ridge, Elias Boudinot, and a small delegation of Cherokees. After due notice the treaty was submitted to the Cherokee National Council at New Echota, Georgia, for approval and sent to the President for submission to the Senate. The draft stipulated that the Cherokees surrender to the United States all its land east of the Mississippi River for a sum of $5 million, an amount that one modern historian has called "unprecedented generosity." This cession comprised nearly eight million acres of land in western North Carolina, northern Georgia, northeastern Alabama, and eastern Tennessee. A schedule of removal provided that the Cherokees would be resettled in the west and receive regular payments for subsistence, claims, and spoliations, and would be issued blankets, kettles, and rifles.[24]

At approximately the same time this draft treaty was drawn up and considered at New Echota, a large delegation of Cherokee chiefs—in the desperate hope that their assembled presence would make a difference and prevent the treaty from going forward to the Senate—went to Washington and asked to speak to their Great Father. In contrast to his grudging granting of Ross's request, Jackson was anxious to meet the delegation and give the chiefs one of his celebrated "talks."

The Indians arrived at the White House at the designated hour, and Jackson treated them with marked respect, as though they really were dignitaries of a foreign nation. Yet he did not remotely say or do anything that would indicate an acceptance of their independence or sovereignty. Once the Indians had assembled, they faced the President as he began his talk.

"Brothers, I have long viewed your condition with great interest. For many years I have been acquainted with your people, and under all variety of circumstances, in peace and war. Your fathers are well known to me. . . . Listen to me, therefore, as your fathers have listened. . . ."

Jackson paused. He turned from side to side to look at and take in all the Cherokees standing around him. After a few moments he began again.

You are now placed in the midst of a white population. . . . You are now subject to the same laws which govern the citizens of Georgia and Alabama. You are liable to prosecutions for offenses, and to civil actions for a breach of any of your contracts. Most of your people are uneducated, and are liable to be brought into collision at all times with your white neighbors. Your young men are acquiring habits of intoxication. With strong passions . . . they are frequently driven to excesses which must eventually terminate in their ruin. The game has disappeared among you, and you must depend upon agriculture and the mechanic arts for support. And yet, a large portion of your people have acquired little or no property in the soil itself. . . . How, under these circumstances, can you live in the country you now occupy? Your condition must become worse and worse, and you will ultimately disappear, as so many tribes have done before you.

These were his usual arguments, but he judged them essential for success.

You have not listened to me, he scolded. You went to the courts for relief. You turned away from your Great Father. And what happened? After years of litigation you received little satisfaction from the Supreme Court and succeeded in earning the enmity of many whites. "I have no motive, Brothers, to deceive you," he said. "I am sincerely desirous to promote your welfare. Listen to me, therefore, while I tell you that you cannot remain where you are now. . . . It [is] impossible that you can flourish in the midst of a civilized community. You have but one remedy within your reach. And that is, to remove to the West and join your countrymen, who are already established there." The choice is yours. "May the great spirit teach you how to choose."

Jackson then concluded by reminding them of the fate of the Creeks, that once great and proud Nation. How broken and reduced in circumstances their lives had now become because they resisted. It was a not-so-subtle threat that also struck home. Would the Cherokees be so foolish as to follow the path of the Creeks? "Think then of these things," he concluded. "Shut your ears to bad counsels. Look at your condition as it now is, and then consider what it will be if you follow the advice I give you."[25]

That ended the talk, and the Indians filed from the room more disappointed and depressed than ever. Jackson would not budge, and they knew their kinsmen were dead set against removal. It was a stalemate that could only end in tragedy.

Meanwhile Schermerhorn called "a council of all the people" to meet him at New Echota in Georgia during the third week of December 1835 to approve the draft treaty, making sure that a large contingent of Treaty Party members attended. Like Jackson, he had the temerity to warn other Cherokees that if they stayed away their absence would be considered a vote of consent for the draft.

Despite the threat and the warning, practically the entire Nation stayed away. As a consequence the treaty was approved on December 28 by the unbelievable low number of 79 to 7. The numbers represented only the merest fraction of the Nation. A vast majority—perhaps fifteen-sixteenths of the entire population—presumably opposed it and showed their opposition by staying away. The entire process was fraudulent, but that hardly mattered. Jackson had the treaty he wanted, and he did not hesitate to so inform the Senate.

The Treaty of New Echota closely, but not completely, resembled the draft treaty in that the Cherokees surrendered all their eastern land and received $4.5 million in return. They would be paid for improvements, removed at government expense, and maintained for two years. Removal was to take place within two years from the date of the treaty's approval by the Senate and President.

A short while later some twelve thousand Cherokees signed a resolution denouncing the Treaty of New Echota and forwarded it to the Senate. Even the North Carolina Cherokees, in a separate action, added 3,250 signatures to a petition urging the Senate to reject it.[26] But Jackson was assured by the Treaty Party that "a majority of the people" approved the document "and all are willing peaceable to yield to the treaty and abide by it." Such information convinced the President that the Principal Chief and his "half-breed" cohorts had coerced the Cherokees into staying away from New Echota under threat of physical violence.[27]

At New Echota the Treaty Party selected a Committee of Thirteen to carry the treaty to Washington, and the committee was empowered to act on any alteration required by the President or the U.S. Senate. This committee invited Ross to join the group and either support the treaty or insist on such alterations as would make it acceptable. "But to their appeal [Ross] returned no answer," which further convinced the President that the treaty represented the genuine interests and the will of the majority of Cherokees.[28]

Although Henry Clay, Daniel Webster, Edward Everett, and other senators spoke fervently against the treaty in the Senate, a two-thirds majority of members voted for it, 31 to 15 against. It carried by a single vote on May 18. Jackson added his signature on May 23, 1836, and proclaimed the Treaty of New Echota in force.

Remarkably, the debate in the Senate over this issue did not begin to compare with the verbal brawl unleashed by the removal bill in 1830. Even the American Board of Commissions for Foreign Missions, whose purpose was the "civilizing" and Christianizing of the Indians, failed to provide any meaningful effort to defeat the treaty. The Cherokees had been abandoned even by their friends.

And they had two years—that is until May 23, 1838—to cross over the Mississippi and take up their new residence in the Indian Territory. But every day of that two-year period, John Ross fought the inevitable. He demanded to see the President and insisted that Jackson recognize the authority of the duly elected National Council, but Sharp Knife would have none of him and turned him away. Back home the Principal Chief advised his people to ignore the treaty and stay put. "We will not recognize the forgery palmed off upon the world as a treaty by a knot of unauthorized individuals," he cried, "nor stir one step with reference to that false paper."

Not everyone listened to him. They knew Andrew Jackson better. Some two thousand Cherokees resigned themselves to the inevitable, packed their belongings, and headed west. The rest, the vast majority of the tribe, could not bear to leave their homeland and chose to hope that their Principal Chief would somehow work the miracle that would preserve their country to them.[29]

But their fate could not have been worse. When the two-year grace period expired and Jackson had left office, his handpicked successor, President Martin Van Buren, ordered the removal to begin. Militiamen charged into the Cherokee country and drove the Cherokees from their cabins and houses. With rifles and bayonets they rounded up the Indians and placed them in prison stockades that had been erected "for gathering in and holding the Indians preparatory to removal." These poor, frightened, and benighted innocents, while having supper in their homes, "were startled by the sudden gleam of bayonets in the doorway and rose up to be driven with blows and oaths along the weary miles of trail which led to the stockade. Men were seized in the fields, women were taken from their wheels and children from their play." As they turned for one last glimpse of their homes they frequently saw them in flames, set ablaze by the lawless rabble who followed the soldiers, scavenging what they could. These outlaws stole the cattle and other livestock and even desecrated graves in their search for silver pendants and other valuables. They looted and burned. Said one Georgia volunteer who later served in the Confederate army: "I fought through the Civil War and have seen men shot to pieces and slaughtered by thousands, but the Cherokee removal was the cruelest I ever saw."

In a single week some seventeen thousand Cherokees were rounded up and herded into what was surely a concentration camp. Many sickened and died while they awaited transport to the west. In June the first contingent of about a thousand Indians boarded a steamboat and sailed down the Tennessee River on the first lap of their westward journey. Then they were boxed like animals into railroad cars drawn by two locomotives. Again there were many deaths on account of the oppressive heat and cramped conditions in the cars. For the last leg of the journey the Cherokees walked. Small wonder they came to call this eight-hundred-mile nightmare the Trail of Tears. Of the approximately eighteen thousand Cherokees who were removed, at least four thousand died in the stockades or along the way, and some say the figure actually reached eight thousand. By the middle of June 1838, the general in charge of the Georgia militia proudly reported that not a single Cherokee remained in the state except as prisoners in the stockade.

At every step of their long journey to the Indian Territory, the Cherokees were robbed and cheated by contractors, lawyers, agents, speculators, and anyone wielding local police power. Food provided by the government disappeared or arrived in short supply. The commanding officer, General Winfield Scott, and a few other generals "were concerned about their reputation for humaneness," says one modern historian, "and probably even for the Cherokee. There just wasn't much they could do about it." As a result, many died needlessly. "Oh! the misery and wretchedness that presents itself to our view in going among these people," wrote one man. "Sir, I have witnessed entire families prostrated with sickness—not one able to give help to the other; and these poor people were made the instruments of enriching a few unprincipled and wicked contractors."[30]

And this, too, is part of Andrew Jackson's legacy. Although it has been pointed out many times that he was no longer President of the United States when the Trail of Tears occurred and had never intended such a monstrous result of his policy, that hardly excuses him. It was his insistence on the speedy removal of the Cherokees, even after he had left office, that brought about this horror. From his home outside Nashville he regularly badgered Van Buren about enforcing the treaty. He had become obsessed about removal. He warned that Ross would exert every effort and means available to him to get the treaty rescinded or delayed, and that, he said, must be blocked. But the new President assured him that nothing would interfere with the exodus of the Cherokees and that no extension of the two-year grace period would be tolerated under any circumstance.[31]

Principal Chief John Ross also shares a portion of blame for this unspeakable tragedy. He continued his defiance even after the deadline for removal had passed. He encouraged his people to keep up their resistance, despite every sign that no appreciable help would be forthcoming from the American people or anyone else; and he watched as they suffered the awful consequences of his intransigence.

Some Cherokees escaped the horror. A tiny band of Indians in North Carolina hid away in the uppermost reaches of the mountains where it was difficult to reach them and drag them into a stockade. After years of negotiation by William Thomas, a white trader, with both the state and federal governments, this small group of Cherokees were permitted to remain undisturbed in their cloud-hidden heights, since there were so few of them and since the land they occupied was considered inaccessible and worthless. Their descendants still live in those mountains today.

Despite the obscene treatment accorded the Cherokees by the government, the tribe not only survived but endured. As Jackson predicted, they escaped the fate of many extinct eastern tribes. Cherokees today have their tribal identity, a living language, and at least three governmental bodies to provide for their needs. Would that the Yamasees, Mohegans, Pequots, Delawares, Narragansetts, and other such tribes could say the same.

Chapter 16

The Second Seminole War

In the waning years of Andrew Jackson's presidency the terrible fate visited on the Cherokees was repeated with the other southern tribes. The Creeks had long since surrendered to Sharp Knife's demands, but their removal did not go peacefully. What remained of the Creeks' eastern lands was fraudulently taken from them, and Jackson was so disturbed by the reports of corruption that he ordered Secretary of War Lewis Cass to undertake an investigation and prosecute those involved in the alleged frauds.

But violence suddenly erupted that changed everything. White squatters and speculators crowded into Creek territory, frequently evicting natives from their homes before they had a chance to pack their belongings. Angry exchanges triggered shootings. Finally a full-fledged war broke out in May 1836 when Creek warriors and the Georgia militia clashed in the Chattahoochee Valley. The mail stage, the toll bridge over the Chattahoochee River, and a tavern on the Federal Road were burned.

As a consequence the investigation came to a screeching halt, and Cass ordered General Thomas S. Jesup to assemble regulars and militia troops from Georgia and Alabama and rush them to the area to subdue the Creeks and then remove them. All Creeks, he directed, must be evicted from their country and transported west. It took close to ten thousand soldiers and several bloody engagements in July to stifle Creek armed resistance. Not until Jim Henry, "the most redoubtable of the Creek chiefs," was captured was the "Creek War of 1836" declared at an end.[1]

Enforced removal began with 14,609 Creeks carted off to the Indian Territory, some of them handcuffed and in chains. In 1837, five thousand more were transported west. So what a genuine treaty of removal failed to produce, guns and bayonets and violence did.[2] At Fort Gibson in the Indian Territory a Creek chief walked up to a white leader of the removal operation and said, "You have been with us many moons. Our road has been a long one. . . . On it we have laid the bones of our men, women, and children. . . . You have heard the cries of our women and children. . . . Tell General Jackson if the white man will let us we will live in peace and friendship."[3]

If possible an even more protracted and painful removal awaited the Seminoles in Florida. In 1832 and 1833 a series of treaties (Payne's Landing and Fort Gibson, respectively) had been signed that called for the eviction of the tribe. Pressure mounted almost immediately to begin the process, particularly when a large number of runaway slaves, estimated in the hundreds, were found hiding among the Seminoles. To assist the operation, President Jackson sent the Seminoles one of his "talks" in October 1834 in which he expressed his displeasure that they were taking their time about relocating. While he did not believe any of his "red children" would be "so dishonest and faithless as to refuse to go," still the delay had caused the Great Father considerable distress.

Nothing resulted from his talk. So Sharp Knife sent another. "My Children," he purred at them, "I am sorry to have heard that you have been listening to bad counsels. You know me, and you know that I would not deceive, nor advise you to do any thing that was unjust or injurious. Open your ears and attend to what I shall now say to you. They are the words of a friend, and the words of truth." He then went on to remind them that they had signed treaties to cede their lands in Florida and that they must leave. To prevent "some of your rash young men" from opposing removal, he continued, a large military force had been ordered into the area and would begin to transport one-third of the Seminoles to the Indian Territory. "But should you listen to the bad birds that are always flying about you, and refuse to remove, I have then directed the commanding officer to remove you by force."[4]

And that would surely trigger more bloodshed. But the Treaty of Payne's Landing in 1832 stipulated removal only after a delegation of Seminoles visited their proposed destination and found it acceptable. As it turned out, the delegation did not like the western country; even so, they were forced to sign the Treaty of Fort Gibson and accept the site on threat of being kept in the west. However, once the members of the delegation returned home, they repudiated the agreement and claimed they had signed the treaty under duress.

When General Duncan L. Clinch, who commanded the federal troops assigned to Florida, called on the chiefs to meet him and hear the Great Father's instructions, he acted with such arrogance and spoke with such contempt for Indian rights that he almost provoked bloodshed. Then suddenly the platform on which the officers and chiefs were sitting collapsed and they fell ten feet to the ground. Suspecting a trap, the Indians began screaming and dashed for the swamps. But the audience of warriors and troops standing nearby realized what had happened and started laughing. When order was finally restored, the chiefs asked for a postponement of the meeting so they could consult one another and prepare a suitable reply to Jackson's instructions.

Meanwhile John H. Eaton, the current governor of the Florida Territory and former secretary of war, warned the administration against any provocative act or any show of force. Without doubt, he said, military force would be met with military force. Furthermore, a new and potentially dangerous warrior had emerged, a mixed-blood by the name of Osceola, who was bold and energetic and had attracted a large following. A handsome man of thirty-five, Osceola absolutely opposed removal in any shape or form and favored "proscribing" every Seminole who obeyed the Great Father's command.[5]

So dangerous had Osceola become that federal troops seized him in the late spring of 1835 and placed him in chains. Caged, the Indian raged, tore his hair, and foamed at the mouth. He screamed and ranted like a madman. He actually seemed insane. He terrorized those who watched his ravings. Then, suddenly, his strange antics ceased. He became calm and subdued and even cooperated with his jailers. When he finally signed a statement certifying the validity of the Treaty of Payne's Landing, the federal authorities believed that they had broken his spirit and he was no longer a threat. So they released him, little realizing that his charade had tricked them into letting him go. But now they had to deal with a warrior who breathed a lethal hatred for all whites and swore to exact a bloody revenge.

Killings began that quickly mounted in intensity. And Osceola followed out his threat to punish any Seminole who removed. Chief Charlie Emathla was one such. He and a small party decided to sell their belongings and head west. Just as they prepared to depart, Osceola and his warriors surrounded them, and in the ensuing argument Osceola shot Emathla and left his body to rot on the ground. He emptied the chief's pockets and flung the money in every direction.

It all escalated into outright war on December 18, 1835, when at Kanapaha, along the rim of the Alachua Savannah, Osceola and eighty of his men ambushed a wagon train escorted by thirty mounted militia and killed eight of them and wounded another six. With the contents of the wagon train the chief could now engage in intensified warfare against the government of the United States. And Osceola had every intention of hitting hard and often. Thus began the Second Seminole War.[6]

It lasted for seven agonizing years, and small wonder. The terrain over which the troops and Indians fought was one vast morass of swamp, and the fighting quickly developed into a full-fledged contest between a crafty, energetic, and supremely gifted Seminole chief and a federal army commanded by two generals who were bitter enemies, Winfield Scott and Edmund Pendleton Gaines. General Gaines did not take kindly to serving under Scott after he arrived on the scene, and the two men quarreled incessantly. To further complicate the situation, President Jackson and his war secretary were distracted by a dispute with the French that almost resulted in a declaration of war.[7]

Two weeks after the action at Kanapaha a full-scale engagement occurred at the Battle of Withlacoochee. It was a standoff, but Osceola succeeded in thwarting federal attempts at inflicting serious injury on his Seminole warriors and allies. Meanwhile the wily chieftain spread terror among the settlers across the entire northern frontier of Florida.

As the war showed no sign of letup, General Scott was summoned to the White House and given instructions from the old master of Indian warfare. Jackson told Scott he should first discover where the "Indian women were collected" and "proceed at any hazard & expense" to that location. This action, he said, would draw Osceola out of the swamps into an exposed area where he could be attacked. Also, "have two good spy companies immediately organized, led by gallant men, acquainted with Indian cunning and treachery, and good woodsmen." Spies are essential to any operation, he declared, and will learn where the women and children are located. As you head south, gather militia along the way in South Carolina and Georgia, strap eight days' rations on their backs, and then head directly to "the deposit of women and children," where you will "find all the warriors" and where with "one blow" you can end the war.[8]

When Scott arrived in Florida it did not take him long to get lost in the swamps. He planned to deploy "three grand columns" in a circling movement—that is, if he could find something to encircle. "To surround what," bawled Jackson when he heard about it, "—the Indians?—no—for . . . Gen'l Scott had no positive information where the Indian women and children were." How did he ever expect to succeed with such a strategy? At length Scott abandoned the current campaign and took up winter quarters in St. Augustine.[9]

And so the Second Seminole War dragged on for years. Scott was replaced first by Richard Keith Call, the new governor of the Florida Territory, and then by General Jesup, who the President hoped would end what he had now come to call this "Punic War." In no time the struggle had become an embarrassment. "I have been brooding over the unfortunate mismanagement of *all the military* operations in Florida," he told his acting secretary of war, Benjamin F. Butler, "all of which are so humiliating to our military character, that it fills me with pain, & mortification—the sooner that a remedy can be offorded the better."[10]

His administration was ending—he would leave office on March 4, 1837—and yet this idiotic war continued unabated. "I am mortified," he seethed. In an interview with Joseph M. White, a retiring congressional delegate from the Florida Territory, the President vented his rage. White had dared to comment that the struggle had placed a terrible strain upon his people, whereupon Jackson burst out, "Let the damned cowards defend their country." They had done nothing to help, he roared, not even placing a brigadier general's command in the field. Why, he boasted, "with fifty *women*" he could "whip every Indian that had ever crossed the Suwannee." Floridians had done less to end the war or defend themselves "than any other people in the United States." Had they been "men of spirit and character" they could have crushed the Seminoles in a single blow. Male Floridians ought to go out and let the Indians shoot them, he raged, then at least the "women might get husbands of courage, and breed up men who would defend the country."[11]

This insanity demonstrated not only Jackson's anguish over the war but the level of his obsession about removing Native Americans. Over the years he had become fixated upon this single idea. Fortunately Jesup fulfilled the President's great desire, but it did not happen until Sharp Knife had left office and until Osceola was tricked into attending a meeting under a flag of truce to negotiate the release of three captured chiefs. The great chief was seized and interned at Fort Marion in St. Augustine. After a few months he died on January 31, 1838.

Jackson departed the presidency with the war still raging. By this time its cost had reached $10 million, and every month it cost another $458,000. Andrew Jackson alone was responsible for this bloodbath, lamented Congressman Caleb Cushing of Massachusetts on the floor of the House, both the loss of treasure and the loss of lives. What a stain to leave on one's presidential record. What a tragedy to carry to one's grave.[12]

Chapter 17

Jackson's Indian Legacy

The Second Seminole War dragged on until 1842 before the last battle was fought. Jesup had been replaced by General Zachary Taylor, who brought it to an end during the administration of John Tyler. Approximately four thousand Seminoles were removed to the Indian Territory, although a number escaped removal by hiding in the Everglades. About fifteen hundred regular soldiers died in the effort out of approximately ten thousand who participated. It is not possible to calculate the mortality among volunteers or Native Americans.

This war was the fiercest, bloodiest, and costliest operation to relocate the Indians west of the Mississippi and marked the end of Jackson's efforts to clear the Gulf Coast of Native Americans. The Five Civilized Tribes—that is, the Cherokees, the Creeks, the Choctaws, the Chickasaws, and the Seminoles—had all been effectively removed. But they were not the only ones. During Jackson's administration the Sac and Fox Indians, the Quapaws, the Apalachicolas, the united tribes of Otos and Missouri, the four confederated bands of Pawnees of the Platte, the Senecas of Sandusky River, and the Chippewas, Ottawas, Potawatomis, Winnebagos, Miamis, Caddos, Wyandots, Menominis, Saginaws, Kickapoos, Kaskaskias, Piankishaws, Delawares, Shawnees, Osages, Iowas, Pinkeshaws, Weas, and Peorias surrendered valuable land in Illinois, Michigan, Iowa, Wisconsin, Louisiana, Kentucky, Indiana, Ohio, Kansas, Minnesota, and Nebraska.[1]

In all, approximately 45,690 Indians were relocated beyond the Mississippi during the eight years of Jackson's presidency. Even as he left office a number of treaties had been signed, but not yet executed, that would raise that total by several more thousands. According to the Indian Office, only about 9,000 Native Americans were without treaty stipulations requiring their removal when Jackson departed Washington. These Indians lived mostly in the Old Northwest and New York. In sum, from 1789, when the American government began under the Constitution, to 1838, a year after Jackson left office, about 81,282 Indians were relocated to the west.

The operation of removal provided the American people with the land they had hungered for over the past hundred and more years. Jackson acquired for the United States approximately 100 million acres of land for about $68 million and 32 million acres of western land.[2] It was one of the unhappiest chapters in American history.

———

From the beginning of the national experience when George Washington assumed the office of President of the United States, the government adopted a policy toward native peoples that was dictated by perceived necessity and the peculiar circumstances of the time. The country was weak, militarily and economically, and many fierce and warlike tribes lived within its territorial limits and understandably resisted the constant encroachment of white settlers on their land. The government could not adequately police these tribes, so it periodically fought them and then signed treaties with them. By signing treaties and then submitting them for ratification by the Senate the government acted as though the tribes were sovereign and independent nations, even though it had no intention of recognizing them as such. It believed that the tribes fell under the sovereignty of the United States, a view that was confirmed later by the Supreme Court. Yet the Indians actually lived under their own laws and their own governments and their own leaders.

It was a hopelessly muddled situation right from the beginning. And when the United States signed treaties with the tribes (which were invariably violated by white settlers), it could not enforce them. It had not the will or the strength, and this only led to further misunderstanding and conflict. As the country expanded with the admission of new states into the Union, the problems became more acute and the pressure for more land by settlers intensified.

With the purchase of Louisiana in 1803 a possible solution seemed feasible when President Jefferson suggested a program of exchange. Some Native Americans took advantage of the proposal and moved to the west, but they were relatively few. Following the War of 1812, as the United States began the process of industrialization and thousands of immigrants from Europe flooded into the country, the relationship between Indians and whites rapidly deteriorated. In terms of population approximately five million people lived in the United States at the start of the nineteenth century. By the time Andrew Jackson became President the population had tripled to fifteen million, and the number of states had increased from the original thirteen to twenty-four—with Jackson adding two more before he left office. By comparison the population of native tribes had steadily dwindled.

Obviously the policy first adopted by the George Washington administration of treating Indian tribes as though they were sovereign and without any allegiance to the United States could no longer suffice. As Jackson himself said, the country was weak at the turn of the century but over the years had grown strong, strong enough now to dictate what the Indians must do if they wished to remain within the territorial boundaries of the United States.

What Jackson did to the Indians as President was take advantage of that strength and end the drift and indecision of previous administrations by instituting a policy of removal that included an exchange of land. With the lessening of hostilities the tribes begged to be left alone, pleaded for protection and to be spared the necessity of contending with the power of the surrounding states whose citizens continually crowded in on them. But what they asked was impossible to provide in 1830. Perhaps it was never possible. As it turned out, the American people as a whole sided with the government and approved Jackson's policy. They did so because of their racism, their decades-old fear and mistrust of Native Americans, and their insatiable desire for the land they occupied. What resulted constitutes one of the great tragedies in the history of the United States, a tragedy for which the American people and their President must be held accountable. Like Jackson, they agreed that removal (which would make Indian land theirs) was also the only way to preserve Indian life and culture. Thus by shunting them off to the wilderness where they would no longer threaten the safety of the United States or hinder its westward and southern expansion, Americans felt they could resolve the problem of the Indian presence in a humanitarian manner that would not conflict with their Christian conscience or moral sensibility.

The distinguished scholar of Native American history Francis Paul Prucha has argued that four courses of action were available to the government in ending the everlasting white/red crisis. And four courses only. First, genocide. Exterminate the race. But no one in his right mind seriously proposed such a solution, certainly not Jackson or any other responsible official in government. Second, integrate the two societies. But Native Americans had no desire to become cultural white men. They had their own customs, laws, language, religion, government, and leaders and wanted to keep them. White man's culture was an abomination, except for those skills that could improve their standard of living. Nor did whites favor integration. As racists they feared that integration with red people would ultimately lead to integration with blacks. And that possibility horrified them. Third, protect the natives where they lived by enforcing existing treaties. Jackson knew such a policy was doomed from the start and had fifteen years of personal experience to attest to its impossibility. There was not army enough to keep squatters from invading Indian country. And future confrontations with southern states, similar to the one with Georgia, would undoubtedly follow, particularly in Alabama and Mississippi. Fourth, removal. That was the course Jackson knew would work and therefore adopted. No other alternative existed if Indians were to survive.[3]

It needs to be remembered that removal was never just a land grab. That is too simplistic an explanation. Jackson fully expected the Indians to thrive in their new surroundings, educate their children, acquire the skills of white civilization so as to improve their living conditions, and become citizens of the United States. Removal, in his mind, would provide all these blessings.

At one point in this sad story a delegation of Chippewa, Potawatomi, and Ottawa chiefs came to Jackson in the White House and movingly described to him their suffering. "Your agent," they said, "told us at the Treaty made at Chicago in 1833 that the country assigned to us west of the Mississippi was equally good as the lands in Illinois. . . . Father—we have been deceived and we feel disappointed & dissatisfied. . . . There is scarce timber enough to build our Wigwams, and that some of our land is too poor for snakes to live upon. Our men are not accustomed to the Prairie. They have always lived in the woods."[4]

Jackson listened to this recitation but did not hear. A long time before, he had made up his mind about what should be done with Native Americans, and nothing would change his mind, even though the eastern tribes no longer posed a danger to the country, nor was national security the issue. He believed the good of the nation and the tribes required their removal, and so thousands of men, women, and children suffered not only the loss of their property, but physical agony and even death.

To his dying day on June 8, 1845, Andrew Jackson genuinely believed that what he had accomplished rescued these people from inevitable annihilation. And although that statement sounds monstrous, and although no one in the modern world wishes to accept or believe it, that is exactly what he did. He saved the Five Civilized Nations from probable extinction.

Notes

Chapter 1. The Making of an Indian Fighter

1. John Sugden, *Tecumseh: A Life* (New York, 1998), p. 237.
2. The quotations here and in the following pages are obviously from unfriendly white sources, in this case J.F.H. Claiborne, known as the "Father of Mississippi History." He was born in 1807 and died in 1884. He claims he wrote his *Mississippi as a Province, Territory and State* (Jackson, Miss., 1880) from newspapers, books, government documents, and the reminiscences and manuscripts of participants in the events he describes. As for the Indians, the information, he says, was "derived from citizens who resided among them, and from my own observations when officially associated with them." Introduction, p. xi. The quote in the text is taken from p. 316.
3. All of these quotations are taken from Claiborne, *Mississippi*, I, 315–18. The author merely cites "an intelligent witness." But much of this information, except for Tecumseh's speech, can also be found in an earlier book, Albert James Pickett, *History of Alabama, and Incidentally of Georgia and Mississippi* (Charleston, 1851), pp. 240–45. For Tecumseh's speech Claiborne simply says that it is compressed. Whether his source is a Creek or a mixed-blood or someone else is not known. Admittedly the speech is "awfully cinematically dramatic and florid" and difficult to swallow whole, but there it is.
4. H. S. Halbert and T. H. Ball, *The Creek War of 1813–1814* (University, Ala., 1969), pp. 79–80.
5. James W. Holland, *Andrew Jackson and the Creek War: Victory at the Horseshoe* (University, Ala., 1968), p. 7.
6. Sources do not agree as to the actual number of men, women, and children killed. One figure runs as high as 517. Frank Lawrence Owsley, Jr., *Struggle for the Gulf Borderlands: The Creek War and the Battle of New Orleans, 1812–1815* (Gainesville, 1981), pp. 30, 33, 34, 36–39; Green, *Politics of Indian Removal*, pp. 40–42; Claiborne, *Mississippi*, p. 324; Halbert and Ball, *Creek War*, p. 156; Albert J. Pickett, *History of Alabama . . .* (Charleston, 1851), II, 275. Holland, *Jackson and Creek War*, p. 10.
7. Blount to AJ, September 14, 1813, in John Brannon, ed., *Official Letters of the Military and Naval Officers of the United States During the War with Great Britain* (Washington, 1823), p. 215; Blount to AJ, September 25, 1813, Jackson Papers, LC.
8. Of the four armies, two came from Tennessee: one from east Tennessee under General John Cocke, and one from west Tennessee under General Jackson. These two armies were to converge under Jackson's command in northern Alabama. In addition one army would invade from Georgia under Major General John Floyd, and another from the Mississippi Territory under General Ferdinand L. Claiborne. Overall command was given to Major General Thomas Pinckney. Owsley, *Struggle for the Gulf*, pp. 43–46.
9. Robert V. Remini, *The Battle of New Orleans* (New York, 1999), pp. 10–12.
10. James Parton, *The Life of Andrew Jackson* (New York, 1861), III, 699.
11. The argument that the Jacksons arrived in Charleston is provided in John Reid and John H. Eaton, *The Life of Andrew Jackson* (University, Ala., 1975), p. 9; Parton, *Jackson*, I, 48; and John Spencer Bassett, *The Life of Andrew Jackson* (New York, 1967), p. 4, but other biographers of Jackson insist the family arrived in Pennsylvania. See Marquis James, *The Life of Andrew Jackson* (Indianapolis and New York, 1938), pp. 789–90; Robert V. Remini, *Andrew Jackson and the Course of American Empire* (New York, 1977), p. 3.
12. Arrel Morgan Gibson, *The American Indian: Prehistory to the Present* (Lexington, Mass., 1980), pp. 210–12; Douglas Summers Brown, *The Catawbas Indians* (Columbia, S.C., 1966), pp. 3, 136.
13. Gibson, *American Indian*, p. 226; Brown, *Catawbas*, pp. 246–47.

14. Brown, *Catawbas,* pp. 209–15, 246–47, 252, 254; Charles M. Hudson *Catawba Nation,* (Athens, Ga., 1970), p. 51.

15. This area later became part of Union County, North Carolina, so named to honor President Jackson, who had faced down the nullifiers of South Carolina in 1833 when they threatened to secede from the Union.

16. Parton, *Jackson,* III, 699.

17. Susan Alexander, "The Fugitives from the Waxhaws," in *National Intelligencer,* August 1, 29, 1845, reprinted in William A. Graham, *General Joseph Graham and His Papers on North Carolina Revolutionary History* (Raleigh, 1904), p. 71. I am grateful to Dr. Hendrik Booraem for alerting me to this source. Jackson's remark about his mother can be found in John Trotwood Moore, *Taylor Trotwood Magazine* (May 1907), V, 142–43.

18. Alexander, "Fugitives from the Waxhaws," p. 71.

19. Hendrik Booraem, who is about to publish a study of Jackson's early life, tells me that Alexander is quite reliable on matters concerning which he can confirm her statements with other sources. Her memory was faulty about the eldest son, which she realized, so she qualified her remarks about him with words like "I thought her eldest son was killed by Indians." Not "they said" or "I know," but "I thought." Ibid., pp. 71, 76.

20. Ibid., pp. 71, 76, 78. Since there had not been a serious Cherokee raid in the county for several years it would appear that the consciousness of past raids remained vivid in their memories, much as southerners remembered Yankee atrocities long after the Civil War. Booraem to author, June 16, 2000.

21. Ibid., pp. 72–73.

22. Parton, *Jackson,* I, 123.

23. It was not so much the presence of the Catawbas who helped inculcate these ideas in the inhabitants of the Waxhaws, given their weakened condition by the end of the eighteenth century; rather it was the Cherokees living farther west who might at any moment swoop down on a white settlement and obliterate it.

24. Parton, *Jackson,* I, 64–65, III, 695.

25. Quoted in Tom Hatley, *The Dividing Paths: Cherokees and South Carolinians Through the Era of Revolution* (New York, 1993), p. 193.

26. Drayton to Francis Salvador, July 24, 1776, in Gibbes, *Documentary History of the American Revolution* (New York, 1971), II, 29.

27. Alexander, "Fugitives from the Waxhaws," p. 73; Amos Kendall, *The Life of Andrew Jackson* (New York, 1844), p. 14.

28. Parton, *Jackson,* I, 72; Kendall, *Jackson,* p. 25; Remini, *Jackson,* I, 16–17.

29. Kendall, *Jackson,* p. 45.

30. Ibid., p. 51; AJ to Sam Houston, July 1824, James McLaughlin to Amos Kendall, January 2, 1843, Jackson Papers, LC.

31. Alexander, "Fugitives from the Waxhaws," p. 72.

32. McLaughlin to Kendall, January 2, 1843, Jackson Papers, LC.

Chapter 2. Fighting Cherokees, Chickasaws, and Creeks

1. Parton, *Jackson,* I, 104–5.

2. Ibid.

3. Stanley W. Hoig, *The Cherokees and Their Chiefs in the Wake of Empire* (Fayetteville, Ark., 1998), p. 58.

4. For further details of this duel, see Remini, *Jackson,* I, 37–39.

5. Parton, *Jackson,* I, 121.

6. Ibid., I, 123–24.

7. J.G.M. Ramsey, *The Annals of Tennessee to the End of the Eighteenth Century* (Charleston, 1853), p. 484.

8. For further details about the divorce and the Jackson marriage see Remini, *Jackson,* I, 57–69.

9. Ramsey, *Annals of Tennessee,* p. 484; Reid and Eaton, *Jackson,* p. 16.

10. Albigence W. Putnam, *History of Middle Tennessee* (Nashville, 1859), pp. 317–18.

11. Kendall, *Jackson,* 85–86.

12. McLaughlin to Kendall, March 13, 1843, Jackson Papers, LC.
13. Putnam, *History of Middle Tennessee,* pp. 318–19.
14. Arrell Morgan Gibson, *The American Indian* (Lexington, Mass, 1980), p. 268.
15. Robertson to McGillivray, August 3, 1788, *American Historical Magazine* (January 1896), I, 81.
16. AJ to Daniel Smith, February 13, 1789, in Jackson, *Papers,* I, 16. To do business within Spanish territory, an American had to take an oath of loyalty to the King of Spain. Jackson took such an oath on July 15, 1789, when he offered his services as lawyer and trader to the residents of Natchez. Cuba 2361, Archivo General de Indias, Seville, Spain.
17. Theda Perdue and Michael D. Green, *The Cherokee Removal* (Boston and New York, 1995), pp. 10–11.
18. Blount to Henry Knox, August 1, 1793, in Clarence E. Carter, ed., *The Territorial Papers of the United States* (Washington, 1936–), IV, 291.
19. Any transaction by Blount "with Respect to my Business," Jackson wrote, "[will] be perfectly pleasing to me [as] I know from Experience that my interest will be attended to." AJ to John McKee, May 16, 1794, in John Spencer Bassett, ed., *The Correspondence of Andrew Jackson* (Washington, D.C., 1926–1933), I, 12, hereafter cited as Jackson, *Correspondence.*
20. AJ to John McKee, May 16, 1794, in Jackson, *Correspondence,* I, 12–13. See also his letter to McKee, January 30, 1793 in ibid., I, 12.
21. Blount to Robertson, January 2, 5, 1792, January 18, 1794, in *American Historical Magazine* (July 1896), III, 280, 282, (July 1898), III, 280.
22. Blount to Robertson, October 28, 1792, in *American Historical Magazine* (January 1897), II, 81.
23. Ramsey, *Annals of Tennessee,* pp. 602–17. A number of Indian prisoners were taken, mostly women, girls, and boys, and marched toward the canoes in the river. Suddenly one "squaw loosed her clothes, sprang head foremost into the river, disengaging herself artfully from her clothes and leaving them floating upon the water." A skillful swimmer, she rapidly out-distanced the militia. "Shoot her— shoot her," cried some of the men. But others, awed by her boldness and her strength and determination, responded, "'she is too smart to kill' and allowed the heroine to escape." Ibid.
24. Ibid., pp. 614–15. The author states his source as the Willie Blount Papers.
25. Putnam, *History of Middle Tennessee,* p. 478 note.
26. Blount to Robertson, November 22, 1794, quoted in Alice B. Keith, "The North Carolina Blount Brothers in Business and Politics, 1783–1812," unpublished doctoral dissertation, University of North Carolina at Chapel Hill, 1940, p. 412.
27. Ramsey, *Annals of Tennessee,* p. 648.
28. Remini, *Jackson,* I, 76–85; Sam B. Smith and Harriet Chapelle Owsley, eds., *The Papers of Andrew Jackson* (Knoxville, 1980–), I, 98–99, hereafter cited as Jackson, *Papers.*
29. *Annals of Congress,* 4th Congress, 2nd Session, p. 1737.
30. Ibid., pp. 1738–39.
31. Ibid., p. 1742.
32. Ibid., p. 2155. The draft is in Jackson's handwriting. Jackson Papers, LC.
33. Claiborne to AJ, July 20, 1797, Jackson Papers. LC. Jackson also won praise from his constituents by keeping them informed of his efforts on their behalf. "Assure my fellow Citizens," he told Robert Hays, "that when those Claims are acted upon they shall have the Earliest information, and those claims I will always keep in View untill I have a decision on them." As promised, he reported regularly to them during each step of the process until the Congress finally authorized payment. AJ to Hays, December 16, 1796, Jackson Papers, LC.
34. AJ to Ore, March 4, AJ to David Henley, February 17, 1797 in Jackson, *Papers,* I, 128, 124–25.
35. AJ to Robert Hays, January 8, 1797, in Jackson, *Correspondence,* I, 24–25.
36. Jackson took a very dim view of George Washington. He objected to his Indian policy and blamed him for accepting the miserable terms offered by the British in the Jay Treaty. He therefore refused to vote in favor of a formal reply to the President's farewell address.
37. Sevier to AJ, January 29, AJ to Sevier, February 24, 1797, in Jackson, *Papers,* I, 120–21, 126–27.
38. Sevier to AJ, November 19, 1797, Anderson, Jackson, and William C.C. Claiborne to Adams, March 5, 1798, Governors' Papers, Tennessee State Library. Copies in Jackson, *Papers,* I, 153–54,185–86.
39. Sevier to AJ, November 26, 1797, January 12, 1798, in Jackson, *Papers,* I, 154–55, 166.

40. The delegation also suggested to the new secretary of war, James McHenry, that "from our knowledge of Indian pursuits" the best time to conduct negotiations would occur between March 20 and May 1, because more chiefs and warriors would attend. By March 20 the Indians would have returned from their "winter hunt," and not until May 1 would they take off again for their "spring hunt." Adams to Anderson, Jackson, and Claiborne, December 1, 1797, Anderson, Jackson, and Claiborne to James McHenry, February 12, 1798, in ibid., I, 156, 181; Adams to U.S. Senate, January 8, 1798, *American State Papers, Indian Affairs (ASPIA)*, I, 631.

41. This time he wanted "the indian claim on the north side of Clinch as low down as the mouth of Emery's river or the Cumberland road, up to the top of that mountain, and along the extreme height up to the Kentucky road—from the mouth of Clinch up the Tennessee to the Chilhowa mountain, and along the extreme height thereof to the late line run by the commissioners." Sevier to AJ, January 12, 1798, in Jackson, *Papers*, I, 166.

42. Kendall, *Jackson*, p. 101.

43. Parton, *Jackson*, I, 227–29.

44. Sevier to AJ, May 8, 1797, in Jackson, *Correspondence*, I, 31.

45. "Elections Returns of Mero District for Major General of the Tennessee Militia," in Jackson, *Papers*, I, 277.

46. For an indication of the support Jackson received see David Campbell to AJ, January 25, 1802, Jackson, *Papers*, I, 274.

47. In retaliation for this unexpected defeat, Sevier's friends in the legislature rushed through a bill dividing the state's military command and creating two military districts, one in the east and one in the west, and permitted Jackson to retain command over the western district.

48. There are several versions of this so-called duel, but see the affidavit of Andrew Greer, October 23, 1803, in *American History Magazine*, V, 208; Kendall, *Jackson*, p. 107; and Parton, *Jackson*, I, 234–35.

49. This county was named for Jackson in 1801 and formed from a portion of Smith County. It was another indication of his popularity and importance in the district.

50. AJ to McKinney, May 10, 1802, in Jackson, *Papers*, I, 294–95.

51. AJ to Winchester, May 10, 1802, in ibid., I, 295–96.

52. Return Jonathan Meigs, the Indian agent to the Cherokees and highly respected by the natives for his help and support, arranged a number of such cessions. One of them involved a tract north of the Tennessee River in middle Tennessee and Kentucky for which the Cherokees were paid $15,600 in goods and $3,000 in annuities. Grace Steele Woodward, *The Cherokees*, (Norman, Okla.), pp. 127–29.

Chapter 3. Old Hickory

1. AJ to John Coffee, March 25, 26, 1813, and enclosure from John Childress, in Jackson, *Papers*, II, 294–95.

2. Parton, *Jackson*, I, 349–54.

3. The Dinsmore incident is described in full in Parton, *Jackson*, I, 349–59; see AJ to Campbell, September 12, 1812, pp. 357–58.

4. AJ to George W. Campbell, September 12, 1812, in ibid., I, 357–58.

5. For these treaties see Charles C. Royce, *Indian Land Cession in the United States* (Washington, D.C., 1904), pp. 648–51, 652–53; Michael Green to the author, July 27, 1999.

6. Blount to AJ, December 28, 1809, in Jackson, *Papers*, II, 226–27.

7. Blount to AJ, February 26, 1811, in ibid., II, 259.

8. Halbert and Ball, *Creek War*, pp. 86, 104.

9. Ibid., pp. 86–87; AJ to Blount, June 4, 1812, Jackson, *Papers*, II, 300–1.

10. AJ to Colbert, June 5, 1812, in Jackson, *Papers*, II, 302–3.

11. AJ to Crawford, June 10, 1816, in Jackson, *Correspondence*, II, 244.

12. Michael Paul Rogin discusses this point at length in his book, *Fathers & Children: Andrew Jackson and the Subjugation of the American Indian* (New York, 1975).

13. AJ to Blount, July 3, 1812, in Jackson, *Papers*, II, 307.

14. AJ to Blount, July 3, 1812, in ibid., II, 307–8.

15. AJ to Graham, July 22, 1817, in Jackson, *Correspondence*, II, 308–9.

16. Halbert and Ball, *Creek War,* pp. 100, 103.
17. Quoted in George Dangerfield, in *The Era of Good Feelings* (New York, 1952), p. 39.
18. Armstrong to AJ, February 5, 1813, Jackson, *Correspondence,* I, 280.
19. Reid and Eaton, *Jackson,* p. 19.
20. AJ to Grundy, March 15, 1813, in Jackson, *Papers,* II, 385.
21. Remini, *Jackson,* I, 178.
22. AJ to Rachel, March 15, 1813, Jackson Papers, LC.
23. Ibid.
24. For details of the gunfight see Remini, *Jackson,* I, 180–86.
25. General Order, September 24, 1813, Jackson Papers, LC; Reid and Eaton, *Jackson,* p. 33.

Chapter 4. The Creek War

1. Remini, *Jackson,* I, 190–91; Owsley, *Struggle for the Gulf,* p. 43; Reid and Eaton, *Jackson,* p. 33; AJ to Chief Chennabee, October 19, AJ to Pathkiller, October 23, 1813, Jackson, *Papers,* LC.
2. AJ to Coffee, September 25, November 2, 1813, Jackson Papers, LC; AJ to Rachel, November 4, 1813, in Jackson, *Papers,* II, 444; Davy Crockett, *Life of Davy Crockett* (New York, 1854), p. 75; Coffee to AJ, November 4, 1813, in Thomas H. Palmer, ed., *The Historical Register of the United States* (Washington, 1816), I, 333–35; John Reid to Nathan Reid, November 21, 1813, Reid Papers, LC; Call's "Journal," quoted in Herbert J. Doherty, Jr., *Richard Keith Call: Southern Unionists* (Gainesville, 1961), p. 6; AJ to Blount, November 4, 1813, Jackson Papers, LC. Jackson estimated that the probable number of Creeks killed at Tallushatchee was two hundred or more.
3. AJ to Rachel, November 4, 1813, Miscellaneous Jackson Papers, Harvard University Library; AJ to Rachel, December 19, 1813, in Jackson, *Papers,* II, 494–95; AJ to Rachel, December 29, 1813, Huntington Library; Parton, *Jackson,* I, 439.
4. Kendall, *Jackson,* p. 201.
5. Reid and Eaton, *Jackson,* pp. 52–53.
6. Halbert and Ball, *Creek War,* p. 269; Reid and Eaton, *Jackson,* p. 53; AJ to Blount, November 15, 1813, in Jackson, *Correspondence,* I, 348.
7. AJ to Blount, November 13, 1813, in Jackson, *Correspondence,* I, 349; Reid and Eaton, *Jackson,* pp. 56–57.
8. AJ to Blount, November 13, 1813, in Jackson, *Correspondence,* I, 349; Reid and Eaton, *Jackson,* pp. 55–58; AJ to Blount, November 11, 1813, in Brannan, *Official Letters,* p. 265; Coffee to John Donelson, November 12, 1813, in *American Historical Magazine* (April 1901), VI, 176; John Reid to Nathan Reid, December 24, 1813, Reid Papers, LC; AJ to Blount, November 15, 1813, and AJ to Thomas Pinckney, December 3, 1813, Jackson Papers, LC.
9. Reid and Eaton, *Jackson,* p. 58; Owsley, *Struggle for the Gulf,* p. 66.
10. Grierson to AJ, November 13, AJ to Grierson, November 17, 1813, in Jackson, *Papers,* II, 451, 456–57.
11. AJ to Cocke, November 18, 1813, in Jackson, *Papers,* II, 457–58.
12. White to Cocke, November 24, 1813, in *Niles' Weekly Register,* December 25, 1813; Cocke to AJ, November 27, 1813, in Jackson, *Papers,* II, 451, 462; Parton, *Jackson,* I, 452.
13. Parton, *Jackson,* I, 453; AJ to Cocke, December 6, 1813, Jackson, *Papers,* II, 469–70.
14. Blount to AJ, November 24, 1813, in Jackson, *Papers,* II, 460–61; Reid and Eaton, *Jackson,* pp. 101–6.
15. Reid and Eaton, *Jackson,* p. 66.
16. Reid and Eaton, *Jackson,* pp. 69–71; Kendall, *Jackson,* pp. 216–17.
17. Kendall, *Jackson,* p. 217.
18. Reid and Eaton, *Jackson,* pp. 83–85; Kendall, *Jackson,* p. 219–20; AJ to Rachel, December 29, 1813, Jackson Papers, Huntington Library; AJ to Thomas Pinckney, December 13, 1813, in Jackson, *Papers,* II, 485.
19. Upon their return, the soldiers published an elaborate defense of their conduct, which Jackson later responded to in an article written by John Reid and published in the Nashville *Whig* of January 11, 1814. Copy of Jackson's address in Jackson, *Papers,* II, 482–83.
20. Coffee to AJ, December 20, Blount to AJ, December 22, 1813, Jackson Papers, LC; Reid and Eaton,

Jackson, p. 89; AJ to Blount, December 29, AJ to Coffee, December 31, 1813, in Jackson, *Correspondence*, I, 416–20, 431.

21. AJ to Blount, December 29, 1813, in Jackson, *Correspondence*, I, 416–20.
22. Remini, *Jackson*, I, 194–97, 207–8; Reid and Eaton, *Jackson*, p. 128; AJ to Thomas Pinckney, January 29, 1814, in Jackson, *Correspondence*, I, 448–501.
23. Reid and Eaton, *Jackson*, p. 136.
24. AJ to Pinckney, March 14, 1814, Jackson Papers, LC; Halbert and Ball, *Creek War*, pp. 246–47.
25. Holland, *Jackson and the Creek War*, p. 19.
26. Reid and Eaton, *Jackson*, p. 149; AJ to Blount, March 31, 1814, in Jackson, *Correspondence*, I, 490; AJ to John Armstrong, April 2, 1814, National Archives.
27. General Orders, March 24 (?), 1814, AJ to Pinckney, March 28, 1814, in Jackson, *Correspondence*, I, 488–89; Halbert and Ball, *Creek War*, p. 275.
28. AJ to Pinckney, March 28, AJ to Blount, March 31, 1814, in Jackson, *Correspondence*, I, 488–91. Jackson always warned his men against being intimidated by the horrifying din set up by the Indians. The racket was intended to frighten white men, he said. But the men should not let it achieve its purpose.
29. AJ to Blount, March 31, AJ to Pinckney, March 28, 1814, in ibid., I, 491, 489; AJ to Blount, April 1, 1814, Jackson Papers, LC; Reid to Elizabeth Reid, April 1, 1814, Reid to Nathan Reid, April 5, 1814, Reid Papers, LC; Coffee to AJ, April 1, 1814, Jackson Papers, LC.
30. AJ to Blount, August 31, 1814, in Jackson, *Correspondence*, I, 491; Charles E. Lester, *The Life of Sam Houston* (Philadelphia, 1866), quoted in Holland, *Jackson and the Creek War*, p. 30; Halbert and Ball, *Creek War*, p. 277; AJ to Rachel Jackson, April 1, 1814, in Jackson, *Correspondence*, I, 493.
31. AJ to Blount, March 31, 1814, in Jackson, *Correspondence*, I, 491–92; Holland, *Jackson and the Creek War*, p. 31.
32. AJ to Blount, March 31, AJ to Rachel Jackson, April 1, 1814, in Jackson, *Correspondence*, I, 491–92, 493.
33. AJ to Blount, March 31, 1814, in Jackson, *Correspondence*, I, 492; Halbert and Ball, *Creek War*, pp. 276–77.
34. AJ to Pinckney, March 28, 1814, in Jackson, *Papers*, III, 52–53; AJ to Rachel, April 1, 1814, Jackson, *Correspondence*, I, 493.
35. AJ to Rachel, April 1, 1814, Jackson, *Correspondence*, I, 493.

Chapter 5. Sharp Knife

1. Green, *Politics of Indian Removal*, p. 42; Coffee to Mrs. Coffee, April 2, 1814, in *Tennessee Historical Magazine* (September 1916), II, 283; AJ to John Armstrong, May 8, 1814, in Jackson, *Papers*, III, 70.
2. AJ to Rachel, April 14, 1814, Jackson Papers, LC; Thomas S. Woodward, *Woodward's Reminiscences of the Creek, or Muscogee, Indians . . .* , quoted in Holland, *Jackson and the Creek War*, p. 15
3. Reid and Eaton, *Jackson*, pp. 155–57; AJ to Rachel, April 6, 1814, Miscellaneous Jackson Papers, Harvard University Library.
4. Green, *Politics of Indian Removal*, p. 42; Memorandum in Major John Reid's handwriting, Reid Papers, LC; AJ to David Holmes, April 18, 1814, in Jackson, *Correspondence*, I, 505. *Lex talionis* is the law of retaliation.
5. McQueen was captured but escaped.
6. C. L. Grant, ed., *Letters, Journals and Writings of Benjamin Hawkins* (Savannah, 1980), p. 684; AJ to Blount, April 18, 1814, in Jackson, *Correspondence*, I, 503.
7. Anne Newport Royall, *Letters from Alabama, 1817–1822* (University, Ala., 1969), p. 91; George Cary Eggleston, *Red Eagle and the Wars with the Creek Indians of Alabama* (New York, 1878), pp. 334–37; Reid and Eaton, *Jackson*, pp. 165–67.
8. Reid and Eaton, *Jackson*, pp. 165, 167; Royall, *Letters from Alabama*, pp. 91–92.
9. AJ to Pinckney, April 18, Pinckney to Hawkins, April 23, AJ to David Holmes, April 18, 1814, in Jackson, *Correspondence*, I, 504, 505, II, 1–2; Secretary of War to Pinckney, March 17, 20, 1814, *ASPIA*, VI, 338; Pinckney to AJ, April 7, 1814, in Jackson, *Correspondence*, I, 496–97; Florett Henri, *The Southern Indians and Benjamin Hawkins, 1796–1816* (Norman, Okla., 1986), p. 296; Merritt B. Pound, *Benjamin Hawkins: Indian Agent* (Athens, Ga., 1951), pp. 234–35.

10. Doherty et al. to Campbell, April 18, 1814, in Jackson, *Correspondence,* I, 497–98 note 2; AJ to John Williams, May 18, 1814, in Jackson, *Papers,* III, 74–75.
11. Reid and Eaton, *Jackson,* pp. 173–76.
12. Armstrong to AJ, May 22, 28, AJ to Armstrong, June 8, 1814, Jackson Papers, LC.; AJ to Armstrong, June 20, 1814, Jackson, *Correspondence,* II, 9.
13. AJ to Rachel, August 10, 1814, in Jackson, *Papers,* III, 114.
14. Armstrong to AJ, May 24, 1814, in Jackson, *Correspondence,* II, 4–5; Henri, *Southern Indians,* p. 297.
15. AJ to Rachel, July 16, 1814, in Jackson, *Papers,* III, 89; AJ to Pinckney, May 18, 1814, in Jackson, *Correspondence,* II, 3.
16. AJ to Hawkins, July 11, 1814, Jackson Papers, LC; Merritt P. Pound, *Benjamin Hawkins* (Athens, Ga., 1951), p. 236; AJ to Coffee, July 17, 1814, Jackson Papers, LC; AJ to Armstrong, July 24, 1814, in Jackson, *Papers,* III, 92.
17. Jackson's talk in Jackson, *Papers,* III, 109–10; Henri, *Southern Indians,* pp. 300–1.
18. Big Warrior to Hawkins, [August 1814], AJ to Big Warrior, [August 1817], in Jackson, *Papers,* III, 106–11; Reid and Eaton, *Jackson,* pp. 184–89; Remini, *Jackson,* I, 227–28; Owsley, *Struggle for the Gulf,* pp. 87–89. In his "talk" to Big Warrior, Jackson is reported as saying that Tecumseh should have been "delivered to the United States as a prisoner, or shot." Jackson, *Papers,* III, 109. Owsley quotes the Augusta *Chronicle* of August 26, 1814, in stating that Jackson used the words "or have cut his throat." Owsley, *Struggle for the Gulf,* p. 89.
19. Reid and Eaton, *Jackson,* pp. 173, 190–91; AJ to Coffee, August 10, 1814, in Jackson, *Papers,* III, 113.
20. Hawkins to Pinckney, August 16, 1814, in *ASPIA,* VI, 341.
21. Big Warrior to AJ, August 8, 1814, in *ASPIA,* I, 837.
22. Henri, *Southern Indians,* pp. 303–4.
23. Big Warrior to AJ, August 8, 1814, in *ASPIA,* I, 837.
24. Statement of Benjamin Hawkins in ibid. Jackson never received the land offered to him. The Senate failed to act on the matter when it ratified the treaty.
25. AJ to Rachel, August 10, 1814, in Jackson, *Papers,* III, 114.
26. Treaty of Fort Jackson, August 9, 1814, can be found in *ASPIA,* I, 837–38.
27. AJ to Coffee, August 10, AJ to Rachel, August 23, 1814, in Jackson, *Papers,* III, 113, 117. Jackson added that Hawkins "is certainly a man of fine understanding, of great experience."
28. AJ to Rachel, August 10, 1814, in Jackson, *Papers,* III, 114.

Chapter 6. *"Brothers, Listen . . . I Am Your Friend and Brother"*

1. John K. Mahon, *The War of 1812* (Gainesville, 1972), p. 341.
2. Frank L. Owsley, "Role of the South in the British Grand Strategy in the War of 1812," *Tennessee Historical Quarterly* (Spring 1972), XXXI, 33.
3. AJ to Rachel, August 5, 1814, Jackson Papers, Huntington Library.
4. For a complete history of the battle see Remini, *The Battle of New Orleans* (New York, 1999).
5. Hawkins to AJ, February 27, 1815, in Jackson, *Papers,* III, 289.
6. Fred Israel, ed., *Major Peace Treaties of Modern History, 1648–1967* (New York, 1967), I, 704.
7. Jesse Wharton to AJ, February 16, 1815, in Jackson, *Papers,* III, 280. The treaty had been submitted to the Senate on November 18, 1814, and referred to a select committee on December 13.
8. A. J. Dallas to AJ, June 12, 1815, in Clarence E. Carter, ed., *The Territorial Papers of the United States,* (Washington, D.C., 1936–), XV, 62.
9. Gaines to AJ, June 8, 1815, in Jackson, *Papers,* III, 361.
10. AJ to Zúñiga, April 23, 1816, in Jackson, *Correspondence,* II, 266.
11. Dallas to AJ, May 22, 1815, ibid., *Correspondence,* II, 206.
12. AJ to Edwards and Clark, June 27, 1815, in Jackson, *Papers,* III, 367–68.
13. General Daniel Bissell to AJ, July 2, AJ to Livingston, July 5, AJ to Edwards and Clark, June 27, AJ to Alexander J. Dallas, July 11, 1815, in ibid., III, 368–69, 370, 372.
14. AJ to Dallas, June 20, 1815, in Jackson, *Correspondence,* II, 211; AJ to Dallas, July 11, 1815, in Jackson, *Papers,* III, 372.

15. Nicholls to Hawkins, June 12, 1815, in Jackson, *Correspondence,* II, 211 note 2.
16. AJ to Hawkins, August 14, 1815, in ibid., II, 214.
17. Return J. Meigs to AJ, October 9, 1815, Jackson Papers, LC; Big Warrior to AJ, April 16, 1816, Jackson, *Papers,* IV, 20. Big Warrior's talk at Tuckabatchie was duly reported to the general, whereupon he called the Indian "an Artful, cunning, double faced man, and a great coward; and capable of plotting, but not of executing mischief." AJ to Crawford, June 9, 1816, ibid., IV, 44.
18. Jackson's Talk to the Creeks, September 4, 1815, in Jackson, *Correspondence,* II, 216–17.
19. Gaines to AJ, October 8, AJ to Gaines, September 30, November 22, 1815, Jackson, *Papers,* III, 387–88, 386, 394.
20. John Reid to Elizabeth Reid, November 18, 1815, in ibid., II, 391–92.
21. AJ to Crawford, December 17, 1815, in ibid., III, 396.
22. Reid to Elizabeth Reid, December 16, 1815, Reid Papers, LC.
23. Coffee to AJ, January 21, February 3, 1816, in Jackson, *Correspondence,* II, 225, 232; AJ to Coffee, February 2, 13, 1816, Jackson, *Papers,* IV, 6–7, 11.
24. Statement of Creek Chiefs and Head Men, January 22, 1816, in Jackson, *Correspondence,* II, 226.
25. AJ to Colbert, February 13, 1816, in Jackson, *Papers,* IV, 13.
26. Colbert to AJ, March 1, 1816, in Jackson, *Correspondence,* II, 234.
27. Crawford to AJ, March 8, 1816, Jackson, *Correspondence,* II, 235; Protest of the Tennesseans, *American State Papers, Indian Affairs,* II, 89. Jackson felt certain that Return J. Meigs, the Cherokee agent, had bamboozled Madison and Crawford with inaccurate accounts of what had happened during the treaty negotiations at Fort Jackson.
28. Monroe was appointed secretary of state in 1811 and held that office to the end of the Madison administration. In 1814 he also assumed the office of secretary of war. On August 1, 1815, William H. Crawford became secretary of war, but on October 22, 1816 he moved over to the Treasury Department, leaving the War Department under the guidance of the chief clerk, George Graham.
29. AJ to Monroe, May 12, 1816, with Monroe's handwritten endorsement, Jackson Papers, LC.
30. Crawford to AJ, May 20, June 19, 1816, Jackson Papers, LC; AJ to Crawford, June 10, 1816, in Jackson, *Correspondence,* II, 245–46.
31. AJ to Crawford, [June 13?], 1816, in Jackson, *Correspondence,* II, 248.
32. Crawford to AJ, July 1, 1816, in ibid., II, 251.
33. AJ to Coffee, July 19, 1816, in ibid., II, 253–54.
34. AJ to Coffee, July 21, 26, 1816, in ibid., II, 254–55, 256; AJ to Isaac Thomas, July 24, in Jackson, *Papers,* IV, 54–55.
35. AJ to Coffee, September 19, McMinn to AJ, September 2, 1816, in Jackson, *Correspondence,* II, 260, 258.

Chapter 7. The Indian Commissioner

1. AJ to Coffee, September 19, 1816, in Jackson, *Correspondence,* II, 260.
2. Instructions to a deputation of our Warriors, September, 19, 1817, in *ASPIA,* II, 145; Journal of the Convention held in September, 1816, Jackson Papers, LC.
3. Commissioners to Crawford, September 20, 1816, in Jackson, *Papers,* IV, 65–67; Cocke to Crawford, September 22, 1816, *ASPIA,* II, 106. Before the convention concluded, Jackson, as instructed by the secretary, asked the chiefs their opinion of Cocke. There had been numerous complaints of incompetence and nepotism about Cocke by the Colbert brothers. Tishomingo, speaking for the Nation, responded that his people had no confidence in Cocke and did not want him as agent. He said they wanted an agent "capable of doing justice to their red & white Brethren." Jackson could not have been more delighted with the response and added his endorsement. Cocke was subsequently replaced by Colonel Henry Sherburne. Cocke answered the charges, claiming that only James Colbert and Tishomingo "disliked him" and that all the other Chickasaws had "unbounded confidence" in him. Cocke to Crawford, September 22, 1816, ibid., 106–7; R. S. Cotterill, *The Southern Indians: The Story of the Civilized Tribes Before Removal* (Norman, Okla., 1954), pp. 200–201 note 28.

4. Journal of the Convention, September 1816, Jackson Papers, LC.

5. This was Jackson's term for them.

6. Journal of Convention, September 1816, Jackson Papers, LC; Commissioners to Crawford, September 20, AJ to Coffee, September 19, 1816, in Jackson, *Papers,* IV, 63–67; Woodward, *Cherokees,* p. 135. A draft for the amounts paid the chiefs and interpreters was drawn by Jackson on John Brahan.

7. Journal of the Convention, September 1816, Jackson Papers, LC.

8. Commissioners to Crawford, September 20, 1816, in Jackson, *Papers,* IV, 66–67; Gibson, *Chickasaws,* pp. 104–5.

9. Commissioners to Crawford, September 20, 1816, Jackson, *Papers,* IV, 67.

10. AJ to Rachel, September 18, 1816, in ibid., IV, 62–64.

11. Chase Mooney, *William H. Crawford* (Lexington, Ky., 1974), p. 4.

12. AJ to Monroe, October 23, November 12, 1816, Jackson, *Papers,* IV, 69–70, 74; AJ to Monroe, March 4, 1817, New York Public Library.

13. Journal of the Convention, September 1816, Jackson Papers, LC.

14. Commissioners to the secretary, October 4, 1816, in Journal of the Convention, September–October 1816, Jackson Papers, LC.

15. Journal of the Convention, September–October 1816, Jackson Papers, LC; Instructions to a deputation of Cherokee warriors, September 19, 1817, in *ASPIA,* II, 145.

16. On this point see Anthony F. C. Wallace, *Jefferson and the Indians: The Tragic Fate of the First Americans* (Cambridge, Mass., 1999).

17. Woodward, *Cherokees,* p. 131; Hoig, *Cherokees and Their Chiefs,* pp. 102–4. For a full discussion of how Jefferson made removal central to the government's Indian policy, see Anthony F. C. Wallace, *Jefferson and the Indians.*

18. Commissioners to the secretary, October 4, 1816, in Journal of the Convention, September–October 1816, Jackson Papers, LC.

19. Cotterill, *Southern Indians,* p. 236.

20. *ASPIA,* II, 92; Arthur H. De Rosier, Jr., *The Removal of the Choctaw Indians* (Knoxville, 1970), p. 37; Charles Kappler, *Indian Affairs: Laws and Treaties* (Washington, D.C., 1904), II, 137.

21. Crawford had became secretary of the treasury. Graham acted as interim secretary until replaced by the new secretary of war, John C. Calhoun.

22. AJ to Graham, December 21, 1816, in *ASPIA,* II, 123.

23. AJ to Livingston, October 24, 1816, in Jackson, *Papers,* IV, 71–72.

24. Monroe to AJ, December 14, 1816, in Jackson, *Correspondence,* II, 266.

25. AJ to Monroe, March 18, 1817, AJ to Edward Livingston, October 24, 1816, in Jackson, *Papers,* IV, 102–3, 71.

26. AJ to Graham, June 11, 1817, *ASPIA,* II, 142; AJ to Calhoun, January 4, 1821, Jackson Papers, LC; AJ to Livingston, October 24, 1816, Jackson, *Papers,* IV, 71–72; Gordon Chappell, "John Coffee: Surveyor and Land Agent," *Alabama Review* (October 1961), XIV, 243; William A. Love, "General Jackson's Military Road," *Publications of the Mississippi Historical Society* (1910), XI, 402–17.

27. AJ to Coffee, December 26, 1816, AJ to Monroe, January 6, 1817 in Jackson, *Correspondence,* II, 270–71, 272; AJ to Richard Butler, December 6, AJ to William B. Lewis, December 8, 1817, in Jackson, *Papers,* IV, 159, 160.

28. AJ to Monroe, March 4, 1817, Jackson, *Papers,* IV, 93–97.

29. Monroe to AJ, October 5, 1817, in ibid., 147.

30. Gaines to AJ, April 2, AJ to Graham, April 22, 1817, in ibid., 107, 111.

31. *ASPIA,* II, 123–24.

32. Graham to AJ, January 13, March 25, May 14, 16, 1817, *ASPIA,* II, 140–42; AJ to Coffee, June 21, 1817, in Jackson, *Correspondence,* II, 298.

33. AJ to Robert Butler, June 21, Arkansas Cherokees to AJ and Meigs, [April 18], 1817 in Jackson, *Papers,* IV, 118, 107–8.

34. Meigs to AJ, May 24, 1817, Jackson, *Correspondence,* II, 295–96.

35. Minutes of the Proceedings of the Commission, 1817, Jackson Papers, LC.

36. AJ to Graham, July 8, 1817, Jackson Papers, LC.
37. Arkansas chiefs to the commissioners, June 28, 1817, Jackson Papers, LC.
38. Eastern Cherokees to the commissioners, July 2, 1817, *ASPIA*, II, 142–43.
39. Journal of the Convention, July 3, 1817, AJ to Graham, July 8, AJ to Coffee, July 13, 1817, Jackson Papers, LC; Instructions to Cherokee Deputation, September 19, 1817, *ASPIA*, II, 145.
40. Journal of the Convention, July 6, 1817, Jackson Papers, LC.
41. Commissioners to Graham, July 8, 1817, Jackson Papers, LC.
42. *ASPIA*, II, 130.
43. Journal of the Convention, July 3, 1817, AJ to Graham, July 8, AJ to Coffee, July 13, 1817, Jackson Papers, LC.
44. AJ to Coffee, July 13, 1817, Jackson Papers, LC; Graham to Commissioners, August 1, 1817, *ASPIA*, II, 143; *Journal of the Executive Proceedings of the Senate*, III, 107. The arguments cited by Graham that might be advanced against the treaty are answered in AJ to Graham, August 19, 1817, in Jackson, *Correspondence*, II, 322. He claimed that with the exception of Pathkiller, who was too ill to attend, every Principal Chief in the Nation and all the members of the Council of Thirteen had signed the treaty.

Chapter 8. To Seize Florida

1. AJ to Coffee, August 12, 1817, in Jackson, *Papers*, IV, 132.
2. Gaines to AJ, May 14, 1816, in ibid., IV, 31.
3. Zúñiga to AJ, May 26, 1816, *American State Papers, Military Affairs (ASPMA)*, I, 714–15; Captain Ferdinand Amelung to AJ, June 4, 1816, in Jackson, *Correspondence*, II, 242–43.
4. AJ to Zúñiga , April 23, in *American State Papers, Foreign Relations (ASPFR)*, IV, 499, 555–56; AJ to Gaines, April 8, 1816, in Jackson, *Correspondence*, II, 239.
5. Gaines to D. C. Clinch, May 23, 1816, in *American State Papers, Foreign Affairs (ASPFA)*, IV, 558; Francis Paul Prucha, *Sword of the Republic* (New York, 1968), p. 130; James W. Silver, *Edmund Pendleton Gaines, Frontier General* (Baton Rouge, 1949), p. 63.
6. Cotterill, *Southern Indians*, p. 8, for the meaning of "Seminole." Other sources claim it means "runaways" or "people of distant fires." See Virginia Bergman Peters, *The Florida Wars* (Hamden, Conn., 1979), pp. 29–30, 286 note 6. On the Seminole raids see W. W. Bibb to AJ, May 19, 1818, in Carter, *Territorial Papers*, XVIII, 331–33, and Monroe to the U.S. Senate, March 25, 1818, in *ASPIA*, II, 154.
7. Gaines to AJ, July 10, Arbuthnot to Commanding Officer, May 3, 1817, in Jackson, *Correspondence*, II, 305–306 and note 1, 305–6.
8. Gaines to AJ, August 31, 1817, in ibid., II, 323–24 and note 1.
9. Gaines to AJ, November 21, 1817, in *ASPIA*, I, 686; Silver, *Gaines*, p. 69.
10. Gaines to AJ, November 21, 1817, in *ASPIA*, I, 686; Silver, *Gaines*, p. 69.
11. Gaines to AJ, December 2, 1817, in Jackson, *Papers*, IV, 153–54; Remini, *Jackson*, I, 346. John K. Mahon in his article "The 1st Seminole War, November 21, 1817–May 24, 1818," in *Florida Historical Quarterly*, LXXVII (Summer 1998), states that the First Seminole War began with the burning of Fowltown (p. 64).
12. AJ to Calhoun, December 16, 1817, in Jackson, *Papers*, IV, 161.
13. Calhoun to AJ, December 26, Calhoun to Gaines, December 16, 1817, in Jackson, *Correspondence*, II, 341–42 and note 2.
14. AJ to Monroe, March 4, 1817, in Jackson, *Papers*, IV, 97.
15. Parton, *Jackson*, I, 219.
16. Monroe to AJ, October 5, December 2, 1817, in Jackson, *Papers*, IV, 144–48, 155.
17. AJ to Monroe, October 22, December 20, 1817, in Jackson, *Correspondence*, II, 332–33, 340–41.
18. Order by John C. Calhoun, December 29, NA-RG 107 (M6-9); Calhoun to AJ, December 29, 1817, in Jackson, *Correspondence*, II, 343.
19. Rhea to AJ, November 27, December 24, 1817, in Jackson, *Correspondence*, II, 335–36, 341.
20. AJ to Monroe, January 6, 1818, in Jackson, *Correspondence*, II, 345–46.

21. Monroe to Calhoun, January 12, 1818, NA, RG 107, M221-79, quoted in Jackson, *Papers,* IV, 165.
22. David S. Heidler and Jeanne T. Heidler in their book *Old Hickory's War: Andrew Jackson and the Quest for Empire* (Mechanicsburg, Pa, 1996) state that Jackson is a liar, that there never was such a letter, that he made it up (p. 121). But they have no proof. As the editor of the Jackson Papers says, "the existence or non-existence of Rhea's letter can probably never be established with certainty." *Papers,* IV, 166.
23. Rhea to AJ, January 12, 1818, in Jackson, *Correspondence,* II, 348.
24. Monroe to AJ, December 28, 1818, Monroe Papers, NYPL.
25. Monroe to Calhoun, January 30, 1818, in W. Edwin Hemphil et al., eds., *The Papers of John C. Calhoun* (Columbia, S.C., 1963–), II, 104; Calhoun to AJ, February 6, 1818, in *ASPMA,* I, 697. Italics mine. The Heidlers agree that Monroe wanted Florida but conclude that he really expected to get it through diplomatic channels, not outright seizure. If that is true, why in the world would he order someone like Jackson to invade the country? And why would Calhoun fail to send such an order— not once but twice? *Old Hickory's War,* p. 129.
26. Luis de Onís, *Memoria sobre las negociaciones entre España y Estados Unidos de América, que dieron motivo al tratado de 1819* (Madrid, 1820, Mexico, 1826), p. 18. An English edition was published in the United States (Baltimore, 1821) in a translation by Tobias Watkins entitled *Memoir upon the Negotiations Between Spain and the United States, Which Led to the Treaty of 1819.*
27. *Annals of Congress,* 15th Congress, 2nd Session, p. 863. Rhea also wrote to Jackson and said, "I will for one support your conduct, believing as far as I have read that you have acted for public good." Rhea to AJ, December 18, 1818, ibid., II, 404. For further information on this dispute see Benton, *Thirty Years View,* I, 169–80; AJ to Richard J. Dunlap, July 18, 1831, Jackson Papers, LC; *United States Telegraph,* February 17, 1831.
28. AJ to Robert Henry Dyer et al., January 11, 1818, *ASPMA,* I, 767.
29. Lacock's Report to the Senate, February 24, Storrs Report to the House, February 28, 1819, in *ASPMA,* I, 740, II, 99–103; Jackson's Memorial to the Senate, February 23, 1820, *Annals of Congress,* 15th Congress, 2nd Session, Appendix, pp. 2320–24; Calhoun to AJ, December 18, 1817, in Jackson, *Correspondence,* II, 341.
30. AJ to Calhoun, January 27, 1818, in Jackson, *Papers,* IV, 172–73.
31. AJ to Calhoun, February 10, 26, 1818, in *ASPMA,* I, 697–98.
32. AJ to Rachel Jackson, March 26, 1818, Miscellaneous Jackson Papers, Harvard University Library, also in Jackson, *Papers,* IV, 183–85; AJ to Calhoun, February 10, 26, March 25, 1818, in *ASPMA,* I, 697, 698–99.
33. *ASPMA,* I, 690.

Chapter 9. The First Seminole War

1. AJ to Rachel, March 26, 1818, Miscellaneous Jackson Papers, Harvard University Library; AJ to Calhoun, March 25, 1818, in *ASPMA,* I, 699.
2. AJ to Calhoun, March 25, 1818, in *ASPMA,* I, 698.
3. Cappachemicco and Boleck to Cameron, [no date], in *The United States and the Indians, 11th–15th Congress, 1810–1819* (Washington, 1820), Supplement, XIV, 134. See also the Petition of the Chiefs of the Lower Creek Nation to Cameron, [no date], in ibid., 154.
4. Chiefs of the Muscogee Nation to the King of England, in *United States and Indians,* Supplement, XIV, pp. 45–47. The document is signed by Hopoath Mico, "king of the four nations," and twenty-nine other chiefs.
5. Hubert B. Fuller, *The Purchase of Florida* (Gainesville, 1964), p. 247; Edwin C. McReynolds, *The Seminoles* (Norman, Okla., 1957), p. 78; J. Leitch Wright, Jr., "A Note on the First Seminole War," p. 375; Frank L. Owsley, "Role of the South in the British Grand Strategy in the War of 1812," *Tennessee Historical Quarterly* (Spring 1972), XXXI, 33; Arbuthnot to David B. Mitchell, January 19, 1818, Arbuthnot to Nicholls, August 26, 1817, in *United States and the Indians,* Supplement, XIV, 156–57, 133.
6. Chiefs to King George, *United States and the Indians,* Supplement, XIV, 45–47; Mahon, "The 1st Seminole War," p. 63.

7. AJ to Masot, March 25, 1818, in *ASPFA,* IV, 562; Masot to AJ, April 15, 1818, in Jackson, *Correspondence,* II, 359–60.

8. AJ to Calhoun, April 8, 1818, in Jackson, *Correspondence,* II, 358–59; Virginia Bergman Peters, *The Florida Wars* (Hamden, Conn., 1979), p. 47.

9. Bibb to Calhoun, March 27, 1818, in *ASPMA,* I, 699.

10. AJ to Caso y Luengo, April 6, 1818, in *ASPMA,* I, 704–5, and Jackson, *Papers,* IV, 186–87.

11. Caso y Luengo to AJ, April 7, 1818, in *United States and the Indians,* Supplement, XIV, 112–13.

12. AJ to Caso y Luengo, April 7, 1818, in ibid., 114.

13. AJ to Masot, May 23, 1818, in Jackson, *Papers,* IV, 207–8.

14. AJ to Calhoun, April 8, AJ to Rachel, April 6, 1818, in Jackson, *Correspondence,* II, 357–59; AJ to Calhoun, May 5, 1818, AJ to Caso y Luengo, April 7, 1818, in *ASPMA,* I, 701–2, 706.

15. AJ to Rachel, April 8, AJ to George W. Campbell, October 5, 1818, in Jackson, *Correspondence,* II, 358, 396; AJ to Calhoun, May 5, 1818, in *ASPMA,* I, 702; AJ to Masot, May 23, 1818, in Jackson, *Papers,* IV, 209–10.

16. *Niles' Weekly Register,* August 21, 1819.

17. AJ to Calhoun, April 20, 1818, in *ASPMA,* I, 700; Jackson, *Papers,* IV, 193 note 1; AJ to Calhoun, April 26, 1818, in Jackson, *Correspondence,* II, 363.

18. General Order, April 15, 1818, in Jackson, *Papers,* IV, 192.

19. AJ to Calhoun, April 20, 1818, in ibid., IV, 193–95.

20. Jackson, *Papers,* IV, 193 note 1.

21. AJ to Calhoun, May 5, 1818, in *ASPMA,* I, 701–2. Gadsden sailed the schooner to Fort St. Marks, arriving on April 25.

22. Ibid., I, 702; AJ to Calhoun, April 26, 1818, in Jackson, *Correspondence,* II, 363.

23. AJ to Calhoun, April 20, 1818, in *ASPMA,* I, 701; AJ to Rachel, April 8, 1818, in Jackson, *Correspondence,* II, 357.

24. AJ to Calhoun, April 26, 1818, in *ASPMA,* I, 701.

25. Arbuthnot to his son, John, April 2, 1818, in ibid., I, 722.

26. "Minutes of the proceedings of a special court," April 26, 1818, in ibid., I, 721–34.

27. Ambrister to Cameron, March 20, 1818, "Minutes of the proceedings," April 26–28, 1818, in ibid., I, 721–34.

28. Ibid., I, 734; *Niles' Weekly Register,* June 6, 1818.

29. AJ to Calhoun, May 5, 1818, in Jackson, *Correspondence,* II, 367.

30. The House report, dated January 12, 1819, disapproved the proceedings of the special court. The Senate report of February 24, 1819, declared the proceedings a departure from normal forms of justice and "calculated to inflict a wound on the national character." Both reports and a minority House report can be found in *ASPMA,* I, 735–43.

31. Masot to AJ, April 15, 1818, in Jackson, *Correspondence,* II, 359.

32. AJ to Calhoun, May 5, 1818, in *ASPMA,* I, 702.

33. Glascock to AJ, April 30, 1818, in ibid., I, 776.

34. Parton, *Jackson,* II, 491.

35. AJ to Rabun, May 7, 1818, in Jackson, *Papers,* IV, 202.

36. Talk to the Chehaw Indians, May 7, 1818, in *ASPMA,* I, 776–77.

37. AJ to Rachel, June 2, 1818, in Jackson, *Papers,* IV, 213.

38. AJ to Masot, April 27, May 23, 1818, in *ASPMA,* I, 706–7, 712–13; Masot to AJ, May 18, 1818, in Jackson, *Papers,* IV, 203–5.

39. Masot to AJ, May 22, 1818, in Jackson, *Papers,* IV, 205–9; AJ to Masot, May 23, 1818, in *ASPMA,* I, 712–13.

40. Masot to AJ, April 24, 1818, in *United States and Indians,* XIV, 117–18.

41. AJ to Piernas, May 24, 1818, in Calhoun, *Papers,* II, 371.

42. AJ to Calhoun, June 2, 1818, in *ASPFR,* IV, 602–3; AJ to George W. Campbell, October 5, 1818, in Jackson, *Correspondence,* II, 397.

43. Jackson's Proclamation, May 29, 1818, in Jackson, *Correspondence,* II, 374–75.

44. AJ to Monroe, June 2, 1818, in Jackson, *Papers*, IV, 214. Calhoun agreed with Jackson. "I entirely agree with you, as to the importance of Cuba to our country. It is . . . the key stone of our Union. No American statesman ought ever to withdraw his eye from it." Had there been a war with Spain at this time, the administration was prepared to seize it. Calhoun to AJ, January 23, 1820, in ibid., IV, 352. See also AJ to George Gibson, February 1, 1820, in ibid., IV, 356.

45. AJ to Calhoun, June 2, 1818, in *ASPFR*, IV, 603.

Chapter 10. Despoiling the Chickasaws

1. AJ to Rachel, June 2, 1818, in Jackson, *Papers*, IV, 212–13.
2. Charles Francis Adams, ed., *Memoirs of John Quincy Adams* (Philadelphia, 1874–1877), IV, 102–3.
3. Ibid., IV, 105.
4. Ibid., IV, 107.
5. Monroe to AJ, July 19, 1818, in Monroe, *Memoirs*, VI, 54–61.
6. AJ to Monroe, August 19, 1818, in Jackson, *Correspondence*, II, 389–91; Margaret L. Coit, *John C. Calhoun, American Portrait* (Boston, 1950), p. 124; AJ to Richard Keith Call, August 5, 1818, in Jackson, *Papers*, IV, 230.
7. Calhoun to AJ, September 8, 1818, in Jackson, *Correspondence*, II, 393.
8. Ibid; AJ to Thomas Cooper, August 24, 1818, Jackson Papers, LC; James, *Jackson*, p. 294.
9. AJ to Call, August 5, 1818, in Jackson, *Papers*, IV, 230.
10. See for example *National Intelligencer*, July 17, 20, 22, 30, August 1, 5, 1818.
11. The general himself thought the Spanish would never relinquish it without a fight. See his letters to Monroe, January 15, AJ to Calhoun, January 17, 21, Calhoun to AJ, January 23, 1820, in Jackson, *Correspondence*, III, 7–12.
12. *Annals of Congress*, 15th Congress, 2nd Session, pp. 631–55.
13. Ibid., pp. 1136–38.
14. Parton, *Jackson*, II, 566.
15. Calhoun to Shelby and AJ, May 2, 1818, in *ASPIA*, II, 173–74.
16. Shelby to AJ, June 27, AJ to Shelby, July 7, 1818, Jackson Papers, LC.
17. Shelby to AJ, June 27, AJ to Shelby, July 7, 1818, Jackson Papers, LC; Calhoun to Shelby and AJ, May 2, 1818, in *ASPIA*, II, 173–74. Shelby agreed that $4,500 was inadequate. Shelby to AJ, July 22, 1818, Jackson Papers, LC.
18. Colbert to AJ, July 17, [1818], in *ASPIA*, II, 102–3.
19. AJ to Graham, December 1, 1817, in Jackson, *Papers*, IV, 151–52.
20. Calhoun to AJ, July 30, Calhoun to Shelby, July 30, 1818, in *ASPIA*, II, 178.
21. AJ to Shelby, August 25, 1818, in Jackson, *Correspondence*, II, 391.
22. AJ to Colbert, July 24, 1818, in Jackson, *Papers*, IV, 228–29.
23. AJ to Shelby, August 11, 1818, in ibid., 234–35.
24. AJ to Crawford, September 20, 1816, in ibid., IV, 67.
25. AJ to Shelby, August 11, 1818, in ibid., IV, 234–35.
26. Samuel Cole Williams, *Beginnings of West Tennessee in the Land of the Chickasaws, 1541–1841* (Johnson City, Tenn., 1930), p. 87.
27. Confidential Journal, Chickasaw Treaty, September 29–October 20, 1818, Jackson Papers, LC.
28. Confidential Journal, September 29–October 20, 1818; Alexander Fanning to E. P. Gaines, October, 1818, Jackson Papers, LC; Sherburne to Calhoun, August 22, 1818, in Calhoun, *Papers*, III, 64.
29. Shelby and AJ to Lewis, October 9, Lewis to Shelby and AJ, October 10, 1818, in Confidential Journal, Jackson Papers, LC.
30. Winchester to Shelby and AJ, October 9, 1818, Confidential Journal, Jackson Papers, LC.
31. Confidential Journal, Jackson Papers, LC.
32. A "Bill has been drawn and accounted in my presence on Mr. Thomas Kirkland of Philadelphia in favour of Martin Colbert for twenty thousand dollars worth of merchandise to meet the Bond given within Sixty days after the ratification of the Treaty; should the Executive not advance the amount on

account of the reservations. Signed Robert Butler, Secretary." This was done when the treaty was finally signed on October 19, 1818. Confidential Journal, Jackson Papers, LC.

33. Confidential Journal, Jackson Papers, LC.
34. Confidential Journal, Jackson Papers, LC.
35. General Winchester surveyed the boundary, but his line ran over four miles north of the 35th parallel that comprised an area of 215,927 acres. A subsequent treaty (1834) determined that the Winchester line would be the true boundary of the cession. Royce, *Indian Land Cessions*, p. 695.
36. *Niles' Weekly Register*, December 12, 1818. Thomas Shelby, the son of Isaac, also attended the negotiations and later contended that Jackson paid too much for the land. *Truth's Advocate & Monthly Anti-Jackson Expositor*, August 1828.
37. AJ to McMinn, August 25, 1819, in Jackson, *Correspondence*, II, 426. John Williams of Tennessee was Jackson's most vociferous critic, and the general called his statements "false, malicious and without the slitest foundation." AJ to William Williams, September 25, 1819, in ibid., II, 430.
38. Confidential Journal, Jackson Papers, LC.
39. Arrell M. Gibson, *The Chickasaws* (Norman, Okla., 1971), p. 105.

Chapter 11. Despoiling the Choctaws

1. Shelby and AJ to Calhoun, October 30, 1818, in Calhoun, *Papers*, III, 245; AJ to Shelby, November 24, 1818, in Jackson, *Papers*, IV, 250 and note 1, 251.
2. AJ to Shelby, November 24, AJ to Monroe, October 30, Robert Butler to AJ, December 15, 1818, in Jackson, *Papers*, IV, 250, 245, 256; AJ to Monroe, June 20, 1820, in Jackson, *Correspondence*, III, 28; Calhoun to AJ, November 30, 1818, in Calhoun, *Papers*, III, 318–19.
3. Pitchlynn to AJ [December], AJ to Calhoun, December 30, 1818, in Jackson, *Correspondence*, II, 405–7.
4. Calhoun to AJ, March 29, 1819, in Jackson, *Correspondence*, II, 414.
5. The names of these three chiefs have various spellings.
6. Gideon Lincecum, "Life of Apushimataha," *Publications of the Mississippi Historical Society* (Oxford, Miss., 1906), IX, 415, 417.
7. AJ to McKee, April 22, 1819, in Jackson, *Papers*, IV, 288.
8. AJ to Monroe, November 16, 1819, Monroe Papers, New York Public Library; AJ to Calhoun, June 19, 1820, Jackson Papers, LC; AJ to Monroe, November 29, 1819, in Jackson, *Papers*, IV, 343.
9. McKee to AJ, August 13, 1819, in *ASPIA*, II, 230.
10. AJ to Lewis, August 17, Jefferson to AJ, November 22, 1819, in Jackson, *Papers*, IV, 315, 337; AJ to Calhoun, June 19, 1820, Jackson Papers, LC. The report by the legislative committee has not been found. For Jackson's defense see his letter to William Williams, September 25, 1819, in Jackson, *Papers*, IV, 325–28. The controversy became an issue in the presidential election of 1824. See Thomas Hart Benton, *An Address to the People of the United States on the Presidential Election*.
11. Notice, May 29, 1820, Jackson Papers, LC.
12. AJ to Return J. Meigs, February 28, Call to AJ, July 8, 1820, in Jackson, *Papers*, 358, 372–74; AJ to Calhoun, June 15, 1820, with Notice to Intruders, May 29, 1820, Jackson, *Correspondence*, III, 26 and note 2.
13. AJ to Calhoun, May 17, 1820, in Jackson, *Papers*, IV, 369; Alexander Macomb to Calhoun, November 2, 1818, in Calhoun, *Papers*, III, 250–51.
14. Edmund P. Gaines to AJ, September 24, 1820, Jackson Papers, LC.
15. Rodgers to AJ, June 7, 1820, with AJ's endorsement, in Jackson, *Papers*, IV, 371. Rodgers's son, John Rodgers, Jr., later became an important western Cherokee chief.
16. January 8, 1820, quoted in Arthur H. DeRosier, Jr., *The Removal of the Choctaw Indians* (Norman, Okla., 1970), p. 54.
17. Pitchlynn to Calhoun, March 18, 1819, in *ASPIA*, II, 229.
18. Hinds had also been recommended by the governor, legislature, and congressional delegation of Mississippi. Calhoun to AJ, May 24, AJ to Calhoun, June 19, 1820, Jackson Papers, LC. See also his acceptance to the Mississippi delegation in AJ to Christopher Rankin, June 19, 1820, in Jackson, *Correspondence*, III, 27.

19. AJ to Calhoun, June 19, 1820, Jackson Papers, LC.
20. AJ to Monroe, June 20, 1820, in Jackson, *Correspondence,* III, 28.
21. Calhoun to Jackson, July 12, 1820, Jackson Papers, LC; Calhoun to AJ and Hinds, July 12, 1820, *ASPIA,* II, 231–32. The United States received the Quapaw land in a treaty signed in 1818 for approximately $4,000 plus a $1,000 annuity. Royce, *Indian Land Cession,* pp. 688–90.
22. AJ to Calhoun, August 2, 1818, in Jackson, *Papers,* IV, 384; AJ to Calhoun, September 15, 1820, Jackson, *Correspondence,* III, 32; Agreements, August 24, 31, 1820, and Vandeventer to AJ, August 21, 1820, in *ASPIA* II, 232, 223, 234; DeRosier, *Removal,* p. 61; Calhoun to Jackson and Hinds, July 12, 1820, Jackson Papers, LC.
23. AJ to Calhoun, August 25, 1820 in Calhoun, *Papers,* V, 336–37; AJ to Calhoun, September 2, 1820, in Jackson, *Correspondence,* III, 31–32.
24. Calhoun to AJ, November 16, 1821, in Jackson, *Correspondence,* III, 132.
25. Parton, *Jackson,* II, 578–81.
26. Lincecum, "Life of Apushimataha," pp. 420, 421.
27. Journal of the Convention, October 3, 1820, *ASPIA,* II, 234.
28. Edmund Folsom to AJ, September 13, "Talk," October 3, 1820, in *ASPIA,* II, 232, 234.
29. Ibid., II, 234–35.
30. AJ to Calhoun, October 11, 1820, in Jackson, *Papers,* IV, 392–93. Calhoun approved Jackson's action. Calhoun to AJ, November 6, 1820, Jackson Papers, LC.
31. Journal of the Convention, October 1820, in *ASPIA,* II, 235; Lincecum, "Life of Apushimataha," p. 418.
32. Journal of the Convention, in *ASPIA,* II, 235-37; Lincecum, "Life of Apushimataha," pp. 466–67.
33. Lincecum, "Life of Apushimataha," p. 470.
34. Ibid., pp. 471–72.
35. See the map on page 182 for the "small slip of your land" in Mississippi.
36. As it turned out, white settlers had, as Pushmataha claimed, already settled on the land in question, and they promptly condemned what had been offered the Choctaws. It necessitated a renegotiation of the treaty in 1825.
37. Statement of Propositions, October 13, 1820 in *ASPIA,* II, 238.
38. *ASPIA,* II, 239; DeRosier, *Removal,* p. 66.
39. *ASPIA,* II, 239–40; DeRosier, *Removal,* pp. 66–67.
40. Treaty of Doak's Stand, in *ASPIA,* II, 225; Kappler, *Indian Affairs,* II, 191–95; Royce, *Land Cessions,* pp. 700–1, plate 36; Angie Debo, *The Rise and Fall of the Choctaw Republic* (Norman, Okla., 1961), p. 49.
41. DeRosier, *Removal,* pp. 397–98.
42. The treaty traded to the Choctaws all the land they would ever receive from the government in present-day Oklahoma. Robert B. Ferguson, "Treaties between the United States and the Choctaw Nation," in Carolyn Keller Reeves, ed., *The Choctaw Before Removal* (Jackson, Miss., 1985), pp. 218–19.
43. Eden Brashears to AJ, November 10, AJ to Calhoun, November 30, 1820, McKee to Calhoun, January 1, 1822, in Calhoun, *Papers,* V, 430–31, 461, 569.
44. Not that the administration did not haul in other large tracts of land from northern and western Indians. In 1818 alone, treaties were signed "upon advantageous terms" with the Quapaws, Wyandots, Senecas, Delawares, Shawnees, Potawatomies, Ottawas, Chippewas, Peorias, Kaskaskias, Mitciganias, Cahokias and Tamarois, Great and Little Osages, Weas, Miamis, and the four Pawnee tribes. Calhoun to Monroe, November 27, 1818, Calhoun, *Papers,* III, 306–7.

Chapter 12. The Making of a President

1. AJ to Calhoun, November 13, 1820, in Calhoun, *Papers,* V, 434.
2. Calhoun to AJ, January 25, 1821, in Calhoun, *Papers,* V, 572–73; AJ to Monroe, February 11, 1821, in Jackson, *Papers,* V, 10.
3. Calhoun to AJ, March 31, 1821, in Calhoun, *Papers,* V, 706.
4. AJ to Adams, April 2, 1821, in Jackson, *Papers,* V, 26; Calhoun to AJ, May 14, 1821, in Calhoun, *Papers,* VI, 115–16.

5. AJ to Calhoun, September 2, 1821, in Calhoun, *Papers,* VI, 363.

6. AJ to Adams, November 22, 1821, in Jackson, *Correspondence,* III, 139; AJ to Calhoun, July 29, 1821, in Jackson, *Papers,* V, 86. For a full discussion of Jackson's tenure as Florida governor see Remini, *Jackson,* I, 399-424.

7. This cliché about a forked tongue, along with other questionable sounding "Indian talk," are in the documents themselves, as are all the quotations of spoken dialogue in this book.

8. Jackson's Talk with Indian Chieftains, September 20, 1821, in Jackson, *Correspondence,* III, 118–21.

9. U.S. Statutes, 17th Congress, 1st Session, p. 65, and House Reports, No. 450, 27th Congress, 2nd Session; AJ to Adams, October 6, 1821, in *ASPM* (Miscellaneous), II, 909–10; AJ to Monroe, October 5, 1821, in Jackson, *Correspondence,* III, 123.

10. AJ to Calhoun, July 14, August 17, Calhoun to AJ, July 31, 1823, in Calhoun, *Papers,* VIII, 163–64, 200–1, 233–34.

11. Calhoun to AJ, May 19, AJ to Calhoun, May 22, September 20, 1821, in Calhoun, *Papers,* VI, 130–31, 142–44, 376–77; Adams to AJ, May 22, 23, 1821, in *ASPFR,* IV, 753–54; James Gadsden to AJ, June 8, 12, 1823, Jackson Papers, LC; Cotterill, *Southern Indians,* pp. 232–33.

12. AJ to Calhoun, January 12, 1822, in Calhoun, *Papers,* VI, 618–19.

13. Grundy to AJ, June 27, 1822, in Jackson, *Correspondence,* III, 163–64.

14. AJ to Bronaugh, July 18, 1822, Jackson Papers, LC; AJ to A.J. Donelson, August 6, 1822, Donelson Papers, LC.

15. AJ to Richard Keith Call, June 29, 1822, in Jackson, *Papers,* V, 198–99. The same sentiments can be found in Jackson's letter to James Bronaugh, August 1, and to Donelson, August 6, 1822, in ibid., 210–11, 213.

16. Robert V. Remini, *Andrew Jackson and the Course of American Freedom, 1822–1832* (New York, 1981), II, 52–53.

17. AJ to James K. Polk, October 25, 1835, Jackson Papers, LC; AJ to Coffee, October 5, 1823, in Jackson, *Papers,* V, 302; B. Coleman to Coffee, October 24, 1823, in Jackson, *Correspondence,* III, 210 note 1.

18. AJ to Andrew Jackson Donelson, March 19, 1824, Donelson Papers, LC; Houston to Abram Maury, December 13, 1825, Miscellaneous Houston Papers, LC; J. D. Steele, Manuscript Journal, 1820–1829, Harvard University Library; Eaton to Rachel, December, 18, 1823, AJ to George W. Martin, January 2, 1824, in Jackson, *Correspondence,* III, 217, 222.

19. AJ to Rachel, December 7, 11, 1823, AJ to Donelson, January 14, 18, 1824, in Jackson, *Papers,* V, 322, 325, 336, 340; AJ to Rachel, December 28, 1823, March 27, 1824, in Jackson, *Correspondence,* III, 220, 241.

20. Lyncoyer to AJ, December 29, 1823, Hurja Collection, Tennessee Historical Society. Many years ago I examined this letter, and as I said in the second volume of my Jackson biography I had grave suspicions as to its authenticity. It is a copy and there is too much fake-sounding "Indian talk" in it. The copy is in poor condition and has been edited. However, it seems to have been written at an early date and appears to have been written in response to Jackson's request of December 7. It is the only known Lyncoya letter in existence.

21. *United States Telegraph,* July 3, 1828. The site of Lyncoya's grave is not known but the Ladies' Hermitage Association, which maintains the Jackson property, has been making a determined effort to locate it.

22. AJ to Rachel, March 17, 1824, in Jackson, *Papers,* VI, 376; *National Intelligencer,* March 17, 1824, reprinted in Jackson, *Papers,* V, 377.

23. AJ to Samuel Swartwout, March 4, 1824, in Jackson, *Papers,* V, 370.

24. Eaton to Rachel, December 18, 1823, in Jackson, *Correspondence,* III, 217; AJ to Donelson, March 6, 19, 1824, Donelson Papers, LC; AJ to Coffee, June 18, 1824, Coffee Papers, Tennessee Historical Society; AJ to Samuel Swartwout, March 25, 1824, in Jackson, *Papers,* V, 381.

25. Remini, *Jackson,* II, 61.

26. AJ to Samuel Swartwout, March 4, 1824, in Jackson, *Papers,* V, 370.

27. Joseph McMinn to AJ, February 9, 1824, Jackson Papers, LC.

28. William Cocke to AJ, July 10, 1824, in Jackson, *Papers,* V, 430; James Taylor Carson, *Searching for the Bright Path: The Mississippi Choctaws from Prehistory to Removal* (Lincoln, 1999), pp. 91–92.

29. Lincecum, "Life of Apushimataha," pp. 420, 478.
30. McMinn to AJ, February 9, AJ to Calhoun, February 26, 1824, in Calhoun, *Papers*, VIII, 531, 553.
31. For a full discussion of the election of 1824–1825 see James F. Hopkins, "Election of 1824," in *History of American Presidential Elections*, Arthur M. Schlesinger, Jr., Fred L. Israel, and William P. Hansen, eds. (New York, 1971), I, 349–81.
32. AJ to Overton, December 19, 1824, in Jackson, *Papers*, V, 455; AJ to Swartwout, December 14, 1824, in Jackson, *Correspondence*, III, 269.
33. AJ to Coffee, January 10, 1825, Coffee Papers, Tennessee Historical Society; Adams, Memoirs, VI, 464–65. The meeting between Clay and Adams is one of the most controversial and hotly debated events in the lives of the two men. My biography of *Henry Clay: Statesman for the Union* (New York, 1991), pp. 251–72, attempts to explain what happened.
34. AJ to Coffee, February 19, 1825, Coffee Papers, Tennessee Historical Society.
35. AJ to William B. Lewis, February 14, 1825, in Jackson, *Correspondence*, III, 276; AJ to Lewis, February 10, 1825, Jackson-Lewis Papers, New York Public Library.
36. Letters reprinted in *Niles' Weekly Register*, July 5, 1828.
37. For an extended study of the reworking of the political parties see Robert V. Remini, *Martin Van Buren and the Making of the Democratic Party* (New York, 1959), and *The Election of Andrew Jackson* (New York, 1963).
38. Adams, *Memoirs*, VII, 89–90, 92; Remini, *Henry Clay*, pp. 313–14.
39. Royce, *Indian Land Cessions*, pp. 708–9, 714–15; Bemis, *Adams and the Union*, pp. 79–87; Albany *Argus*, September 5, 1827; New York *Advocate*, October 28, 1827.
40. AJ to Terrill, July 29, 1826, in Jackson, *Correspondence*, III, 308–9.
41. AJ to Coffee, August 20, September 2, 25, and an undated letter, 1826, in Jackson, *Correspondence*, III, 310, 312, 314–16.
42. Remini, *Election of Jackson*, pp. 186–90; *Niles' Weekly Register*, December 6, 1828.
43. Parton, *Jackson*, III, 144, 153; *National Journal*, May 24, 1828.
44. Parton, *Jackson*, III, 158; AJ to Coffee, January 17, 1829, Coffee Papers, Tennessee Historical Society.

Chapter 13. The Indian Removal Act

1. Remini, *Jackson*, II, 168–69, 171, 184–85, 200; James D. Richardson, *A Compilation of the Messages and Papers of the Presidents* (Washington, 1897) II, 1011.
2. Richardson, *Compilation of the Messages and Papers of the President*, II, 1001.
3. AJ to James Gadsden, October 12, 1829, in Jackson, *Correspondence*, IV, 81.
4. Ronald N. Satz, *American Indian Policy in the Jacksonian Era* (Lincoln, 1975), pp. 3, 9; Wilson Lumpkin, *The Removal of the Cherokee Indians from Georgia* (New York, 1907), I, 43; Instructions to Generals William Carroll and John Coffee from Secretary of War John H. Eaton, May 20, 1829, *Senate Documents*, 21st Congress, 1st Session, Document # 1, serial 160; AJ to James Gadsden, October 12, 1829, in Jackson, *Correspondence*, IV, 81; Parton, *Jackson*, III, 279–80. A very convincing argument supporting Jackson's actions can be found in Francis Paul Prucha, "Andrew Jackson's Indian Policy: A Reassessment," *Journal of American History* (December 1969), LVI, 527–39.
5. Satz, *American Indian Policy*, p. 13; Cotterill, *Southern Indians*, pp. 237–38; Annie H. Abel, "The History of Events Resulting in Indian Consolidation West of the Mississippi," American Historical Association, *Annual Report for the Year 1906* (Washington, 1908), I, 370–71.
6. Herman J. Viola, *Thomas L. McKenney: Architect of America's Early Indian Policy, 1816–1830* (Chicago, 1974), pp. 200, 202–22.
7. Ibid., p. 223–24; Satz, *American Indian Policy*, p. 18.
8. Satz, *American Indian Policy*, p. 18.
9. Cherokees to AJ, March 26, 1830, RG 75, Office of Indian Affairs, microfilm, National Archives.
10. AJ to [secretary of war], October 5, 1831, RG 75, ibid.
11. Creek chiefs to AJ, February 1, 1830, ibid.
12. F. E. Plummer to Lewis Cass, May 22, 1832, in *Correspondence on the Subject of the Emigration of Indians* (Washington, 1835), II, 361–62.

13. Tuskinihah-haw to AJ, May 21, 1831, RG 75, Office of Indian Affairs, microfilm, NA.
14. Richardson, ed., *Messages of the Presidents*, pp. 1021–22.
15. Thomas Hart Benton, *Thirty Years' View* (New York, 1854–1856), I, 164.
16. *Register of Debates*, 21st Congress, 1st Session, pp. 310–11.
17. Ibid., pp. 325, 345, 354–57, 359, 360.
18. Ibid., p. 383.
19. Ibid., pp. 1002, 1021–23, 1032–34; Satz, *American Indian Policy*, p. 27.
20. Ibid., p. 30; John C. Fitzpatrick, ed., *The Autobiography of Martin Van Buren*, (Washington, 1920), p. 289; *Register of Debates*, 21st Congress, 1st Session, pp. 1145–46.
21. Lea to the editor of the Knoxville *Register*, May 27, 1830 quoted in Satz, *American Indian Policy*, p. 30; Van Buren, *Autobiography*, p. 289.
22. U.S. *Statutes*, IV, 411–12.

Chapter 14. "Remove and Be Happy"

1. "We will no more beg, pray and implore, but we will *demand* justice," it said. *Phoenix*, May 15, 1830.
2. AJ to William B. Lewis, August 25, 1830, in Jackson, *Correspondence*, IV, 177; Eaton to John Donnelly, August 11, Pitchlynn to AJ, August 11, 1830, Jackson Papers, LC; Eaton to Chiefs, June 1, 1830, in *Correspondence on the Subject of the Emigration of Indians* (Washington, 1835), II, 3–5.
3. Quotation from Satz, *American Indian Policy*, pp. 152, 156; Viola, *McKenney*, pp. 222–23. Samuel S. Hamilton replaced McKenney, followed by Elbert Herring.
4. AJ to Coffee, June 14, July 9, 1830, in Jackson, *Correspondence*, IV, 146, 160; DeRosier, *Removal of Choctaw*, pp. 113-17; Eaton to Gilmer, June 1, 1830, in *Correspondence on the Subject of the Emigration of Indians*, II, 1-3.
5. AJ to Lewis, August 25, 1830, in Jackson, *Correspondence*, IV, 177.
6. LeFlore to Eaton, August 10, 1830, Choctaw Chiefs to AJ, August 16, 1830, Records of the Bureau of Indian Affairs, Letters Received, Choctaw Agency, NA; Choctaw Chiefs to Eaton, August 15, 1830, Jackson Papers, LC.
7. AJ to Lewis, August 25, 1830, in Jackson, *Correspondence*, IV, pp. 177-78; DeRosier, *Removal of Choctaws*, pp. 117-18.
8. Colberts et al. to AJ, August 25, 1830, Record Group 75, Office of Indian Affairs, NA.
9. Journal of Proceedings with Chickasaws and Choctaws, August 23-30, 1830, in *Correspondence on the Subject of the Emigration of Indians*, II, 240-51; Jackson's Talk, August 1830, Jackson Papers, LC; *Niles' Weekly Register*, September 18, 1830.
10. *Correspondence on the Subject of the Emigration of Indians*, II, 246-47.
11. Ibid.; "Journal of the proceedings had with the Chickasaw and Choctaw Indians, at the late treaties," Jackson Papers, LC.
12. AJ to Lewis, August 25, 1830, Jackson–Lewis Papers, NYPL; Arrell M. Gibson, *The Chickasaws*, pp. 172–73.
13. Gibson, *Chickasaws*, pp. 174–76.
14. *Missionary Herald* (August 1830), XXVI, 253; AJ to J. Pitchlynn, August 5, Eaton to Pitchlynn, August 5, 1830, Jackson Papers, LC.
15. *Missionary Herald* (August 1830), XXVI, 255; H. S. Halbert, "The Story of the Treaty of Dancing Rabbit," in *Publications of the Mississippi Historical Society* (1902), VI, 375-76.
16. H. S. Halbert, "The Story of the Treaty of Dancing Rabbit," in *Publications of the Mississippi Historical Society* (1902), VI, 399.
17. Halbert, "The Story of the Treaty of Dancing Rabbit," in *Publications of the Mississippi Historical Society* (1902), VI, 389; DeRosier, *Removal of Choctaws*, pp. 120-22.
18. DeRosier, *Removal of Choctaws*, pp. 124-26; Royce, *Indian Land Cessions*, pp. 726-27.
19. H. S. Halbert, "The Story of the Treaty of Dancing Rabbit," in *Publications of the Mississippi Historical Society* (1902), VI, 396.
20. DeRosier, *Removal of Choctaws*, p. 128.
21. Ibid., pp. 129-47; Satz, *American Indian Policy*, p. 78.

22. Satz, *American Indian Policy*, p. 152.
23. For Cass's tenure as secretary see Willard Carl Klunder, *Lewis Cass and the Politics of Moderation* (Kent, Ohio, 1996), pp. 59-95.
24. Satz, *American Indian Policy*, pp. 151-68; Laurence F. Schmeckebier, *The Office of Indian Affairs* (Baltimore, 1927), pp. 27-43; "Report on Regulating the Indian Department, May 20, 1834," *House Report* #474, 23rd Congress, 1st Session, pp. 23-27; Secretary of War Lewis Cass to Benjamin F. Curry, September 1, 1831, and Cass to James Montgomery, September 3, 1831, Return J. Meigs Papers, LC. Cass replaced Eaton as secretary of war in 1831.
25. Mary Young, "The Creek Frauds: A Study in Conscience and Corruption," *Mississippi Valley Historical Review* (1955), XLII, 411-37; Enoch Parsons to Cass, February 10, 1833, quoted in Green, *Politics of Indian Removal*, pp. 170-73, 181-82.
26. Royce, *Indian Land Cessions*, pp. 738-39.
27. AJ to Coffee, November 6, 1832, Coffee Papers, Tennessee Historical Society.
28. Chiefs of the Big and Little Osage to AJ, January 1832 in *Correspondence on the Subject of the Emigration of Indians*, III, 354-56.

Chapter 15. Andrew Jackson Versus the Cherokee Nation

1. Address of Cherokee Nation to the people of the United States, July 17, 1830, in *Niles' Weekly Register*, August 21, 1830. An excellent study of this period is William C. McLaughlin, *Cherokee Renascence in the New Republic* (Princeton, 1986).
2. The case can be found in 5 *Peters* 1ff. See also Joseph C. Burke, "The Cherokee Cases: A Study in Law, Politics and Morality," in *Stanford Law Review* (February 1969), XXI, 500–31.
3. 5 *Peters* 15–20.
4. Ross's annual message to the Nation, October 10, 1832, in Gary E. Moulton, *The Papers of Chief John Ross* (Norman, Okla., 1978) I, 251–52.
5. John Ross's Annual Message to the Cherokees, October 24, 1831, in ibid., I, 226. Marshall's opinion can be found in 6 *Peters* 515. See also John Hutchins, "The Trial of Reverend Samuel A. Worcester," in *Journal of Cherokee Studies* (Fall 1977), II, 356–74.
6. Edwin Miles, "After John Marshall's Decision: *Worcester* v. *Georgia* and the Nullification Crisis," *Journal of Southern History* (1973), XXXIX, 519–44; Richard P. Longaker, "Andrew Jackson and the Judiciary," *Political Science Quarterly* (1956), LXXI, 348–50, 363–64; Satz, *American Indian Policy*, p. 49; Remini, *Jackson*, II, 276–77; AJ to Coffee, April 7, 1832, Coffee Papers, Tennessee Historical Society.
7. Miles, "After John Marshall's Decision," pp. 530, 537; Van Buren to AJ, December 22, 1832, Van Buren Papers, LC; B. F. Butler to Wilson Lumpkin, December 17, 1832, Gratz Collection, Historical Society of Pennsylvania. For further details see Remini, *Jackson*, II, 278.
8. Ross to the Cherokee People [October 11, 1830], [July 1, 1829], in Moulton, ed., *Papers of John Ross*, I, 202, 166; Letter of Dr. Butler, September 22, 1830, in *Missionary Herald*, (1830), XXVI, 381–82.
9. Although the annuities were technically controlled by the Cherokee Committee (upper house) and Council (lower house), Ross usually proposed how they should be distributed. Ross's annual message to the Nation, October 10, 1832, in Moulton, ed., *Papers of John Ross*, I, 254. There are two useful biographies of Ross: Rachel C. Eaton, *John Ross and the Cherokee Indians* (Menasha, Wis., 1914), and Gary E. Moulton, *John Ross, Cherokee Chief* (Athens, Ga., 1978).
10. Ross to the Cherokee People [October 11, 1830], [July 1, 1829] in Moulton, ed., *Papers of John Ross*, I, 202, 166.
11. For the Black Hawk War see Ellen M. Whitney, comp. and ed., *The Black Hawk War, 1831–1832* (Springfield, Ill., 1970–1975).
12. Black Hawk, *Autobiography* (Rock Island, Ill., 1833), pp. 116–17; Washington *Globe*, April 27, 1833.
13. Frances A. Kemble, *Journal* (London, 1835), II, 157, 159.
14. *Niles' Weekly Register*, June 15, 1833.
15. Journal of a Young Irishman, Huntington Library, Pasadena, Calif.
16. AJ to Coffee, April 7, 1822, Coffee Papers, Tennessee Historical Society; Amos Kendall to William L. Marcy, November 1845, Amos Kendall Papers, LC.

17. Morris L. Wardell, *A Political History of the Cherokee Nation, 1838–1907* (Norman, Okla., 1977), p. 16.

18. Ross to the Cherokees, April 14, 1831, Annual Message, October 24, 1831, in Moulton, ed., *Papers of John Ross*, I, 218, 230.

19. Ross to AJ, February 3, 1834 in Moulton, ed., *Papers of John Ross*, I, 273.

20. AJ to Van Buren, October 5, 1839, Van Buren Papers, LC.

21. Ross to AJ, March 12, 1834, in Moulton, ed., *Papers of John Ross*, I, 278. Over several weeks Ross persisted in his efforts to get Jackson to agree to allowing the Cherokees to keep a portion of their land and enforce protection of their rights on the remainder of their territory for a definite period.

22. Eaton, *John Ross*, pp. 83–84; Moulton, *John Ross*, pp. 60–61; Grace Steele Woodward, *The Cherokees* (Norman, Okla., 1963), pp. 178–79; Ross et al. to Cass, February 14, 25, 27, 28, 1835, Cass to Ross et al., February 16, 27, 1835, in *House Documents*, 23rd Congress, 2nd Session, No. 286.

23. Memorial of the Cherokee Delegation, March 3, 1835, and Memorial and Protest of the Cherokee Nation, in *House Documents*, 23rd Congress, 2nd Session. See also documents 292 and 315. See also Ross et al. to AJ, March 28, 1834, Record Group, 46, E, 327, 23 A-G 6, National Archives.

24. Mary Young, "Friends of the Indian," lecture given at Mary Baldwin College, October 8–9, 1980, II, 26. For provisions of this draft treaty see *House Documents*, 23rd Congress, 2nd Session, No. 292.

25. Jackson's talk, March 1835, Jackson Papers, LC.

26. *Senate Documents*, 24th Congress, 1st Session, No. 120; Charles C. Royce, "Cherokee Nation of Indians," in Bureau of American Ethnology, *Fifth Annual Report* (1887), Part 2, p. 281; Major Ridge et al. to AJ, December 1, 1835, in Records of the U. S. Senate: Executive Messages Relating to Indian Relations, 1829–1849, Record Group 46, National Archives; Moulton, *John Ross*, 70–77; Young, "Friends of the Indian," II, 26.

27. Major Ridge and John Ridge to AJ, June 30, 1836, in Records of the Bureau of Indian Affairs, Record Group 75, National Archives.

28. Amos Kendall to William L. Marcy, November 1845, Kendall Papers, LC.

29. Young, "Friends of the Indian," II, 26; Moulton, *John Ross*, pp. 72–74.

30. Robert V. Remini, *The Revolutionary Age of Andrew Jackson* (New York, 1976), pp. 113–18; James Mooney, *Myths of the Cherokees* (Chicago, 1972), pp. 130, 133; *Senate Documents*, 27th Congress, 3rd Session, No. 219; Van Buren to AJ, June 17, AJ to Van Buren, July 8, 1838, Van Buren Papers, LC; Perdue and Green, eds., *Cherokee Removal*, pp. 160–73. See also Grant Foreman, *Indian Removal: The Emigration of the Five Civilized Tribes of Indians* (Norman, Okla., 1932) and William L. Anderson, ed., *Cherokee Removal: Before and After* (Athens, Ga., 1991).

31. Robert V. Remini, *Andrew Jackson and the Course of American Democracy* (New York, 1984), 436–37.

Chapter 16. The Second Seminole War

1. Creek Chiefs to AJ, April 14, 1836, Record Group 233, E 281, National Archives; *National Intelligencer*, July 12, 1836.

2. Green, *Politics of Indian Removal*, pp. 183–85; Angie Debo, *The Road to Disappearance* (Norman, Okla., 1941), pp. 98–102. The best account of the Creek War is Kenneth LL. Valliere, "The Creek War of 1836: A Military History," *Chronicles of Oklahoma* (1979), LVII, 463–85.

3. Quoted in Foreman, *Indian Removal*, p. 176.

4. AJ to the Seminole Chiefs, February 16, 1835, in [Woodburne Potter], *The War in Florida* (Baltimore, 1836), pp. 78–80.

5. [Potter], *War in Florida*, pp. 81–82; John K. Mahon, *History of the Second Seminole War, 1835–1842* (Gainesville, Fla., 1967), pp. 91, 95.

6. Mahon, *Second Seminole War*, p. 101; Peters, *Florida Wars*, p. 105.

7. This dispute involved spoliation claims resulting from the Napoleonic Wars. See Remini, *Jackson*, III, 201–36.

8. AJ to Francis P. Blair, July 28, 1840, private collection, Jackson Papers Project, University of Tennessee, Knoxville.

9. Ibid.

10. AJ to Jesup, August 3, November 5, 1836, private collection, copy Jackson Papers Project; AJ to Call, November 1, 5, 1836, Jackson Papers, LC; AJ to Butler, November 2, [1836], Butler Papers, New York State Library, Albany.
11. AJ to Jesup, November 5, 1836, private collection, copy Jackson Papers Project; White to J. Knowles, February 15, 1837, in Clarence E. Carter, ed., *The Territorial Papers of the United States, Florida* (Washington, 1936–   ), XXV, 378.
12. Memorandum, Jackson, *Correspondence,* V, 468–71; AJ to Blair, July 28, 1840, private collection, copy Jackson Papers Project; *Congressional Globe,* 25th Congress, 2nd Session, 42ff; Mahon, *Second Seminole War,* p. 244.

Chapter 17. Jackson's Indian Legacy

1. Royce, *Indian Land Cession,* pp. 748–66.
2. Ronald N. Satz, "Indian Policy in the Jacksonian Era: The Old Northwest as a Test Case," *Michigan History* (1976), LV, 81–82 note 38, and *American Indian Policy,* pp. 97, 115 note 1; Report from the Office of Indian Affairs, December 1, 1836, *Senate Documents,* 24th Congress, 2nd Session, No 15, p. 420; Records of the Office of Indian Affairs, December 1, 1836, Miscellaneous Records, I, 300–1, II, 6–8, 90–100, Record Group 75, National Archives; *House Document,* 25th Congress, 3rd Session, No 347.
3. For a complete and better statement of Prucha's argument see his article "Andrew Jackson's Indian Policy: A Reassessment," *Journal of American History* (1969), LVI, 527–39. A magisterial study of Indian policy for the entire course of American history can be found in Prucha's *The Great Father: The United States Government and the American Indians,* 2 vols. (Lincoln, 1984).
4. Petition of Chippewa, Ottawa and Potawatomi Chiefs to AJ, March 10, 1835 [?], Record Group 75, NA, copy Jackson Papers Project.

Bibliography

I n the past few decades the literature on Native Americans has happily increased at an extraordinary rate. When I first began my study of the Jacksonian era there were only a few pioneering studies that dealt with the life, customs, and history of Indians. That has all changed. Today there exists a vast amount of information available in print that trace the origins and development of almost every tribe in North America. But since this book is narrowly focused on Andrew Jackson's relations with Native Americans—in particular the Five Civilized Tribes—this bibliography is necessarily limited to that topic.

For documentary materials directly related to Native Americans I relied heavily on the manuscripts to be found in the National Archives, especially the records, reports, and correspondence of the Office of Indian Affairs and the Bureau of Indian Affairs. In addition, the record groups in the National Archives of the secretary of war, secretary of state, attorney general, the headquarters of the army, and the adjutant general's office proved invaluable.

The personal manuscript collections of Andrew Jackson, John C. Calhoun, Henry Schoolcraft, Martin Van Buren, Amos Kendall, William Mendill, and William Wirt in the Library of Congress were especially important, as were those of John Coffee and Lewis Cass in the Tennessee Historical Society and the James Monroe and Jackson–Lewis Papers in the New York Public Library.

Among printed primary sources a good place to start in understanding Jackson as a man and President is John Spencer Bassett's six-volume *Correspondence of Andrew Jackson* (Washington, D.C., 1926–1935), because it includes letters written by and to him over the entire course of his life. However, the first five volumes of *The Papers of Andrew Jackson*, edited by Sam Smith et al. (Knoxville, 1980–), provide a great many more documents that deal with Jackson's relations with Native Americans from approximately 1770 to 1824.

Other printed primary materials can be found in *House Journals; House Reports; House Executive Documents; Senate Journals; Senate Documents; American State Papers; Indian Affairs* and *Military Affairs;* the *Annals of Congress;* the *Register of Debates;* the *Congressional Globe* and *Statutes at Large;* James D. Richardson, comp., *A Compilation of the Messages and Papers of the President, 1789–1902* (Washington, D.C., 1905); *The United States and the Indians, 11th–15th Congress 1810–1819* (Washington, 1820); and *Correspondence on the Subject of the Emigration of Indians* (Washington, 1835).

The following printed primary sources were regularly consulted in writing this book: Clarence E. Carter and John P. Bloom, comps. and eds. *The Territorial Papers of the United States* (Washington, D.C., 1944–); Charles J. Kappler, ed., *Indian Affairs: Laws and Treaties* (Washington, D.C., 1892–1899); Charles C. Royce, *Indian Land Cessions in the United States* (Washington, D.C., 1900); Charles Francis Adams, ed., *Memoirs of John Quincy Adams* (Philadelphia, 1874–1877); Robert L. Meriwether et al., *The Papers of John C. Calhoun* (Columbia, S.C., 1959–); Wilson Lumpkin, *The Removal of the Cherokee Indians from Georgia* (New York, 1907); Thomas L. McKenney, *Memoirs, Official and Personal* (Lincoln, Neb., 1973); Francis Paul Prucha and Donald Carmony, eds., "A Memorandum of Lewis Cass Concerning a System for the Regulation of Indian Affairs," *Wisconsin Magazine of History* (August 1968), II, 35–50; Henry R. Schoolcraft, *Personal Memoirs of a Residence of Thirty Years with the Indian Tribes on the American Frontiers* (Philadelphia, 1851); C. L. Grant, ed., *Letters, Journals and Writings of Benjamin Hawkins* (Savannah, 1980); Black Hawk, *Autobiography* (Rock Island, Ill., 1833); Gary F. Moulton, ed., *The Papers of Chief John Ross* (Norman, Okla., 1985); and Theda Perdue, ed., *The Writings of Elias Boudinot* (Knoxville, 1983).

It is not possible to list all the secondary works that inform this study. There are so many new books on the history of Native Americans and their relations with white settlers that I can only mention a few.

On Jackson, my own three-volume biography, *Andrew Jackson and the Course of American Empire, 1767–1821* (New York, 1977), *Andrew Jackson and the Course of American Freedom, 1822–1832* (New York, 1981), and *Andrew Jackson and the Course of American Democracy, 1833–1845* (New York, 1984), provides a more detailed discussion of Jackson's career. But see also John Reid and John H. Eaton, *The Life of Andrew Jackson, Major General in the Service of the United States, Comprising a History of the War in the South from the Commencement of the Creek Campaign to the Termination of Hostilities Before New Orleans* (Philadelphia, 1817); Amos Kendall, *The Life of Andrew Jackson* (New York, 1844); and James Parton, *The Life of Andrew Jackson* (New York, 1861). One of the first historians to deal directly with Jackson's relations with Indians is Michael Paul Rogin, *Fathers and Children: Andrew Jackson and the Subjugation of the American Indian* (New York, 1975), a work that explores psychological motivation.

Biographies of other important individuals include John Sugden, *Tecumseh: A Life* (New York, 1998); Merritt B. Pound, *Benjamin Hawkins: Indian Agent* (Athens, Ga., 1951); Rachel C. Eaton, *John Ross and the Cherokee Indians* (Menasha, Wis., 1914), and Gary E. Moulton, *John Ross, Cherokee Chief* (Athens, Ga., 1978); Herman J. Viola, *Thomas L. McKenney, Architect of America's Early Indian Policy: 1816–1830* (Chicago, 1974); Gideon Lincecum, "Life of Apushimataha," *Publications of the Mississippi Historical Society* (1906), IX; Cecil Lamar Sumners, *Chief Tishomingo: A History of the Chickasaw Indians* (Iuka, Miss., 1974); Florett Henri, *The Southern Indians and Benjamin Hawkins, 1796–1816* (Norman, Okla., 1986); Herbert J. Doherty, *Richard Keith Call: Southern Unionist* (Gainesville, Fla., 1961); and Willard Carl Klunder, *Lewis Cass and the Politics of Moderation* (Kent, Ohio, 1996).

For the actual wars Jackon waged with and against the Indians see Frank Owsley, Jr., *Struggle for the Gulf: The Creek War and the Battle of New Orleans 1812–1815* (Gainesville, Fla., 1981); H. S. Halbert and T. H. Ball, *The Creek War of 1813 and 1814* (Chicago and Montgomery, Ala., 1895); James W. Holland, *Andrew Jackson and the Creek War: Victory at the Horseshoe* (University, Ala., 1968); George Cary Eggleston, *Red Eagle and the Wars with the Creek Indians of Alabama* (New York, 1878); David S. Heidler and Jeanne T. Heidler, *Old Hickory's War: Andrew Jackson and the Quest for Empire* (Mechanicsburg, Pa., 1996); [Woodburne Potter], *The War in Florida* (Baltimore, 1836); Virginia Bergman Peters, *The Florida Wars* (Hamden, Conn., 1979); John K. Mahon, "The 1st Seminole War, November 21, 1817–May 24, 1818," in *Florida Historical Quarterly*, XXVII (Summer 1998), and *History of the Second Seminole War, 1835–1842* (Gainesville, Fla., 1967); and Ellen M. Whitney, comp. and ed., *The Black Hawk War, 1831–1832* (Springfield, Ill., 1970–1975).

For studies on government policy toward the Indians see the many works of Francis Paul Prucha, especially *American Indian Policy in the Formative Years: The Indian Trade and Intercourse Act, 1790–1834* (Cambridge, Mass., 1962), *The Great Father: The United States Government and the American Indians* (Lincoln, Neb., 1984), and "Andrew Jackson's Indian Policy: A Reassessment," *Journal of American History* (December 1969), LVI, 527–39. See also Bernard W. Sheehan, *Seeds of Extinction: Jeffersonian Philanthropy and the American Indian* (New York, 1973); Anthony F. C. Wallace, *Jefferson and the Indians: The Tragic Fate of the First Americans* (Cambridge, Mass., 1999); Wilcomb Washburn, *Red Men's Land, White Men's Law* (New York, 1971); and R. S. Cotterill, *The Southern Indians: The Story of the Civilized Tribes Before Removal* (Norman, Okla., 1954). Of particular value is Ronald N. Satz, *American Indian Policy in the Jacksonian Era* (Lincoln, Neb., 1975).

For studies of individual tribes see Douglas Summers Brown, *The Catawbas Indians* (Columbia, S.C., 1966); Charles M. Hudson, *Catawba Nation* (Athens, Ga., 1970); Marion L. Starkey, *The Cherokee Nation* (New York, 1946); Thurman Wilkins, *Cherokee Tragedy* (New York, 1970); Henry T. Malone, *Cherokees of the Old South* (Athens, Ga., 1956); Grace S. Woodward, *The Cherokees* (Norman, Okla., 1963); Stanley W. Hoig, *The Cherokees and Their Chiefs in the Wake of Empire* (Fayetteville, Ark., 1998); Morris L. Wardell, *A Political History of the Cherokee Nation, 1838–1907* (Norman, Okla., 1977); James Mooney, *Myths of the Cherokees* (Chicago, 1972); William L. Anderson, ed., *Cherokee Removal: Before and After* (Athens, Ga., 1991); Michael D. Green, *The Politics of Indian Removal: Creek Government and Society in Crisis* (Lincoln, Neb., and London, 1982); Joel W. Martin, *Sacred Revolt: The Muskogees' Struggle for a New World* (Boston, 1991); Mary Elizabeth Young, *Redskins, Ruffleshirts and Rednecks: Indian Allotments in Alabama and Mississippi, 1830–1860* (Norman, Okla., 1961); Horatio B. Cushman, *History of the Choctaw, Chickasaw and Natchez Indians* (New York, 1972); Albert J. Pickett, *History of Alabama* (Charleston, 1851); J.G.M. Ramsey, *The Annals of Tennessee to the End of the Eighteenth Century* (Charleston, 1853); Albigence W. Putnam,

History of Middle Tennessee (Nashville, 1859); J.F.H. Claiborne, *Mississippi, as a Province, Territory and State* (Jackson, Miss., 1880); Arrell M. Gibson, *The Chickasaws* (Norman, Okla., 1971); Samuel Cole Williams, *Beginnings of West Tennessee in the Land of the Chickasaws, 1541–1841* (Johnson City, Tenn., 1930); Edwin C. McReynolds, *The Seminoles* (Norman, Okla., 1957); Brent Richards Weisman, *Unconquered People: Florida's Seminole and Miccosukee Indians* (Gainesville, Fla., 1999); James W. Covington, *The Seminoles of Florida* (Gainesville, Fla., 1993); Hubert B. Fuller, *The Purchase of Florida* (Gainesville, Fla., 1964); Angie Debo, *Rise and Fall of the Choctaw Republic* (Norman, Okla., 1934) and *The Road to Disappearance* (Norman, Okla., 1941); Robert B. Ferguson, "Treaties Between the United States and the Choctaw Nation," in Carolyn Keller Reeves., ed., *The Choctaw Before Removal* (Jackson, Miss., 1985); and James Taylor Carson, *Searching for the Bright Path: The Mississippi Choctaws from Prehistory to Removal* (Lincoln, Neb., 1999).

The removal of the Indians is treated in most of the works cited above. But see also Reginald Horsman, *The Origins of Indian Removal* (East Lansing, Mich., 1970); Grant Foreman, *Last Trek of the Indians* (Chicago, 1946), *Indian Removal* (Norman, Okla., 1942), and *The Five Civilized Tribes* (Norman, Okla., 1934); Theda Perdue and Michael D. Green, *The Cherokee Removal* (Boston and New York, 1995); John Ehle, *Trail of Tears: The Rise and Fall of the Cherokee Nation* (New York, 1988); Arthur H. DeRosier, *The Removal of the Choctaw Indians* (Knoxville, Tenn., 1970); Annie H. Abel, "The History of Events Resulting in Indian Consolidation West of the Mississippi," American Historical Association, *Annual Report for the Year 1906* (Washington, D.C., 1908), I; and Wilber R. Jacobs, *Dispossessing the American Indian* (New York, 1972).

Index